# YOUR ORGANIC GARDEN

## WITH JEFF COX

**By the Editors of Rodale Garden Books**

Rodale Press, Emmaus, Pennsylvania

If you have any questions or comments concerning this book, please write to:
Rodale Press, Inc.
Book Readers' Service
33 East Minor Street
Emmaus, PA 18098

---

## Our Mission

We publish books that empower people's lives.

RODALE BOOKS

---

**Executive Editor:** Margaret Lydic Balitas
**Managing Editor:** Barbara W. Ellis
**Editor:** Cheryl Winters Tetreau
**Copy Editors:** Barbara McIntosh Webb and Sarah Sacks Dunn
**Copy Manager:** Dolores Plikaitis
**Art Director:** Michael Mandarano
**Design Director:** Linda Jacopetti
**Office Manager:** Karen Earl-Braymer
**Administrative Assistant:** Susan Nickol
**Editorial assistance:** Deborah Weisel and Cindy Cadle
**Book Designers:** Rebecca K. McClimans and Mary Kaye Nilan
**Cover Photographer:** Mitch Mandel
**Interior Illustrators:** John Carlance, Pamela Carroll, Rae Chambers, Julia Child, Frank Fretz, Kathy Kester, and Elayne Sears
**Indexer:** Cheryl Namy Dickason

Library of Congress
Cataloging-in-Publication Data
Cox, Jeff.
    Your organic garden: with Jeff Cox/by the editors of Rodale Garden Books.
        p.   cm.
    Includes bibliographical references and index.
    ISBN 0–87596–623–3  hardcover
    ISBN 0–87596–624–1  paperback
    1. Organic gardening. 2. Organic gardening—United States. I. Rodale Press. II. Title.
SB453.5.C68  1994
635'.0484—dc20                          93-21061
                                             CIP

**Distributed in the book trade
by St. Martin's Press**

2  4  6  8  10  9  7  5  3  1  hardcover
2  4  6  8  10  9  7  5  3  1  paperback

# CONTENTS

# PART 1

## GARDENING BASICS

# PART 2

## PLANT SELECTION AND CARE GUIDE

# WHAT IS ORGANIC GARDENING?

Gardening organically is a skill that draws on farming traditions of the past as well as modern scientific discoveries. Simply stated, organic gardening is a method that uses our understanding of nature as a guide for gardening, and caring for the plants in our gardens without using synthetic chemical pesticides or fertilizers.

Have you ever wondered how a forest or meadow grows and thrives with no added fertilizer? The answer is that natural ecosystems make their own fertilizers. Nature's cycle of growth, death, and decay is continuous. As plants and animals die, rodents, insects, earthworms, and microscopic soil creatures consume their bodies, and nutrients are released. These nutrients feed new generations of plants.

In a natural ecosystem, natural predators and parasites help keep plant-eating insects in check. In organic gardens, similar cycles and natural balances exist. However, gardeners harvest and remove crops from the garden, breaking the cycle. To keep the natural processes that feed plants working, they add organic materials such as compost or purchased organic soil amendments. Also, gardeners demand better appearance or yield from their plants than they would from those growing in the wild. But by encouraging biological diversity in their yards and gardens, they can minimize the need for artificial pest control. When organic gardeners do intervene, they choose control tactics that have little impact on natural systems.

Many gardeners choose the organic method because they want to be good stewards of the environment. They are concerned about pollution of air, water, and soil and about protecting the health of their families and communities. They know that using synthetic pesticides can destroy wildlife, bees, and other beneficial insects and may have an effect on food quality and safety. Tending an organic garden connects them with the soil and makes them feel close to nature. If you share these concerns about our environment and about the health of your family and community, organic gardening is for you.

## ORGANIC IN A NUTSHELL

If you're new to organic gardening, here are some basic suggestions to help you get started:

**Read about gardening and growing plants, especially using the organic method.** Learning about gardening is an ongoing process that gardeners enjoy throughout their lives.

**Use a plan and keep records.** Find out about the plants you want to grow and which types will grow best in your area. Draw a sketch of your garden and decide what will go where, then revise it as you work. Begin a garden journal for keeping records through the season. Stock up on supplies and tools you may need during the gardening year.

**Learn more about your soil.** You may want to have it tested by the Cooperative Extension Service or by a private laboratory. Use the results as a guide to bring your soil into balance with a long-term approach—biological changes aren't instant and may take several years! Add lime, compost, or organic fertilizers as needed. Maintain soil balance by growing green manure crops and adding organic matter each season.

**Start a compost pile.** Recycling garden wastes and increasing soil organic matter are two fundamentals of organic gardening. Composting helps you do both. There are many simple designs for compost enclosures, or you can just make a compost heap in a corner of your yard.

**Keep the garden clean.** Garden sanitation protects plants against pests and diseases. Clearing crop waste out of the vegetable garden and pruning diseased branches from trees and shrubs not only helps the appearance of your garden but also makes for a healthy garden. Having a clean garden also means carefully inspecting any newly bought plants to ensure that they aren't carriers of diseases or insects. Make garden cleanup part of your usual gardening routine, rather than a once-in-the-fall extravaganza.

**Learn to manage pest problems.** The idea behind most organic techniques is to sidestep the insect problem one way or another or to let natural controls kill off the pests. Keep plants healthy with timely feeding and watering. Encourage beneficial insects. Use row covers to exclude pests; build a fence to exclude animals. Try biological control techniques. As a last resort, use botanical insecticides.

**Practice disease prevention.** Prevention and protection are the keys to organic disease control. If you keep plants healthy, they will be robust and vigorous enough to resist most diseases. Whenever possible, use disease-resistant or disease-tolerant plants. Clean up the garden

regularly and put diseased plant materials in the trash or a hot compost pile. It's also important to rotate crops, not handle plants when they're wet, and be gentle when you pick and cultivate so you don't create wounds where disease organisms can gain entry. Reserve sprays and dusts for fighting disease organisms that could wipe out yields or kill your plants.

**Banish weeds.** The organic gardener's first line of attack against weeds is to prevent them from getting a foothold in the garden. For existing weed problems, organic gardeners begin by identifying the weed, and then use specific techniques that will be most effective for eradicating that plant. So, set aside some time for good old-fashioned weeding, and learn about other techniques for controlling weeds that don't require a hoe and a strong back.

# How This Book Can Help

Whether you're a seasoned organic gardener or just getting started, this book is your guide to a healthy, bountiful, organic garden.

We'll take you through the steps for putting pencil to paper and planning your garden and landscape, then show you how to improve your soil and choose the plants that will work best for you. Along the way you'll find plenty of information on making compost, starting seeds, transplanting, propagating, controlling pests and diseases, watering, mulching, and other techniques to make your organic garden a success.

In addition, you'll learn how to select and care for plants for your vegetable garden, fruit and berry garden, herb garden, and flower garden, as well as care and maintenance tips for trees, shrubs, vines, lawns, and groundcovers.

Even a quick look through these pages will provide you with enough ideas to make you want to pull out your hoe and get going. So head on out to the garden and dig in!

# INTRODUCTION

I didn't learn to garden organically all at once. Rather, I learned my way into it. I discovered that it takes a special way of thinking about the soil and the life in it, the things that grow in it, those who garden and eat from it, and the nature of which it's a part.

This book, and the television series that it augments, is designed to help you learn the practices and the parts of the organic method so that you can grasp the big idea. Once you understand the special way of thinking behind the organic method, you'll be able to fly on your own and make decisions in your garden based on your understanding of the system, rather than by simply applying pre-set solutions to a problem. You will find that this way of thinking affects more than your gardening. It can come to color the way you look at life in general, as it has for thousands and thousands of people who have learned the organic method.

It began in the early 1940s when J. I. Rodale was reading about the work of agriculturist Sir Albert Howard. Sir Albert had written about two herds of cattle in India. One herd had a bad outbreak of hoof-and-mouth disease. The other did not. The only difference was that the healthy herd was eating grass from pasture fertilized with compost. "It hit me like a ton of bricks," J. I. later wrote, describing the moment when he first saw in a lightning flash the connection between soil and health. Health is built from the ground up. A healthy soil grows healthy plants. Healthy plants make for healthy animals and the human beings who eat them.

Organic gardeners know how to create a healthy soil and grow plants that will bring home a bounty of produce to benefit their families. From the healthy soil, all else follows. The secret, of course, is to think of the soil as a living organism that must be fed properly to be healthy. What to feed it? Lots of organic matter, for the same reason that we eat big salads: They're good for us.

This organic matter, turned into the soil or mounded into compost piles, is colonized by microorganisms, which multiply and reproduce furiously. As these tiny creatures die, their cell contents spill into the soil as the perfect organic fertilizer, feeding plants what they want, in the form they want it, as they want it. The rule is, feed the soil and the soil will feed the plants.

Species diversity is all-important, too, whether we're talking about soil organisms, the plants in a garden, or the insects that live on those plants. The greater the number and the more diverse the species in a system, the healthier it is. For instance, a healthy wilderness contains most of the native species that can live there. Very few pest outbreaks threaten the health of wilderness, because along with native pests come native predators—good bugs that eat the bad bugs. There's a built-in system of checks and balances that keeps pest insects from wreaking havoc in the system.

Contrast this with an agrichemical monoculture, such as that found in a large cornfield, where only corn is allowed to grow. It shouldn't surprise us that corn pests appear there in abundance. If we spray insecticides to kill the corn pests, we also kill off the beneficial bugs that would otherwise help keep the pests in check. We also kill off all the pests who are susceptible to the insecticide, but not the ones who are resistant. We are, in effect, selecting for pesticide resistance in the bugs. In addition, pesticides destroy other forms of life besides the target insect and also pollute water and food up and down the food chain. Thus we destroy nature's carefully constructed system of health.

The story is similar in the soil: Nitrogen-fixing bacteria colonize plant roots in a healthy soil, pulling nitrogen from the air and feeding it to the plants in a carefully balanced natural system that allows plants to thrive even when there may not be great amounts of nitrogen in the soil. If we flood the soil with chemical fertilizer, we trigger a reaction in the nitrogen-fixing bacteria that turns them off. They sense that the soil has enough nitrogen, and they stop working—permanently. Thus we shut down a natural system that gives us free nitrogen in favor of an artificial injection of nitrogen for which we must pay. In addition, chemical nitrogen has deleterious effects on other soil life and can contribute to water pollution as it seeps into wells and runs off into streams. Again we thus destroy nature's carefully constructed system of health.

Eventually organic gardeners are granted the great privilege of perceiving nature's healthy cycles and systems at work and trying to work with them instead of against them. We discover that when we use a chemical shortcut to achieve a garden goal, we get a short-term solution that carries with it a group of unwanted negative side effects. But when we work with nature, we get a long-term solution that carries a host of unexpected beneficial consequences.

Organic gardeners don't refuse to use chemicals because we are rabid, red-eyed true believers in a cause—though there are some among us who might feel that way. Rather we refuse to use these chemical shortcuts because we know that in the long run, they won't work. Nature will have her way. It's much smarter and much easier to try to understand the natural systems operating in the garden, and to protect and cherish them, than to subvert them with toxic chemicals. It just makes sense: environmentally, financially, commonsensically, and ethically.

The organic garden is one piece of the natural world that we actually, physically have under our care. Rather than trying to control it, we need to celebrate it. We need to use its systems and cycles to our advantage—build our health with it. That's why it is there. That's why it has the capability of giving us health and making us happy.

Nature—of which we are a part—has designed it for our benefit. But we only get the full benefit if we understand the system and do the work.

Happy gardening!

Jeff Cox

# Part I

# GARDENING BASICS

# Chapter 1

# GARDEN PLANNING

The best and most satisfying gardens are the result of careful planning and sound design. Whether you want to design a flower garden, plant a shrub border to screen an outdoor patio, or add plantings of vegetables, fruits, and herbs to your yard, there are some basic principles that will help you make decisions as you plan.

You don't have to be an artist to create an attractive and useful environment around your home. Landscaping is a form of personal expression, an extension of the care you put into arranging the inside of your house. There is no "right" landscape; what works for your neighbor may not suit your needs or look good on your site.

Having a beautiful and unique property depends on five basic steps: gathering ideas, creating a design, taking a close look at your site, installing plants and structures, and maintaining the landscape. Attractive landscaping will help you enjoy your home and increase its value as well.

## GATHERING IDEAS

Start the design process by looking around for ideas. Great landscaping ideas are all around you. Look at homes in your community and take note of landscapes that catch your eye. See whether a garden club in your area sponsors tours of local gardens; these "open gardens" are a great way to get a close view of plants and design ideas that are appropriate for your area.

Public parks and botanical gardens can also give you planting ideas. Check out the wide variety of gardening books available; they're packed with photographs and tips about other people's success stories.

When you look at a landscape, try to visualize it as a series of garden "rooms." Like a room in a house, each part of the landscape has walls, a floor, and a ceiling. The walls could be a hedge, a row of trees, a fence, or a trellis. The floor might be turf, mulch, groundcover, crushed stone, or wooden decking. The sky or an arbor may serve as the ceiling.

Breaking a landscape down into rooms makes it easier to identify the elements you need to add or change. For example, if you want to separate the vegetable garden from the rest of your yard, you need some sort of wall. If you don't want to see the garden, you could plant a hedge or install a solid wood fence. If you are enclosing the garden to protect it from animals, you might try a woven wire fence planted with attractive vines. These rooms need doorways, too—don't forget to think about gates or openings in the walls.

When you view a landscape as a combination of these solid elements, the whole process of planning a design is much more manageable. If you see a landscape that you particularly like, try to figure out what makes it special. Is there an attractive fence that makes a nice backdrop for the plants? Is there a beautiful tree or shrub you would just love to have for your own property? Has your neighbor come up with a clever way to screen the front yard from the street? You may not want to copy any of these ideas exactly, but they will give you some idea of what is possible for your own home. The unlimited combinations of these elements make it easy to create a landscape that is unique to your property. And that's what landscaping is all about: making the best of your site.

## CREATING A DESIGN

Creating a design starts with a wish list, based on the ideas you've gathered from books and neighboring properties. This list should include design ideas, garden structures, and specific plants. This isn't the time to be realistic—go ahead and put down anything that you'd like to see in your yard.

The next step is figuring out what you really need in the landscape. If you have children, a play area may be the most important use of the yard. If you do a lot of entertaining, a shady arbor might be just the place for parties. For a large family, parking may be a major consideration. Besides play areas, entertaining, and parking, think about privacy, security, noise reduction, pets, flowers, and food production.

## LIST YOUR LANDSCAPE NEEDS

Once you've started thinking about your yard and what you want it to do, it's time to start a garden notebook. You'll find that keeping all your records in one place is invaluable as you make plans and review the progress of your garden. A good garden notebook doesn't need to

---

### ✳ Landscape-Needs Checklist

Here's a list of of ways you can use plants and gardens to enhance your landscape, along with features you might want to add to your yard. In your garden notebook, jot down all that apply in your situation, but use this list only as a starting point. To unlock all the potential your yard has to offer, try to think about what activities you would like to have space for and what you would like it to do for you. If reducing maintenance is at the top of your landscape-needs list, see "Reducing Landscape Maintenance" on page 7.

- ❑ Screen a patio or deck from the neighbors.
- ❑ Hide a bare foundation, or transform a dull or ugly foundation planting.
- ❑ Add a vegetable garden.
- ❑ Add interest along the front of the yard.
- ❑ Create a welcoming entrance to the house.
- ❑ Create a sitting area under shade trees.
- ❑ Add a colorful planting along the driveway.
- ❑ Make the front entrance to the house more appealing.
- ❑ Create a quiet sitting area outdoors.
- ❑ Make an area for composting or tool storage.
- ❑ Beautify a lamppost or mailbox.
- ❑ Create a boundary around the property.
- ❑ Hide an unattractive view or element (like a utility pole, laundry line, or chain-link fence).
- ❑ Make an attractive view into the yard from a prominent window indoors.
- ❑ Fill a bare spot.
- ❑ Create a place to walk to in the yard.
- ❑ Beautify a garage or outbuilding.
- ❑ Surround a bench, trellis, or arbor.
- ❑ Give a new home a more finished look.

be anything fancy—a loose-leaf notebook with a pocket or two to hold pencils and notes will do fine. Don't worry if it gets cluttered and messy as time goes on; you can still get what you need from it as long as you can read it and find things.

Use the "Landscape-Needs Checklist" on page 3 to help you start thinking about what features you'd like to have in your yard. As you review the list, make sure you look at your yard from every perspective: Look out at the yard from inside the house, including the upstairs windows; look at it from the street, from down the street, from the front door, from the sides, from the back door, from the back boundary line; look back at the house from the yard. Taking a fresh look at your yard will help you identify features you'd like to hide or views

 **Inventory Your Site**

You may think you know everything about your yard, but once you start really looking at it, you may be surprised at how many details you've forgotten. Here's a list of important facts and features you'll want to keep in mind as you make your design. As you read about them, use a page in your garden notebook to make notes about them. When you're finished, you'll have a much clearer idea of where you could put a garden or gardens in your yard.

**The Vital Statistics**

Before you draw up your garden plan and goals, collect some facts about your property. Doing this will help you organize your priorities and make realistic plans. You'll need to know about:

■ Hardiness zone and local weather conditions

■ Soil condition (See "Investigating the Soil" on page 26 for tips on assessing your soil.)

■ Drainage, including both wet and dry sites around your yard

■ Exposure, such as areas with full sun, partial shade, or full shade

■ Property dimensions, including a breakdown of the space available for gardens, recreation areas, pet runs, and other areas

■ Existing insect and disease problems

■ Areas to avoid, such as septic tank fields and underground utility cables or waterlines

■ Locations of essential features, such as a water source, tool shed, or compost pile

■ Established plants and their condition, as well as possible effects on new plants, such as shade or competition for nutrients

■ How much time you have to spend on your yard and garden

**Know Your Microclimates**

Knowing about the microclimates on your property—places that are warmer or cooler than the rest—can be valuable when it comes to siting all your plantings. Planting a vegetable garden in a frost pocket, where frost settles late in spring and early in fall, can shorten your harvest season tremendously, for example. A sheltered, south-facing site, on the other hand, can be quite a pleasant place to sit on a cool winter day. Such sites will also encourage spring flowers to bloom earlier than in cooler parts of your yard. To verify your hunches about warmer or cooler pockets that would affect your plans, take temperature readings at different times of day throughout the year in various locations in the garden.

you'd like to improve—such as the view out your kitchen window, for example. Date your list; you might want to add or change things later.

Then compare your wish list and landscape-needs list. Some things will probably appear on both lists. The rose hedge on your wish list, for example, may match your need to keep romping pets out of the vegetable garden. Other wants and needs may be totally incompatible. If your yard is a popular place for neighborhood football or volleyball games, a delicate rock garden might be out of the question. Discuss the lists with your family, and decide which elements are acceptable to everyone. Also, don't forget to consider maintenance needs. A lovely perennial border can quickly deteriorate into a tangled mess if you don't have time to take care of it. (See "Reducing Landscape Maintenance" on page 7 for ideas on making your yard easier to maintain.)

# SIZING UP YOUR SITE

Now that you've looked at what features and plantings you'd like to have on your property, it's time to take stock of what conditions you have to work with. Taking a careful look at your site—its soil, climate, and exposure—will make it easier to decide where to locate your vegetable garden, plantings of flowers or fruit, trees, hedges, or other plantings you'd like to add. (You'll find specific suggestions for selecting sites for vegetable gardens and fruits in Chapters 9 and 10, respectively.)

See "Inventory Your Site" on the opposite page to help you get a better idea of what you have to work with. Take note of wet, shady, and rocky spots, and try to take advantage of them. A wet spot may not be desirable in a play area, but it could be a good place for a group of moisture-loving plants. Also, think of the land-

scape as it changes through the seasons. Evergreens and berried shrubs, along with a bench in a sunny spot, can make your yard a pleasant winter retreat. A little careful planning can give the landscape four-season appeal. Don't forget details like specimen plants, interesting rocks, or sculpture to give the garden character.

## HOW TO MAKE A GARDEN MAP

You don't need professional skills to draw a map of your garden. Using lined graph paper, any gardener can make a usable garden map.

Your first step should be to measure the boundary lines of your property, using a flexible measuring tape that's 25 feet or longer. It's easiest to do this with a helper to hold one end of the tape. If you work alone, stick a pencil through the loop at the end of the tape and push it into the ground to secure it. If you have a survey of your property, you can skip this step. Just use the dimensions on your survey or make a photocopy of the survey to use as a base map.

You'll also want to take measurements of the size of your house and note its location with regard to boundary lines. Make sure to note the size and location of existing garden beds and plantings as well.

Next, sit down with your list of measurements and your graph paper. Choose a scale, such as one square on paper equals 1 foot of actual space. If you have a large property, you may need to tape a few sheets of paper together to work on that scale. Or you can choose a different scale, such as 1 inch on paper equals 5 feet of actual space.

Draw your boundaries, and then fill in the location of existing buildings and plantings. Make as accurate a plan as possible, and include all your garden's features—paths, trees, buildings, fences, and walkways. Double-check your counting to be sure you've drawn things accurately. With this base map, you'll have a template to use when sketching in your plans and dreams for the ideal yard and garden.

Rather than drawing your plans directly on your base map, however, it's best to draw on overlays. Use sheets of thin tracing paper as overlays to sketch in ideas and see how they fit while you work on the design. That way, you can use your master plan again and again until you decide on the best arrangement of pathways, flower beds, and other features. Then transfer the final design to your master plan.

# PLAN FOR PRACTICALITY

Whether you design your home landscape yourself or leave it to a professional, make sure that the finished plan fits your needs. Don't add a deck just because all your neighbors have them in their backyards if what you really want is a dooryard herb garden. And while you don't want to copy your neighbors exactly, try to keep the general theme of the area in your design. A woodland garden in the Southwest would look as out of place as a cactus garden in New England. By using plants that are best adapted to your area, your landscape will have the appropriate regional look, and your plants will be healthier, too.

There are some basic practical considerations to keep in mind while you're designing your garden. A variety of people need to have access to your property. Oil or gas delivery people

**Plan before you plant.** One way to reduce maintenance in the long run is to make a plan before you buy foundation plants and then choose among the many low-growing and dwarf cultivars of trees and shrubs that mature at the size you would like. Providing plants with the room they need to develop properly allows them to display their natural beauty, and you won't need to shear them into cubes or cones in an attempt to keep them in bounds. If the planting looks too sparse at first, fill in spaces with annuals, perennials, or bulbs until the shrubs develop.

##  Reducing Landscape Maintenance

Keep these timesaving pointers in mind when designing and caring for your yard:

■ On a steep, hard-to-mow slope, build terraces to break the slope into steps or plant the incline with groundcovers.

■ Use the right tool for the job. A good tool can make a tiresome chore a pleasure.

■ Don't struggle with sparse, weedy grass under trees; surround trees with beds of shade-loving plants.

■ Avoid using sharp angles or fussy curves when laying out flower beds; mowing is less difficult along straight lines and smooth curves.

■ Reduce lawn area and cut down on mowing time by installing low-maintenance groundcovers or decking.

■ If you really want to grow fruit, try easy-to-grow bush cherries, blueberries, strawberries, or raspberries.

■ Choose disease- and insect-resistant plants to reduce pest control problems.

■ Use edgings. Edgings can keep grass out of flower beds, prevent gravel from scattering over a flagstone walk, and cut down on trimming. Brick or plastic mowing strips, which are set flush with the soil around lawn areas, make it much easier to maintain a neat edge. One wheel of your mower rides on the strip, so the mower can cut the grass right at the lawn's edge. This eliminates hand-trimming.

■ Choose hedges, shrub borders, and specimen plants that have natural-looking, informal shapes. Sheared hedges and other plantings require frequent trimming to keep them looking neat.

■ To save yourself pruning time, choose slow-growing plants and pick species that won't outgrow their site.

■ Keep up with yard maintenance by doing a little bit at a time. Fifteen minutes a day can take the place of a whole afternoon of yard work once a week.

■ Set pavers in mortar, or plant something like creeping thyme between them to keep weeds from growing up. It saves tedious weeding.

■ Choose plants that don't make a mess by dropping seedpods, sap, or lots of large leaves. Also avoid plants that are prone to problems in your area. They will look messy and take up your time as you try to keep them healthy.

■ Choose plants suited to your site and climate, so you won't need to spend time cosseting finicky plants.

■ Make a few large beds around a number of trees and shrubs, rather than dozens of little planting islands that take lots of time to mow and trim around.

■ Choose the best—not necessarily the most expensive—materials possible; they will last longer and require less maintenance, and you won't have to replace them so soon.

■ Confine high-maintenance features such as lawns and rose gardens to small areas.

■ Install drip irrigation systems for areas that you have to water; plant most of your landscape with plants that can grow well without supplemental water.

■ Mulch under trees, shrubs, and plants. It reduces weeding, watering, and trimming.

■ Use a mulching lawn mower. As you mow, it finely chops the grass clippings and scatters them on the lawn, so your lawn gets mulch and you don't have to deal with grass clippings. Grass clippings are also a free source of nitrogen for your lawn!

need to get to the tank or inlet. Meter readers need to get to the meters. Be sure to accommodate their needs when you plan. An element as simple as a short stepping-stone path through a flower bed to a meter enables the reader to get in and out without damaging your plantings.

**Informal design.** Even a rectangular lot can have an informal design. Parts of the garden—terraces, lawn areas, groundcover beds, flower gardens, or plantings of shrubs and trees—all have free-form shapes that flow together in a unified, informal design.

**Formal design.** Because they can be unfussy and simple, formal designs are often very effective on a small lot. Rectangular beds filled with herbs and edged with dwarf shrubs, straight walks, and symmetrical design are all characteristic of a formal garden.

Electric, telephone, and cable television service people may trim trees that grow near their lines. It pays to design plantings that they will be able to work around.

Don't forget to consider your own everyday needs, either. Have you planned your paths so you will be able to get your mower and garden cart where you need to go? Is it easy to take out the garbage? What about someone delivering bulk garden supplies like mulch—is there a place for that?

And of course, don't plan, and certainly don't dig, before finding out where underground utilities run. Not only do you want to avoid injuring them or yourself, but you may not even be allowed to build or plant permanent features over them.

# UNDERSTANDING DESIGN

Your site will determine some of your design choices. For example, the style of your home may influence the feel of the design you'd like to have. If you have a brick house, the landscape might include brick paths and clipped evergreen hedges. A house with natural wood siding lends itself to wood-chip paths and rail fencing. You'll also need to plan access areas, such as paths, steps, and ramps.

There are two general types of garden design styles—formal and informal. Formal gardens exhibit classical symmetry. Flower beds, terraces, pools, and other features are generally rectangular (or sometimes round), and walks are straight. Formal gardens are not necessarily grand; gardens designed in this manner can be unfussy and simple.

Informal gardens feature curved, free-form flower beds that sweep along the land's features. Lawns, terraces, walkways, and other features are also irregularly shaped, with one gentle arc leading to another. Natural-looking woodland

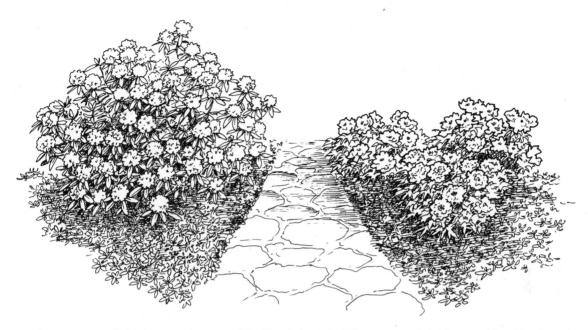

**Balance.** Asymmetrical balance can be accomplished by placing two different types of plantings on either side of a central point. Several good-sized clumps of peonies will balance one large shrub, but a single peony paired with a large shrub would be out of balance.

wildflower gardens and free-form island beds of perennials are both examples of informal style. If the lay of your land is irregular, it will lend itself to an informal design.

## BASIC DESIGN PRINCIPLES

Regardless of style, all well-designed gardens make use of three essential principles—balance, proportion, and repetition—to blend the various parts of the garden into a harmonious whole.

**Balance** When elements on two sides of a central point are similar in size or visual weight, they are balanced. Balanced design gives the viewer a peaceful, restful feeling; unbalanced, lopsided design is unsettling. Balance doesn't necessarily mean symmetry; you don't need mirror-image plantings to accomplish it. Several good-sized clumps of a plant can balance one large one, for example. Symmetrical balance is a

hallmark of formal gardens; and asymmetrical balance, of informal gardens.

**Proportion** Garden features (plants, flower beds, terraces, and so forth) are in proportion when their scale is in good relationship to their surroundings. For example, a large clump of 9-foot-tall giant reed planted in a bed with low-growing, 2- to 3-foot perennials creates a picture that is out of proportion. Similarly, a huge shed would be out of proportion in a small yard.

**Repetition** Repeating an element—color, texture, shape, or even building materials like landscape timbers—throughout a garden adds unity and harmony to a design, so the parts of the garden fit together more closely. For example, repeating the color red at intervals in a flower bed leads the eye through the design and creates a feeling of wholeness and rhythm. You can repeat the same plant, or use different species with similarly colored blooms, to achieve the same effect.

# PLANTS AND DESIGN

The color, height, form, and texture of plants play a vital role in any garden. All plants change from season to season and year to year. They may grow taller than planned, spread too vigorously, or not bloom when expected. Balancing and working with these changes is what makes gardening an art. Even the most carefully designed gardens are never static; their owners adjust and develop the design over time.

## USING COLOR

In a garden, color can be used in many different ways. One gardener may prefer bright reds and yellows; another, soft pinks, blues, and lavenders. Color can influence the mood of a garden. Hot colors—vibrant reds, oranges, and yellows—are cheerful and bright. Cool colors—greens, blues, and purples—are more serene.

Color can influence perceived perspective. Hot or warm colors appear to bring an object or scene closer. Cool colors tend to recede and push the object farther away, so they're a good choice for making a small garden seem larger. Use them in large clumps to catch the eye, and remember that they can be easily overwhelmed by warm colors.

Use balance, proportion, and repetition to design your color scheme. Strive for balanced distribution of color. A large planting of one color can overwhelm a design. Repeating a color at intervals can unify the design. Use clumps of a single plant or several different species with the same flower color.

## BALANCING HEIGHT AND FORM

Plant height and plant form should be balanced and in proportion. In a planting in front of a fence or other backdrop, plant the tallest plants in the back, the shortest in front. If the planting bed's shape is free-form, put the tallest plants at the widest parts of the border. In island beds, which can be viewed from all sides, plant the tallest plants in the center, with shorter plants around the edges.

Form refers to a plant's shape—round, vertical, creeping, or weeping, for example. It's used to describe the entire plant or just the flowers.

**Proportion and repetition.** Plants in a design are in proportion when they are all in scale with one another and with nearby garden elements such as fences or other structures. Repeating a flower color or foliage texture throughout will unify a design.

For example, delphiniums are vertical plants with spike-shaped bloom stalks; marigolds are mound-shaped with round blooms. Intersperse different plant forms throughout a design for balance and interest. Form can be used like color, although it's more subtle. Repeating a form at intervals strengthens unity and harmony. You needn't repeat the same plant to achieve this effect; several plants with similar forms will do.

## INCORPORATING TEXTURES

Plant leaves can look coarse, crinkled, glossy, fuzzy, or smooth. Flowers can be feathery and delicate or waxy and bold. Using plants with a variety of textures—and repeating interesting textures at intervals—adds interest and appeal. Like form, texture is a subtle characteristic.

# GARDEN SIZE

Several factors play a role in determining the best size for the individual gardens in your design. Available space may be the main consideration, but keep in mind what landscape purpose the garden is to serve. For example, if you need a shrub border to screen an unattractive view or create a private patio space, determine the size by walking around your yard and studying where the largest plants need to be planted to accomplish your purpose. Smaller shrubs and perennials that connect these larger plants into a continuous border can be filled in later, as time and budget permit. The beauty of having an overall plan is that nothing is planted haphazardly and you'll be able to work gradually toward your goal.

For a flower garden that blooms all season, you will need enough space to accommodate a variety of plants that will provide an extended bloom period. About 125 square feet will give you enough room to mass flowers for a succession of color. For a formal garden, a 5-foot

× 25-foot rectangle, two 5-foot × 12½-foot beds, or a 12-foot-diameter circle all provide about 125 square feet. In an informal garden, make the shapes free-form, or plan several related beds divided by paths. In general, don't plan gardens that are less than 4 or 5 feet wide if you want a lush effect. Don't plan them any wider if you want to be able to tend the plants without stepping into the bed, or else plan on an access path on either side.

## CONSIDER TIME AND MONEY

These last considerations are critical: How much time and money do you want to spend? You can plan for features that reduce maintenance, but any garden will require basic care—especially in

 **Help for Problem Landscapes**

If you're having trouble settling on a landscape design because you have to deal with factors such as hot sun, too much shade, wet sites, or other troublesome conditions, don't despair. You'll find that this entire book is a gallery of garden ideas. Here's a rundown of where to look for solving your particluar landscaping problems.

**Shade gardening:** Turn to the following pages for lists of shade-tolerant plants: flowers, page 273; herbs, page 254; groundcovers, page 333.

**Plants for sunny sites:** Turn to the following pages for lists of sun-tolerant plants: flowers, page 292; herbs, page 251; groundcovers, page 332.

**Ideas for attracting beneficial insects and animals:** Turn to the following pages for information on attracting beneficials to your garden: insects, page 118; animals, page 124.

##  Budget-Stretching Ideas

There are many ways to stretch your gardening dollar. Here are a few to consider:

■ Renting can be much less expensive than buying tools or equipment you may need, especially large power equipment such as shredders and tractors that you may need only occasionally. Renting also may make the difference between being able to do a job or having to hire someone to do it for you.

■ For a soil-enriching boost of almost-free fertilizer and organic matter, plant a green manure crop like annual ryegrass, soybeans, or buckwheat and till it under before planting.

■ Making a nursery bed is a great way to save money on plants. If your design calls for lots of groundcovers or hostas, for example, buy only a plant or two. Then systematically propagate them for a year or more by division, cuttings, or layering, depending on the species, until you have a small nursery of plants to move to your garden. A nursery bed is perfect for young seedlings, too. Keeping the young plants together ensures they get the care they need, since they're easier to water and weed en masse. Transplant to the garden when the plants are large enough to thrive on their own.

To make a nursery bed, prepare the soil and add plenty of compost or leaf mold; a raised bed is ideal. Shade if the bed is in hot sun.

■ Make shady and sunny nursery beds. Don't make the beds too small—you'll be propagating your plants and growing them on, so you'll need more space than seems likely at first.

■ Don't be afraid to invest in top-quality cultivars if you can divide or propagate them.

■ Look for special packages from nurseries—group offers of daffodils, hostas, and other popular perennials. You can save money with these packages, but be aware of the trade-offs: If you buy a group of unnamed plants, don't expect cultivar quality—put them on a slope or distant area that needs color rather than in a nearby bed or border. If you buy a "named, our choice" special, you won't sacrifice quality—you just won't know exactly what you're getting.

■ Make compost. It saves money on purchased mulch and soil amendments, makes great fertilizer, and recycles valuable nutrients.

■ Ask your local utility company who does their tree work, and call. Many will dump wood chips on your property for free mulch.

■ Spend your money on the best—not necessarily the most expensive—materials possible; they will last longer and be a better investment.

■ Start with smaller plants. Small plants are easier to plant and are less expensive.

■ Order plants with a friend or group to take advantage of volume discounts.

■ Plan before you shop, and buy only what you need. Impulse shopping is costly.

■ Include some edibles in your design. You'll harvest tasty food and save money. Many edible plants are ornamental, too. (See "Edible Landscaping" on the opposite page.)

■ Recycle what you have, use found materials, and make the best use of existing plants and features.

■ Trade plants with neighbors. Almost everybody has too much of something, and these "extra" plants are often fast-growing—take up just what you need for quick color.

■ Buy from reputable nurseries. You'll find healthier plants, often for little more than those found at bargain-basement sales. Reputable nurseries will often replace plants for free if they don't thrive.

the early stages. Consider how much time you want to devote to such tasks as weeding, staking, watering, and pruning. Look for tough, low-maintenance plants if you want to keep these chores to a minimum.

Plants and supplies also cost money; decide on your budget before you start to dig. (See "Budget-Stretching Ideas" on the opposite page for tips on getting the most from your gardening dollar.) If you're not realistic about what size garden you can control, it will end up controlling you. Once you have a plan, you can plant each area as time and budget permit. Plan your garden so you'll have time to enjoy it.

# INSTALLATION

Once you actually have a plan, the next step is to carry it out. The first consideration in installation is often the cost. If you can't or don't want to do everything at once, consider carrying the plan out over several years. It's usually best to start with structures, such as fences and buildings. Next, add the trees and hedges. Eventually, add smaller shrubs, flowers, and groundcovers. This approach makes it fairly easy to install the landscape on your own.

If you do want to carry out the plan all at once, it may be best to hire a professional; this is especially true if the plan includes grading and drainage changes or irrigation and lighting systems. For your protection, get three bids for large projects, and make sure you have signed contracts before work begins. Also, don't forget to check local regulations and get necessary permits before starting.

## MAINTAINING THE LANDSCAPE

After you have spent all this time developing and installing your landscape, you'll certainly want to take good care of it. In new landscapes, watering is probably the most important task.

Regular watering for the first year or two helps plants to settle in. After that, water your plants less frequently to encourage strong root systems. Pruning, applying mulch and fertilizer, and controlling insects and diseases are all routine maintenance tasks that keep your landscape looking its best.

# EDIBLE LANDSCAPING

While many gardeners would like to grow their own fresh produce, not all have time or space for a separate food garden. Edible landscapes do double duty—they produce food and make our yards attractive at the same time. An edible landscape is also convenient. Slogging out to the vegetable garden on a rainy evening after work is a chore. Picking a few ripe tomatoes on your way in from the car or gathering a handful of fragrant herbs from a small garden beside the back door is a pleasure.

The concept of edible landscaping is not new. Ancient Egyptian pleasure gardens included fish ponds, flowers, grape arbors, fruit trees, and places to sit and enjoy the serenity. But by the Renaissance, gardeners began to exclude edible plants from their formal ornamental gardens. They planted separate herb gardens, vegetable gardens, and orchards. Edible landscaping concepts came to the fore in the 1980s. Gardeners recognized that many edible plants are also beautiful, and they reintroduced them to the general landscape.

## MAKING THE TRANSITION

Only those who move into newly built homes have the luxury of designing the landscape from scratch. Most likely, your yard already has many permanent plantings. While you won't want to redesign and uproot your whole yard overnight, there are many ways to gradually transform your existing plantings into an edible landscape. Keep

**Kitchen gardens.** A dooryard kitchen garden is a great place to start your edible landscape. Planting a small bed with herbs, salad greens, and even edible flowers close to your kitchen door makes it easy to include fresh ingredients in your daily meals.

in mind that an edible landscape is one in which *most,* but not necessarily all, of the plantings are food-producing plants.

Start by including some edibles with your annual flowers. Remember, you don't have to plant vegetables in rows—they'll grow just as well interplanted among ornamentals and herbs. Use the same design rules you would with flowers alone. Try accenting a flower bed with deep green rosettes of corn salad, small mounds of 'Spicy Globe' basil, or crinkly red leaf lettuce.

Plant perennial herbs and vegetables in your existing ornamental borders—make room by relocating or replacing existing plants. For example, lavender and rosemary have upright forms with thin leaves and will add four-season

interest to a border. Artichokes are perennial in Zones 9 and 10; their silvery, spiky foliage makes an interesting foil for other plants.

If you need to remove an existing tree or shrub that has died or outgrown its site, consider a fruit or nut tree as a replacement. A nut tree (pecan, hickory, English walnut, hazelnut—whatever is suitable for your climate) can replace a large shade tree. A full-sized fruit tree might be a good replacement for a medium-sized tree. Many of the spring-flowering pears, cherries, and crab apples used in landscaping are sterile hybrids that do not produce fruit. Their fruiting cousins are equally attractive in bloom and do produce fruit.

There are several other special ways to incorporate edibles into your existing landscape:

■ Convert areas of lawn into new garden beds and include edibles in the design.

■ Replace grass with food-producing groundcovers in some areas. Alpine strawberries produce fruit all summer and tolerate light shade.

■ Make use of existing walls and fences, or add new ones. Train dwarf fruit trees against them, or use them to support raspberries, blackberries, or vegetables.

■ Plant a fruiting hedge. Shrub roses such as rugosa roses (*Rosa rugosa*) make a lovely and intruder-resistant barrier.

■ Build an arbor or trellis. Grapes are traditional, but hardy kiwi would also be a good choice for a large arbor. Vegetables like cucumbers, melons, and beans work well, too, but some need special support for the fruit.

■ Add containers to your landscape. Many dwarf fruit trees are now available and can be grown in large tubs. Dwarf citrus will grow even in northern climates if the trees are moved to a cool, sunny, indoor location during the winter. Strawberry jars are good for strawberries or herbs. For more suggestions on incorporating edibles in your container plantings, see "Colorful and Tasty, Too" on this page.

## SELECTING PLANTS

When you become an edible-landscaper, you'll find that bringing vegetables and fruit trees out of hiding and into the total landscape makes your gardening even more rewarding.

There are food-producing plants to satisfy every need in your landscape. Fruit and nut trees come in a wide range of sizes and shapes, provide shade, and may provide spring blooms and/or fall color. Berry-producing shrubs, such as blueberries and wild plums, also provide flowers and fall color. Some blueberries even have attractive red branches in the winter. The flowers of certain annual and perennial flowers, such as nasturtiums and chives, are edible. Many herbs and vegetables have interesting foliage and some have showy flowers or brightly colored fruit. Fruiting vines such as grapes, melons, and climbing beans will cover fences and trellises. Some edibles, such as creeping thyme and alpine strawberries, make good groundcovers.

Your personal tastes and how much space

 **Colorful and Tasty, Too**

Once you begin working with edible landscaping designs, you'll discover there are nearly limitless possibilities for attractive combinations of food-producing and ornamental plants. The combinations listed here are suitable for container plantings or for garden beds:

■ Curly parsley and yellow pansies (*Viola* spp.)

■ Red leaf lettuce with dwarf yellow marigolds (*Tagetes erecta*)

■ Red chard and New Zealand spinach

■ 'Spicy Globe' basil with 'Nantes' carrots and dwarf orange marigolds (*Tagetes erecta*)

■ Dwarf curly kale with dusty miller and pink nemesia (*Nemesia versicolor*)

■ Sorrel with curly parsley, trailing lobelia (*Lobelia erinus*), and alpine strawberries

■ Eggplant and ageratum

■ Yellow zucchini and coreopsis (*Coreopsis* spp.)

■ 'Royal Burgundy' bush beans with 'Royal Carpet' alyssum and oregano

■ Red geraniums (*Pelargonium* × *hortorum*) with white alyssum and trailing blue lobelia

you have available will determine what you plant. Consider these factors as you select plants:

■ What foods do you like and use most? You're defeating the purpose of an edible landscape if you plant crops you won't eat.

■ How big is each plant and how much will it produce? Fresh homegrown sweet corn is a treat without comparison, but those large cornstalks yield only two or three ears apiece.

■ Do you have a location suitable for growing edibles? Many fruit and vegetable crops will thrive only if they have direct sun for at least six hours daily. Your choice will be limited if you have a shady yard.

■ What fresh foods can you buy locally, and which are expensive or difficult to find? You may decide to plant raspberry canes and forego zucchini plants. Good raspberries are next to impossible to buy at the grocery store, while zucchini in season is cheap (or available free from friends).

## A GALLERY OF EDIBLES

Almost all food-producing plants have ornamental value. The following listings are only a small sampling of the many excellent edible landscape plants.

**Trees**  In warm climates, citrus (orange, lemon, lime, grapefruit) are versatile trees. They

are large enough to provide good shade, cooling the house or an area of the garden during the heat of the day. They retain their shiny deep green leaves through the winter, and they have fruit in various stages of development and ripeness on their branches year-round. When in flower, their fragrance perfumes the air. The flowers of the orange tree are extremely sweet and can be used to flavor honey, sugar, and tea, or as a beautiful garnish.

In the East, if your flowering dogwood (*Cornus florida*) trees are in decline, replace them with Korean dogwood (*Cornus kousa*). It blooms in June (later than the flowering dogwood), the flowers are longer-lasting, and it has brilliant fall foliage. The edible fruit resembles a pale strawberry. It is tartly sweet, with a pearlike, mealy texture, and is favored by birds and wildlife. Figs make interesting foundation plants, but they need a sheltered location and winter protection in the North. Dwarf fruit trees work well in small areas.

**Shrubs**  A blueberry bush makes a good foundation plant but must have acid soil to thrive. Bush cherries, wild plums, gooseberries, currants, hazelnuts, and highbush cranberries (*Viburnum trilobum*) make good hedges. Tightly planted raspberries or blackberries create a living fence. Some shrub-type roses, such as rugosa roses, produce large, bright orange or red, edible rose hips with 60 times the vitamin C of an orange. The hips can be used to make tea, jam, or jelly.

**Ornamentals with Edible Parts**  Leaves of amaranth (especially 'Love Lies Bleeding', 'Red Stripe Leaf', and 'Early Splendor'), leaves and flowers of anise hyssop (*Agastache foeniculum*), young leaves of balloon flower (*Platycodon grandiflorus*), seeds of love-in-a-mist (*Nigella damascena*), and leaves and flowers of nasturtium and violets are edible.

**Showy Edibles**  The following edibles have

## More on Edible Landscapes

If you would like in-depth information for planning and planting an edible landscape, try reading Kate Rogers Gessert's *The Beautiful Food Garden*, Rosalind Creasy's *The Complete Book of Edible Landscaping*, or Robert Kourik's *Designing and Maintaining Your Edible Landscape Naturally*.

colorful and attractive flowers: amaranth (green, purple, red), artichoke (lavender), beans (red, purple, white), cardoon (lavender), chives (lavender, white), dill (yellow-green), eggplant (lavender), garlic (white), Jerusalem artichoke (yellow), nasturtium (orange, red, yellow), okra (white, yellow), rosemary (pale blue), salsify (blue), and sugar peas (purple, white).

The foliage of edibles also comes in many interesting colors and forms. Various cultivars of artichoke, cabbage, cardoon, kale, lavender, leeks, marjoram, onion, rosemary, and sage feature shades of gray and blue. Beets, purple basil, red cab-bage, red chard, pink cress, purple ornamental kale, red lettuces, and purple mustard feature pink and red shades. Carrots, endive, white ornamental kale, variegated lemon balm, nas-turtiums, and thyme feature light green, yellow, and white. Asparagus has attractive green fernlike foliage.

**Vines**   Peas are lovely trained on a fence, and they can be followed by cucumbers or squash as the season progresses. Hardy kiwi is a vigorous climber. 'Scarlet Runner' beans have bright red-orange flowers and are pretty planted with white flowering cultivars of beans. Indeterminate tomatoes can be trained on a trellis or arbor; let the side shoots grow in for maximum coverage.

**Groundcovers**   Alpine strawberries produce tasty fruit. Many herbs are also low-growing and vigorous and can be used as groundcovers as well.

**Fragrant Edibles**   Certain fragrances may be attractive to some people and annoying to others. The most fragrant edibles include basil, chamomile, chives, fennel, mint, oregano, parsley, sage, strawberry, thyme, and tomato. Creeping varieties of thyme and oregano are low-growing and work well planted between stepping stones, where they may be lightly stepped on, releasing their fragrance.

# WILDLIFE AND BIRDS

While you're planning and dreaming about your yard and garden, don't overlook the joys of attracting wildlife and birds. Your yard can become a veritable Noah's ark if you provide the basics for nature's creatures: food, water, shelter, and a safe place in which to reproduce and raise the next generation. With careful planning, you can develop even a tiny yard to attract a surprising array of wildlife and birds. Small occupants, such as rabbits, squirrels, and birds, can become near-permanent breeding residents. Animals with larger territories, such as deer and foxes, may appear for a visit as their travels come to include your backyard as a regular stop.

## ATTRACTING WILDLIFE

Although wild birds have been welcome back-yard and garden visitors for decades, other

### ❀ More on Wildlife

In 1991, the National Wildlife Federation registered its ten-thousandth backyard habitat. That number represents only those gardeners who took the time and trouble to officially register the wildlife-friendly habitats they had developed. Millions of others—the Federation estimates more than 12 million—are enjoying the fruits of attracting wildlife into their backyards without any official recognition whatsoever. For information on registering your backyard, write to Backyard Wildlife Habitat Program, National Wildlife Federation, 1400 16th Street NW, Washington, DC 20036-2266.

You'll find information on attracting beneficial insects and on controlling unwanted wildlife in Chapter 7.

**Backyard wildlife.** A garden alive with wild creatures is interesting in all seasons. Make your yard a haven for wildlife by supplying the essentials—food, water, and shelter.

forms of wildlife have generally been greeted with much less warmth. But growing numbers of gardeners across the country are developing a new attitude toward squirrels, rabbits, mice, toads, salamanders, crickets, and all the rest that the neighborhood ark might hold.

Look at your backyard from a new perspective—one of wildlife in search of food, water, cover, and a safe place for their young. When viewed in this light, tangled brush, tall weeds, and dead trees take on a much more essential role than manicured lawns and rows of flowers.

**Food**  To make your sanctuary attractive to a number of species, you'll need to include a variety of plants. The cottontail rabbit, for example, eats herbaceous plants such as grasses and clovers for much of the year and in winter adds the twigs and bark of young trees and

shrubs. The eastern gray squirrel is most decidedly a nut eater—primarily acorns, hickory nuts, and beechnuts—but corn is also a great attraction. Birds depend on insects as their mainstay, adding seeds, berries, and fruits.

Raccoons relish crayfish, grasshoppers, frogs, and birds' eggs, but almost any living creature that is smaller and slower than a 'coon will find its way into its diet. Acorns, corn, and fleshy fruits also are favorite raccoon foods. Most of the diet of the red fox is small rodents, such as mice, voles, and rabbits. In summer and fall, fox diets also include as much as 25 percent fleshy fruits. The browsing diet of the white-tailed deer consists largely of twigs from trees and shrubs but is supplemented in spring and summer by many of the same herbaceous plants cottontail rabbits eat.

**Shelter**   Tall and mid-sized trees, shrubs, tall herbaceous plants, grasses, and groundcovers all provide for varying needs of different species. Weeds and wildflowers also play their part where local ordinances and neighbors will allow.

Consider seasonal diversity, too. Different plants produce their buds, fruits, and seeds at different times of the year. Some plants, such as evergreens, supply shelter year-round. The brambly interior of a blackberry patch makes a good escape route for small animals such as rabbits, even in winter.

You'll attract the most wildlife by mimicking the plantings of nature. Wild animals stay safe from predators by moving from place to place through protective cover. An isolated berry bush may attract a migrating group of cedar waxwings, but a grouse who tries to reach it could soon become hawk food. If you add another few bushes, and perhaps a hemlock (*Tsuga* spp.), and front the shrubs with meadow grasses and wildflowers, you'll make the planting attractive to a variety of wild creatures.

To this living landscape add snags, logs, brush piles, and rock piles to provide places for smaller creatures to hide and to rear their young. You can camouflage these elements by planting vines like wild grapes or Virginia creeper (*Parthenocissus quinquefolia*) to trail over them. In the process, you'll provide additional food sources.

**Water**   Water is the most overlooked aspect of backyard wildlife habitats. Food and cover preferences vary widely, but nearly all creatures need water. A birdbath will serve many birds, many insects, and some mammals. A ground-level fountain will provide for even more drinkers and might also attract some amphibians. A small pond of varying depth will find use by nearly every creature that you can expect to draw into the backyard and can even provide a permanent home for frogs and turtles.

# ATTRACTING BIRDS

Birds are most gardeners' favorite visitors, with their cheerful songs, sprightly manners, and colorful plumage. Birds are also among nature's most efficient insect predators, making them valuable garden allies. In an afternoon, one diminutive house wren can snatch up more than 500 insect eggs, beetles, and grubs. Given a nest of tent caterpillars, a Baltimore oriole will wolf down as many as 17 of the pests per minute. More than 60 percent of the chickadee's winter diet is aphid eggs. And the swallow lives up to its name by consuming massive quantities of flying insects—by one count, more than 1,000 leafhoppers in 12 hours.

Unless your property is completely bare, at least some birds will visit with no special encouragement from you. Far more birds, however, will come to your yard and garden if you take steps to provide their four basic requirements: food, water, cover, and a safe place in which to raise a family. Robins, nuthatches, hummingbirds, titmice, bluebirds, mockingbirds, cardinals, and various sparrows are among the most common garden visitors.

## LANDSCAPING FOR BIRDS

Feeders, birdbaths, and birdhouses play important roles in attracting birds. But trees, shrubs, and other vegetation can do the whole job naturally. Plants provide food, cover, and nest sites, and because they trap dew and rain and control runoff, they help provide water, too.

When adding plants to your landscape, choose as many food-bearing species as possible, with enough variety to assure birds a steady diet of fruit, buds, and seeds throughout the year. Mix plantings of deciduous and evergreen species in order to maintain leafy cover in all seasons. Species that are native to your region are generally best because the local birds evolved with them and will turn to them first for food and cover. Combine as many types of vegetation as possible: tall trees, shorter trees, shrubs, grasses, flowers, and groundcovers. The greater the plant diversity, the greater the variety of birds you will attract to your yard.

Hummingbirds have their own landscape favorites. Preferred trees and shrubs include tulip tree (*Liriodendron tulipifera*), mimosa (*Albizia julibrissin*), cotoneasters (*Cotoneaster* spp.), orange-eye butterfly bush (*Buddleia davidii*), flowering quinces (*Chaenomeles* spp.), and rose-of-Sharon (*Hibiscus syriacus*). Favored perennials include columbines (*Aquilegia* spp.), common foxglove (*Digitalis purpurea*), alumroots (*Heuchera* spp.), cardinal flower (*Lobelia cardinalis*), penstemons (*Penstemon* spp.), torch lilies (*Kniphofia* spp.), sages (*Salvia* spp.), and delphiniums (*Delphinium* spp.).

Of course, there is the flip side to landscaping for the birds, especially if you grow berries for your family. Bird netting may be a necessity if you don't want to share your cherries and blueberries with your feathered friends.

## PROVIDING FEEDERS

Food is the easiest of the four basic requirements to supply. Even if you live in a city apartment, you can attract birds by putting a feeder filled with seed on your balcony. If your landscape is mostly lawn and hard surfaces, you can use feeders as the main food supply while you add plantings of fruiting trees and shrubs. And if your yard is a good nature habitat, where plants are the primary food source (as they should be), feeders can provide crucial nourishment during winter, drought, and other times when the natural food supply is low. Besides, carefully placed feeders allow you and your family to watch and photograph birds.

Some birds, including juncos, mourning doves, and towhees, feed on the ground, while others, including finches, grosbeaks, nuthatches, titmice, and chickadees, eat their meals higher up. In order to attract as many different birds as possible, use a variety of feeders—seed tubes, broad platforms, and shelf and hanging types. Place them at varying heights, widely separated from one another, and near the protective cover of a tree or shrub if possible. No matter what the style, the feeder should resist rain and snow, should be easy to fill and clean, and should hold enough birdseed so that you don't have to refill it every day, but not so much that the food spoils before it can all be eaten.

## WATER ALL YEAR

Under normal conditions, most birds get all the water they need from the food they eat, from dew, and from rain. Nonetheless, a reliable water source makes life easier for birds—and can be critical during drought or in arid regions.

A birdbath or shallow pan set in the open and at least 3 feet off the ground, with shrubs or overhanging branches nearby to provide an escape route from cats or other predators, is ideal. The water in the bath should be no deeper than 3 inches. Birds are particularly attracted to the sound of moving water, so it helps to hang a dripping hose (or a leaky can or jug, filled with water daily) from a branch over the bath.

Birds need water in winter, too. Commercial immersion water heaters will keep the water in birdbaths thawed in winter. They are available from stores and mail-order supply houses that sell bird supplies. You can try to keep water from freezing by pouring warm water into the baths as needed, but on very cold days this requires a lot of pouring.

## COVER AND NEST SITES

Cover is any form of shelter from enemies and the elements. Different bird species favor different kinds of cover. Mourning doves, for example, prefer evergreen groves; others prefer the refuge of densely twiggy shrubs. Likewise, most species require a particular kind of cover in which to raise a family. Some birds, including red-winged blackbirds, nest in high grass; others, such as cardinals, nest in dense foliage; and still others, such as woodpeckers, need wooded land.

You can add more nest sites and attract many types of birds to your yard with birdhouses. Different species have different housing require-ments, but there are ready-made birdhouses and build-your-own plans for everything from blue-birds to barn owls. Whichever birdhouse you choose, make sure that it is weather-resistant, that its roof is pitched to shed rain, and that there are holes in the bottom for drainage and in the walls or back for ventilation. A hinged or removable top or front makes cleaning easier. Position birdhouses with their entrance holes facing away from prevailing winds, and clean out the nesting materials from the boxes after every nesting season.

 ## Trees and Shrubs for Birds

To attract birds to your landscape, look at plants from a bird's point of view. Do they provide food and shelter? Nest sites? Try to plant a variety to provide birds with protective cover and a varied diet throughout the year. The following trees and shrubs are excellent food sources—producing berries, nuts, or seeds that birds will flock to. Evergreen species provide food but are also especially important for winter cover. These species will grow in most regions of the country.

### Evergreen Shrubs

Chinese holly (*Ilex cornuta*)
Cotoneasters (*Cotoneaster* spp.)
Japanese yew (*Taxus cuspidata*)
Oregon grape (*Mahonia aquifolium*)

### Deciduous Shrubs

American elder (*Sambucus canadensis*)
Bayberries (*Myrica* spp.)
Blueberries (*Vaccinium* spp.)
Common buckthorn (*Rhamnus cathartica*)
Japanese barberry (*Berberis thunbergii*)
Pyracanthas (*Pyracantha* spp.)

Raspberries and blackberries (*Rubus* spp.)
Red-osier dogwood (*Cornus sericea*)
Sand cherries (*Prunus pumila, P. besseyi*)
Viburnums (*Viburnum* spp.)

### Evergreen Trees

American holly (*Ilex opaca*)
Canada hemlock (*Tsuga canadensis*)
Douglas fir (*Pseudotsuga menziesii*)
Eastern red cedar (*Juniperus virginiana*)
Pines (*Pinus* spp.)
Spruces (*Picea* spp.)

### Deciduous Trees

American beech (*Fagus grandifolia*)
Cherries (*Prunus* spp.)
Common persimmon (*Diospyros virginiana*)
Crab apples (*Malus* spp.)
Flowering dogwood (*Cornus florida*)
Hackberries (*Celtis* spp.)
Hawthorns (*Crataegus* spp.)
Hickories (*Carya* spp.)
Oaks (*Quercus* spp.)
Serviceberries (*Amelanchier* spp.)
White ash (*Fraxinus americana*)

# Chapter 2

# IMPROVING YOUR SOIL

Healthy soil is the key to successful organic gardening. The basic principle that organic gardeners live by is to feed the soil, and let the soil feed the plants. The challenge for organic gardeners is to balance the soil so that it provides all the conditions plants need to thrive.

You may wonder why the soil in your yard and garden would be out of balance. There are several possible reasons:

■ The surface soil around many homes may have been disturbed—or even removed—during construction, and nothing was done to restore the soil afterward.

■ Driving equipment, such as a lawn tractor, or repeatedly walking on soil compacts it, harming its structure.

■ Your soil's natural characteristics may not be favorable for gardening. For example, you may have a soil that is so sandy that it does not hold sufficient water and nutrients to support vigorous plant growth. Or your soil's pH may be so acidic that many kinds of plants won't thrive.

■ Unless you're a longtime organic gardener, the soil may be depleted by years of cropping without replenishing organic matter, the soil's natural storehouse of nutrients.

■ If you've used chemical fertilizers, the soil microorganisms that play an important role in maintaining natural fertility may have died off.

The first step in the process of improving your soil organically is to learn about its characteristics. There are many tests that will help you analyze your soil. After testing, you'll know what problems your soil has, and you can take steps to remedy them. Your soil improvement process will include adding organic matter and other soil amendments. While you work on improving your soil, you may want to use organic fertilizers to boost plant performance.

## HOW SOIL WORKS

Organic gardeners know that soil is much more than just dirt. Soil is an intricate mix of fine rock particles, organic matter, water, air, microorganisms. A *healthy* soil is especially full

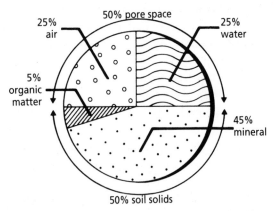

**Soil components.** Soil is nearly half minerals and half water and air. Organic matter makes up only a small percentage of the soil. But for successful gardeners, maintaining organic matter content is critical. Soil life, including mammals, reptiles, insects, and microorganisms, transforms organic matter into nutrients that can be taken up by your plants.

of living things: plant roots, animals, insects, bacteria, fungi, and other organisms. Managing your soils to keep this living system thriving can make the difference between gardening success and failure.

## TEXTURE AND STRUCTURE

Although we might assume that the size differences between soil particles—sand, silt, and clay—are too small to have any significance, they are actually of great importance. The relative proportion of these tiny rock fragments—referred to as soil texture—influences soil water retention, air drainage, and fertility. The tiny spaces between these particles are the holding areas for soil water and for the dissolved nutri-

ents that can be absorbed by roots.

The spaces between sand particles are comparatively large, so they do not tend to granulate, or stick together. Thus, sandy soils often do not hold enough water to support the growth of many kinds of plants. Sandy soils may also tend to be less fertile because they have less surface area where nutrients can be held.

Clayey soils are rich in very tiny particles that are attracted to each other when wet. While these clay particles can hold large reserves of water and dissolved nutrients, too much clay also can create problems. When clay particles dry, they stick together and form a hard layer. Clayey soils tend to form surface crusts that water cannot penetrate easily. A clay layer deep-

 **Words to Know**

**Sand, silt, and clay:** Tiny fragments of rock or minerals that make up nearly half the material in the soil. They are distinguished by size. Sand particles are from 0.05 to 2.0 millimeters in diameter, silt particles are from 0.002 to 0.05 millimeters, and clay particles are less than 0.002 millimeters in diameter.

**Soil texture:** The relative proportions of sand, silt, and clay in the soil.

**Soil structure:** The arrangement of soil particles in the soil.

**Loam:** Soil that has moderate amounts of sand, silt, and clay. Loam soils are generally considered the best garden soils.

**Soil pH:** A measurement of the acidity or alkalinity of the soil.

**Organic matter:** Various forms of living or dead plant and animal material.

**Microorganisms:** Animals and plants that are too small to be seen clearly without use of a microscope.

**Decay cycle:** The changes that occur as plants grow, die, and break down in the soil. The action of soil animals and microorganisms breaks down plant tissues to release nutrients that new plants then take up to fuel their growth and development.

**Nitrogen cycle:** The transformation of nitrogen from an atmospheric gas to organic compounds in the soil to compounds in plants, with eventual release of nitrogen gas to the atmosphere.

**Humus:** A dark-colored, stable form of organic matter that remains after most of the plant and animal residues in it have decomposed. When soil animals and microbes digest organic matter, such as chopped leaves or weeds, humus is the end product.

**Erosion:** The wearing away of soil by running water, wind, ice, or other geological forces. Erosion can be accelerated by the activity of people or animals.

er in the soil can form a hardpan that impedes water drainage.

It takes a huge effort to change soil texture. For example, to have a beneficial effect on clayey soil in a 20-foot × 50-foot garden bed, you'd have to add about 3 to 5 tons of sand to the top 6 inches of soil.

Fortunately, there are steps you can take to improve another important characteristic, soil structure. Soil structure determines how well water is retained in the soil and how well it drains, how much air is available in the soil, and how easily nutrients are released for uptake by plant roots.

Many factors contribute to the creation of soil structure. Soil water freezes and thaws, plant roots grow and die, earthworms move through the soil. All these processes contribute to formation of soil pores and soil clumps, or aggregates. Soil structure is also affected by soil pH, the amount of humus in the soil, and the combination of minerals in the soil. The ideal soil is friable—the soil particles clump together in clusters with air spaces between them. This allows water to drain through, and oxygen and carbon dioxide can easily move from the air above into the spaces below. Pore space can vary from 30 to 50 percent of soil volume.

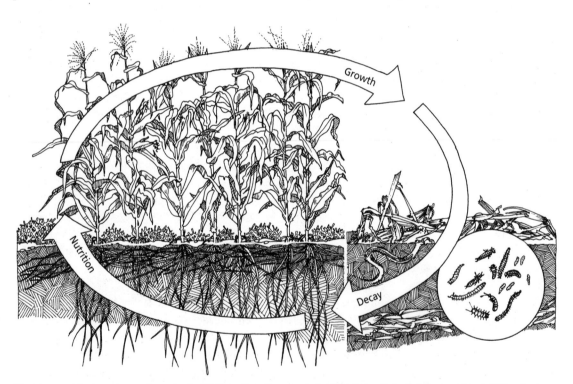

**The decay cycle.** In nature, when plants die, they literally are returned to the soil via the decay process. Mites, beetles, millipedes, earthworms, bacteria, and fungi feed on the dead and dying tissues. These organisms physically and chemically break the plant tissues down into simpler components. The waste products and, in their turn, the dead bodies of the soil-dwelling animals and microorganisms become part of soil organic matter. Proteins are converted to simple nitrogen compounds that can be absorbed by plant roots. Minerals such as phosphorus, potassium, and calcium are also changed into soluble compounds that are then absorbed by root cells and used by new growing plants.

## Should You Squash or Save?

Turn a shovelful of garden soil or just scratch the surface, and you'll discover an underground living world. Here's a rundown of common garden insects:

**Armyworms:** Armyworms are greenish brown caterpillars with white stripes on their sides and dark- or light-colored stripes on their back. They feed on garden plants at night. During the day, they hide in plant foliage or just beneath the soil surface.

**Centipedes and millipedes:** These are serpentine creatures from ½ inch to 5 inches long, with  many legs. Both are important predators and decomposers in the soil ecosystem. They consume dead plant materials. You'll find them among leaf litter or in any damp, dark spot.

**Colorado potato beetles:** Adults have yellow wing covers with ten black stripes. Larvae are orangey, humpbacked grubs, with black spots on their sides. Larvae eat potato foliage, quickly defoliating potato plants. You'll find adults and pupae in soil where potatoes are grown.

**Cutworms:** These are fat, greasy-looking, gray or dull brown, 1- to 2-inch caterpillars with shiny heads. They are often confused with armyworms. They chew through stems of vegetable and flower seedlings at night. During the day, they rest just below the soil surface.

**Earthworms:** Most garden species are less than 5 inches long. Look for red, gray, and brown garden worms at and beneath the soil surface. Many feed upon decompos-ing organic matter, transporting it through their burrows and redistributing it throughout the soil.

**Ground beetles:** Adults are blue-black or brown, ¾- to 1-inch-long beetles. Larvae are dark brown or black and grublike but slender. Adults and larvae prey on other insects and pests, including slugs. Some species eat weed and vegetable seeds. Spread organic mulches to attract them.

**Grubs:** Grubs are the larvae of Japanese beetles, June or May beetles, and other beetles. They are wormlike, fat, C-shaped, and most often white with a dark-colored head. They munch on both living and dead plant roots. You'll find them in soil beneath lawns.

**Rove beetles:** These resemble earwigs without rear pincers. The hard wing covers are shortened, leaving the abdomen exposed. Length ranges from ¹⁄₂₅ to ¹⁄₁₀ inch. Most rove beetles are insect predators. You'll find them under rocks, in moss or fungi, and in compost piles and organic mulches.

**Slugs and snails:** Both slugs and snails are soft-bodied and wormlike, measuring ⅛ to 8 inches long. Snails have a spiral-shaped shell into which they can 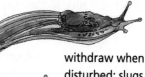 withdraw when disturbed; slugs lack a shell. Both lay clear, jellylike egg masses under stones and other debris. They feed at night on most aboveground plant parts, leaving behind a shiny trail of mucous slime.

The best way to improve soil structure is to add organic matter—lots of it. See "Adding Organic Matter" on page 32 to learn more about adding organic matter to your soil.

All too often, gardeners also unthinkingly harm soil structure by tilling excessively or by walking on or working soils that are too wet. These activities can ruin soil structure, and the damage done is not easily undone.

## AIR AND WATER

Oxygen is critical in the soil because many beneficial soil organisms cannot live without it. Gaseous nitrogen, another component of soil air, is a raw material for nitrogen-fixing bacteria that manufacture protein materials. These are later broken down to yield nitrogen compounds that can be absorbed by plant roots. Plant roots also "breathe" and need good air exchange between soil air and the atmosphere for good development.

Water also occupies soil pore space. Plant roots absorb this water and pass it on to leaves and stems, where it serves as a nutrient, a coolant, and an essential part of all plant cells. Water is also the carrier for mineral nutrients, allowing them to enter plant roots and be transported through the plants. If soil doesn't drain well, water occupies all the soil pore space. This suffocates the plants because their roots cannot get the air they need.

Soil pore spaces should vary in size and be evenly distributed. Soil with sufficient organic matter will have this quality. Walking on the soil or driving yard and garden equipment over it can cause these pore spaces to collapse.

## ORGANISMS

Although they are only a minute portion of the soil by weight and volume, the living organisms in soil play a vital role. Soil microorganisms power the decay cycle—nature's perfect system for recycling organic matter and maintaining healthy soils.

Soil microorganisms include nematodes, protozoa, fungi, bacteria, and actinomycetes (threadlike bacteria). These microorganisms convert plant material into humus. The illustration on page 24 explains how.

Earthworms serve as natural "tillers" and soil conditioners. Many soil-dwelling insects are parasites and predators of insects that harm crop plants. And soil animals, including the much-maligned mole, also help improve soil aeration and eat some harmful insects.

# INVESTIGATING THE SOIL

One question home gardeners frequently ask is, "Should I be adding anything to the soil this spring?" The best way to answer that question is to investigate your soil—to learn about its structure and content by observation and testing.

There are several simple tests you can do yourself to learn about your soil's structure, drainage, and earthworm activity (earthworms are a key indicator of soil health). You can also submit soil samples from your yard for soil analysis. Privately run soil testing laboratories and the Cooperative Extension Service perform soil analyses for home gardeners and offer recommendations on soil improvement based on the results of their tests.

## PREPARING A SOIL SAMPLE

You may want to collect many samples from around your yard and combine them to submit for a single test and report. Or you may want to prepare separate samples from your vegetable garden soil, your lawn, and an area where you hope to create a flower border, for example. However, you'll have to pay three times as much to get the three separate sets of recommendations.

Follow these steps to prepare a sample that will accurately reflect the content of your soil:

1. Scrape away any surface litter or plant growth from a small area of soil. Use a soil probe to cut a core of soil, or dig a hole with a stainless steel trowel or other tool (if you don't have stainless steel tools, use a large stainless steel spoon) and collect a slice of soil from the side of the hole. For cultivated areas, collect a core or slice to a depth of 6 inches. For lawns, collect your samples only from the top 4 inches of soil.

2. Repeat the sampling procedure at 10 to 15 different locations around your yard or the particular area you are sampling.

3. Mix the soil cores or slices in a clean plastic or stainless steel container.

4. Place some of the mixed sample in a plastic container or bag and put it in the bag supplied by your Cooperative Extension Service or the soil testing laboratory for shipment.

Don't touch the sample with soft steel, galvanized, or brass tools, or with your bare skin. The content of some minerals in soil is so small that minerals picked up from these metals or your skin could throw off test results.

You'll send your sample, along with an information sheet concerning your soil's history and your future gardening plans, to the testing laboratory by mail. Be sure to write on the information form that you want recommendations for organic soil amendments.

## INTERPRETING RECOMMENDATIONS

After analyzing your soil, the test lab will send you a report on the results of their analysis and recommendations for improving your soil.

Test results may include: soil pH, organic matter content, and content of calcium, magnesium, nitrogen, phosphorus, potassium, sodium, sulfur, and trace minerals.

Soil labs make recommendations based on results of their research programs on plant responses to additions of mineral amendments. Making the recommendations is an imprecise science because the researchers must try to relate the data from the research soils they study to your individual soil. However, all soils are different. They do not all respond equally to applications of minerals or organic materials.

Typically, soil fertility studies are performed on soils that have low organic matter content. Analysis of such low organic matter soils may be more accurate because organic matter makes the soil more biologically diverse and complex.

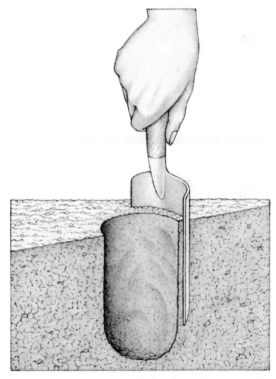

**Taking a soil sample.** To collect a soil sample with a soil probe, first push the probe straight down into the soil to the proper depth. Then pull it completely out of the soil and remove the sample from the probe. If you're using a trowel, begin by digging a hole at least 6 inches deep. Then use the trowel to cut a slice of soil from the side of the hole; the slice is the soil sample.

If you have built up your soil's organic matter content, the test results and recommendations you receive may be less than fully accurate. In general, if you have been adding organic matter regularly to your soil for years and had healthy crops and good yields, don't add as much nitrogen, phosphorus, and potassium as recommended. Soil with high organic content uses soil amendments more efficiently, and organic soil amendments are less likely to leach quickly out of the root zone. You can reduce the amounts recommended by soil labs by as much as 75 percent. For example, if the recommendation you receive is for 2.5 pounds of nitrogen per 1,000 square feet of garden, you could add 1 pound per 1,000 square feet.

If you are just beginning an organic soil management program, be prepared to add soil-building materials in the amounts recommended by the testing service. Ask clearly for recommendations for organic amendments. That way, you won't have to guess whether to add smaller amounts than those on the lab report.

## DO-IT-YOURSELF TESTS

Another way to learn about your soil's condition is to try simple tests that rely not on precise chemical analysis, but rather on your observations of the soil. With these tests, there is little or no cost and no waiting for results.

**The Squeeze Test** This test helps you determine soil texture. Do this test two or three days after a rainy spell. Take a loose ball of soil about the size of a Ping-Pong ball in the palm of your hand. Gently squeeze it between the ball of your thumb and the lower outside edge of your index finger. Sand feels gritty, silt feels like moist talcum powder, and clay feels slippery.

Squeeze the ball in your hand, and release. If it crumbles, it has a reasonably balanced texture. If the soil ball can hold its shape, it has a substantial percentage of clay. If you can roll it into

a sausage shape, it has even more clay.

Run the palm of your other hand firmly over the handful of soil. If you see scratch marks on the surface of the soil, there is a sizable proportion of sand present. If the soil feels greasy, this indicates silt.

**The Perc Test** This test is an easy way to assess water drainage through your soil. Dig a hole 6 inches across and 1 foot deep. Fill the hole with water and let it drain. As soon as the water has drained completely, fill it again. This time, keep track of how long it takes for the hole to drain. If it takes more than eight hours, you have a drainage problem that needs attention.

**The Watering Test** A variation on the perc test will tell you whether your soil drains too rapidly. Start by watering a small area of your lawn or garden bed very thoroughly. Two days later, dig a small hole 6 inches deep where you watered. If the soil is already dry to the bottom of the hole, your soil likely doesn't retain enough water for good plant growth.

Another way to monitor soil moisture is to use a manual or automatic moisture sensor. These are small, electronic devices that measure available water in the soil, letting you know how long water levels are adequate for your plants' needs. If a meter indicates that the soil needs rewatering only a few days after you've watered thoroughly or after a soaking rain, then you need to improve the soil's water-retention capacity.

**The Undercover Test** The best way to learn about some aspects of your soil is to get right down into it. If you plan to plant a new tree or shrub, kill two birds with one stone and check out your soil as you prepare the hole. Your new plant will benefit from the extra-large planting hole, and you'll get valuable information about what's happening beneath the soil surface.

Dig a hole at least 2 feet deep and 2 feet

across so you can get a view down into it. Pile soil on a ground cloth as you dig, so you can neatly refill the hole when you're done. Then observe your soil closely. For some ideas on what to look for, see the illustration on page 32.

## OTHER TESTS

If you have your soil tested, the test results will include a measurement of your soil's pH. However, pH is something you may want to measure separately from the mineral content. For example, if you plan to plant blueberries, which

require acid soil, you may want to quickly check pH at several sites to see if the soil pH needs adjusting. For more information about pH testing and changing soil pH, see "Understanding pH" on page 30.

An indirect way to find out about nutrient levels in your soil is to analyze the content of the plants growing in it. Plant analysis is not a do-it-yourself test. Many Cooperative Extension Service offices and some private labs will analyze samples of leaf tissue for nutrient content. This type of testing may give more accurate results

*(continued on page 32)*

---

 ### Soil Tests: Which One, When?

How can gardeners tell when they should go to the effort and expense of having their soil tested? And if they need a test, should they do it themselves or have a lab do the work?

**Cooperative Extension soil tests:** Extension soil tests are generally inexpensive (or free in some states). Soil test kits are available from your local Cooperative Extension Service office or at many garden centers. Their analysis will probably not be as complete as that offered by private testing labs.

**Private laboratory soil tests:** Private soil test labs usually charge $30 or more for their analyses. However, the extra money you spend often will translate to a more complete soil test and final report. It may also be easier to find a soil lab familiar with making organic, rather than chemical, fertilizer recommendations.

**Commercial home test kits:** Results from home test kits will be less accurate than those from a soil lab, because soil labs factor in individual differences in soil samples, such as moisture content and soil density, when doing analyses. But the more sophisticated (and

expensive) home test kits will give fairly accurate results. If your home results indicate soil imbalances, you may want to confirm the results with a professional soil test.

**When to test:** When is it worthwhile for you to pay for a private soil test lab? Answer that question by thinking about the general picture of your garden's health. Are your plants growing vigorously? If you've had plant problems, have they been limited to just one area or to a few types of plants? If yields have been disappointing, the lawn is filled with weeds, or many plants suffer from repeated disease problems or show deficiency symptoms, consider testing your soil. Some deficiency may well be at the heart of the problem.

Also, if your observations or home tests indicate an imbalance that could be corrected by adding mineral amendments such as rock phosphate, lime, or gypsum, get a professional test before you act. If you add too much of any of these materials, you can create problems that won't be easy to correct. If you add too little, you won't fix the problem.

## Understanding pH

Soil acidity or alkalinity affects plant growth by influencing the availability of nutrients in soil for uptake by plants. The measure of acidity or alkalinity is called pH. Many gardening books and catalogs list the preferred pH for specific plants. The good news is that with a few exceptions, most plants will tolerate a fairly wide range of soil pH. The illustration on the opposite page shows how pH values relate to soils.

### Nutrient Uptake and pH

Plant roots absorb mineral nutrients such as nitrogen and iron when they are dissolved in water. If the soil is too acid or alkaline, some nutrients won't dissolve easily and therefore are unavailable for uptake.

Most nutrients that plants need are readily available when the pH of the soil solution ranges from 6.0 to 7.5. Below pH 6.0, some nutrients, such as nitrogen, phosphorus, and potassium, are less available. When pH exceeds 7.5, iron, manganese, and phosphorus are less available.

### Regional Differences

Many environmental factors, including amount of rainfall, vegetation type, and temperature, can affect soil pH. In general, areas with heavy rainfall and forest cover such as states in the East and the Pacific Northwest have moderately acid soils. Soils in regions with light rainfall and prairie cover such as the Midwest tend to be near neutral. Droughty areas of the western United States tend to have alkaline soils. However, the pH of cultivated and developed soils often differs from that of native soil. During construction, topsoil is frequently removed and may be replaced by a different type of soil. So your garden soil pH could be different from a garden across town.

### Changing pH

Most horticultural plants grow well in slightly acid to neutral soil (pH 6.0–7.0). Some common exceptions include blueberries, potatoes, and rhododendrons, which prefer moderately acid soil. You can make small changes to soil pH by applying soil amendments. However, you'll have best success if you select plants that are adapted to your soil pH and other soil characteristics. Adding organic matter to the soil also tends to make both acid and alkaline soils more neutral.

If you have your soil analyzed by a lab, the lab report will include soil pH. You can also test soil pH yourself with a home soil test kit or a portable pH meter. Home kits and portable meters vary in accuracy but can be helpful in assessing the general pH range of your soil. See "Soil Tests: Which One, When?" on page 29 for more information about testing.

The quantity of liming or acidifying material needed to change soil pH depends on many factors, including current pH, soil texture, and the type of material. A soil lab report will recommend types and quantities to use.

You can spread liming or acidifying materials with a garden spreader or by hand for small areas. If hand-spreading, be sure to wear heavy gloves to protect your skin.

### Correcting Acid Soil

If your soil is too acid, you must add alkaline material, a process commonly called liming. The most common liming material is ground limestone. There are two types: calcitic limestone (calcium carbonate) and dolomitic limestone (calcium-magnesium carbonate). In most instances, you'll use calcitic lime. Apply dolomitic lime only if your soil also has a magnesium deficiency. Ground limestone breaks down slowly in the soil. Apply it in the fall to allow time for it to act on soil pH before the next growing season. A rule of thumb for slightly acidic soils is to apply 5 pounds of lime per 100 square feet to raise pH by 1 point. In general, sandy soils will need less limestone to change pH; clay soils will need more.

The amount of lime you must add to correct pH depends not only on your soil type but also on its initial pH. For example, applying 5 pounds of limestone per 100 square feet will raise the pH of a sandy loam soil from 6.0 to 6.5. It would take 10 pounds per 100 square feet to make the same change in a silty loam soil. However, if 5.6 was the initial pH of the soil, 8 pounds per 100 square feet would be required for the sandy loam soil, and 16 pounds per 100 square feet for the silty loam soil. There is no simple rule of thumb that applies to all soils. The safest approach to take if you plan to apply limestone is to have your soil tested and follow the lab recommendations.

Applying wood ashes also will raise soil pH. Wood ashes contain up to 70 percent calcium carbonate, as well as potassium, phosphorus, and many trace minerals. Because it has a very fine particle size, wood ash is a fast-acting liming material. Use it with caution, because overapplying it can create serious soil imbalances. Limit applications to 25 pounds per 1,000 square feet, and apply ashes only once every 2 to 3 years in any particular area.

### Correcting Alkaline Soil

If your soil is too alkaline, add a source of acidity. The most common material to add is elemental sulfur. As with lime, there is no simple rule on how much sulfur to add to change pH by a set amount. Testing your soil and following lab recommendations is the best approach.

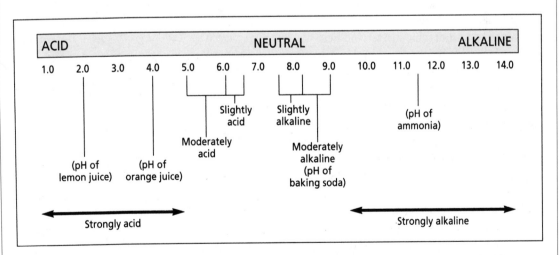

**The pH scale.** The pH scale ranges from 1.0 to 14.0. Soils are called acid or alkaline, but the degree of acidity or alkalinity in soils is not great enough to pose any hazard to humans. Most soils are less acidic than orange juice and less alkaline than baking soda. Gardeners generally refer to alkaline soils as "sweet" and acid soils as "sour."

for certain nutrients, including nitrogen, than soil analysis does. The labs analyze the nutrient content in the samples and compare the readings with compiled research data that show the normal range of nutrients required for optimal growth of that species. Based on that comparison, they make recommendations for treatment.

# IMPROVING YOUR SOIL

There are no overnight or even single-season organic solutions for an imbalanced soil. Unlike gardeners who rely on soluble synthetic chemical fertilizers to keep their plants green and growing, organic gardeners boost the soil's natural fertility through a two-, three-, or four-year program that results in a fertile, rich soil. However, your plants don't have to suffer during the soil-building years. You can supplement your soil-building program with organic fertilizers to meet your plants' needs for nutrients.

## ADDING ORGANIC MATTER

The single most important step you can take to improve your soil is to increase its organic matter content. Adding organic matter will help improve your soil's structure and biological activity. Organic material stimulates the growth and reproductive capacity of the bacteria and

**A worm's-eye view.** There are many clues both above and below ground level about the health of your soil. Vigorous plants with strong, deep root systems are among the best indicators of soil health. Soil color is also important. Generally, dark browns, reds, and tans indicate good soils. Soils that have a high humus content will usually be darker in color than soils low in humus. Soil color is also a clue to drainage. Tinges of blue and gray indicate poor aeration, often the result of poor water drainage. Generally, brown soils will drain much better than gray-colored soils. Brown and red colors reflect the oxidized iron content of the soil.

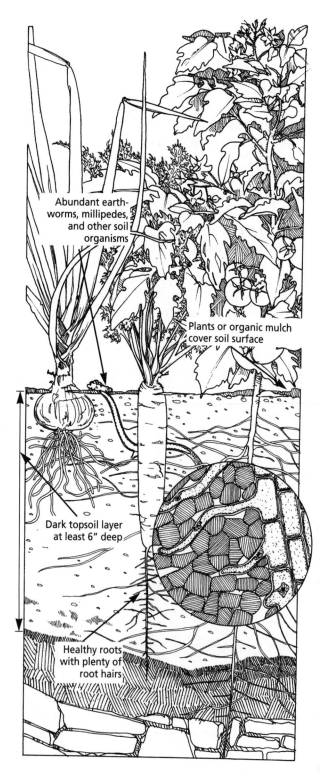

Abundant earthworms, millipedes, and other soil organisms

Plants or organic mulch cover soil surface

Dark topsoil layer at least 6" deep

Healthy roots with plenty of root hairs

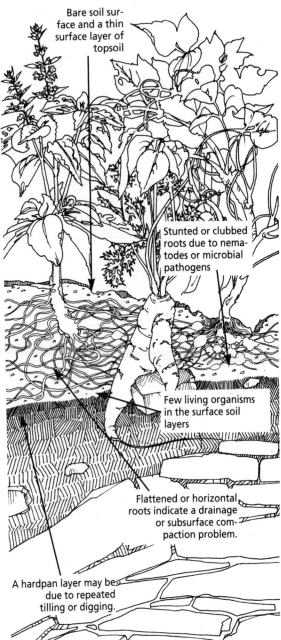

Bare soil surface and a thin surface layer of topsoil

Stunted or clubbed roots due to nematodes or microbial pathogens

Few living organisms in the surface soil layers

Flattened or horizontal roots indicate a drainage or subsurface compaction problem.

A hardpan layer may be due to repeated tilling or digging.

**Subsurface problems.** It's no surprise that the scene below the soil surface in this garden is not pretty—or healthy. The leggy plants and stunted carrots are sure signs of soil that needs help.

other microorganisms that help create a vital and productive soil. Adding finished compost or other partially decayed organic material can also go a long way toward helping solve mineral deficiencies in your soil and can even modify soil pH.

There is a wide range of organic materials available to gardeners. The best of these is compost—a mixture of decayed organic materials. Other good organic materials include aged manure, chopped leaves, straw, grass clippings, and peat moss. To learn how to make and use compost, see Chapter 3.

**How to Add Organic Matter**  You can add organic matter by digging or tilling it into the surface of the soil, by planting green manure crops, or simply by applying mulches and allowing them to break down over time. For more information on these methods, see "Using Green Manure" on page 36 and "Double Digging" on page 40.

It's relatively easy to increase the humus content of vegetable gardens because they are usually cleared of plants every year. But how do you increase the organic material under an existing lawn? Or around trees and shrubs? Wherever you have existing plants, including lawn grass, shrubs, or perennials, you can lay compost or other decayed organic material on the surface. In a few months, the soil organisms will have begun to work that organic material down into the soil. The other method for gardens and around trees and shrubs is to use some kind of organic mulch and let it break down naturally, giving the soil an organic material boost as it does. You can do this at any convenient time of year. Remember, a soil filled with plants also is gaining organic matter from the growth and decay of the plant root systems. However, that may not be adequate to give the soil the amount of organic material it needs.

**How Much to Add**  Five percent organic matter is a good goal to strive for in your soil. One inch of compost or other fine-textured organic material spread over the soil surface equals about 5 percent of the volume of the first foot of soil. As a rule of thumb, if you add about 1 inch of fine organic matter to a garden every year, you will gradually increase that soil's organic matter content to a desirable level. If you use a bulkier material such as chopped leaves or straw, you will have to apply a thicker layer because there is less actual organic matter per volume. A 4-inch layer of bulky organic

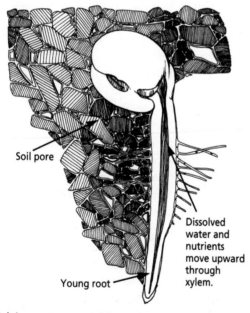

Soil pore

Dissolved water and nutrients move upward through xylem.

Young root

**Helping roots grow.** Adding organic matter to soil and working the soil to make it loose and friable improve the soil's structure and biological activity, enabling plant roots to thrive. Roots extend through soil pore space, absorbing water and nutrients from the water, dissolved minerals, and organic compounds that line soil pores. In soil with low organic content, the nutrients that roots need for growth are unavailable. In compacted soil, root growth is retarded or stopped because of lack of pore spaces.

material is equivalent to a 1-inch layer of fine material.

In the South, it's more difficult to maintain soil organic matter levels. Microorganisms break down organic matter, and microbial populations grow faster (and so eat more) in warmer temperatures. Organic material can break down twice as fast in hot southern soils as it does in cooler northern soils.

**Fresh versus Dry**  On the average, fresh organic matter—such as grass clippings, kitchen waste, and green weeds—worked into the soil will be 50 percent decayed in just two months. The material will be 75 percent decayed after four months, and about 87 percent decayed after six months.

Dry materials decompose more slowly than moist. For example, if you dig chopped dried leaves into your garden, it may take four to five months for them to be halfway along the path of transformation to humus.

The decay process works best if there is a constant supply of food for the soil microorganisms that act as the decay "machine." So it's a good idea to mulch areas where you've incorporated partially decayed material with dry organic matter that will decompose slowly. The mulch serves two functions. It protects the decomposing organic matter from excessive heat, which can cause some organic compounds to volatilize and be lost. It also provides a longer-term food source for the soil microorganisms that are stimulated by the dug-in organic matter.

**The Rule of Mulch**  There is one cardinal rule in your efforts to increase the organic content of your soil. Once you've added whatever material your soil needs, there should not be a single square inch of bare soil left anywhere on your property. It should be covered with grass, a groundcover, plants, or mulch. Bare soil loses humus much faster than covered soil because the nutrients created by the decomposition of the organic matter are leached away more readily. In addition, the impact of raindrops on bare soil can destroy the loose soil structure you have worked to obtain. Covered soil is also much less prone to surface erosion by wind or water.

## ADDING MICROBES

If you're a gardener who's switching to organic methods from chemical methods, or if you've inherited a garden that's been treated with pes-ticides, you may have soils with very low biological activity. Give some extra help to the struggling microbial populations by applying bacterial cultures that give your soil and compost piles a biological boost. Some of these cultures are in a dry, dormant, powdered form. After you spread this material over your soil or into a compost pile, the microbes become activated and biological activity accelerates. Keep in mind that you must keep adding sufficient organic matter to feed the increased populations of soil

---

 **Problem Soils**

Two of the most common problems gardeners face are soils that don't drain well and soils that are high in clay.

Finally, you can install a drainage system, but this is a project for which you'll probably need professional help.

### Poorly Drained Soils

If your soil tests and observations have alerted you to a drainage problem in your yard, you have several options. Your first option could be to accept the wet spot and create a small bog garden. If you have other plans for the site, you'll have to find a way to improve drainage.

The drainage problem may be due to a hardpan somewhere in the top 2 feet of soil. You may be able to break up the compaction layer by double digging. If the layer is deeper than you can reach by double digging, try planting deep-rooted sweet clover in spring and allow it to grow for two full growing seasons. The roots may penetrate the deep hardpan and naturally create better drainage.

Another way to sidestep a drainage problem is to create a raised bed in the wet area. You'll have to bring in extra topsoil and build up sides, essentially creating a layer of soil with good drainage for plants to grow in above the poorly drained area.

### Clay Soils

If you have heavy clay soil that is low in organic matter, you will have to add considerable amounts of organic material and energy to make that soil as loose and friable as you can. Double digging (see page 40) is your best option. Some gardeners will add sand along with the organic material to heavy clay soils in beds where they want to grow root crops or flower bulbs. A lot of sand is required to make a significant difference, though. Adding small amounts of sand may actually cause your soil to harden, worsening its condition. To boost the sand component in the top 6 to 8 inches of the soil by 5 to 10 percent, you will need about 3 to 5 tons per 1,000 square feet of garden. If you have a close and convenient source of sand, it may be worth the effort to spread and till in the sand. However, adding sand alone will not remedy problems with heavy clay. Using green manures and incorporating organic matter are the best long-term solutions.

microbes, or you won't get any lasting benefit from your investment.

If your earthworm count is low, don't despair. Once you provide more organic material to feed them, they will usually return. Earthworm egg casings can lie dormant as deep as 20 feet in the soil for as long as 20 years.

Dry or granular, a fast-acting chemical fertilizer can repel earthworms when it dissolves in soil water and leaches down into the soil. Earthworms are highly sensitive to changes in the environment and will avoid the salty conditions created by the chemical fertilizers. If you are making the transition from chemical fertilizers to organic soil amendments and fertilizers, have patience. As your soil reaches a healthy balance, you will see more earthworm activity.

### ADDING MINERALS

There are several organic soil amendments you can add to correct specific pH and mineral

imbalances. In most cases, you should only add these amendments according to recommendations from soil tests or plant analyses. If you add too much of a natural mineral supplement such as rock phosphate, you can create an excess of a particular nutrient. The excess may damage plants or may interfere with uptake of some other nutrients.

# USING GREEN MANURE

Green manure crops can be a great supplement to an organic soil improvement program. If you can't get animal manures, or if your compost supply isn't equal to demand, try planting green manures in the garden areas you till annually, such as vegetable or annual flower beds. Many gardeners plant a green manure crop such as buckwheat or clover in the fall, after finishing the harvest and clearing debris from the beds. Others make green manures part of their regular crop rotation, planting them during the growing season.

Cover crops are plantings of grasses or legumes that cover the soil surface. Cover crops help prevent soil erosion and stop weeds from taking over unplanted garden beds. Gardeners often use the term *cover crop* interchangeably with the term *green manure crop*, although their technical definitions are not the same.

A green manure crop sown in the fall and grown through the winter also functions as a cover crop, protecting the soil from erosion and compaction. Plan to till or dig the crop into the soil in early spring, about three to four weeks before you begin your vegetable garden.

In soils that are wet in early spring, dig the green manure into the soil late in the fall and let it decompose over the winter. Otherwise, the damage done by working soil when it's wet could outweigh the benefit of the green manure.

---

 **Words to Know**

**Green manure:** A crop that is grown and then incorporated into the soil to increase soil fertility or organic matter content.

**Cover crop:** A crop grown to protect and enrich the soil or to control weeds.

**Nitrogen fixation:** The capture and conversion of atmospheric nitrogen gas into nitrogen compounds, stored in soil, that can be used by plants.

**Legume:** A plant whose roots form an association with soilborne bacteria that can capture atmospheric nitrogen.

**Inoculant:** A seed treatment medium that contains the symbiotic rhizobial bacteria to capture nitrogen when in contact with legume roots.

---

# Green Manures for Home Gardens

One of the best ways to improve your soil is to grow green manure crops. Incorporating green manures into the soil increases organic matter content, improves tilth, and feeds earthworms and soil microorganisms. Try combining plantings of more than one species for best results.

| Crop | When to Sow | Rate per 1,000 sq. ft. | Cultural Requirements | Comments |
|---|---|---|---|---|
| **LEGUMES** | | | | |
| **Crimson clover** (*Trifolium incarnatum*) | Spring or fall | 8–12 oz. | Likes neutral, well-drained soils. | Tall clover with dense root system. Annual. |
| **Hairy vetch** (*Vicia villosa*) | Late summer or fall | 1–2 lb. | Tolerates moderate drainage. Winter cover with rye. | Good nitrogen capture; grows well in northern climates. Annual. |
| **Red clover** (*Trifolium pratense*) | Spring or late summer | 4–8 oz. | Somewhat tolerant of acidity and poor drainage. | Good phosphorus accumulation; grows quickly for incorporating during same season. Biennial. |
| **Soybeans** (*Glycine max*) | Spring or summer | 2–3 lb. | Tolerate poor drainage. | Inoculate for nitrogen fixation. Annual. |
| **White clover (Dutch)** (*Trifolium repens*) | Spring or late summer | 4–8 oz. | Tolerates droughty soils. | Good for undersowing in row crops as a living mulch. Perennial. |
| **NONLEGUMES** | | | | |
| **Annual ryegrass** (*Lolium multiflorum*) | Spring | 1–2 lb. | Tolerates a wide range of soils. | Provides fast cover; good for establishing slow-growing crops. Annual. |
| **Buckwheat** (*Fagopyrum esculentum*) | Spring or summer | 2–3 lb. | Tolerates infertile and acid soils. | Accumulates phosphorus. Annual. |
| **Oats** (*Avena sativa*) | Spring or summer | 2–3 lb. | Prefer well-drained loamy soil. Tolerate some acidity. | Quick-growing summer crop. Provides quick cover. Annual. |
| **Winter rye** (*Secale cereale*) | Late summer or fall | 2–3 lb. | Prefers well-drained soil. | Winter-hardy; grows well in early spring. Annual. |

The table "Green Manures for Home Gardens" on page 37 will guide you in choosing the green manure crop that is best suited to your garden. If you select a legume, it's a good idea to apply a bacterial inoculant so your soil will get maximum benefit from the crop's nitro-

---

### ❀ How to Covercrop

Leaving a cover crop in place for a full growing season gives the most added benefit, but even a short-term cover crop helps to reduce the potential for soil erosion and compaction. Here's how to raise a cover crop:

1. Till or rake the planting site smooth. As a rule, cover crops don't require added fertilizers unless soil test results indicate that soil is extremely poor. However, cover crops *will* benefit from a light application of compost. Treat legumes with the proper inoculant before sowing.

2. Broadcast seed by hand. A shallow pass (1 inch deep) with a rotary tiller will help to bury seeds and improve seed distribution. You can create the same effect by raking lightly after sowing.

3. If weeds outgrow the cover crop, mow the area with your lawn mower set on high. The mower will skim over the tops of low-growing cover crops while chopping away the taller weeds. In a raised bed, use a scythe or other hand tool to cut away weeds, or pull them by hand.

4. Use a rotary tiller to mix in cover crops when they're less than 6 inches tall. You can mow the crop first to chop the green matter before tilling. You can also dig it in by hand with a garden fork or shovel. If the crop is taller than 6 inches, working it into the soil will take more effort.

---

gen-collecting ability. Different crops require different strains of inoculant. Use the specific strain required by the legume you're planting or a product that's a blend of many types of nitrogen-collecting bacteria. You'll find inoculants at well-stocked garden centers, or order them by mail.

## PLANTING GREEN MANURES

If possible, sow seed when rain is forecast. The stand will not establish well if the soil surface dries during the germination period. Remove all crop residues and rake the soil free of clumps before sowing. You can sow seed with a manually powered seeder that consists of a bag or reservoir for holding seed connected to a crank-operated seed broadcaster. For small areas, try broadcasting seed by hand. If you're sowing less than 1 pound of seed per 1,000 square feet, mix the seed with fine sand, organic fertilizer, or screened soil before spreading. When sowing fine seed by hand, rake the seedbed afterward to cover the seed. Cover larger-seeded crops, such as Austrian peas or soybeans, with $\frac{1}{4}$ to $\frac{1}{2}$ inch of soil.

After seeding, tamp the soil with the back of a hoe or spade to ensure good contact between soil and seed. You can cover the newly seeded area with loose straw or grass clippings to help prevent drying. For large plots (1 acre or more), a small seed drill pulled by a farm or garden tractor will plant and cover the seed in one pass.

## PLANTING LIVING MULCHES

Some gardeners plant green manures such as white clover between rows of young squash or corn to add nitrogen to the soil and to help control weeds. The green manure acts as a living mulch—it's a growing crop, but it serves all the functions of a standard mulch. You can plant living mulches between many types of vegetable row crops.

This system works well only if you seed the green manure plant in a weed-free seedbed. After planting the main crop, keep the areas between rows and between plants clear of weeds for about one month. Till or dig just before planting the mulch crop, and pick out any exposed weed roots to prevent rerooting. Work carefully to avoid disturbing the root systems of your vegetable plants. The annual green manure will die down at frost or can be tilled or dug in when you prepare the soil for winter cover.

Late-season plantings of broccoli and cauliflower can benefit from underseeding with a winter-hardy green manure such as hairy vetch. To underseed, let the vegetable crop get established for about one month, keeping the area weed-free. Then broadcast the green manure seed over the entire area, not just between the rows, when the vegetable plants are 6 to 8 inches tall. By the time the plants are ready to harvest, you will be able to walk on the green manure without damaging it. Till or dig it several weeks before planting the following spring.

Don't let vetch go to seed, or it could become a nuisance.

Oats are also effective as an undersown or living mulch crop. Planted anytime from the middle to the end of summer, the crop will suppress weeds but won't set seed itself. The oats will die down during winter, leaving a thick layer of mulch to prevent soil erosion and suppress late-fall and early-spring weeds. Shallowly till or dig in the oats two weeks before planting the following spring. Or to conserve time and effort, hand-pull the mulch back in spots and transplant established seedlings into it. It will retard weed growth until it decomposes, by which time the plant's leaves will be shading the area.

# WORKING THE SOIL

To many gardeners, working the soil means using a rotary tiller. While a tiller is a powerful and helpful tool, it's not the only, or the best, way to work the soil.

Many gardeners use their rotary tillers several

## Give Soil a Squeeze

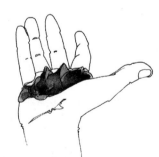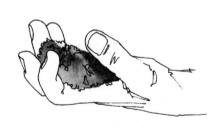

Always check soil moisture content before you work the soil. If the soil is too wet or too dry, cultivating can destroy soil structure. You can do a rough moisture test by picking up a handful of soil and squeezing it. If the soil crumbles apart when you open your fingers (left), it's too dry.

If the soil forms a solid ball (center), it's too wet.

If the soil holds together without packing densely (right), it's just right, and it's time to get out in the garden.

times during the season. They may till in a green manure crop in early spring and then till again a few weeks later to make a fine seed bed for planting. During the season, they may get out a smaller tiller for weed control and then till the garden under again in fall. While tillers are valuable time- and back-saving machines, their use does have a cost to your soil's health.

Tilling or hand-digging, no matter how carefully done, has a major impact on soil microorganisms. When you turn the soil, you add an enormous amount of oxygen to it. This creates an environment primed for an explosion of microbial activity. In most soils, more than 80 percent of the aerobic bacteria are present in the top 6 inches; more than 60 percent are in the top 3 to 4 inches. If you add organic matter as you till, you supply fuel for the population explosion, and your soil will remain in balance. If you till repeatedly without supplying more food for the rapidly increasing microbial population, you'll speed the decomposition of your soil's organic reserves. Soil organic matter levels will decrease.

Cultivating the soil when it is too wet or too dry is even more harmful. Tilling or digging at these times is disastrous for soil structure. Wet soils will form large clumps when tilled. The clumps will dry hard and solid, without the many tiny pores that hold soil water and air. Dry soils can turn to fine dust when tilled. So for the sake of your soil and plants, reserve the tiller for when you really need it. Use mulches to reduce weed problems and conserve soil moisture, avoid walking on growing beds to reduce compaction, and cultivate shallowly when weeds are small.

## DOUBLE DIGGING

Double digging a garden bed takes considerable time and effort, but it's work well rewarded by more vigorous, higher-yielding plants. The process improves the structure and fertility of the top 2 feet of the soil.

When you double dig, you remove a spadeful of topsoil from a garden bed, loosen the soil layer below the topsoil, and then restore the topsoil layer. During the process, you can incorporate organic matter into the soil. See "How to Double Dig" on the opposite page for step-by-step directions.

Double digging is hard work. If you have back problems, it's probably best not to double dig your garden. And if you've never double dug a bed before, start small. Try working a 3-foot × 3-foot bed and build up from there.

# RAISED BED GARDENING

If your garden soil is difficult—poorly drained, heavy clay that's low in organic matter, very alkaline, or full of rocks—raised beds offer a solution. By bringing in topsoil mixed with organic amendments, you can avoid having to deal with the soil in your yard.

Raised gardening beds are higher than ground level and separated by paths. Plants cover the bed areas; gardeners work from the paths. The beds are 3 to 5 feet across to permit easy access and may be any length. You can grow any vegetable in raised beds, as well as herbs, flowers, or berry bushes.

You may wonder whether it's worth your while to build raised beds. In many cases, the answer is a resounding yes. Raised beds can: solve problems of difficult soils; improve production; save space, time, and money; and improve your garden's appearance and accessibility. While that sounds like a tall order, raised beds can do it all. Crops produce better because they grow in deep, loose, fertile soil that is never walked upon. And you can grow twice as many crops in the same space: In a row garden, the crops occupy only one-third of the garden area; the paths, two-thirds. In a raised bed garden, the proportions are reversed.

Raised beds save time and money because you need only dig, fertilize, and water the beds, ignoring the soil in the paths. You don't need to weed as much when crops grow close together, because weeds can't compete as well.

The quickest and easiest way to make a raised bed is simply to add lots of organic matter, such as well-rotted manure or compost, to your garden soil to mound up planting beds.

Shape the soil in an unframed bed so that it is flat-topped, with sloping sides (this shape helps conserve water), or forms a long, rounded mound. (You may need to add extra materials

to raised beds if you want them to be tall enough for a gardener in a wheelchair to reach easily.) Frames prevent soil from washing away and allow you to add a greater depth of improved soil. Wood, brick, rocks, or cement blocks are popular materials for framing. Choose naturally rot-resistant woods such as cedar, cypress, or locust. If you don't use rot-resistant woods, you may eventually need to replace the frame. Another option is to use wood treated with borax-based preservatives. This natural mineral is toxic to insects and fungi but relatively nontoxic to humans. For information about these preservatives, write to U.S. Borax, 3075 Wilshire Boulevard, Los Angeles, CA 90010.

## How to Double Dig

Double digging improves the structure of the top foot of soil. It's hard work, but it pays off in high plant yields. Here's the best technique:

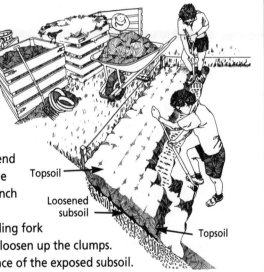

1. Several days in advance, mark off the area you plan to dig, and soak the soil with water. A few days later, remove weeds or sod and loosen the top 1 foot of soil with a spading fork.

2. The next day, begin digging, starting at one end of the marked area. With a spade, dig a 1-foot-wide × 1-foot-deep trench. Pile the topsoil from that trench onto a ground cloth or garden cart.

3. To loosen the exposed subsoil, stick your spading fork deeply in the soil and twist and wiggle the fork to loosen up the clumps. Spread a shovelful of organic matter over the surface of the exposed subsoil.

4. Slide the topsoil from the next 1-foot section of the bed onto the subsoil in the first trench. Loosen the subsoil in the second trench.

5. Continue down the bed, shifting the topsoil and loosening the subsoil.

6. At the end of the bed, use the reserved topsoil from the first trench to fill in the last trench.

7. Spread compost or other organic matter over the entire bed, and use a spading fork to work it into the top 4 to 6 inches of the soil.

# Chapter 3

# COMPOSTING

Inside a compost pile, billions of decay organisms feed, grow, reproduce, and die, recycling household and garden wastes into an excellent organic fertilizer and soil conditioner. This process of decomposition occurs constantly and gradually in nature. When you build a compost pile, you intervene to speed things up and create a valuable soil amendment.

Compost systems range in size from small, home-built bins used to recycle one household's food scraps to industrial systems capable of handling hundreds of tons of municipal waste daily. Your choice of a composting method depends on what materials you plan to use, how much money you're willing to spend, how much space you have available, and how much time and effort you want to devote to it.

Composting offers benefits to both the environment and your pocketbook. By making compost, gardeners create a source of high-quality nutrition for their garden and eliminate the need to buy commercial fertilizers. Compost improves soil structure and moisture retention and can actually protect plants from certain diseases. As an alternative to landfills and incinerators, composting attracts interest even from nongardeners seeking to reduce their trash-collection bills. As much as three-fourths of a household's waste is compostable. On the farm, composting is a practical, cost-effective way to conserve the nutrients in manure. The composting process also allows the farmer to make use of free sources of soil fertility such as municipal yard wastes and food processing wastes.

**Good compost starts at home.** You can make excellent compost in a pile (*left front*), a bin (*left back*), or a barrel tumbler (*right back*). Match your compost style to your space, garden style, or neighbors' ideas of neatness. Begin your search for compost ingredients in your own backyard, kitchen, and neighborhood. You probably won't have to travel far to find a wealth of nutrient-rich materials such as grass clippings, pine needles and cones, hay, manure, kitchen scraps, coffee grounds, and dried leaves to turn into soil-nourishing compost.

## BUILDING A COMPOST PILE

Your goal in building a compost pile is to provide the best possible conditions for the proliferation of a hardworking microherd of composting organisms. Introduce organisms to your compost pile with a starter culture of rich garden soil or finished compost, or apply a commercial compost activator. Composting organisms' needs are simple: a balanced diet, water, air, and warmth. Understanding a few basic composting principles will help you get the best possible results from the labors of your microherd.

## INGREDIENTS

Anything of living origin can be composted, but the quality and quantity of the materials you use affect the process and determine the nutrient value of the finished compost. Compost organisms require the correct proportion of carbon for energy and nitrogen for forming protein—called the C/N ratio—to function efficiently. If the C/N ratio is too high (excess carbon), decomposition slows down and nitrogen is depleted. Too low a C/N ratio (too much nitrogen) wastes nitrogen by letting it escape into the air, causing unpleasant odors, and into the water, creating pollution problems.

The ideal C/N ratio of 25:1 to 30:1 is readily reached by building your pile in alternating layers of high-carbon materials, such as sawdust, and high-nitrogen materials, such as fresh grass clippings. The illustration on page 44 shows the ratio of carbon to nitrogen in some common compostable materials. In general, high-carbon materials are brown or yellow and are dry and bulky. High-nitrogen materials tend to be green, moist, and often sloppy. If you find you have an abundance of either high-nitrogen or high-carbon wastes on hand, make the effort to locate ingredients that provide your microherd with the right balance of nutrients.

Most organic materials supply a wide range of the other nutrients needed by compost organisms and plants. The greater the variety of materials you include in your compost, the greater your certainty of creating a nutritionally balanced product. Use additions of mineral-rich materials such as rock phosphate or greensand to tailor the nutrients in your compost to match the needs of your soil and plants. See "Adding Minerals" on page 36 for information on mineral sources you can add to your compost pile.

Although lime is often used to moderate pH and odors in compost, it is not always a desir-

---

### 🍂 Words to Know

**Aerobic:** Describes organisms living or occurring only in the presence of oxygen.

**Anaerobic:** Describes organisms living or occurring when oxygen is absent.

**Composting:** The art and science of combining organic materials under controlled conditions so that the original raw ingredients are transformed into humus.

**C/N ratio:** The proportion of bulky, dry, high-carbon materials to dense, moist, high-nitrogen materials. The ideal C/N ratio for stimulating compost organisms is 25:1 to 30:1; finished compost's C/N ratio is 10:1.

**Cold, slow, or passive pile:** A compost pile that receives little or no turning, allowing some anaerobic decomposition to occur; composting proceeds at cooler temperatures over a longer period of time.

**Hot, fast, or active pile:** A compost pile that is turned or otherwise aerated frequently, creating high temperatures and finished compost in a relatively short time.

**Sheet composting:** A method of spreading undecomposed organic materials over the soil's surface, then working them into the soil to decompose, rather than piling them and spreading the resulting compost.

**Windrow:** A long, low, broad compost pile often used in large-scale composting systems; dimensions are limited only by the equipment available to turn the pile and the weight of the materials being composted.

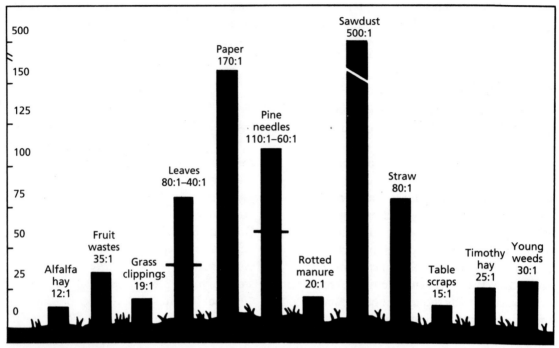

**C/N ratios of common compost ingredients.** Composting organisms need carbon for energy and nitrogen for growth. It's the composter's job to supply both kinds of materials in roughly the proportions the microorganisms prefer. Carbonaceous ingredients are almost always plant materials; many nitrogen sources, such as manure and blood meal, come from animals, although fresh plant matter is also nitrogenous.

able addition to the compost pile. Particularly when manure is being composted, lime causes the release of nitrogen into the atmosphere in the form of ammonia, reducing the nitrogen available to compost organisms and plants. Replace the calcium supplied by lime with crushed eggshells, bonemeal, or wood ashes, which also provide potash. Like lime, wood ashes are alkaline and will raise the pH of your compost. Use wood ashes in moderation to avoid high pH levels that inhibit microorganism activity and limit nutrient uptake by some plants.

There are some organic materials to avoid when composting. Human and pet feces may carry disease organisms; meat scraps and fatty materials break down very slowly and attract animals. Some municipal or industrial wastes are contaminated with high levels of heavy metals, pesticide residues, or other highly toxic substances. If your composting plan includes industrial-waste products, obtain a complete laboratory analysis for possible contaminants before you add such waste products to your pile.

## MOISTURE

All living organisms need water, but too much moisture drives out air, drowns the pile, and washes away nutrients. Good compost is about as damp as a moist sponge. There are several ways to control moisture levels in compost piles:

■ Build your pile on a site that is well drained. If necessary, begin your compost pile with a bottom layer of sand or gravel to make sure the pile never sits in a puddle.

■ Sprinkle each layer with a watering can or garden hose as you construct the pile. The composting process requires water; check the moisture level every few days and, if necessary, add water when you turn your compost.

■ Layer very wet, sloppy materials such as fruit wastes with absorbent ingredients such as sawdust or shredded dry leaves.

■ Turn your pile to release excess moisture that prevents proper heating.

■ Protect your pile from the weather. Compost in a covered bin, or place a layer of hay or straw over your pile.

■ Shape your pile to work with weather conditions. In humid climates, a pile with a rounded, or convex, top repels excess water; a sunken, or concave, top lets the pile collect needed water in dry climates.

## AERATION

Supplying enough air to all parts of a compost pile to encourage thorough decomposition is perhaps the key to successful composting. Frequent turning is the most straightforward way to do this, but there are other aerating techniques to use in addition to or even in place of turning:

■ Build a base of coarse material such as brush or wood chips under your pile to allow air penetration from below.

■ Shred leaves, hay, and garden debris before composting. Use materials such as paper and grass clippings sparingly, because they tend to form impermeable mats when wet.

■ Insert sticks into the pile when building it, then pull them out later to open air passages. You can also poke holes in the compost with a garden fork or crowbar.

■ Bury perforated drainpipe at intervals in a passive compost pile as an excellent way to improve aeration. Sunflower stalks and straw also conduct air into compost; cornstalks don't hollow out as they decay and won't work for this purpose.

 **Common Compostables**

Build your compost pile from a mixture of "green" (wet, high-nitrogen) materials and "brown" (dry, high-carbon) materials.

### "Greens"

Coffee grounds
Cover crops
Eggs and eggshells*
Feathers*
Fish and seafood scraps*
Fruit wastes and grains
Grass clippings
Hair (pet or human)
Leaves
Manure
Milk
Seaweed
Vegetable scraps
Weeds

### "Browns"

Corncobs and cornstalks
Hay
Nutshells
Paper
Pine needles
Sawdust
Straw
Vegetable stalks and seeds

---

*Most animal scraps will attract animal pests and slow decomposition. Also, some communities have regulations restricting ingredients allowed in backyard piles.

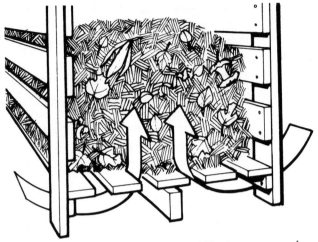

**Build a bottom-heated pile.** One way to avoid having to turn your compost pile frequently is to make it on recycled wooden pallets. Air rises from beneath the pallets, and as the compost heats up, air is pulled up through the compost by natural convection, reducing the need to turn the pile.

■ Limit the height and width of the pile to 5 to 6 feet to avoid compression. There is no limit on length—large-scale compost systems frequently employ windrows hundreds of feet long.

## TEMPERATURE AND CRITICAL MASS

Too large a compost pile interferes with aeration, but a minimum size of 3 feet in each dimension is needed in order for heating to occur. Given the proper C/N ratio, moisture, and aeration, your compost will heat up even in cold winter weather. A hot pile can reach temperatures of 160°F but will produce satisfactory results if it cooks along at about 120°F. Northern composters sometimes insulate their piles with hay bales or leaves to help composting continue throughout the winter.

## STRUCTURES

The type of structure used for composting can vary greatly, depending on the materials available, the needs of the composter, and the climate.

A structure isn't essential—many composting methods employ free-standing piles or heaps. As long as the volume of materials is at least 3 cubic yards, the container is relatively unimportant. Compost bins are made of wood, plastic, concrete, bricks, or just about any durable, weatherproof material. Whether permanent or portable, bins can protect compost from the weather, conserve heat during composting, and keep out scavenging animals. They are also more aesthetically pleasing. Composting structures made of wire fencing or wood and wire frames are sometimes called pens. Pens may be somewhat more portable than bins, but the terms are often interchangeable.

# MAKING HOT COMPOST

Methods that meet the requirements of compost organisms range from quick, hot composting that requires effort and attention, to slow, cool techniques that take less trouble. Many people perceive quick, hot composting as the only way to compost, but such methods have drawbacks as well as advantages.

Quick compost is generally ready to use in less than eight weeks and can be finished in as little as two weeks. Frequent turning is the secret: It keeps the compost well aerated so that decomposer organisms can work efficiently. Keep your compost working properly by monitoring the temperature and turning the pile again as soon as the temperature drops. The object is to maintain temperatures of 113° to 158°F until decomposition is complete. A thermometer is helpful but not essential; you can stick your hand down into the pile to see how

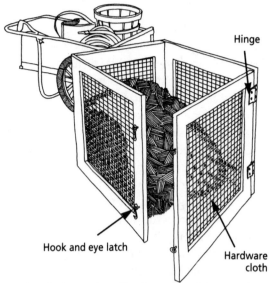

**Wood and wire compost bin.** Construct a 3-foot × 3-foot portable bin using four sides made of 3-foot × 3-foot pieces of ½-inch hardware cloth fastened to 2 × 4s. Hinge one of the sides, and place hooks and eyes on the edge opposite the hinges, creating a door for your bin. Set up this bin close to your garden; when the bin is full, move it to another convenient location and begin a new pile.

hot it is. Or insert a metal rod into your compost. If the rod feels hot to the touch after a few minutes in the pile, your compost is heating properly.

The main advantage of hot composting is its speed—even in cooler climates you can process six or more batches in a season. It's the most effective way to build fertility when you are just starting out in a new location or have limited room for composting. The other major benefit of this method is its heat. Hot composting temperatures, maintained over several weeks, kill most weed seeds and pathogens. Perfect your hot-composting skills before you include diseased plants or seed-bearing weeds on your list of compost ingredients. Weeds such as Canada thistle that sprout readily from small pieces of

root also are better left out of the compost bin. It's better to miss out on some plant material than to risk putting weed- and disease-carrying compost on your garden.

The major disadvantage of quick composting is the labor involved in turning the compost every few days. It is also a less forgiving process than others; if the moisture level or C/N ratio is wrong, you have to make adjustments. Another drawback is that the whole pile must be built at once. If your compost pile is also your household garbage disposal system, compostables

## Compost Troubleshooting

Is your compost heap just not cooking? The King County Solid Waste Division in Seattle, which runs one of the most successful municipal composting programs in the country, offers this guide to solving common composting problems.

| Symptom | Problem | Solution |
| --- | --- | --- |
| Compost has bad odor. | Not enough air | Turn the pile. |
| Center of pile is dry. | Not enough water | Moisten materials while you turn the pile. |
| Pile is damp and warm only in middle. | Pile is too small | Build a larger pile; mix new materials with the old. |
| Pile is damp and sweet-smelling but remains cool. | Lack of nitrogen | Add a nitrogen source, such as fresh grass clippings, manure or blood meal. |

must be saved up until you're ready to start a new pile.

Hot composting conserves less nitrogen than cooler methods because fast bacterial growth requires extra nitrogen, some of which inevitably drifts off in the form of ammonia. Finally, studies have shown that compost produced at high temperatures is less able to suppress soil-borne diseases than is cool compost, since the beneficial bacteria and fungi that attack pathogens can't survive the higher temperatures.

# SMALL-SCALE COMPOST

You don't need a lot of space to compost successfully. If you have a small yard, a single 3-foot-diameter circle of rigid wire fencing is all that is necessary.

Make a simple outdoor composter by cutting out the bottom of a trash can and setting the can firmly into the ground to prevent tipping. Use several such cans for continuous waste

---

 **Blender Compost**

For extra-quick results, start with pureed kitchen scraps for your compost pile. As kitchen scraps accumulate, put them in the blender, add enough water to cover them, and blend until finely chopped. Then, pour the "liquid compost" into a bucket with a lid to keep it until you can take it out to the garden. Pour it into a shallow hole dug in your pile and cover it with a shovelful of compost. Or, if your gardening space is limited and you don't have room to make conventional compost, dump your liquid gold directly into trenches dug in the garden and cover with a shovelful of dirt.

---

composting; simply wait six months to a year, depending on your climate, for the finished product. Chopping your wastes first speeds up the process, as does occasional turning or fluffing of the can's contents. Air holes, drilled into the sides and lid, provide aeration to keep the system working and encourage earthworms to inhabit your garbage can composter.

Compost tumblers, also called barrel or drum composters, offer many of the benefits of hot composting, while virtually eliminating the effort of turning. Compost tumblers work quickly; used properly, they produce finished compost in about two weeks. Their capacity tends to be limited, however; once the drum is full, you have to wait until composting is complete before adding new materials. Store kitchen wastes in plastic buckets with tight-fitting lids during this time, using sawdust or similarly absorbent materials to minimize odors.

## WORM BOXES

You can make compost indoors with the help of earthworms. A worm box, with air holes, drainage, and a healthy earthworm population, helps turn food wastes into compost with very little effort and little or no odor. A general rule of thumb suggests that 1 square foot of surface area is needed to digest each pound of waste material generated per week—a box 3 inches square and 1 inch deep can accommodate most of a family's food wastes. You can also use a plastic garbage can, modified to allow drainage and aeration, as a worm-powered indoor composter.

## GARBAGE CAN COMPOSTING

To compost kitchen scraps in winter, or for year-round composting for a small yard and garden, try a garbage can. Start by using a hammer and a large nail to punch holes in the bottom, sides, and lid of a metal garbage can.

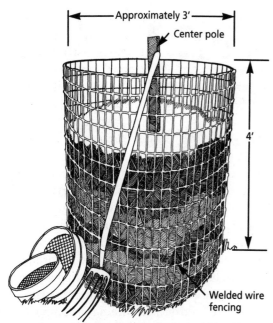

**Compost pen.** A 10-foot length of 4-foot-wide welded wire fencing forms a circular compost pen slightly larger than 3 feet in diameter. Fasten the ends of the fencing together with wire or reusable clips. Turn the compost by unfastening the fencing and setting up the pen next to the freestanding pile; turn into the now-empty pen. To direct moisture into the center of your compost pile, drive a pole or length of pipe into the ground in the center of your pen so that it extends slightly above the top edge of the pen and your compost.

Place the can on a large tray to catch any draining liquid. Then place a 3-inch layer of finished compost or soil in the bottom of the can. Add finely chopped kitchen scraps, followed by an equal amount of shredded newspaper, grass clippings, and/or shredded leaves. Add more materials as available until the can is full, then layer new materials into another prepared can and allow the first to finish composting—about three to four months.

Here are a few tips for making your garbage can composter work its best:

■ Protect the composter from freezing tem-peratures—put it in a garage or cellar.

■ Start with soil or finished compost and add a little more on top of each addition of other materials.

■ Chop, shred, or even blend all additions as finely as possible.

## 🌼 Kitchen Compost Collector

Store kitchen wastes for the compost pile indoors without odor problems by layering the scraps with sawdust or soil in a bucket or other container. Each day, add kitchen scraps to the container and then top with a 1-inch layer of sawdust, soil, or coffee grounds to absorb and hold odors. Continue layering until you have enough materials to warrant a trip to the compost pile. Smaller households might get by with a single clay pot for a collector.

A new product that eliminates worries about odors is a biodegradable compost bag developed jointly by Wood's End Research Laboratory in Mount Vernon, Maine, and Stone Container Corporation of Louisville, Kentucky. The bag looks like a brown paper grocery bag. Inside, it's lined with natural cellulose to hold liquids and prevent leaks. The surface allows air penetration to the wastes inside, which inhibits the development of odors. The bag stands upright on your kitchen counter; when it's full, just drop it into the compost bin. Within one week, bacteria and fungi will be eating holes through the bag's surface, turning everything into rich, dark compost. To find out how to obtain the composting bags, contact:

Stone Container Corporation
P.O. Box 37020
Louisville, KY 40233

■ Add kitchen scraps before they start to smell.

■ Mix the composting material after each addition and every few days. If you don't, it may produce unpleasant odors. Stir with a stick, roll the can back and forth on its side a few times, or use a compost-turning tool.

■ Add water sparingly and only if your materials are very dry.

A plastic garbage can can also serve as a compost bin. A plastic can will last longer than a metal one because it won't rust. However, if you have rodent problems, use a metal can because rodents can chew through plastic. These instructions will work for both metal and plastic cans:

1. Drill several ¼- to ½-inch holes in the bottom of a 30-gallon garbage can. Drill holes 4 to 6 inches apart all around the sides of the can.

2. Place the garbage can on bricks or cement blocks to ensure the best possible aeration. Place 2 to 3 inches of dry sawdust, wood chips, or chopped straw in the bottom of the garbage

**Using a compost-turning tool.** The compost-turning tool works by mixing materials from the bottom up as it is pulled through the compost pile.

can to absorb any excess moisture.

3. Add food wastes in 2-inch-thick layers. Keep in mind that food wastes will compost more quickly if you chop them into small pieces before adding. Top each food layer with 3 to 4 inches of shredded leaves, shredded newspaper, or straw, and a 1-inch layer of soil or sawdust.

4. Between additions, use a bungee cord to hold the lid securely closed to prevent animals from getting into your compost.

5. If you want to keep the compost active, mix weekly with a compost-turning tool to add air and mix materials. Properly managed compost should be ready in six to eight months.

## Using Compost

Finished compost is a versatile material that you can apply freely at any time of year without any fear of burning plants or polluting water. For most garden applications, use compost that is well finished—aged long enough so that the decomposition process has stabilized. Unfinished compost retards the germination and growth of certain plants, although others, such as corn and squash, seem to thrive on partly finished compost. Try these tips for using compost

**Garbage can bin.** With a garbage can composting "bin," you can make compost in your basement or garage if you don't have room in your yard for a pile.

around your garden and yard:

**Vegetables and annuals:** Incorporate compost liberally into the top inch or two of all annual beds (including your vegetable garden) before seeding or transplanting. Apply compost during the growing season as a mulch or side-dressing, and work it into the soil when you turn under cover crops.

**Trees and shrubs:** If your soil is poor, avoid backfilling the planting hole with compost-enriched soil, since roots will tend to ball up inside the hole instead of branching out in search of nutrients. Top-dress with compost around the root zone, and bore plugs of compost into the soil around the drip line.

**Lawns:** Spread compost when establishing new seedings and rejuvenating your lawn in spring. Add fine compost when you aerate so it comes in contact with roots.

**Potting mixes:** Compost provides an excellent medium for starting seeds and growing houseplants. Contrary to popular belief, pasteurization is unnecessary—heating compost actually suppresses disease-fighting microbes, allowing airborne pathogens to populate the growing medium. Simply screen your compost to remove any large pieces, and mix the fine compost with sand, peat moss, or other amendments to create a custom potting mix. (Use the large pieces that you screen out either as mulch or to "seed" a new compost pile.)

**Compost tea:** When plants need some immediate care, perk them up with nutrient-rich water made by soaking a cloth bag full of compost in a watering can or barrel for a couple of days. Dilute the resulting solution to a weak-tea color; reuse your compost "tea bag" a few times, then apply the remaining solids to your garden.

 **Gardening in Compost**

Nowhere is it written that gardeners have to till, spade, and generally churn up more soil than an army of earthworms to have successful gardens. Several well-known and respected organic gardeners advise just the opposite. They are firm advocates of no-dig gardening.

So how do you garden without regular digging or cultivating? It's easier than you might think. Simply start collecting all manner of organic wastes—leaves, grass clippings, kitchen scraps, shredded tree trimmings, even weeds—and compost them. Many municipalities now collect yard wastes and even make compost, which is available free or for a small charge.

Spread all of this material evenly on your garden plot, sprinkle on organic high-nitrogen substances such as cottonseed meal, and if the weather is dry, sprinkle it with water. Then mix it up with a garden fork, or till shallowly and simply let it rot.

This combination of heavy mulching and sheet composting is especially helpful if you have heavy clay soil. Experienced gardeners advise first working up the soil for better drainage and then letting nature and earthworms work their magic on the smorgasbord of organic materials you'll heap on the soil surface.

Other gardeners don't even till the compost into the soil. They leave it on the soil surface, continuing to apply organic materials in strips to form raised beds. They then plant seeds or transplants into the beds, rather than into the soil, and cover them with finished compost or heavy mulch.

# Chapter 4

# SEEDS AND SEEDLINGS

Seeds come in an amazing variety of forms and sizes, from the dustlike seeds of begonias to the hefty coconut. But all seeds have one quality in common: They are living links between generations of plants, carrying the vital genetic information that directs the growth and development of the next plant generation. Seeds are alive. They even carry on respiration—absorbing oxygen and giving off carbon dioxide.

As long as a seed is kept cool and dry, its life processes hum along on low. Most seeds remain viable for one to three years after they ripen on a plant. Some, such as parsnip seed, can't be counted on to sprout after more than one year, but others, like muskmelon seeds, can germinate after five years or more if storage conditions are favorable. In fact, certain seeds recovered from archaeological digs have sometimes proven to be viable after many hundreds of years.

Growing your own plants from seed can be one of the most satisfying and intriguing aspects of gardening. Almost all gardeners have grown vegetables from seed. But if you're interested in a challenge, you can start your own perennials, herbs, and even trees from seed. For tips on buying seeds, see "Buying the Best Seeds" on this page.

## SEED GERMINATION

Moisture and warmth encourage seeds to germinate. When the seed absorbs water, its internal pressure rises, rupturing the seed coat. Growth

hormones within the seed go into action, directing vital compounds to where they are needed and encouraging the growth of new tissue.

 **Buying the Best Seeds**

Here are some tips to help you to get the most from your seed order:
- Send for several seed catalogs so you can compare offerings and prices.
- Keep seed catalogs for reference.
- Some companies offer small seed packets at reasonable prices. Seed mixtures give you a wide variety of plants from a single packet.
- Days to maturity is an average—the actual days in your area may be different.
- Hybrids may offer advantages such as early harvest or high yields but are usually more expensive. Open-pollinated cultivars may taste better and produce over a longer season, and they tend to be cheaper.
- Some seed is routinely treated with synthetic chemical fungicide. Specify untreated seed if you prefer it.
- Read descriptions and choose cultivars with qualities that are important to you.
- Certain catalogs specialize in plants suited to specific regions of the country.
- All-America Selections seeds grow and produce well over a wide range of conditions.

All of these changes depend on temperature as well. Most garden seeds started indoors germinate best at a soil temperature of 75° to 90°F. Sprouting seeds also need air. A porous soil kept evenly moist (but not swampy) will provide enough air to support the germination process. Seeds often rot if they are submerged in water for days or if they are planted in completely waterlogged soil, so control the moisture.

After the germination process has been in action for several days (or, in some cases, for a week or more), the seed will change in ways that we can see. The root emerges and starts to grow, the stem grows longer, and then the cotyledons unfold. Once germination has begun, you can't reverse the process. If the sprouted seed continues to receive moisture, warmth, air, and light, it keeps growing. If not, it dies.

Most seeds have no specific light requirement for germination. However, some kinds of seeds need light to break dormancy and germinate, including many tiny seeds such as begonia, columbine, snapdragon, and petunia. Some larger seeds such as impatiens, spider flower, sweet alyssum, and dill are also best left uncovered. Sow light-sensitive seeds on the surface of fine, moist soil or seed-starting mix. Cover them loosely with clear plastic to retain moisture, or mist frequently.

 **Words to Know**

**Seed:** A plant embryo and its supply of nutrients, often surrounded by a protective seed coat.

**Seed germination:** The beginning of growth of a seed.

**Viable:** Capable of germinating; alive.

**Dormancy:** A state of reduced biochemical activity that persists until certain conditions occur that trigger germination.

**Seedling:** A young plant grown from seed. Commonly, plants grown from seed are termed seedlings until they are first transplanted.

**Cotyledon:** The leaf (or leaves), present in the dormant seed, that is the first to unfold as a seed germinates. Cotyledons often look different than the leaves that follow them. In seeds such as beans, they contain stored nutrients. Also called seed leaves.

**Endosperm:** Specialized layer of tissue that surrounds the embryo.

**Scarification:** Nicking or wearing down hard seed coats to encourage germination.

**Stratification:** Exposing seeds to a cool (35° to 40°F), moist period to break dormancy.

**Damping-off:** A disease caused by various fungi that results in seedling stems that shrivel and collapse at soil level.

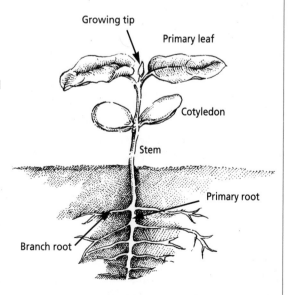

A few types of seeds require darkness to germinate. For example, Madagascar periwinkle (*Catharanthus roseus*) will germinate far better if the flat is covered with black plastic or kept in a dark closet until seeds sprout.

Other seeds will germinate readily only if planted soon after they ripen. Angelica, hawthorn, and Solomon's-seal are three types of seed best sown soon after they are collected.

Check seed packet information to find out whether the seeds you want to raise have special germination requirements.

## PRETREATING SEEDS

Some kinds of seeds require certain treatments before they'll start to germinate. No matter how ideal conditions are for germination, the seeds will remain dormant if pre-germination requirements have not been met. This characteristic, called innate dormancy, helps ensure survival in nature, because the seeds wait out the winter or the dry season before sprouting.

Certain seeds require a period of moist cold. This mechanism is common in plants native to climates with cold winters, especially perennials, trees, and shrubs. Other seeds have chemicals in their seed coats that must be soaked away before the seeds will germinate. Some seeds are slow to absorb enough water to start germination because of thick or impermeable seed coats. Plants native to areas with seasonal dry spells often have this type of dormancy. If you understand these dormancy mechanisms, you can work around them and coax the seeds to germinate.

Even seeds that don't have dormancy requirements may be slow to germinate.

**Stratifying seeds.** To stratify seeds, put them in damp sphagnum moss, peat moss, or vermiculite and keep them in a cold place (34° to 40°F) for one to four months. Layer large seeds between damp sphagnum moss in a covered container. Mix smaller seeds with damp moss or other seed-starting medium in a plastic bag and close with a twist tie. Be sure to label the seeds with name and date.

---

### ✿ Anti-Fungal Compost Tea

Researchers at the University of Bonn in Germany report that soaking seeds in tea made from well-rotted compost containing both animal and plant material results in a much lower incidence of damping-off.

Stir together 1 part well-rotted compost (made from a mixture of plant material and manure) and 6 parts water in a 1-gallon bucket or other container. Allow the mixture to steep for a week, then strain it through cheesecloth. Soak seeds overnight in the tea before sowing.

Appropriate pretreatment can significantly increase germination rate and reduce germination time.

**Stratification**   Some seeds must be exposed to cold for a certain period before they will break dormancy and germinate. Stratification simulates natural conditions when a seed over-winters in cold, moist ground.

Seeds of various perennials, including wild bleeding heart, gas plant, and cardinal flower, need a cold period. You can plant them outdoors in fall, or spring plant after giving them a cold treatment. The illustration on the opposite page shows how to prepare seeds for cold treatment. Many woody plant seeds also require stratification, including birch, dogwood, false cypress, and spruce. Some tree and shrub seeds, including arborvitae, cotoneaster, and lilac, are double-dormant, which means they require a warm, moist period followed by a cold period to germinate. If planted outdoors in fall, these seeds may not germinate for two years.

**Scarification**   Some seeds, such as morning-glory, sweet pea, okra, baptisias, lupines, and others, have hard seed coats that inhibit water absorption. To make a hard-coated seed absorb water more readily, nick the seed coat. Be careful not to damage the embryo inside the seed. On large seeds, use a knife to cut a notch in the seed coat, or make several strokes with a sharp-edged file. If you have only a few seeds to treat, you can scrape the seed coats with a nail file. Or, you can scarify medium-sized or small seeds by rubbing them between two sheets of sandpaper. Yet another method involves putting a sheet of medium-grit sandpaper inside a cookie sheet or rectangular metal cake pan (one you don't mind getting scraped up), putting a layer of seeds on top of the sandpaper, and rubbing over them with a sanding block to wear down the seed coats.

After scarifying, soak seeds in lukewarm

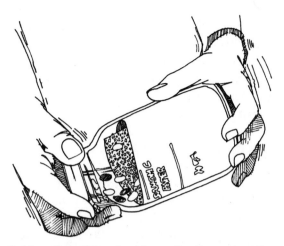

**Quick seed scarifying.** A sandpaper-lined jar works well for processing many seeds at a time. Slip a sheet of coarse-grit sandpaper inside the jar, add seeds, screw the lid on, and shake until the seed coats wear down.

water for several hours before planting.

**Presoaking**   Even seeds that have thin seed coats can benefit from a soak in lukewarm water for several hours before planting. Large seeds such as peas, beans, and okra will germinate faster if soaked overnight first. Before planting, drain the seeds and dry them briefly on paper towels to make them easier to handle.

**Presprouting**   Presprouting takes seeds one step further than presoaking. It's a good way to handle such seeds as melons, squash, and their relatives, which need plenty of warmth for germination. Because sprouted seeds can tolerate cooler temperatures, you can concentrate your population of germinating seeds in one warm place and farm out the presprouted seedlings to cooler spots where they will receive plenty of light. "Presprouting Seeds" on page 57 gives step-by-step instructions for this technique.

Presprouted seeds are fragile; handle them with great care. Be sure to plant them before their roots grow together and tangle. Plant sprouted seeds in individual containers of premoistened potting mix. Cover them gently but firmly with potting mix and treat them as you would any container-raised seedling. Presprouted seeds may be planted directly in the garden, but it is better to keep them in containers until the roots become established.

# STARTING INDOORS

Starting seeds indoors will give you earlier vegetables and flowers, and your cultivar choices will be endless. The process of germination may seem awesomely complex, but the act of seed planting is reassuringly simple. Just take it step-by-step, and you'll soon be presiding over a healthy crop of seedlings.

Select your work area—a surface at a comfortable height and close to a water supply where you'll have room to spread things out. Assemble your equipment: seed-starting con-

tainers, starting medium or soil mix, watering can, labels, marking pen, and seed packets.

## CHOOSING CONTAINERS

You can start seeds in almost any kind of container that will hold 1 to 2 inches of starting medium and won't become easily waterlogged. Once seedlings form more roots and develop their true leaves, though, they grow best in containers that provide more space for root growth and have holes for drainage.

You can start seedlings in open flats or in individual sections or pots. Individual containers are preferable, because the less you disturb tender roots, the better. Some containers, such as peat pots, paper pots, and soil blocks, go right into the garden with the plant during transplanting. Other pots must be slipped off the root ball before planting.

Square or rectangular containers make better use of space and provide more root area than round ones do. However, individual containers dry out faster than open flats. Many gardeners start seeds in open flats and transplant seedlings to individual containers after the first true leaves unfold. Choose flats and containers to match the number and types of plants you wish to grow and the space you have available.

Excellent seed-starting systems are available from garden centers and mail-order suppliers. You can also build your own wooden flats. If you raise large numbers of seedlings, it's useful to have interchangeable, standard-sized flats and inserts.

You can reuse your seedling containers for many years. To prevent problems with damping-off, you may want to sanitize flats at the end of the season by dipping them in a 10 percent solution of household bleach (1 cup of bleach plus 9 cups of water).

You can recycle milk cartons and many types

**Homemade seeding flats.** Construct a four-sided wooden frame 3 to 4 inches deep to fit your growing area. Nail slats across the bottom, leaving ⅛- to ¼-inch spaces between them. Fill the flat with potting mix, and sow seeds. Bend three lengths of wire coat hanger, and insert them in the mix to support a plastic bag that encloses the entire flat. Close the bag with a twist tie.

of plastic containers as seed-starting pots. Just be sure to poke a drainage hole in the bottom of each. Plastic wrap or plastic bags make good mini-greenhouses for starting seeds. The illustration on the opposite page shows one idea for a homemade seed-starting system.

To make your own at-home seed-starting container, follow these instructions for simple newspaper pots. To make seed-starting pots from newspaper, begin by cutting bands of newspaper about twice as wide as the desired height of your pot (about 4 inches wide for a 2-inch-high pot). Wrap a band of newspaper around the lower half of a jar a few times, and

## Presprouting Seeds

Sprouting seeds before you plant them can boost germination rates and give you more control when working with expensive or scarce seeds. It's also an alternative to the stratification technique discussed on page 55, and it's a good way to test the viability of seeds that you've stored for a while. Here's how to presprout seeds:

1. Spread a double layer of damp paper towels on a flat surface.

2. Evenly space seeds 1 inch or so apart on the moist towels, making sure they don't touch one another. If you're testing for viability, place only ten seeds on the towels.

3. Roll up the towels, being careful to keep the seeds from bunching up.

4. Label the seed roll and enclose it in a plastic bag. Close the bag loosely—germinating seeds need some air. You can put several rolls in one bag.

5. Put the seeds in a warm place—near a water heater or on top of a refrigerator. Check them in two to three days.

6. After the first inspection, check the seeds daily for signs of sprouting, and remove them from the towels as soon as they're sprouted. Transplant immediately.

For the viability test, multiply the number of sprouted seeds by 10 to determine the percentage of germination. If eight of the ten seeds sprout, the germination rate is 80 percent. Anything under 70 percent is considered poor, but that doesn't mean you can't use the seeds. Just sow more thickly to compensate for the ones that don't come up.

Plant sprouted seeds in individual containers using a fine, loose potting soil mix, or plant them directly in the garden. Handle them gently: The fleshy roots and stems are easily broken. Then treat as you would other newly germinated seedlings.

secure it with masking tape. Then form the bottom of the pot by creasing and folding the paper in around the bottom of the jar. You can also put a piece of tape across the pot bottom to hold it more securely in place. Slip the newspaper pot off the jar. Set your pots in high-sided trays with their sides touching. When you fill them with potting mix, they will support one another. There are also commercial molds for making newspaper pots.

---

 **Sterilizing Containers**

To prevent damping-off and other soilborne diseases, you must sterilize pots and seedling flats before you sow. To disinfect plastic pots and flats, fill a washtub, laundry sink, or small wading pool with warm water and dish detergent. Scrub the pots and flats clean. Be sure to remove old fertilizer salts that may have accumulated around the pot rims. Drain the tub and rinse everything in clean water. Refill the tub with 10 gallons of water and stir in 1 gallon of chlorine bleach. Place the pots or flats in the solution and soak for 10 minutes. Remove and rinse. Reuse the bleach solution for succeeding batches of pots or flats.

To disinfect only a few pots or flats, use the ratio of 1 part bleach to 9 parts water. One cup of bleach and 9 cups of water makes about 2½ quarts of solution.

To disinfect clay or metal plant containers, immerse them in boiling water or heat them briefly in a 180°F oven. Allow them to cool; store in a clean dry place. Before planting in clay pots, soak them in clean water for a few hours; otherwise, they will draw water out of the potting mix and possibly harm your plants.

---

## POTTING MIXES

Seeds contain enough nutrients to nourish themselves through sprouting, so a seed-starting mix does not have to contain nutrients. It should be free of weed seeds and toxic substances, hold moisture well, and provide plenty of air spaces. Don't use plain garden soil to start seedlings; it hardens into a dense mass that delicate young roots can't penetrate.

The following soil-free materials are good for starting seeds. Try them alone, or mix two or more together: vermiculite, milled sphagnum moss, peat moss, perlite, and compost. Let your seedlings grow in such a mixture until they develop their first true leaves, and then transplant into a nutrient-rich potting mix.

Some gardeners prefer to plant seeds directly in potting mix and eliminate transplanting. Planting in large individual pots is ideal for plants such as squash and melons that won't grow well if their roots are disturbed. You can use a commercial potting mix (which may contain synthetic chemical fertilizer) or make your own.

To make your own potting mix, combine equal parts compost and vermiculite. For more recipes for mixes, see "Simple Seed-Starting Mixes" on page 61.

Moisten the planting mix before you fill your containers, especially if it contains peat moss or sphagnum moss. Use warm water and allow the mix time to absorb it. When you squeeze a handful of mix it should hold together and feel moist, but it shouldn't drip.

If you're sowing directly in flats, first line the bottom with a sheet of newspaper to keep soil from washing out. Scoop premoistened planting medium into the containers and spread it out. Tap the filled container on your work surface to settle it in, and smooth the surface with your hand. Don't pack it down tightly.

## SOWING SEEDS

Space large seeds at least 1 inch apart, planting two to three seeds in each pot. Plant medium-sized seeds ½ to 1 inch apart and tiny ones about ½ inch apart. If you're sowing only a few seeds, use your fingertips or tweezers to place them precisely. To sprinkle seeds evenly, try one of these methods:

■ Take a pinch of seeds between your thumb and forefinger and slowly rotate thumb against finger—try to release the seeds gradually while moving your hand over the container.

■ Scatter seeds from a spoon.

■ Sow seeds directly from the corner of the packet by tapping the packet gently to make the seeds drop out one by one.

■ Mix fine seeds with dry sand and scatter the mixture from a saltshaker.

To sow seeds in tiny furrows or rows, just make shallow ¼- to ½-inch-deep depressions in the soil with a plant label or an old pencil. Space the seeds along the bottom of the furrow.

Cover the seeds to a depth about equal to their diameter by carefully sprinkling them with light, dry potting soil or seed-starting medium. Don't cover seeds that need light to germinate. Instead, gently pat the surface of the mix so the seeds and mix have good contact.

Write a label for each kind of seed you plant and put it in the flat or pot as soon as the seeds are planted, before any mix-ups occur.

Set the flats or pots in shallow containers of water and let them soak until the surface of the planting medium looks moist. Or you can gently mist the mix. If you water from the top, use a watering can with a rose nozzle to get a gentle stream that won't wash the seeds out of place.

Cover the container, using clear plastic or a floating row cover for seeds that need light, or black plastic, damp newspaper, or burlap for those that prefer the dark.

Finally, put the containers of planted seeds in a warm place where you can check them daily. Unless the seeds need light to germinate, you can save space the first few days by stacking

 **The Difficult-to-Transplant**

Some plants are harder to transplant successfully than others. Sowing recommendations on seed packets will often serve as warning—either they state, "Difficult to transplant, do so with care," or they advise outdoor sowing where the plants are to grow. These plants can be started indoors if you choose the proper container and take extra care to handle them gently during the transplanting process. Peat pots are a good choice for plants that don't transplant well because seedlings can be set in the garden, pot and all, with little disturbance. Be sure the rim of the pot doesn't extend above the soil level, however, because it can act as a wick, sucking all of the water out of the peat and creating a nearly impenetrable prison for the roots.

Difficult-to-transplant vegetables include beans, Chinese cabbage, corn, cucumbers, melons, pumpkins, squash, and most root crops (excluding beets, turnips, and celeriac). Perennials with taproots, including balloon flower (*Platycodon grandiflorus*), butterfly weed (*Asclepias tuberosa*), and flax (*Linum* spp.), are hard to move, too. Difficult-to-transplant annuals include California poppy (*Eschscholtzia californica*), cockscomb (*Celosia cristata*), and moss rose (*Portulaca grandiflora*). Annual and perennial poppies resent transplanting, also. Hard-to-transplant herbs include borage, burnet, caraway, chervil, coriander, and dill.

flats. Just be sure the bottom of a flat doesn't rest on the planting mix of the flat below. Check flats daily; unstack as soon as the seeds sprout. Keep the soil moist but not water-logged. As soon as you notice sprouts nudging above the soil surface, expose the flat to light.

## ❀ Cylinders for Seedlings

Soil cylinders make inexpensive substitutes for commercial peat pellets sold for seed starting. In this formula, gelatin binds the soil, stabilizes the cylinders even after repeated waterings, and supplies nitrogen for the young seedlings.

To make 80 to 100 soil cylinders, place 20 pounds of your choice of soil mix in a 5-gallon bucket. Place 1 quart of water in a 2-quart saucepan, bring to a boil, remove from heat, and add two envelopes of unfla-vored gelatin, stirring until thoroughly dis-solved. Cool. Add enough of the gelatin mix-ture to the soil mix so that a handful forms a small clod when squeezed. Depending on the type of soil mix you choose, you may need more or less gelatin. One quart of gelatin mixture will set 20 pounds of fairly dry loam and perlite.

Remove both ends from a clean 6-ounce tomato paste can and save one end. Place the tomato paste can upright at one end of an empty seed flat and fill it about two-thirds full of the soil mix. Cover the mix with one of the can's cut-off ends and push down to compact the soil slightly. Push again, gen-tly, to eject the newly formed soil cylinder from the can. Continue making soil cylinders in this manner until the seed flat is full. Allow an hour or two for the soil cylinders to set before planting seeds.

## RAISING HEALTHY SEEDLINGS

Seedlings need regular attention. Provide the right amount of light, heat, and humidity to grow robust, healthy seedlings.

**Light** Seedlings need more intense light than full-grown plants. If they don't get enough light or if the light isn't strong enough, they will become spindly and leggy. Sixteen hours of light a day is ideal, 14 hours is acceptable, and plants can get along with 12 hours in a cool location. Up to 18 hours will do no harm, but most plants won't thrive in continuous light.

Windowsills are a popular spot for starting seedlings. Wide windowsills are ready to use, but you can also widen narrow windowsills by installing shelf brackets and boards. Keep in mind that the air close to the window glass can be too cold for some tender seedlings, especially at night. Pull curtains orprop up cardboard next to the glass at night for protection. Short winter days provide inadequate light for many plants. Turn plants regularly to prevent them from developing a one-sided leaning, or rig up a mir-ror or a reflector made of aluminum foil and cardboard. A sunporch offers more room and often longer exposure to the sun than do win-dowsills, and the cooler temperatures in a sun-porch can be great for cold-loving plants.

If you have a greenhouse, you can easily raise high-quality seedlings in quantity. Cold frames can shelter small batches of cold-hardy seedlings like pansies and broccoli early in the season, followed by tomatoes and annual flowers as the season progresses. The addition of heating can transform a cold frame into a hotbed.

Fluorescent lights use energy and will raise your electric bill, but they do help in raising good seedlings. Special plant-growth lights, often called grow-lights, are expensive. The light from less-expensive cool-white tubes pro-duces comparable plants. Light from incandes-

##  Simple Seed-Starting Mixes

Seedlings and young plants are prone to a number of soilborne diseases, commonly lumped together under the term *damping-off*. A disease-free medium and sterilized containers are a basic part of producing healthy young plants. Here are tips on sterilizing potting soil, plus recipes for four easy-to-make mixes.

### Easy Soil Sterilization

If you make your own potting medium, especially out of ingredients such as garden soil, you will probably want to pasteurize it. Exposure to temperatures from 160° to 180°F for 30 minutes will kill most insects, weed seeds, and pathogenic bacteria and fungi. Higher temperatures, however, can also destroy beneficial organisms, deplete soil organic matter, and release toxic salts into the soil; monitor soil temperature carefully during treatment.

To pasteurize your potting mix indoors in a conventional oven, fill a clean, shallow pan with moist soil. Cover the pan with aluminum foil, insert a meat thermometer into the soil, and place the pan in an oven heated to 200°F. Start timing when the soil temperature reaches 140°F, and continue heating for 30 minutes. Remember that the soil temperature should not exceed 180°F; if necessary, remove the pan from the oven and let it cool to below 180°F before returning it to the oven.

### All-Purpose Mix

Seeds generally require only warmth and moisture to germinate. After the first small root and tiny leaves have appeared, they also need light and a growing mix that provides sufficient nutrients for continued growth. This formula makes a good all-purpose seed-starting mix that's suitable for almost any type of seed.

**Ingredients:**
  1 part sterilized potting soil
  1 part vermiculite
  1 part sterilized sand

Children's play sand is usually sterilized; follow the soil sterilization directions on this page if you are using topsoil. To mix, simply combine the ingredients in a suitably sized container.

### Three Quick Mixes

These seed-starting mixes are equally good. Just remember that mixtures such as these don't contain compost or other nutrient-rich ingredients. You'll need to feed seedlings germinated in these mixes regularly until they're transplanted to a richer mix.

**Mix I**
**Ingredients:**
  1 part vermiculite
  1 part milled sphagnum moss
  1 part perlite

**Mix II**
**Ingredients:**
  1 part milled sphagnum moss
  1 part vermiculite

**Mix III**
**Ingredients:**
  1 part milled sphagnum moss
  2 parts vermiculite
  2 parts perlite

Combine all ingredients in a suitably sized container. Stir with a clean stirring stick.

cent lightbulbs will not stimulate growth as well as grow-lights or cool-white fluorescent tubes do.

**Water**  Seedlings need a steady supply of moisture. Dry air in a heated house can suck moisture rapidly from the shallow soil in seedling flats. Check for dryness by poking your finger into the soil and by lifting the flats. A flat with dry soil weighs less than one that's well watered. For delicate seedlings, bottom-watering is best, since it does not disturb roots and helps prevent disease problems such as damping-off. Use tepid water rather than cold water to water seedlings, especially warmth-loving plants like okra, eggplant, and melons. In a warm, dry house, seedlings may need to

be watered every two to three days or even more frequently.

**Temperature**  Young plants require less warmth than germinating seedlings do. Average room temperatures of about 60° to 70°F, dropping by about 10°F at night, will keep most seedlings growing steadily. Slightly lower temperatures will make seedlings stocky but more slow-growing. Cool-weather plants such as cabbage and lettuce prefer cooler temperatures.

Temperatures of 30° to 45°F can cause chilling injury in some warmth-loving flowers and vegetables. Temperatures higher than about 75°F tend to produce weak, spindly plants that are vulnerable to harsh outdoor conditions.

**Ventilation**  Remove any plastic or other coverings as soon as seeds sprout. Lack of air circulation can lead to damping-off.

**Fertilizer**  Seedlings growing in a soilless or lean mix will need small doses of plant food, starting at the time the first true leaves develop. Use a half-strength fertilizer solution once a week for the first three weeks. Fish emulsion and compost or manure teas are good. After that, use a full-strength solution every 10 to 14 days. Seedlings grown in a potting mix that contains compost or other nutrients may not need supplementary feeding for several weeks. If the seedlings start looking pale, feed as above. For recipes for making compost tea or manure tea, see "Anti-Fungal Compost Tea" on page 54 and "Fertilizing Seedlings" on page 66.

**Transplanting**  Most gardeners tend to sow seeds thickly, but seedlings grow faster, develop better, and are less prone to disease if they have plenty of space and good soil. Transplanting gives you a chance to select the best seedlings and to move them into a larger container of richer soil. You can transplant seedlings from their nursery flat to another flat with wider

 **Troubleshooting**

If your seeds fail to germinate or if only a few sprout, it is probably due to one or more of these factors:

- Old seed that is no longer viable
- Seed produced under poor growing conditions and is not viable
- Seed that is damaged
- Too much or not enough moisture
- Temperature too high or too low
- Germination-inhibiting substances in the soil (herbicide residues, for example) or high salt content in soil
- Top-watering or heavy rain washed seeds out of soil mix or covered them too deeply, or seed was planted too deeply to start with
- Damping-off disease
- Seeds not in good contact with soil
- Lack of light or lack of darkness for seeds that need these for germination
- Dormancy requirement not met

spacing, or you can move them to individual pots. Seedlings are ready for transplanting when they have developed their first set of true leaves. For details on how to handle seedlings, see "Transplanting" on page 65.

## PLANTING OUT

Before you can plant your seedlings in the garden, you must prepare them for life outdoors.

Sheltered plants are unaccustomed to wind, strong sun, cold air, and varying temperatures. They will do better if you help them develop tougher tissues gradually, before you plant them outside.

When it's time to plant the hardened-off seedlings in the outdoor garden, wait for an overcast or drizzly day, or plant them in the late afternoon. Seedlings will suffer less stress if they

## Getting the Most from Your Grow-Lights

Grow-lights get your seedlings off to a good start. Follow these guidelines:

■ Growing seedlings need lots of light. Keep the lights on 16 hours a day and suspend the lights as close to the leaves of the seedlings as possible without allowing the tubes to touch the leaves—never more than 3 or 4 inches away. Buy an inexpensive timer so you won't have to remember to turn them on and off.

■ Since tubes produce less light at the ends than in the middle, choose the longest ones you have room for and rotate seedlings near the ends into the middle every few days. Shop light fixtures, which generally have two 48-inch bulbs, reflect more light toward the seedlings, where you want it to go, than bulbs without reflectors.

■ Keep the tubes clean because dust can decrease the amount of light available. Reflecting surfaces, in addition to the reflectors on the fixtures, increase efficiency. Paint surfaces near the fixtures such as shelves and walls with white paint to reflect more light.

■ Tubes last longest if they aren't turned on and off unnecessarily. As they age, however, they produce less light, so it's a good idea to replace them before they burn out completely.

■ Use a mirror to make double use of the light from a window or fluorescent fixture. Just position it so that it will reflect light back onto your seedlings. If you are growing seedlings on a windowsill, this technique helps them grow more evenly, so you won't have to turn them as often. You can also use sheets of cardboard covered with aluminum foil to reflect light onto plants.

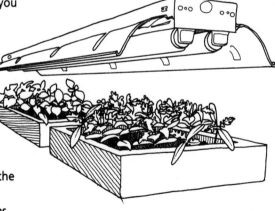

**Grow-lights.** Use cool-white fluorescent tubes or grow-lights to light indoor seedlings. Keep tubes close to the seedlings—no more than 3 inches away— for their first few weeks. Then raise the lights to 4 to 6 inches above the seedlings.

are not set out during a hot, sunny day. If you plant transplants out just before a rain, they'll get off to a good start, and you'll have less watering to do.

After planting out, you may want to put berry baskets or cut-open plastic jugs over seedlings or drape the row with a floating row cover to protect them from sun, wind, or frost. If the sun is strong or the plants are in an exposed location, water the soil around them several times during their first week in the ground, until their roots take hold. If plants wilt, water the soil promptly and shade the plants from the sun for a day or two.

## Scheduling Seed Starting

To plan the best time to start seedlings indoors in spring, you need to know the approximate date of the average last spring frost in your area. Count back from that date the number of weeks indicated below to determine the appropriate starting date for various crops.

| Flower | Weeks until Transplant Time | Vegetable | Weeks until Transplant Time |
|---|---|---|---|
| Ageratum | 6–8 | Broccoli | 4–5 |
| Aster | 6–8 | Brussels sprouts | 4–5 |
| Celosia | 6–8 | Cabbage | 4–5 |
| Centaurea | 4–6 | Cauliflower | 4 |
| Cosmos | 4–6 | Celery | 10 |
| Marigold | 4–6 | Chinese cabbage | 3–4 |
| Morning glory | 4–6 | Cucumbers | 3–4 |
| Pinks | 6–8 | Eggplant | 6–7 |
| Snapdragon | 8–10 | Leeks | 8 |
| Statice | 8–10 | Lettuce | 3–4 |
| Stock | 6–8 | Melons | 3–4 |
| Strawflower | 6–8 | Peppers | 7–8 |
| Sweet pea | 4–6 | Pumpkins | 3 |
| Zinnia | 4–6 | Squash | 3 |
| | | Tomatoes | 4–5 |

| Herb | |
|---|---|
| Basil | 4-6 |
| Chives | 6–8 |
| Dill | 4–6 |
| Lavender | 8–10 |
| Rosemary | 8–10 |
| Sage | 6–8 |
| Thyme | 8–10 |

# TRANSPLANTING

Transplanting simply means moving a rooted plant from one place to another. If you pick out tiny parsley seedlings from a flat into individual pots, you're transplanting. If you move tomato plants from your windowsill into the garden, you're transplanting. And if you decide the big forsythia would really look better in the backyard, you're transplanting, too.

For best results, follow these guidelines for transplanting your seedlings from place to place.

## TRANSPLANTING TO CONTAINERS

If you start seeds in flats, transplant when seedlings are still very young. Watch for the emergence of the first pair of true leaves, and transplant soon after. The choice of planting containers ranges from homemade newspaper cylinders to plastic cell packs and clay pots. Peat

---

 **Tips for Seed-Starting Success**

Gardeners have developed many secrets for successful seed starting. Here are some favorites:

■ Mix clean clay cat-box litter in your potting mix to loosen up a heavy mix; it also retains moisture and nutrients.

■ Try soaking seeds in black tea to scarify tough seed coats—the tannin in the tea does the trick.

■ When starting seeds in a flat, lay them on top of the moistened soil mix and cover with a thin layer of dry soil mix. It's faster than poking holes in the seedbed for planting. Cover the flat with plastic to retain moisture.

■ Cover the soil surface of seedling flats with a thin layer of milled sphagnum moss. Bacteria that live in the sphagnum produce chemicals that prevent damping-off.

■ If your seed flats are in a greenhouse or cold frame, watch out for mice—they love freshly sown seed.

■ When sowing fine seed, mix it with unflavored Knox powdered gelatin, which is orange and easy to see and will actually nourish the seedlings by releasing a little nitrogen as it breaks down. Or try using sand: Add a few teaspoons of clean white sand to the seed packet and shake to mix.

■ Don't go by the planting depth on seed packets—some recommendations are outdated. Instead, follow the rule of thumb that seeds shouldn't be buried any deeper than their diameter. Forget those $1/4$-inch planting depths for all but the biggest seeds like peas and beans.

■ Sow small seeds like those of impatiens, begonias, and snapdragons right on the soil surface. Water the soil first to prevent burying the tiny seeds. For subsequent watering, set the flat in a pan of water for bottom-watering.

■ Use an empty herb or spice shaker bottle with a plastic lid that has large holes to broadcast seeds in the garden. Tops with $1/4$-inch holes are perfect for round seeds such as poppies, radishes, onions, and members of the cabbage family.

■ Use those discarded cell packs (the kind bedding plants are sold in) to save steps in seed starting. Sow one seed in each cell, then just pop the seedlings out when it's time to transplant. If you're not sowing a lot of seeds and have room, this will really reduce transplant shock.

■ Store seeds in Ziploc plastic storage bags in the refrigerator—they take up less space than jars.

pots are a favorite of many gardeners because the pots can be transplanted with the plant. Plastic and clay containers are reusable.

Before you start, collect your transplanting supplies and put down a layer of newspaper to catch spills. Follow these steps:

1. Fill the containers with soil mix. You'll find recipes in "Mixes for Transplants" on the opposite page. The depth of the soil depends on seedling size. Fill nearly to the top for small seedlings; add only 1 inch of soil for large ones.

2. Pour warm water onto the soil mix and let it sit for an hour to soak in. Moist potting soil prevents seedling roots from drying out.

3. Carefully dig out either individual seedlings or small groups of seedlings. A Popsicle stick makes a good all-purpose tool for digging, lifting, and moving tiny plants. A tablespoon or narrow trowel works well for larger transplants.

4. Hold the seedling by one of the leaves, not by (or around) the stem: You could crush the tender stem or, if you grasp the stem tip, you could kill the growing point and ruin the seedling's further growth.

5. For very young seedlings, poke small holes into the soil mix with a pencil. For larger seedlings, hold the plant in the pot while you fill in around the roots with soil. Firm the soil with your fingertips.

6. Return the seedlings to the window, light rack, or cold frame. If seedlings wilt from the stress of transplanting, mist lightly with water and cover loosely with a sheet of plastic wrap. Keep them cool and out of direct sun for a day or two, then remove the wrap and return them to light.

7. Keep soil lightly moist but not soggy by pouring water into the tray holding the containers. Feed regularly with a weak solution of water-soluble organic fertilizer.

8. As the plants grow, pinch or snip off any extra seedlings, leaving only the strongest one.

If you miscalculated the seed-starting date or if the weather turns nasty, you may need to transplant your plants again to larger containers so plants won't stop growing and become stunt-

 **Fertilizing Seedlings**

Most seedlings respond well to a weak "starter solution," which provides a quick dose of readily available nutrients. Starter solutions help young plants recover quickly from the shock of transplanting. Try one of these.

**Fish Emulsion and Seaweed Extract**

Mix ½ cup fish emulsion and ½ cup seaweed extract together in a disposable container. Pour into a jar or bottle, seal tightly, and store in a cool, dark place. To use, add 3 tablespoons of starter solution to 1 gallon of water. Use as a soil drench at transplanting time or as a spray for foliar feeding.

**Manure Tea**

If you have a readily available source of poultry, horse, or cow manure, try this starter solution for your young transplants. Fill a large barrel, garbage can, or other waterproof container one-eighth full of manure. Then fill the container to the top with water. Allow it to steep for a day or two; stir the mixture several times during this period. Dip out the liquid with a clean can and dilute it with water to a light amber color. Water each transplant with clear water, then pour about a cup of this solution around the base of each. Repeat at 10- to 14-day intervals to encourage vigorous growth.

**Handling seedlings.** Hold and move seedlings by grasping a leaf between thumb and forefinger. Yanking up seedlings by their stems will damage roots. Also avoid touching the delicate growing top of the stem.

ed. Roots pushing through drainage holes are a clue that it's time to transplant.

## TRANSPLANTING TO THE GARDEN

Toughen your seedlings for outdoor growing conditions by hardening them off. Two weeks before outdoor transplanting time, stop feeding them and slow down on watering. About a week before you plan to plant them out, put them outdoors in a protected area, out of direct sun and wind. Leave them outdoors for only an hour at first, then two hours, then a morning, working up to a full day. Water frequently.

Transplant on a cloudy or drizzly day or in early evening to spare transplants from the sun's heat. Water the plants before you start. Follow these steps for best results:

1. Dig a hole slightly wider than and of the same depth as the container. (Plant tomatoes deeper, so that roots form along the stem.)

2. If your transplants are in plastic or clay pots, turn the pots upside down and slide out the plants. Whack the pot with your trowel to

### ❀ Mixes for Transplants

Good potting mixes don't have to be fancy, but don't be afraid to experiment. Seedlings generally don't live in them longer than eight weeks before they're moved to the garden; so as with seed-starting mixtures, structure and texture matter more than the exact proportion of ingredients. Most have ingredients such as screened compost that contribute to the nourishment of growing plants, however. If you suspect your compost or leaf mold is extremely acidic, be sure to test the pH of the mix.

Use one of the basic potting-mix formulas listed here, or develop your own:

■ 1 part screened, finished compost or leaf mold and 1 part vermiculite or perlite.

■ 1 part finished compost or leaf mold; 1 part good potting soil; and 1 part of sharp sand, perlite, vermiculite, or a mixture of all three

■ 1 part commercial potting soil, compost, or leaf mold; 1 part sphagnum moss or peat moss; and 1 part perlite or sharp sand. You can make a richer version of this mix by combining 1 part good potting soil; 1 part compost or leaf mold; 1 part sphagnum moss; and 1 part sharp sand or perlite.

■ 1 part compost or leaf mold; 2 parts good potting soil; and 1 part compost or well-rotted, sifted manure. This makes an especially rich potting mix.

## Dos and Don'ts When the Seeds Come Up

Here's what to do—and what not to do—to ensure healthy seedlings:

■ **Do** remove plastic or glass covers to bring the humidity down and give the seedlings as much light as possible.

■ **Do** cut down on water—let the top ¼ inch of soil dry between waterings—and resist the urge to feed the emerging plants. Both overwatering and fertilizing result in soft, tangled growth and rot.

■ **Do** water seedlings carefully—remember that damping-off threatens seedlings. If you are watering from above, water next to the row of seedlings rather than on top of them. Water as gently as possible—you can use a nozzle to break the force of the water. If possible, water seedlings from below by pouring water into the tray or saucer in which the flats or pots are sitting and letting it soak up into the soil. Also, water in the morning, not in the evening.

■ **Do** thin new seedlings in flats by cutting them off at soil level with a sharp pair of pointed nail scissors. It's quick and it doesn't disturb the roots of the seedlings left behind.

■ **Do** transplant before the roots of adjacent seedlings get tangled together. The best time is when the seedlings have developed their first set of true leaves. When seedlings sprout, they first send up seed leaves, called cotyledons, which are shaped like the seed coat. The next set of leaves, the true leaves, often look very different from the seed leaves. All the rest of the leaves will be true leaves.

■ **Don't** handle seedling stems—they're very fragile and easy to crush. Instead, dig up the seedling with a houseplant trowel or Popsicle stick, then hold it by the leaves to move it.

■ **Do** plant each seedling in a clean cell pack, Styrofoam cup (with drainage holes added), or plastic pot of its own. Replant the seedling at the depth at which it grew in the flat, and firm the soil to make sure there's good root-to-soil contact.

■ **Do** handle seedlings as little and as quickly as possible, and don't leave them lying out. Have your pots set up and ready before you start to transplant, and transplant one seedling at a time. The roots can dry out in a matter of minutes.

■ **Do** protect newly transplanted seedlings until they've re-established themselves. Keep them in bright but indirect light.

■ **Don't** fertilize the plants until they're established or you'll shock them. Once they're growing again, you can give them a boost with one-third- to one-half-strength liquid seaweed.

■ **Don't** let your seedlings overheat. Seedlings prefer cooler temperatures than you might think—around 60°F is fine for most species. When in doubt, keep them cool.

■ **Do** start hardening off the plants when frost danger is over and the soil has warmed by setting them outside during the day and bringing them in again at night. Select a protected location, such as a spot against a north-facing wall. If possible, mist them in the heat of the day and put them in the shade or cover them with moist newspaper or a spunbonded row cover like Reemay. Continue the hardening off process for about one week.

■ Do put seedlings in a cold frame or nursery bed after hardening off until they're big enough to hold their own in the garden.

dislodge stubborn ones. Plants in peat or paper pots can be planted, pot and all.

3. Gently place the plant in the hole. Spread out roots of plants not in pots. The illustration on this page shows how to open up peat pots for better root penetration after planting.

4. Fill and tamp with your hands, forming a shallow basin to collect water.

5. Slowly pour water—at least a quart—at the base of each transplant. Keep well watered until they are established and show new growth.

## Starting Outdoors

You can plant seeds of many flowers, herbs, and vegetables directly in the garden. If you live

**Transplanting peat pot plants.** Slit the sides and remove the bottom of the peat pot before transplanting unless many roots have already penetrated. Always tear off the rim above the soil line. If even a small piece of peat pot is exposed after transplanting, it will draw water from the soil surrounding the transplant's roots, leaving the plant in danger of water stress.

where winters are mild, you can sow seeds outside pretty much year-round. In cold-winter areas, the outdoor seed-sowing season begins in spring when the ground thaws and continues until early autumn.

When the soil is soft enough to dig and dry enough to crumble readily in your hand, you can make your first outdoor plantings. Don't try to work the soil while it is wet.

Plant flowers and vegetables in fertile, well-drained soil that is rich in organic matter. If you're starting a new garden, double digging is worth the effort. This technique loosens the top 2 feet of the soil, increasing pore space to hold soil and water. For step-by-step directions, see "Double Digging" on page 40.

Prepare the seedbed with a rotary tiller or turn the earth with a spade or garden fork. If you do the tilling or digging in fall, you'll be one step ahead come spring. Rake the soil to a fine tilth, breaking up clods and removing stones and weeds.

Check seed packages to find out when to sow and if the plants have any special germination requirements. Some plants, such as peas, prefer cool weather; others, such as corn, will rot if planted before the soil warms up. Many will produce flowers or fruit earlier if given a head start indoors or in a cold frame. Start with the hardiest seeds, such as peas and radishes, and gradually work up to more tender crops as the season progresses and frost danger diminishes and finally disappears.

Avoid stepping on the seedbed; compacted soil lacks the air spaces necessary for good root growth. Follow seed packet directions for seed spacing: Thick stands of seedlings compete with each other just like weeds and are more prone to disease problems such as damping-off.

Sow seeds thinly to avoid thinning chores later. Sprinkle flower seeds in long single rows for cutting, or broadcast with a flinging motion over a wider area for a free-form display. Plant small vegetable seeds such as lettuce and spinach in rows, or scatter them in a wide band. Plant large flower and vegetable seeds individually, spaced according to package instructions. Vining plants such as melons and cucumbers can be planted in hills of three to five seeds.

Cover the seeds with fine soil to a depth about equal to the diameter—not the length—of the seed. Firm the soil (use the palm of your hand or the back of your hoe) to establish good contact between seed and soil. Some seeds, such as lettuce, petunias, and begonias, must have light to germinate. Lightly press seeds like these onto the surface of moistened soil.

Always water gently after you plant seeds, taking care not to wash the seeds away. A fine, misty spray is best; you can buy a hose attachment at garden centers and hardware stores. Keep the soil evenly moist until you see stems and leaves popping above the ground.

After you have sown the seeds, mark the spot with a label, and record the planting on your garden calendar or plan.

To figure the latest possible planting date for late-summer seed sowing, subtract the average days to maturity for the crop from the average date of your first hard frost. Subtract five to ten extra days to compensate for cooler fall nights and slower growth. If hard frost comes in mid-October, for instance, make a final planting of 50-day lettuce in early to mid-August. If you use season extenders like floating row covers, delay the final planting date a few weeks.

Hill planting is a good way to provide space for vines like watermelon, squash, melons, pumpkins, and cucumbers because it gives room for them to spread. It also provides them with the rich, loamy soil they require for best performance.

To build a hill, form a 6- to 12-inch-high mound of loamy, fertile soil 1 to 1½ feet square. Amend the soil with plenty of organic matter such as compost to make sure it is porous and loose. Flatten the mound on the top so water won't erode it during heavy rains. A light covering of mulch, such as salt hay, will also help prevent rains from washing the mound away before plant roots bind it together.

Plant six to eight seeds in the mound at the correct depth, spacing them along the tops and sides. Later you can thin out your plants, leaving the two or three strongest. If the soil is poor or if you'd like to provide an especially rich environment for your plants, dig a hole 12

## Ring around the Transplant

A little ring in the soil around new transplants creates a small basin to collect water so it goes right down to the roots. Use your finger to draw a 4-inch-diameter circle around transplants in the soil. The rings don't need to be deep; just draw in the soil with enough pressure to make an indentation the way you do when you write in the sand at the beach. This is also very helpful when applying fish emulsion. To fertilize, water thoroughly first, then apply 2 cups of fish emulsion per transplant. The emulsion is diluted at the rate of 1 tablespoon of emulsion per 1 gallon of water.

## Homemade Seed Tapes

When you need to space seeds uniformly or if you want to avoid thinning seedlings, try homemade seed tapes using cornstarch and ordinary paper towels.

In a small saucepan, dissolve 1 tablespoon of cornstarch in 1 cup of cold water. Cook over medium heat, stirring constantly to prevent the mixture from becoming lumpy. Once it boils and turns translucent and gel-like, remove from the heat, and let it cool to room temperature.

Tear off 4- or 5-foot-long sections of paper towels. Leave the towels attached to each other and cut them into long strips that are ½ to ¾ inch wide.

At this point, check the seed packet or some other source to determine the correct seed spacing for the seeds you're using. If you're making a tape of large seeds, the proper technique is to put dots of cornstarch at the proper spacing on the paper towels and then dab one seed onto each dot.

Begin by putting a few spoonfuls of the cornstarch mix in a plastic bag. Twist the bag until the gel is squeezed into one corner; snip off the tip of that corner. Using the bag as you would a pastry bag, squeeze out dots of cornstarch gel down the length of the paper towel. Place one seed on each cornstarch dot and let the seed tape dry for about 1 hour or until it is no longer sticky. Then, roll the seed tape up and place it in a plastic bag until you are ready to use it. Write the type of seed and the cultivar name in ink on each seed tape, or you may end up with mystery plantings.

For the best results with small seeds, mix the seeds and cornstarch mixture together in the plastic bag. Then, as before, cut a small hole

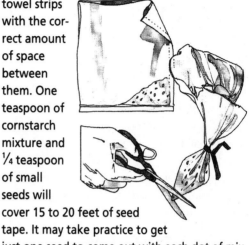

in one corner of the bag and squeeze dots of the seed-and-cornstarch mixture onto paper towel strips with the correct amount of space between them. One teaspoon of cornstarch mixture and ¼ teaspoon of small seeds will cover 15 to 20 feet of seed tape. It may take practice to get just one seed to come out with each dot of mixture. Don't let the seed-and-cornstarch mixture set before making the tapes, or the seeds will become too moist and may sprout. Let the finished seed tapes dry, label them, roll them up, and store them in a plastic bag.

When planting time arrives, check the proper planting depth for each crop, then dig furrows of the appropriate depth in your garden. Unroll the seed tapes, place one in each furrow, and cover the tapes with soil. The cornstarch and paper towels will decompose in the damp earth, and the seeds will sprout evenly spaced along the row.

inches deep and 12 inches square before forming each hill. Fill it with well-rotted compost,
manure, or other organic material. Then build a
mound on top.

# SAVING SEEDS

Saving seeds is fun, and you can save a bit of
money by doing it. You can save seeds from
individual plants with traits you desire, such as
earliness, disease resistance, high yield, or flower
color. By carefully selecting individual plants
each year and saving their seeds, you can develop strains that are uniquely suited to your growing conditions.

Seed saving is also an important way to per-
petuate heirloom plants that are in danger of
becoming extinct.

## SELECTING SEEDS TO SAVE

Only save seeds from plants grown from open-
pollinated seed. Open-pollinated cultivars produce seed that comes true—the seedlings are
very like the parents. They also are somewhat
variable by nature, and repeated selection for
a particular character will yield a strain that is
slightly different from the original one. Seed
harvested from hybrid plants produces seedlings

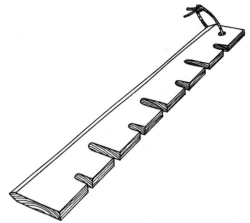

**Planting guide.** It's easier to plant seeds at the correct
spacing than to thin them later. A notched board with
a beveled edge makes a helpful guide for even seed
sowing.

unlike the parents and, in most cases, the seeds
are inferior to the original plant.

When selecting plants to save seed from,
choose those that are vigorous, disease-free,
and outstanding in whatever qualities you wish
to encourage. Mark chosen plants with a stake
or colored string so you won't forget and harvest them for other purposes by mistake.

Some garden plants, such as tomatoes, peas,
and lettuce, are self-pollinated. Each flower pol-
linates itself. You don't have to take any precautions to prevent one cultivar from crossing with
another—just let the seed mature, and then harvest it.

Others, such as corn and plants of the pumpkin, squash, and cabbage families, are cross-
pollinated and can cross with other cultivars of
the same plant. To keep a strain pure, keep
plants from which you want to save seed separate from other blooming cultivars of the same
species by at least 200 feet. Or use bags to cover
the blooms you plan to harvest seed from
before they open, and pollinate them by hand
with flowers of the same cultivar.

---

### ✿ Row Covers for Germination

"Row covers are really handy for boosting
germination rates," says Janet Bachmann, a
co-owner of a small organic farm in
Arkansas. "Not only do they keep the soil
warmer, they also retain a little extra moisture and keep the soil from crusting." Bachmann uses row covers over most of her
direct-seeded crops and says that they are
invaluable for slow germinators like carrots.

---

As you become more interested in seed saving, you may want to try your hand at making some controlled crosses of your own by pollinating protected blossoms with flowers from a different cultivar.

Certain garden plants normally grown as annuals, such as carrots and lettuce, are biennials—these crops will not produce seed the first year. Select superior plants and allow them to overwinter in place if possible. If you can't work around them, transplant them carefully to a new location.

## HARVESTING

Pick seed pods when they have turned dry and brittle but before they break open and scatter the seed. Some plants have very fragile seed pods or ripen unevenly. Cover the pods of these plants with a bag before the seeds ripen completely, and tie it snugly to the stem so seeds can't escape. Remove the seeds from the pods after harvesting. You can split the pods by hand or thresh the seeds out by beating them with a stick onto a large piece of plastic.

Allow fleshy fruits like tomatoes, squash, and cucumbers to get a little overripe on the plant before harvesting them, but don't allow them to start to rot. Separate the seeds from the flesh and wash them clean in water. Some seeds are covered with a thick, jellylike coating. Clean the seeds by removing as much flesh as possible by letting them sit in a jar of water for a few days. The seeds will sink to the bottom of the jar and the pulp will float. Pour off the pulp and dry the seeds.

## DRYING AND STORING

After gathering seeds, spread them on newspaper and let them air dry for about a week. Write seed names on the newspaper so you don't get them confused. Then pack them away in airtight jars and keep them in a cool, dry place.

Remember that heat and dampness will shorten the seed's period of viability. Label packaged seeds with cultivar, date, and any other pertinent information.

## Block Planting for Big Yields

Planting in blocks rather than rows increases yield per square foot. Some crops seem to perform better with this treatment, and once leaves are big enough to shade the growing bed, block-planted crops require much less weeding than row plantings. The following table lists appropriate equidistant spacing in a good soil. The spacing listed is meant as final spacing. With crops such as kale, beets, and radishes, for example, initial spacing can be closer. Thin alternate plants as they grow, and use the thinnings in salads.

| Crop | Spacing (inches) |
| --- | --- |
| Beets | 3–5½ |
| Broccoli | 15–18 |
| Bush beans | 6 |
| Cabbage | 15–18 |
| Carrots | 2–4½ |
| Celery | 6–11 |
| Corn | 15–18 |
| Cucumbers | 12 |
| Kale | 15 |
| Lettuce | 6–12 |
| Melons | 15 |
| Onions | 2½–5 |
| Peas | 3–4 |
| Potatoes | 9–16 |
| Radishes | 1–2 |
| Spinach | 4–6 |
| Squash | 30 |
| Tomatoes | 18–24 |

# Chapter 5

# PLANTING

One of the best ways to ensure that plants will grow well is to do a good job planting them. Preparing planting areas thoroughly, so roots will quickly extend into the soil surrounding the planting holes, is time well spent.

## KNOW YOUR SITE

Before you dig that planting hole or plant those seeds, try to make a good match between the plant and its environment. Getting to know your soil and growing conditions—and using that knowledge to pick the right plants—is just as important as knowing the best planting techniques. So before you plant:

■ Take a close look at your soil. Is it red clay or deep loam? Waterlogged or sandy and dry? Is it acid or alkaline?

■ Check the amount of sunlight your site gets. Is it full sun all day or just afternoon sun? Is the shade dappled through the small, shifting leaves of a birch, or deep and heavy, as beneath a fir? A tomato plant must have six hours of direct sunlight daily for good fruit set, but the same amount of sun fades and burns ferns.

■ Know your hardiness zone. Your local nurseries and garden centers generally stock only plants that are hardy in your area. But if you do any mail-order buying, knowing your zone will save you money and disappointment.

■ Learn the growth rate and size of your plants. Choose a site where they won't cause problems or overgrow your garden. This is

especially important for permanent plants such as trees and shrubs.

■ Be aware of seasonal conditions. Is the spot you picked sheltered by a wall or windbreak, or does it get the full blast of winter winds? Is it low-lying and prone to late-spring frost?

For more information about site selection, see "Sizing Up Your Site" on page 5.

## GET YOUR SOIL IN SHAPE

If you set plants into poorly drained soil, the roots are likely to rot and die. If you plant seeds into poorly drained soil, they may never even germinate. Before you plant a pumpkin seed or a pine tree, be sure that your soil drains well. If drainage is poor, see "Problem Soils" on page 35 for ways to improve it. Or consider growing plants in raised beds. "Raised Bed Gardening" on page 40 explains how to make and plant raised beds. For very wet areas, your best bet may be to grow plants that can tolerate wet conditions.

If you till the soil for a vegetable garden or dig a hole for a tree when the soil is too wet, you'll destroy the soil's structure. Your soil will compact, causing water to run off or lie in puddles rather than penetrate. Without air, root growth suffers. If your soil is too wet, let it dry before planting. Pick up a handful of soil and squeeze it. If it crumbles, it's perfect for planting. But if it forms a muddy ball, the soil is too wet to be worked.

Most plants pay less attention to pH than

# Buying Healthy Annuals

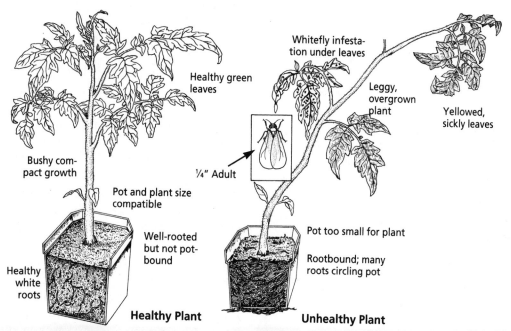

Healthy green leaves

Whitefly infesta-tion under leaves

Leggy, overgrown plant

Yellowed, sickly leaves

Bushy com-pact growth

¼" Adult

Pot and plant size compatible

Well-rooted but not pot-bound

Pot too small for plant

Rootbound; many roots circling pot

Healthy white roots

**Healthy Plant**

**Unhealthy Plant**

If you're buying annual flowers and vegetables, get your garden off to a good start by selecting the healthiest plants you can find. Use these pointers to make your choice:

■ Look for a sales display where the plants are well cared for. Plants subjected to hot, sunny sidewalks, allowed to wilt frequently, and watered unevenly are never a bargain.

■ Look at the entire group of plants being offered for sale. If some seem to be in poor health, shop somewhere else. Those that look healthy today may be diseased tomorrow.

■ Look for plants with deep green leaves and bushy, compact growth. Pale overall color indicates a need for nutrients, which is easy to correct. However, distinct yellow streaks or brown leaf spots indicate presence of disease.

■ Choose plants whose buds aren't yet open. If plants are already in flower, pinch off the

blossoms when you set them out. Pinching will help direct the plant's energy into growing roots, so it will be better able to support more flowers and fruit later in the season.

■ Don't buy by the yard. Bigger isn't necessarily better. Overgrown plants that have long outgrown their pots probably have roots circling the stem and have already had their growth severely checked.

■ Buy plants that are clearly labeled, unless you're game for a gamble. Labels help you choose the cultivars you'd like to grow, and therefore flower color, bloom size, and height.

■ Finally, always look carefully for signs of insect infestations or disease. Don't buy plants that show evidence of whiteflies, aphids, spider mites, or other pests. Disease symptoms to look for include rotted lesions on the stem or leaves and yellowed or spotted foliage.

gardeners do. If your soil is fertile and well drained and not extremely acid or alkaline, most plants will do just fine. But a number of plants are more demanding. Acid-loving azaleas and blueberries, for instance, will do poorly in soil that's alkaline. If you don't know the soil pH in an area you plan to plant, it's a good idea to test it. See "Soil Tests: Which One, When?" on page 29 and "Understanding pH" on page 30 for more information on soil testing and pH.

Enrich flower and vegetable beds with lots of aged manure, compost, or leaf mold before planting. For more about enriching your soil, see Chapter 3.

 **Don't Rush to Transplant**

Every spring, gardeners rush to plant their gardens. But late spring frosts and cool soil conditions can damage new plants. While many plants grow well in cool temperatures—cole crops such as cabbage, broccoli, and cauliflower, as well as peas, lettuce, spinach, and many annuals and perennials—others are very sensitive to cold, which can check growth or kill plants. When you begin the hardening-off process, be sure to bring your plants in each night. Seedlings that thrive in cool weather can be left out all night once they are fully hardened, but have boxes ready to cover them if frost threatens. Warm-weather plants such as tomatoes, peppers, eggplant, melons, and tender annuals and perennials also should be left out all night the last day or so of the hardening process. However, it's often best with these plants to wait an extra few days after the average last frost date before transplanting so that all danger of frost has passed and the soil has warmed.

# SEEDLINGS

There comes a day in early spring when your seedlings have been hardened off or your bedding plants have all been purchased and you're ready to plant them in the garden. Although clear, breezy spring days are beautiful, they're not the best kind for transplanting seedlings. Sun and wind cause seedlings to lose large quantities of water, which newly disturbed root systems have difficulty replacing. It's a far better idea to wait and transplant seedlings at the beginning of a spell of warm, damp, cloudy weather. That way, they'll have a chance to recover and put on root growth before having to withstand sun and wind.

Try not to rush seedlings into the garden if cold weather still threatens, unless you're prepared to cover them nightly with boxes or other protective devices when the weather turns cool. Jumping the average date of last spring frost pays off some years; in others, late spring frosts take their toll on newly transplanted seedlings. Although many plants grow well in cool temperatures, others are sensitive to cold and won't begin growing until the weather (and the soil) warms up. If you can't bear to wait, be sure to hold back a few of each kind of plant as insurance against a late cold snap.

Transplanting is a stressful operation for plants, and the more you can do to ease the stress that a plant suffers in being put out in the garden, the sooner it will be off and growing. (See "Transplanting to the Garden" on page 67.) Here are some tips to make your transplanting day a success:

■ Dig a generous hole for each seedling so there is ample space for the plant's roots.

■ If you're planting an entire bed of plants, work plenty of compost into the soil before planting, or add a handful to each hole as you plant, mix it in, and cover with ordinary garden soil before planting.

■ Water seedlings before you transplant, and try to keep as much soil around the plants' roots as possible so they will not dry out. If the potting mix falls away from the roots, it's a good idea to dip them in a slurry of thick, muddy water to be sure the roots stay moist.

■ As you place each plant in its hole, take time to make sure the roots fan out evenly in all directions. They shouldn't double back on each other or stick up toward the top of the hole.

■ When transplanting seedlings in peat pots, tear off the top inch or so of the pot so the remaining portion will be entirely underground. Cut slits down the sides to help roots penetrate them. Some gardeners prefer to gently tear away the entire pot if roots haven't already grown through. If you've started your seedlings in peat pellets encased in plastic netting, cut the netting off before planting. Then plant as you would any other seedling.

■ Water the seedlings as you go, rather than waiting and watering after you've finished transplanting. If the soil is unusually dry, moisten it slightly before planting because dry soil can quickly pull the water out of tender roots and damage them.

■ To settle seedlings in their holes, fill the hole with loose, well-tilled soil, sprinkle at least a quart of water on each transplant, and gently firm the soil to eliminate large air pockets so the roots will be in contact with the soil and there will be no root-drying air spaces. A shallow, saucerlike depression will help catch rain and direct it toward the roots.

■ As a general rule, set seedlings in the soil at the same depth they were growing in their pots. Tomatoes are an exception to this rule. If they are planted in a shallow trench on their sides with the top one or two sets of leaves above ground, the stems will grow roots and the tomato plants will be less leggy.

## PLANT PROTECTION

The transplanting operation doesn't simply end when the last seedling is in place in the garden, however. Sun and wind can still wreak havoc with your seedlings for the first week or so after transplanting, and occurences such as freak late-spring frosts can reduce your carefully tended plants to mush. Be sure to keep them well watered, and, if possible, screen them from heavy wind. Pale yellow leaves indicate sunscald. Cover afflicted plants promptly with screens,

### A Second Chance

Most of us know the frustration of having a flat of seedlings or transplants turn out to be leggy, with stems flopping in a jumbled mess. Deep transplanting can give lanky cabbage, tomato, and other seedlings a second chance on life. This technique works with seedlings of cabbage-family crops, as well as lettuce. To deep transplant, dig an angled planting trench, strip off lower leaves, and lay the floppy stem in the trench, as shown in the illustration. The plant will form additional roots along the buried stem.

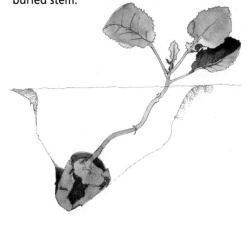

plastic sheeting, or anything else that will provide shade. Then gradually increase exposure to sun over several days.

# HARDY BULBS

Planting hardy bulbs is easy when you do it right. By carefully selecting a site, determining planting times, and using proper spacing and planting techniques, you'll be following the path to foolproof planting.

## SELECTING A SITE

Almost all bulbs are sun lovers and grow best in full sun. However, this is only true when they're actively growing. By the time spring-blooming bulbs go dormant, they can tolerate full shade. That's why spring bulbs like daffodils and crocuses grow well under deciduous trees and shrubs—their active growing season occurs before the trees leaf out. Some bulbs, like pink daffodils, will have better color if they're grown in partial shade.

Bulbs need loose, humus-rich soil for best performance; they won't bloom well in poor, compacted soils. Most bulbs also need well-drained soil and will appreciate the addition of decomposed organic matter like composted pine bark. If you have poorly drained or compacted soil, try growing bulbs in raised beds, which will enhance drainage and make for easier planting. Of course, bulbs will thrive in beds that have been double-dug, since they thrive in well-worked soil, but in most soils this extra effort isn't essential. Bulbs prefer a pH of 6.0 to 7.0 but will tolerate slightly more acidic soils.

## DETERMINING PLANTING TIMES

Plant spring-flowering and early-summer-flowering bulbs in fall so they can develop a root system and meet their cold requirements. (Hardy bulbs usually need a certain number of hours of cold temperatures to bloom.) It's best to wait until soil temperatures are below 60°F at 6 inches deep before planting. Follow these rules of thumb: In Zones 2 and 3, plant bulbs in September; in Zones 4 and 5, September to early October; in Zones 6 and 7, October to early November; in Zone 8, November to early December; and in Zone 9, December. In Zone 9, precooling may be necessary.

You can plant bulbs later in the fall, as long as they're planted before the onset of hard freezes. Late-planted bulbs tend to bloom several weeks later and on shorter stems, and there is the possibility of aborted blooms or bulbs freezing before roots are established.

Soak anemone (*Anemone* spp.) and winter aconite (*Eranthis hyemalis*) tubers overnight in warm water before planting to bring them out of dormancy. Plant anemones in fall in Zones 7 to 9, or in the spring in Zones 4 to 9. Because it is difficult to tell the top from the bottom of anemone tubers, plant them sideways.

## SPACING BULBS

Place bulbs in your flower bed and space according to flower stalk height. For greatest impact, plant in clusters of ten or more rather than singly in rows. Plant large bulbs 5 to 6 inches apart and small bulbs 1 to 3 inches apart. Leave room to interplant with perennials, groundcovers, or annuals.

You can use 6-inch concrete reinforcing wire as a template to make a uniform bulb bed. Put this hardware cloth flat on the ground and place bulbs in the centers of the squares. Remove the hardware cloth before planting.

## PLANTING TECHNIQUES

The general rule for planting depth is three to four times the height of the bulb. This depth will help to protect the bulbs against frost, animals, and physical damage from hoeing.

## Buying Healthy Bulbs

Whether you buy bulbs from a garden center, mail-order catalog, or specialist grower, you want to be sure to get the healthiest bulbs. Here's how:

■ Buy the biggest bulbs you can afford—you get what you pay for. Look for categories like "exhibition size," "jumbo," "top size," and "double- (or triple-) nosed" for the best bloom. Smaller bulbs, often called "landscape size," are less expensive and good for naturalizing.

■ Inspect bulbs as soon as you get them in the mail or before you buy them at a garden center. Healthy bulbs are sound, solid, and heavy. Lightweight, pithy, soft bulbs won't grow well.

■ Buy only dormant bulbs that show little, if any, root development and no topgrowth other than a pale, fat bud. (Lilies, however, are never completely dormant; their bulbs often have fleshy roots attached.)

■ Purchase and plant bulbs at the right time. Reputable dealers sell bulbs in defined seasons: fall for spring-flowering bulbs (daffodils, tulips), spring for summer-flowering bulbs (lilies, glads), and summer for fall-flowering species (some crocuses).

■ Small nicks and loose skins do not affect the development of the bulb. In fact, loose skins (tunics) make it easier for the bulb to sprout. However, don't buy bulbs (especially tulips) that completely lack the protective tunic.

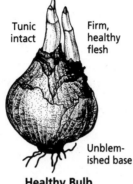

Tunic intact
Firm, healthy flesh
Unblemished base

**Healthy Bulb**

■ Plant bulbs as soon as they arrive. If you can't plant them at once, store bulbs in a dry place with good ventilation and get them in the ground as soon as you can.

■ Avoid bulbs with cuts, mold, dark or water-soaked spots, rotted areas, or discolored or scabby areas.

■ Choose bulbs packaged in materials that permit air to enter. Damp bulbs in plastic bags often rot.

Growing healthy, trouble-free bulbs also depends on good cultural practices. Prepare bulb planting beds well, and make sure the soil is well drained. Handle bulbs carefully when planting to avoid injuries that provide access to diseases. Remove problem plants quickly to keep pests and diseases from spreading. Always let bulb foliage die back naturally to allow food production for growth and flowering in subsequent years. Mark sites where bulbs are planted so you can find them after foliage has faded. Clean up flower beds in fall to remove plant debris that offers shelter to pests and diseases.

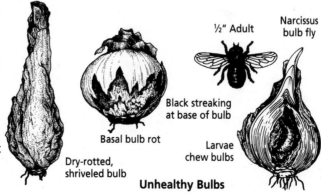

Dry-rotted, shriveled bulb

Basal bulb rot

½" Adult
Narcissus bulb fly

Black streaking at base of bulb

Larvae chew bulbs

**Unhealthy Bulbs**

Deeper planting will also help bulbs naturalize and perennialize.

The thought of planting a boxful of bulbs can be daunting, but with the right tools and techniques, bulb planting is easy. A heavy-duty tubular bulb planter large enough for daffodil bulbs is the ideal tool for prepared beds. It's a cup-shaped steel cylinder with a foot bar and long handle on top. Insert the bulb planter in the soil by stepping on the foot bar. Twist the planter, lift it out, then place the bulb in the bottom of the hole. Fill the hole with dirt from the planter, then repeat with the next bulb.

For planting bulbs in unworked soil, around tree roots, and in groundcovers, you need a stronger tool. Choose a naturalizing tool (a straight steel blade with a forked end, topped by a foot bar and long handle), a crowbar, or a narrow spade with a sharp cutting edge and a foot bar. Push the blade halfway into the soil and pull back, then push down hard so the blade goes completely into the soil. Push forward so the blade lifts up the soil to make a planting slot. Put in a bulb, remove the tool, step down to firm the soil, and repeat with the next bulb.

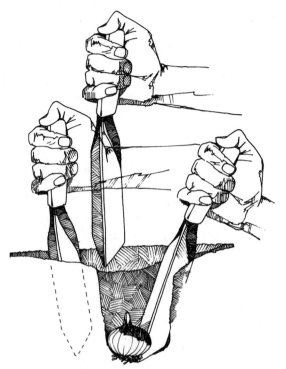

**Planting bulbs in a lawn.** Crocuses and grape hyacinths (*Muscari* spp.) brighten spring lawns and are easy to plant. Here's a fast, effective method: Stab a bulb trowel into the soil like a dagger, and pull toward you to make a hole for the bulb. Drop in a bulb, and step on the spot to close the slot.

 **Which Side Is Up?**

Bulbs get off to the fastest start if you plant them right-side up. The general rule: Plant with the pointed tip up. But not all bulbs have points, and that's where confusion sets in. If you're ever in doubt, you can always plant the bulb on its side. Although you might not be able to tell which side is up, the bulb will know which way to send roots and which way to send shoots. A bulb planted sideways will have a better chance of growing than a bulb planted upside down.

There's a special trick to planting small bulbs. Using a narrow trowel, one person can easily plant several hundred small bulbs in an hour. (See the illustration on this page for a discussion of this technique.)

# PERENNIALS

Because perennials live a long time, it's important to get them off to a good start. Proper soil preparation and care at planting time will be well rewarded at bloom time. Prepare your planting beds before you order or buy plants. It is best to work a season ahead and dig in early fall for a spring planting. Be sure to mulch pre-dug beds, then turn the soil in spring when you're ready to plant.

## SOIL PREPARATION

The majority of perennials commonly grown in beds or borders require evenly moist, humus-rich soil of pH 5.5 to 6.5. A complete soil analysis from your local extension office or a soil-testing lab will give you a starting point. For more on soils and soil testing, see Chapter 2.

Double digging is the best way to prepare a perennial bed. Despite the difficulty of the task, the rewards are unparalleled. Plants' roots will be able to penetrate the friable soil easily, creating a strong, vigorous root system. Water and nutrients will also move easily through the soil, and the bed won't dry out as fast. As a result, your plants will thrive. Have the necessary soil amendments and organic fertilizer on hand before you start. For more on this technique, see "Double Digging" on page 40.

If you can't double dig before you plant, turn the soil evenly to a shovel's depth at planting time. Thoroughly incorporate appropriate soil amendments and fertilizer as required. Break up all clods and smooth out the bed before planting.

## PLANTING

Plant perennials any time the soil is workable. Spring and fall are best for most plants. If plants arrive before you are ready to plant them, be sure to care for them properly until you can get them in the ground.

Planting is easy in freshly turned soil. Choose an overcast day whenever possible. Avoid planting during the heat of the day. Place container-grown plants out on the soil according to your design (see "Designing a Garden" on page 276). To remove the plants, invert containers and knock the bottom of the pot with your trowel. The plant should fall out easily. The

roots will be tightly intertwined. It's vital to loosen the roots—by pulling them apart or even cutting four slashes, one down each side of the root mass—so they'll spread strongly through the soil when planted out. Clip any roots that are bent, broken, or circling. Make sure you place the crown of the plant at the same depth at which it grew in the pot.

Planting bareroot perennials and transplants requires more care. Inspect the roots carefully and prune off any irregularities, then soak the roots in a bucket of lukewarm water for one or two hours to hydrate them before planting. Dig a hole large enough to accommodate the full spread of the roots. Build a mound with tapering sides in the center of the hole. Spread the roots of fibrous-rooted plants evenly over the mound, and rest the crown of the plant at its apex. Check to be sure that the crown will end up just below the soil surface. Build up the mound to raise the crown if necessary. Do not plant too deeply!

Position rhizomes such as those of iris at or just below the surface, depending on the species. Spread the roots evenly over a mound of soil as described above. Spread tuberous

*(continued on page 84)*

 **Pansies Double Bulb Show**

Gardeners in Zones 6 and warmer can plant pansies between tulips, daffodils, and other tall, spring-flowering bulbs. To do this, plant the bulbs first, using toothpicks to mark where the bulbs are planted. Then plant the pansies in the spaces between the bulbs. As the bulbs grow in late winter, they push through the pansies, and you'll have double the show when the weather is mild enough for both to bloom.

##  Smart Shopping for Perennials

Smart shopping, whether in the garden center or through the mail, begins at home. Make a list of the plants you intend to buy, then stick to it. Otherwise, you may come home with a carload of mixed plants that looked great in the garden center but not in your garden design. Or, you will be tempted to order everything the catalog has to offer. Here's a look at how to shop smart in the garden center and through the mail, and what to do with your perennials between purchasing and planting.

### At the Nursery or Garden Center

The advantages of buying perennials from a local nursery or garden center are that you can get your plants the minute you need them and that you can choose the healthiest, most attractive plants. Many garden centers also have display gardens where you can see the mature sizes and forms of the plants. The plants will be larger than those available by mail, so you'll get more "instant gratification" when you put them in the ground (the mail-order plants usually catch up by the end of the season). Here are some tips for getting the most from buying plants at a garden center:

- The best selection is available in spring.
- If you want a specific color, buy a named cultivar.
- Avoid plants that are visibly rootbound. Check the root systems of plants that are leggy or disproportionately large in relation to the size of the pot.
- Choose plants with lush, nicely colored foliage and multiple stems. Avoid plants with dry, pale, or shriveled leaves.
- Check for insects on the tops and undersides of leaves and along stems.

- When buying in the fall, keep in mind that plants will look rough. They have probably been sitting on the bench all summer. Check the root system first. If it is in good shape, the plant is likely to be healthy.
- If you can't plant immediately, keep containers well watered. Check them daily!

### Plants by Mail

There are two big advantages to mail-order shopping: convenience and selection. With mail-ordering, you can have perennials delivered right to your door. And mail-order nurseries offer a much larger selection than most garden centers are able to because the mail-order companies usually have large growing fields.

If you're looking for an unusual species or a particular cultivar, you'll often have the best luck by turning to a catalog. It's fun to compare catalogs, too. Many provide valuable growing tips, information on good plant combinations, entertaining plant anecdotes, and design suggestions, as well as clear descriptions and color photos of the perennials.

The drawback of mail-ordering is that you can't see the plants you're buying until they arrive. The best way to avoid disappointment is to start with a small order from each nursery you want to try. Some nurseries ship plants in containers; others ship bareroot; and others use both techniques. Specify shipping times when ordering by mail to make sure your plants arrive when you can actually plant them. A nursery in another part of the country may not know when planting conditions will be right in your area.

Mail-order shopping is a convenient way to

order a large selection of perennials. But it pays to be cautious—some mail-order nurseries are better than others. Here's how to get the most from mail-order shopping:

■ Order early for the best selection.

■ Specify a desired shipping time so plants will arrive when you want them.

■ When plants arrive, get out your plant journal and write down when you received them, from where, and in what condition they arrived. This information will come in handy when you order next time.

■ Evaluate containerized mail-order plants just as if you were looking them over at the garden center. Don't expect perfect foliage, though—shipping often leads to broken or bruised leaves. If the plants are healthy, they'll recover quickly. Diseased foliage and insects are more serious matters; return plants that show signs of infection or infestation.

■ Examine bareroot plants for pests and diseases, too. Check the roots, crowns, and stems for pests or signs of pest damage.

■ If the roots of your bareroot plants are sparse or in poor condition, return the plants.

■ Rewrap bareroot plants after you've inspected them, and store in a cool place until you are ready to plant them.

■ Before planting, soak the roots of bare-root plants in water for at least one hour.

■ If you receive substandard or damaged plants and want a refund or a replacement plant, contact the nursery immediately.

■ Avoid hype and exaggerated claims. If it sounds too good to be true, it usually is. However, reputable nurseries sometimes offer collections of perennials that are excellent buys (but not *unbelievable* buys).

## When Your Plants Arrive

Let's back up a minute here to stress a vital point: Dig your beds *before* your plants arrive. Don't order plants or buy them locally unless you've prepared a place to put them. You'll be rushed enough at planting time without having to start from scratch, and your plants deserve a better start than you could give them with last-minute bed making.

Even if you've already prepared your garden bed, you still may not be able to put your plants in the ground as soon as they arrive, especially if they're mail-order. More likely, you'll come home after a long day's work, with hours of chores still before you, and find them on the doorstep. You may have to wait until the next day—or even the weekend—before you can plant. It's important to keep your new arrivals healthy. Here's what to do with your plants in the interim:

■ Take mail-order plants out of the box as soon as you get them.

■ Water container-grown plants whenever the soil dries. The smaller the pot, the more often you'll have to water.

■ Set container-grown plants outside in a protected, shaded area until you can plant them in the ground.

■ If bareroot plants are wrapped in a protective material like peat or shredded wood, keep the material damp. If the plants aren't wrapped in protective material, soak the roots in luke-warm water, then cover them with moist soil or compost.

■ Keep bareroot perennials in a protected place until you can plant them.

■ Plant your perennials as soon as you can.

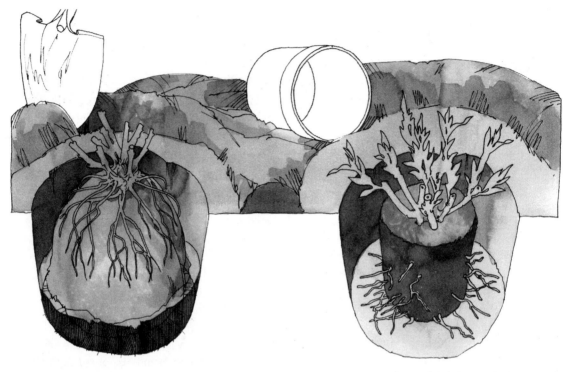

**How to plant perennials.** To plant a bareroot perennial (*left*), mound soil in the bottom of the planting hole and set the plant on top of the mound, spreading its roots down the sides. Fill in around the plant with soil. Plant these perennials at the same depth they grew in the nursery—don't cover the crowns. Container-grown perennials (*right*) are a snap to plant. Plant them at the same depth they sit in the pot. If the surrounding soil is loose, plant them a little high. The plant will sink when the soil settles. If the plant is rootbound, loosen the root ball before planting.

roots like those of daylilies evenly in a similar fashion. Fill in the planting hole with soil, then firm it down and add more soil if necessary before you water the new plant.

Water plants thoroughly after planting so the soil is completely settled around the roots. Give your newly planted perennials a layer of organic mulch to conserve soil moisture. Provide extra water for the first month or so while plants are becoming established.

Here's one last helpful hint that's important but easy to forget: Keep the plant labels that come with your perennials, and stick them firmly in the ground next to each plant as you plant it.

## TREES AND SHRUBS

There's no doubt about it—trees and shrubs can enhance the value of your home, both by increasing your property's monetary worth and by adding beauty and variety to your surroundings. While the cost of a well-planted property can be measured in materials, equipment, labor, and maintenance, the daily impact for most of us comes from the effects of vegetation on our physical and emotional comfort. We plant trees and shrubs because they provide welcome shade, windbreaks, privacy, and—most important—beauty. Their spring flowers, lush summer *(continued on page 87)*

## ❀ Aftercare: A Timetable

How well your plants will thrive depends on the care you give them after planting. Use this care calendar to make sure you're giving your new plants what they need.

### Right Away

**Water:** Water perennials as soon as you've planted them.

**Cut back foliage:** If the nursery hasn't already done this, cut off one- to two-thirds of the foliage on bareroot plants; otherwise plants will wilt. If they wilt even after you've cut them back, cut back to a few inches to give plants a chance to recover.

**Mulch:** Mulch your plants after watering them to maintain soil moisture and guard against wilting. Mulch will keep weeds from competing with your new plants, too.

**Provide shade:** Shade your newly planted perennials from direct sunlight until they've had a chance to recover from the shock of transplanting. Cover them with a spunbonded row cover like Reemay or with shade cloth, screening, or a lath cover.

### The First Week

**Water:** Your plants' primary need will continue to be water. Check at least once a day—before *and* after work is even better.

**Check for bugs:** Check your perennials daily for signs of pests and pest damage. New plants are smaller, so they're particularly vulnerable to pest damage. If you find insects or damage, check in Chapter 7 for the culprit and what to do about it. Animals and birds can decimate a planting, too—if you see signs of their damage, protect your plants with screens.

**Remove shade:** Gradually remove your shade cover after the first few days—ideally, leave it on only during the heat of the day and remove it for the morning and late afternoon. If you can't get home to move the cover, take it off after the third day; make doubly sure that plants are well watered and mulched.

### The First Season

**Water:** Make sure your perennials get 1 inch of water a week, from either rain or the hose.

**Weed:** Weeding is most important the first two years after planting; after that, plants will be large enough to shade out most weed seedlings. Mulch will help control weeds, but check for them every time you're in the garden.

**Feed:** If you've prepared the soil well, your perennials won't need more than an application of compost in the middle of the season, or compost (or manure or seaweed) tea once a month, to grow vigorously.

**Monitor for insects and diseases:** Continue to keep an eye out for pests and diseases, and apply appropriate controls.

**Disbud:** If you buy bareroot perennials in May or June that are late-blooming (like asters and mums), remove all their flower buds. They need to establish themselves the first growing season, not put their energy into flowering.

**Deadhead:** Cut off spent flowers to keep your perennials from wasting energy by setting seed.

**Move things around:** If plants don't look right where you've placed them, don't be afraid to move them around. (Don't move perennials in bloom.) If you find you've left a gap in your bed that won't be filled in by the following season, add more plants to cover the bare spot.

**Enjoy:** Take time to appreciate the beautiful garden you've made.

##  Tips for Healthy Trees and Shrubs

The key to success with trees and shrubs is to know your site. You can't choose plants that will thrive in your yard or garden until you learn about the site and how to prepare it. Here's what you, or the designer or landscape architect who is choosing the trees and shrubs for your property, need to know:

**Soil:** Begin learning about your site with a soil test. The results will tell you your soil's pH and fertility, two of the most important pieces of information that you must have when making a plant selection.

Also look at your soil's consistency and drainage characteristics. Is the soil loose or compacted? Is it clayey, sandy, or loamy? Is it rocky and shallow, or chalky and poorly drained? Is it elevated, depressed, or sloping? Does water stand at any time of the year? Different plants have different tolerances for these conditions, and you're best off planting a tree or shrub that will be happy in the soil you have to offer.

**Soil preparation:** Till the planting area before you dig. This will reduce compaction and encourage aeration and drainage. Since roots tend to stay in the top 1 foot of soil, tilling can make a real difference.

Adding soil amendments to backfill isn't necessary for typical plantings, but it may be appropriate for certain plants in particular sites. For example, if you're planting trees in raised beds or berms (mounds), adding water-holding organic soil amendments can be very beneficial, since beds and berms tend to dry out faster than ground-level plantings.

**Exposure:** Is the planting site sunny or shady? Buildings and nearby vegetation can limit the hours of full sun that fall on a potential planting site. Be sure to check how many hours, and at what time of day, your plant will have direct sunlight.

**Water:** Note the amount of rainfall that you can expect your new tree or shrub to receive, and consider how you will water it during a dry spell. If your resources are limited, select plants that can tolerate occasional drought.

**Other factors:** Other physical factors to watch include overhead and underground utilities (such as electric wires and water pipes); nearby buildings; actual use of the site (is it a quiet, out-of-the-way spot, or right near a path?); and the size of the area, which determines the appropriate size of the plant. Recognizing these physical limitations will enable you to make better choices. If there are overhead utilities, for example, choose plants that are naturally dwarfed or slow-growing, with an ultimate height considerably lower than that of the overhead lines and equipment. Or, if your site is near a path or sidewalk, a tree with low-hanging or pendant branches might pose a problem. Pavement and buildings may cause plants stress by reflecting heat, creating unnatural wind patterns, and limiting root space and water penetration. Finally, does the site have a vast, open, parklike scale or that of an intimate patio or enclosed backyard?

**Site maintenance:** It's important to maintain the planting site *after* planting, as well. If grass grows in the area covered by the mature spread of the tree's crown (the drip line), it can compete with the tree's roots for nutrients and water. To prevent regrowth of grass after you've tilled and planted, spread mulch around the tree as far out as the drip line. Don't allow the mulch to touch the base of the tree because this can encourage disease problems.

foliage, autumn color, interesting bark, and variety of forms add color, texture, and appeal to the landscape.

## GETTING A GOOD START

When you are buying new trees and shrubs, you can avoid a lot of future problems by choosing locally adapted or resistant species. Trees and shrubs that are native to an area are often less prone to problems because they are growing in the environment to which they are best adapted. Read about the trees and shrubs you intend to buy, and avoid very pest-prone species. Look for this information in catalogs, or ask your local nursery owner or extension agent for more information on the trees and shrubs best adapted to your area.

Once you get your tree or shrub home, some basic care will help it get established quickly. Good soil preparation will provide the ideal conditions for strong root development. Providing ample water for the first few years after planting also encourages vigorous growth. A 2- to 3-inch-thick layer of organic mulch such as wood chips helps keep the soil moist and weeds down; just be sure to keep the mulch a few inches away from the trunk or main stem to discourage animal and insect pests from attacking the base of the plant. Do any necessary pruning or staking carefully, and avoid making wounds in the trunk or stems with lawn mowers or string trimmers.

## PLANTING

The trees and shrubs you buy will be bareroot, balled-and-burlapped (B&B), or in containers. Many deciduous trees and shrubs, such as apples, maples, lilacs, and roses, are sold as dormant, bareroot plants. Evergreens are usually sold B&B because even when they're dormant, they have leaves that draw water from the roots. Container-grown plants have roots established in the container (sometimes a little too well established!); these plants are easy to add to your garden, even in full growth. "Settling

 **Group Plants Where Possible**

Consider another strategy for success: safety in numbers. From harsh urban streetsides to country churchyards, plants benefit greatly when arranged together in beds. Trees or shrubs sharing a bed will usually have more rooting space than if each were off in its own planting hole—especially considering the size and quality of the holes a weary gardener might dig at the end of a long day.

A group of plants also tends to create its own microclimate. Humidity in the immediate area is higher, wind is reduced, roots are shaded and cooled, perhaps a duff layer of decomposing fallen leaves is formed and begins to decompose with the mulch. Better yet, plants that are grouped in a bed and that are adequately mulched fare better at avoiding nicks, cuts, and other hardships caused by errant lawn mowers and their operators. Since lawn mower damage is the leading cause of mechanical injury to trees, this aspect alone is reason enough to plant trees and shrubs in groups.

Grouping plants gives you more and better results from your labor. Most home gardeners will agree that preparing one good-sized bed for a group of plants is much less arduous than digging individual holes for the same number of plants, especially in a difficult soil. Maintaining, weeding, fertilizing, mulching, and especially watering a group of plants are more efficient than performing those tasks on several individual plants scattered hither and yon.

Them In" on page 90 explains how to set each of these types of plants in a planting hole. The heeling-in technique illustrated on this page is a good way to hold bareroot or B&B stock until you're able to plant.

Plant a bareroot tree while it is dormant, either in fall or early spring. A few trees have roots so sensitive to disturbance that you should not buy or transplant them bareroot. Your chances of success are best when these trees are container-grown: Kentucky coffee tree (*Gymnocladus dioica*), crape myrtle (*Lagerstroemia indica*), sweet gum (*Liquidambar styraciflua*), black tupelo (*Nyssa sylvatica*), white oak (*Quercus alba*), and sassafras (*Sassafras albidum*).

**Heeling in.** If you can't plant bareroot plants right away, keep the roots moist by heeling them in. Dig a trench with one vertical and one slanted side in a spot sheltered from direct sun and wind. Lay bareroot plants against the slanted side, and cover the roots with soil. Uncover and move to a permanent position while the plant is still dormant.

You can plant most B&B or container-grown trees any time of year except when the ground is frozen. There are a few exceptions, however. A few trees, especially those with thick and fleshy roots, seem to suffer less transplanting shock if planted in the spring in areas where the soil freezes deeply during the winter. Though tree roots will continue to grow until the soil temperature drops below 40°F, these trees are slow to get established and are best reserved for planting in the spring: dogwoods (*Cornus* spp.), golden-rain tree (*Koelreuteria paniculata*), tulip tree (*Liriodendron tulipifera*), magnolias (*Magnolia* spp.), black tupelo (*Nyssa sylvatica*), ornamental cherries and plums (*Prunus* spp.), most oaks (*Quercus* spp.), and Japanese zelkova (*Zelkova serrata*).

A close examination of the roots of your new tree will prevent problems that can limit growth. Trim any mushy, dead, or damaged roots. Comb out potbound roots and straighten or slice through roots that circle the root ball before you set the plant in its hole. Look carefully for girdling roots, which can strangle the tree by wrapping tightly around the base of its trunk. This stops the upward movement of water and nutrients absorbed by the roots and needed by the leaves and branches.

## PREPARE A PROPER PLANTING SITE

Do you know how to dig a proper planting hole? A few minutes of extra preparation can make all the difference. Although some trees' roots may go deep, the small but all-important feeder roots forage mostly through the top 6 to 8 inches of soil. Shape the hole to accommodate the feeder roots. The illustration on page 92 shows how to shape a planting hole for best root development.

**Don't Coddle the Roots** Traditional planting advice once called for digging the biggest hole you could dig and filling it with a rich mixture of topsoil and compost. Now gardeners have learned that the best way to plant is to dig a hole just deep enough for the roots, widening toward the top, and filled with the same soil you took out. While the "big and rich" idea did indeed get the tree off to a good start, the tree roots had no inclination to leave the hole. A hole filled with peat moss and rotted manure encourages roots to grow only in the hole instead of branching out. These pockets of over-

ly amended soil stay too wet during rainy periods and too dry during drought. This means tree roots can suffocate from too much moisture or can be more prone to wilting during drought. Also, since the roots don't spread and anchor the plant strongly, it will be more susceptible to windthrow—being toppled during high winds.

But there may be times when soil amendments are necessary. If the soil in the root ball is

---

 ## Smart Shopping for Trees and Shrubs

Once you've determined which trees and shrubs will thrive in your chosen site, follow these guidelines when shopping to get the healthiest plants:

■ Buy small to medium-sized trees. Big trees are difficult to move and plant. They take longer to get established than smaller trees, because more of their roots were lost when they were dug.

■ Buy only trees and shrubs that are clearly tagged or labeled with the botanical and common names to make sure you get the flowers, fruit, and crown shape you want.

■ When buying trees, look for a relatively straight trunk with a slight natural flare at its base—if no flare exists, the tree has had too much soil placed atop its roots.

■ Buy trees with widely spaced, even branches, not trees with branches that are tightly spaced and mostly at the top of the trunk.

■ Know how to spot a good buy when you go shopping. Look for plump, firm buds and leaves that are the correct size and color. Watch out for broken branches or scratched bark, dry or brown leaf margins, or dry root balls. B&B (balled-and-burlapped) or container-

grown plants may be putting out new leaves; check for healthy growth. Examine leaves and bark for pests and diseases.

■ Buy bareroot trees and shrubs only when they're dormant, and only if the roots have been kept moist. Roots that are evenly spaced around the base of the stem make a secure anchor. On B&B plants, look for a well-wrapped, secure root ball. Container-grown trees may be rootbound, with crowded roots wrapped around the root ball.

■ Avoid trees that pull easily from the container, leaving the potting soil behind. Also avoid those whose roots have left the container and anchored themselves firmly in the soil beneath.

■ Inspect container-grown shrubs, and don't buy rootbound plants. Many large roots on the outside of the root ball or protruding from drainage holes mean the plant may be stunted by growing in a too-small container.

■ Be sure to ask about the nursery or garden center's guarantee. Some offer guarantees only on trees and shrubs that are planted by nursery staff; others will guarantee homeowner-planted stock as well.

## Settling Them In

Your new trees and shrubs may be bareroot, balled-and-burlapped (B&B), or planted in a container. For best results, follow these guidelines when planting:

**Bareroot plants:** As long as you plant bareroot trees or shrubs while the stock is still dormant, your chances of success are good with these generally low-cost plants. Leave a small cone of undisturbed soil in the center of the hole. Remove any circling, broken, or diseased roots from the plants, spread out the roots over the cone of soil, and fill. Water well and mulch.

**Balled-and-burlapped plants:** It's best to get balled-and-burlapped plants in the ground while they're dormant so the roots can get a good start before they have to supply food and water to burgeoning topgrowth. But the B&B method gives you more leeway; even actively growing trees and shrubs can be held until the weekend for planting.

The illustration on page 92 shows how to set a B&B plant in the planting hole. Remove binding ropes or twine and all nails. Leave natural burlap in place: It will eventually rot. Slit synthetic wrapping material in several places so roots can penetrate it. Try to keep the root ball intact. If the root ball is in a wire basket, cut off the loops on top to keep them from sticking up through the soil, and snip and remove the top few wires. If the tree is large, have a helper hold it in place as you fill the hole. After every few shovelfuls of dirt, add water to help settle air pockets.

**Container-grown plants:** Remove any labeling tags to keep the tags or wires from cutting into the stems. Support the plant while you turn it upside down and remove the pot. Even fiber pots of compressed peat or paper are best removed; exposed edges wick away moisture, and the walls slow down root growth.

Carefully snip off dead or sickly roots and use your fingers to comb out any potbound roots. Cut through circling roots. Set the plant as deep as it grew before, fill, water, and mulch.

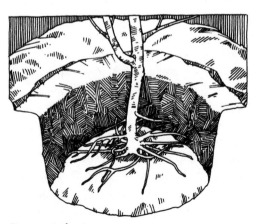

**Bareroot plant**

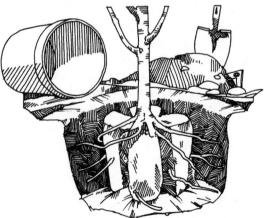

**Container-grown plant**

significantly different from your local soil, your tree may grow better if you amend the soil before planting. Roger Funk, Ph.D., the vice president of human and technical resources at the Davey Tree Expert Company, planted B&B trees that had been grown in sandy clay loam in a landscape where the soil was a heavy blue clay. He didn't amend the soil, and he found that water pooled up in the holes. "Since most nurseries are growing trees in sandy or loamy soil, and lots of gardeners have clay soils—especially in new developments, where they may have sub-soil—this can be a common problem," says Dr. Funk. "It's best to evaluate the specific conditions and decide what to do on a case-by-case basis." See "Tips for Healthy Trees and Shrubs" on page 86.

Encourage roots to reach out beyond the planting hole by loosening ground surrounding the hole. Plunge a garden fork in as deep as the tines allow, and wiggle it slightly to break up compacted soil. Repeat every 1 to 1½ feet to a distance of 5 feet or more on all sides.

**Set It Straight** After settling the plant in the

---

 **Tips on Tree Wraps**

The use of tree wraps is a subject of debate among horticulturists. One thing they do agree on is that when wraps are used on newly planted trees, they should be removed after the first year or two. Wraps are helpful if:

- The trees came from a nursery where they were grown close together (shading one another).
- The trees are thin-barked species such as crab apple (*Malus* spp.), cherry (*Prunus* spp.), peach (*Prunus persica*), pin oak (*Quercus palustris*), birch (*Betula* spp.), and linden (*Tilia* spp.).
- The trees are planted near the street where the heat radiates up off the pavement.
- The trees are exposed to fierce north winds or very hot sun.

Even these trees will suffer if the wrap is left in place too long. Disease, borers, and soggy, peeling bark have been found underneath tree wraps that have been in place two years or longer.

If you decide to use a wrap, you have several materials to choose from:

**Plastic:** The easiest wraps to work with are the plastic spirals. They're easy to put on, and they fit loosely enough to reduce the likelihood of creating a home for borers. For best results, remove the spiral at the end of the growing season, inspect the trunk for insects, then put the spiral back in place. As trees grow and expand, the spiral or any wrap can restrict new growth. If you remove the spiral or wrap each season, and then put it back in place, you can avoid girdled trees.

**Burlap:** For economy, cut long, 3-inch-wide strips of burlap to make your own wrap. Wind the strips around the trunk, spiraling up from the bottom. Keep wrapping until you reach the point where the tree begins to branch. Secure the wrap in place at the bottom and top with electrical tape or panty hose. Don't use wire or any material that binds. It could girdle the trunk. Even tape can restrict tree growth if left on too long. Adjust the tape and wrap each fall.

**Paper:** Watch paper tree wraps, because some have a black interior. This type must be removed as soon as it begins degrading or else the black will absorb sunlight. This will actually make the trunk hotter instead of protecting it from sunscald.

hole, observe it from all angles to be sure it is positioned straight up and down. There's nothing more frustrating than filling your planting hole and then discovering that the plant is set crookedly. Once you're sure the plant is positioned properly, add soil gradually. For bareroot plants, give the tree or shrub an occasional shake as you refill the hole to sift soil among the roots. Level the soil around the base of the plant. Don't stomp all the air out of your newly filled hole: Instead of using your feet, tamp the soil with your hands or the back of a hoe to settle it and eliminate air pockets.

**Water Thoroughly**  Water the soil thoroughly after planting. Apply a 2- to 3-inch layer of mulch to retain moisture, pulling it back a bit from the trunk. Water new plants once a week during their first year, especially if rainfall is less than 1 inch per week. By the time you notice wilting or other signs of stress, it may be too late.

## STAKING

Staking is done to straighten or strengthen the trunk, or to prevent root movement and breakage before the tree anchors itself in the soil. Trees usually don't need staking if they aren't located in windy sites and are under 8 feet with small crowns.

Avoid rigid staking. Allow the trunk to flex or move slightly when the wind hits it. This movement encourages the tree to produce special wood that will naturally bend when the wind hits it. A tree that is rigidly staked will often bend over or break after it is unstaked. Given a choice, avoid buying staked, container-grown trees—you will generally be buying a weak stem.

Unstake all trees one year after planting. Any tree that had an adequate root system and was properly planted will by then be able to stand on its own. If you want to leave the stakes in

**Correct Planting Techniques**

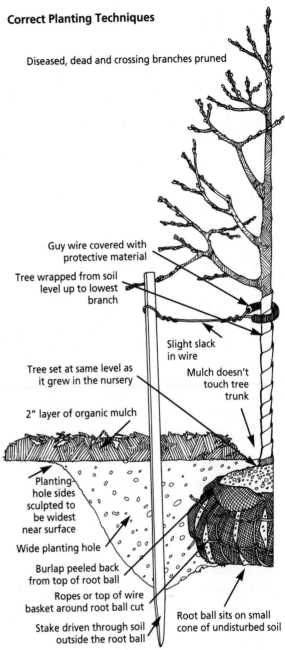

Diseased, dead and crossing branches pruned

Guy wire covered with protective material

Tree wrapped from soil level up to lowest branch

Slight slack in wire

Tree set at same level as it grew in the nursery

Mulch doesn't touch tree trunk

2" layer of organic mulch

Planting hole sides sculpted to be widest near surface

Wide planting hole

Burlap peeled back from top of root ball

Ropes or top of wire basket around root ball cut

Stake driven through soil outside the root ball

Root ball sits on small cone of undisturbed soil

**Planting dos.** In addition to the techniques shown here, rough the surface of the planting hole; this enables the roots to find a crack and take off. When drainage is less than perfect, plant shrubs or trees 2 inches higher than they grew in the nursery.

**Incorrect Planting Techniques**

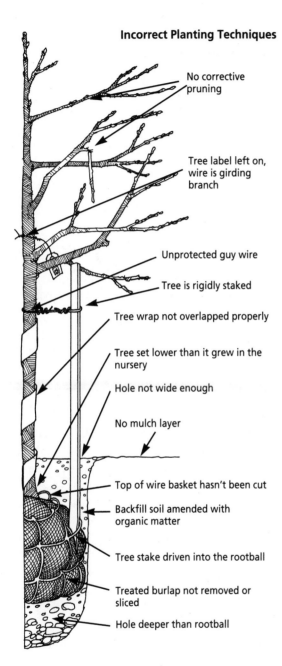

No corrective pruning

Tree label left on, wire is girding branch

Unprotected guy wire

Tree is rigidly staked

Tree wrap not overlapped properly

Tree set lower than it grew in the nursery

Hole not wide enough

No mulch layer

Top of wire basket hasn't been cut

Backfill soil amended with organic matter

Tree stake driven into the rootball

Treated burlap not removed or sliced

Hole deeper than rootball

**Planting don'ts.** Note the poor techniques shown, and remember to drop the wrap holding the roots to the bottom of the hole. Leave it there—sliding it out can crack the root ball and kill the plant. Cut wire baskets down the sides and push them down into the hole.

place to keep lawn mowers and other equipment from hitting the trunk and damaging the tree, remove the guy wires or ropes but leave the stakes for a barrier.

## FINISHING TOUCHES

You don't need to prune newly planted trees and shrubs, except to remove branches that are broken, diseased, narrow-angled, or overlapping. If you cut back all the branches, you may actually slow your tree's or shrub's establishment, because buds produce chemicals that aid root growth. The exception is young fruit trees, which you must prune promptly if you plan to train them for easier harvesting and care. See Chapter 10 for more information on pruning and training fruit trees.

A tree wrap protects the trunk from sunscald, nibbling rodents, and lawn mower nicks. See "Tips on Tree Wraps" on page 91 for a discussion of the pros and cons of wrapping.

### ✿ An Easy Depth Gauge

It's important to plant trees and shrubs at the same depth at which they were previously planted. Before you set the plant into the hole, you can see the dark mark on the plant stem that indicates how deep the plant was grown at the nursery. But once you start digging, checking depth by hauling the tree or shrub in and out of the hole is a lot of wear and tear on you and the plant. Here's an easier way: Measure from the stem mark to the bottom of the roots or root ball to find out how deep the hole should be. As you dig, check depth now and then by laying a board across the hole and measuring from the board's center to the bottom of the hole.

# Chapter 6

# PROPAGATION

Learning to propagate plants—to make new plants from existing ones in your home and garden—is one of the most exciting and rewarding aspects of gardening. Many of the methods are easy, and you don't need fancy or expensive tools. Propagation is cheaper than buying large numbers of plants, so with a little time and effort you can fill your garden quickly at minimal cost. Propagating new plants will keep your house and garden full of vigorous specimens, and you'll probably have plenty to give away, too!

You can reproduce most plants by several methods. There are two major types of propagation: sexual and asexual. Sexual propagation involves seeds, which are produced by the fusion of male and female reproductive cells. Growing from seed is an inexpensive way to produce large numbers of plants. Annuals, biennials, and vegetables are almost always reproduced by seed. You can also grow perennials, shrubs, and trees from seed. For complete information on growing plants from seed, see Chapter 4.

Asexual propagation methods use the vegetative parts of a plant: roots, stems, buds, and leaves. Division, cuttings, and layering are all asexual methods.

With division, you split entire plants into sections; for cuttings, you remove stem tips and root them; and in layering, you root a stem while it is stiill attached to the parent plant.

Select a technique by considering the plant you are working with, the materials you have, the season, and the amount of time you are willing to wait for a new plant.

## DIVISION

Division is a quick and reliable way to propagate many types of multi-stemmed plants with almost guaranteed success. Dividing—separating a plant into several smaller new plants—works well for increasing groundcovers, clump-forming perennials, bulbs, and tubers. You can also divide ornamental grasses and suckering shrubs, as well as houseplants and herbs.

The best time to divide garden plants is when they are dormant. In general, divide spring- and summer-blooming plants in the fall, and fall-blooming plants in the spring. If possible, divide houseplants in the spring as new growth starts. Divide plants with tubers and tuberous roots, such as dahlias and tuberous begonias, before planting in the spring.

The key to division is starting with a vigorous parent plant. If the soil is dry, water the plant thoroughly the day before. Whenever possible, wait for cool, cloudy weather (or at least evening), to reduce moisture loss from the plant during the process.

To divide a hardy plant, lift it from the soil with a fork or spade. Separate small clumps by pulling off the vigorous young plantlets; discard the woody center growth. Use a sharp knife to cut apart small plants. When dividing plants, make sure that each piece you remove has its own root system. Otherwise, new divisions won't grow. Replant divisions as quickly as possible, to the same depth as the original plant, and water them thoroughly. Mulch fall divisions well to protect the developing roots from frost heaving.

## DIVIDING HARDY BULBS

The easiest way to propagate hardy bulbs—especially the ones that are good for naturalizing, such as daffodils—is to dig them when the foliage yellows, separate the offsets on each bulb, and replant. You can plant them at the same depth and location as the mature bulbs, but they might reach flowering size sooner if you grow them in a nursery bed for two to three seasons first.

Propagate crocuses and other bulbs that arise from corms in much the same way: Dig them and separate the small new corms, called cormels, that form alongside the parent corm.

There are two ways to propagate lilies: Pick the small bulbils that form along the stem above the leaves or the bulblets that form at the base of the stem. Then plant them in a nursery bed, where they'll need to grow for several years to attain blooming size. You can also scale lily bulbs to propagate them. Remove the scales one at a time, and place them in a shallow flat or pot filled with moist vermiculite or peat moss. Bury the scales about halfway, and keep them moist. Small bulblets, which can be transplanted to a nursery bed, will form at the base of each scale.

## DIVIDING TENDER BULBS

You can increase your stock of favorite dahlia cultivars in the fall when you've dug the tuberous roots and allowed them to dry, or store the clumps whole and divide them in spring. Use a sharp, sterile knife. Make sure that each division has a piece of stem attached; new shoots sprout only from that part of the plant. Discard any thin or immature roots. Divide tubers such as

tuberous begonias and caladiums in spring. Cut them into pieces, making sure each piece has an eye or bud. Let the pieces dry for two days and

---

 **Best Bets for Division**

Dividing established perennials is a fast and sure way to fill your yard with flowers. Plants with more than one tall stem, especially clump-forming ones like garden phlox or asters, are good candidates for dividing, says Dave Bowman, who grows over 1,000 perennials as a co-owner of Crownsville Nursery in Maryland. Or keep your eye open for ones that root as they wander along the ground, such as snow-in-summer (*Cerastium tomentosum*) and creeping phlox (*Phlox stolonifera*).

The plants listed below are easy to divide by digging up a clump and separating the roots into smaller sections. Some will pull apart by hand with a bit of gentle teasing; for others, you may need a sharp knife or trowel. Replant as soon as possible, and water well. Protect from direct sun for a few days until the roots recover.

Avens (*Geum* spp.)
Bee balm (*Monarda didyma*)
Candytufts (*Iberis* spp.)
Daylilies (*Hemerocallis* spp.)
Evening primroses (*Oenothera* spp.)
Hardy ageratum (*Eupatorium coelestinum*)
Hostas (*Hosta* spp.)
Irises (*Iris* spp.)
Obedient plants (*Physostegia* spp.)
Peonies (*Paeonia* spp.)
Perennial sunflowers (*Helianthus* spp.)
Soapworts (*Saponaria* spp.)
Tansies (*Tanacetum* spp.)
Yarrows (*Achillea* spp.)

# Division Step-by-Step

**1.** To start dividing a clump, cut around the mother plant with a trowel or spade (depending on the size of the plant), or loosen the soil with a garden fork. Then lift the plant from the ground, shaking enough soil from the roots so you can see what you're doing when you divide the plant. If there's still too much soil clinging to the roots, you can hose it off.

**2.** Use a sharp spade to divide perennials or tough clumps of ornamental grasses. Don't chop at the roots, though; try to make single, clean cuts. Another technique for separating hard-to-divide clumps is to

Step 1

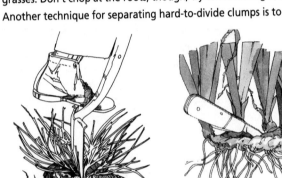

Step 2

plunge two garden forks back-to-back into the clump, then press the handles together until the clump separates into two parts. Divide each part into halves to quarter the perennial, or pull off sections for smaller divisions.

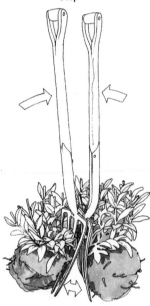

For smaller perennials or plants with thick, fleshy roots, use a sharp knife to cut the plant apart.

**3.** If the center of the plant has become woody and has stopped flowering, divide the clump in half. Cut out and discard the woody center, leaving an outer ring of good plant material. Cut the ring into smaller pieces.

Replant the divisions quickly, water them in, and cover them with damp newspaper or burlap for the first week. Pot up very small divisions until they're growing strongly, then transplant to the garden.

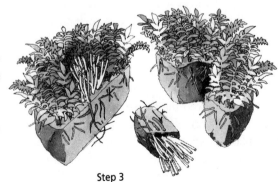

Step 3

then plant them. Gladiolus corms produce small cormels, which you can grow to flowering size in two to three years. Dig, cure, and store the cormels the same way you treat the mature corms. In spring, plant the cormels in a nursery bed at the same time you put the mature corms out in the garden.

# CUTTINGS

Plants have the amazing capacity to regenerate from small pieces of tissue, called cuttings. These small portions of stems, leaves, or roots will form new roots and shoots if given the right treatment.

Taking cuttings is the most common way to propagate many types of ornamental plants. Because raising plants from cuttings is an asexual type of reproduction, the new plants will look exactly like the parent.

There are several ways to make cuttings, but all types of cuttings need a medium to support them while they grow roots, plus some type of structure to protect them during the rooting period. It's also important to observe good sanitation to minimize disease problems.

The best media for taking cuttings are moisture-retentive but well drained and free of insects, diseases, and weed seeds. Commonly used media are sand, perlite, vermiculite, and peat moss. No one medium or combination is ideal for all plants, but an equal mixture of peat and sand or perlite is useful in most situations. Soil is not a good propagation medium, especially in containers. Unlike the other materials, soil is not sterile and can compact severely from frequent waterings. Only very hardy cuttings are planted directly into soil.

Some plants, such as African violets, coleus, and willows (*Salix* spp.), will root directly in water. This method is fun to try, but if you want to save the cutting, plant it in potting soil while

the roots are still small. Plants may have difficulty adapting to soil if their roots are in water too long.

 **Propagation Datebook**

With so many options for propagating plants, it can be hard to decide what to do when. Layering can be done anytime in spring, summer, or fall. In general, divide plants either in early spring, just as new growth begins, or in summer after bloom. Take cuttings after the flush of new spring growth is over. Propagate houseplants anytime. Here are some propagation suggestions to mark on your calendar:

■ In early spring, divide asters, yarrows, and other perennials. In early to midsummer, take softwood cuttings of ornamental shrubs.

■ In July, take root cuttings of oriental poppies (*Papaver orientale*), bleeding hearts (*Dicentra* spp.), bugloss (*Anchusa* spp.), and other plants with thick, fleshy roots.

■ In August, divide peonies (*Paeonia* spp.), digging carefully so you don't damage any more eyes than necessary. Replant with eyes not more than 2 inches below surface.

■ In August, start cuttings of wax begonias, coleus, and geraniums for winter bloom indoors.

■ In August, propagate groundcovers such as pachysandra and periwinkles (*Vinca* spp.) in cold frames.

■ In August, start cuttings of subshrubs like lavender, santolina, sage, and thyme.

■ In late summer, take cuttings of broadleaved evergreens, such as boxwoods (*Buxus* spp.), arborvitaes (*Thuja* spp.), and hollies (*Ilex* spp.).

Cuttings need a protected, high-humidity environment while they root. Cuttings don't have roots to take up water, but they still lose moisture through their leaves. By keeping the surrounding air moist, you minimize water loss and help cuttings survive until they can support themselves.

On a small scale, plastic bags are great for protecting cuttings. Support the bag so the plastic does not rest on the cuttings and encourage rot. Provide ventilation by occasionally opening the bag for an hour or two. In most cases, you won't have to add water until the cuttings form roots. To harden off rooted cuttings, gradually open the bag for longer periods.

For large numbers of cuttings, a cold frame or greenhouse is more practical. You can set pots of cuttings on the soil or plant directly in the soil inside a cold frame. Close the frame and cover the glass with shading material, such as cheesecloth or wooden laths (like snow fencing or lattice); gradually remove the shading when

---

 ### Division Dos and Don'ts

No matter which method of division you use, there are some basics that apply. Remember that division shocks your plants—treat them like the postoperative patients that they are, and follow these guidelines:

■ **Do** prepare the site for your new divisions before you divide your perennials.

■ **Do** take plants out of the ground before you divide them.

■ **Do** make sure your tools are sharp. Sharp knives, trowels, or other tools cause fewer open wounds. Since they damage the roots less, plants are less susceptible to disease.

■ **Do** discard or compost the dead, woody centers of old plants. Cut the remaining section of healthy plant into smaller pieces and replant.

■ **Do** remove one-half to two-thirds of the foliage on your divisions so it won't wick water away from the plant, but **don't** cut off more than that or you'll slow growth and invite rot.

■ **Do** replant divisions as soon as possible. Divisions are vulnerable—**don't** leave them lying in the sun.

■ **Do** plant divisions ½ inch higher than they were planted originally; they'll sink a little as the soil settles. The goal is for them to end up at the same level as the original plants were growing.

■ **Do** water your divisions well. Give them a good soaking as soon as you plant them, and continue to water them regularly until they're established.

■ **Do** shade newly planted divisions to protect them. Cover the plants with moist newspaper or burlap held down with rocks or soil for the first week after planting.

■ **Do** give divided perennials and ornamental grasses a foliar feed of liquid seaweed or fish emulsion to provide trace elements and speed establishment.

■ **Do** heavily mulch plants divided in fall when the soil cools, to prevent shallow freezing and frost heaving.

■ **Don't** divide perennials after early October, since the roots need time to establish themselves while the soil is warm.

■ **Don't** divide taprooted perennials—start them from stem cuttings or seed. These include plants such as butterfly weed (*Asclepias tuberosa*), gas plants (*Dictamnus* spp.), and rues (*Ruta* spp.).

---

roots form. Ventilate and harden off by gradually opening the cold frame for longer periods.

Use a clean, sharp tool to collect and prepare cuttings. Crushed plant tissue is an invitation to rot. Never propagate from diseased or insect-infested plants. Plant cuttings in fresh, sterile propagation mix that is stored in closed containers. Pots and propagation areas should be scrubbed clean and, if possible, sanitized by rinsing with a 10 percent bleach solution (1 part bleach to 9 parts water). Check plants often during rooting, and remove any fallen leaves or dead cuttings. Don't overwater; do provide adequate ventilation.

## SOFTWOOD STEM CUTTINGS

Take softwood cuttings from succulent spring growth of woody plants such as azaleas and

---

## Homemade Propagation Containers

Propagation containers need not be anything fancy. Milk cartons, clear plastic food containers—like the clamshell packs from salad bars—and plastic soda bottles all make mini-greenhouses that are perfect for starting seeds and rooting cuttings. You can reuse plastic containers a few times by disinfecting them after each use. Don't reuse milk cartons. Here's how to get started:

**Milk cartons:** Cut the upper half off of a quart or half-gallon cardboard milk carton, and poke several drainage holes in the base. Fill the base to ½ inch from the rim with a soilless mix, and insert the cuttings.

**Clear plastic food containers:** Punch several drainage holes in the bottom half, and fill to ½ inch from the rim with seed-starting mix. Plant the seeds and close the lid for a humid, greenhouselike

atmosphere. To root cuttings, punch ventilation holes in the top and fill the bottom half to ½ inch from the rim with a soilless mix. Insert the cuttings.

**Plastic soda bottles:** Here are two ways to use soda bottles as greenhouses. Both work equally well, and your preference may depend on how many bottles you have lying around. To use up two at a time, cut off the top third of two bottles. Fill one bottom about ½ inch from the rim with soilless mix, insert the cuttings, and water. Then remove the colored bottom from the other cut bottle, and fit that bottle over the planted base, as shown in the illustration. Another method is to use just one plastic soda bottle. Cut off the bottom, fill it with soilless mix, insert the cuttings, and water. Then replace the bottle's cut-off top, and seal the top and bottom together with tape.

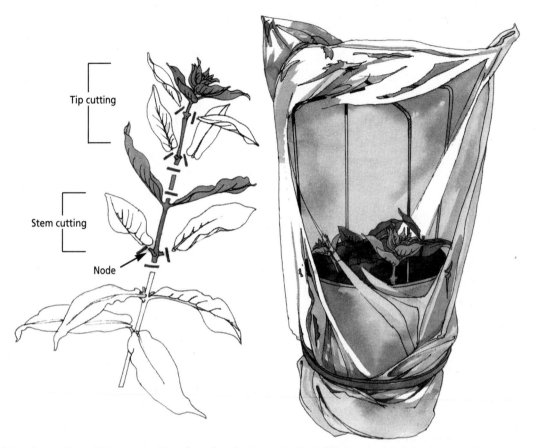

Tip cutting

Stem cutting

Node

**Taking stem cuttings.** Make stem cuttings from first-flush growth that's firm but not hard. Cut 3- to 6-inch-long pieces (shorter if the plant is small) with a sharp, sterile knife. Take softwood and herbaceous cuttings from stems that snap when bent. Remove the cutting just below a node; discard the stem piece left on the parent down to the uppermost node. Remove the lower leaves, and stick the cuttings in a pot or flat in moist, sterile potting medium so the bottom inch of the stem is in the medium and at least one node is at or below the soil surface. When all the cuttings are in the pot or flat, cover it with clear plastic draped over wire hoops so the plastic doesn't touch the plants.

magnolias. Treat stem cuttings of herbaceous plants, including geraniums and impatiens, like softwood cuttings. Because these cuttings are taken from young tissue, they form roots easily but need high humidity to prevent them from wilting.

Take softwood cuttings from April through June, when new leaves are fully expanded but stems are still soft. Take houseplant cuttings anytime.

Water the parent plant a day or two before taking cuttings. Fill a container with moist propagation mix.

Collect cuttings in the morning or on a cloudy, cool day, and keep them moist until planting. Cuttings should be 3 to 6 inches long; they usually include a terminal bud. Remove leaves from the lower half of the stem, and apply rooting hormone if desired. Insert the cutting to about one-third its length, firm the medium, and water to settle the cutting. Enclose the container in plastic, or place it under a mist system in a cold frame or greenhouse.

Ventilate plants; water to keep the medium moist but not wet. Softwood and herbaceous cuttings root quickly, often in two to four weeks. When roots appear, harden off the cuttings and plant them in the garden or in a pot.

## HARDWOOD STEM CUTTINGS

Take hardwood cuttings from woody plants during their dormant period. Hardwood cuttings don't require high-humidity conditions. This method is effective for some types of woody plants and vines, including grapes, currants, willows, and some roses.

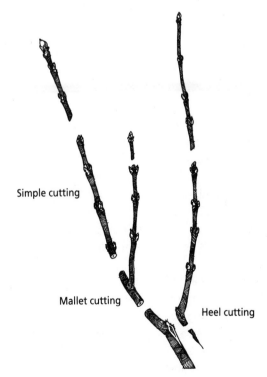

Simple cutting

Mallet cutting

Heel cutting

**Hardwood cuttings.** Take simple cuttings from the midsections of branches. For difficult-to-root plants, take a heel or mallet cutting as shown above. Each has a bit of older wood at the base, which helps promote rooting.

Take cuttings after leaf fall and before new growth begins in spring. Mid-autumn is often the best time to collect and plant cuttings so they can form roots before the buds begin to grow.

For potted cuttings, fill the container with moist propagation mix. If you are planting cuttings outdoors or into a cold frame, prepare a deep, well-drained nursery bed.

Collect 4- to 8-inch cuttings from vigorous, one-year-old wood, a few inches below the terminal bud. Make a straight cut at the top, slightly above a bud, and a sloping cut at the base, slightly below a bud. Stick cuttings 2 to 4 inches apart in the medium, with the top bud about 1 inch above the surface. Be sure the cuttings point upward: Double-check that you've stuck the ends with sloping cuts into the medium. Plant fall cuttings soon after they are taken, or store them upside down in moist peat moss

 **Rooting Hormones**

Rooting hormones—synthetic versions of natural plant hormones—can encourage root formation on stem cuttings of difficult plants and can increase the number of roots on others. Commercial rooting hormones are usually available in garden centers in powder form; be aware that some products contain chemical fungicides. Product labels will suggest uses, or you can experiment with treated and untreated cuttings.

A solution known as *willow water* can also encourage rooting. Cut willow stems into 1-inch pieces and place them in a small container; add about 2 inches of water, cover, and let stand for 24 hours. Remove the stems, insert cuttings, and let the cuttings soak overnight before planting.

or perlite and plant right-side up in spring. Cover fall-planted cuttings with 6 to 8 inches of mulch to prevent frost heaving; remove mulch in spring. Plant late-winter cuttings directly into pots or soil.

Keep cuttings moist. They usually root rapidly in spring, but it is best to leave them at least until fall. Transplant rooted cuttings to the garden or into pots.

## EVERGREEN CUTTINGS

Broad-leaved and needled evergreens are often propagated by stem cuttings. Try this method on plants such as arborvitae, hollies, and boxwood.

Collect broad-leaved cuttings in late summer. Take needled cuttings in fall or winter; yew and juniper cuttings should have had some frost.

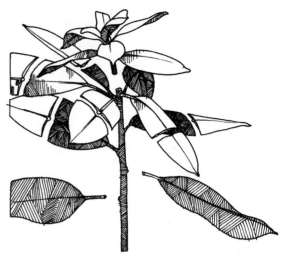

**Broad-leaved evergreen cuttings.** To save space remove up to half of the leaves from a cutting. Some broad-leaved evergreen cuttings benefit from wounding. Use a knife to make a shallow 1-inch cut at the stem base.

---

### ❀ Best (and Worst) Bets for Cuttings

These perennials are easy to start from cuttings; keep the nursery bed or flat well moistened until new growth is well on its way:

 Asters (*Aster* spp.)
 Candytufts (*Iberis* spp.)
 Centaureas (*Centaurea* spp.)
 Chrysanthemums (*Chrysanthemum* spp.)
 Lady's-mantles (*Alchemilla* spp.)
 Lavenders (*Lavandula* spp.)
 Leadworts (*Plumbago* spp.)
 Showy stonecrop (*Sedum spectabile*)
 Thread-leaved coreopsis (*Coreopsis verticillata*)
 Yarrows (*Achilea* spp.)

Some annuals and even a few perennials will root from cuttings stuck directly in the ground. Insert 2- to 4-inch cuttings directly in loose, rich soil where they are to grow, and water well until established. Try these super-easy rooters:

 Ageratum (*Ageratum* spp.)
 Coleus (*Coleus* spp.)
 Dahlias (*Dahlia* spp.)
 Felicias (*Felicia* spp.)
 Golden marguerite (*Anthemis tinctoria*)
 Wax begonias (*Begonia* × *semperflorens-cultorum*)

Many hardwoods are difficult to propagate by cuttings. It's best to buy the following plants from a nursery:

 Birches (*Betula* spp.)
 Firs (*Abies* spp.)
 Flowering dogwood (*Cornus florida*)
 Japanese maple (*Acer palmatum*)
 Maples (*Acer* spp.)
 Oaks (*Quercus* spp.)
 Pines (*Pinus* spp.)
 Spruces (*Picea* spp.)
 Upright junipers (*Juniperus* spp., upright)

Fill a container with moist propagation mix, or prepare a well-drained bed in the base of a cold frame.

Collect 4- to 6-inch tip cuttings in the proper season. Some cuttings benefit from a piece of older wood—a heel—left at the base of the stem. To take a heel, pull sharply downward on the base of a sideshoot as you remove it from the parent plant; trim the excess with a knife.

Wounding is another way to encourage the rooting of difficult plants. Create a wound by cutting a shallow sliver on the side of the cutting near the base. This process stimulates cell division and enhances water uptake but also increases the chance of disease problems.

Before planting, remove lower leaves and

**Needled evergreen cuttings.** Leaving a small bit of the main stem—called a heel—at the base of the cutting stem enhances rooting of needled evergreen cuttings.

sideshoots. To save space with large broad-leaved cuttings, cut each remaining leaf in half. Apply rooting hormone if desired. Plant cuttings about one inch deep, firm the soil, and water to settle the cuttings. Place potted cuttings indoors in a plastic bag or in a greenhouse; alternatively, set pots in a cold frame, or plant directly into the frame.

---

### ❀ Cutting Dos and Don'ts

Fungal problems are the major threat to cuttings. Here are some dos and don'ts for avoiding rots and other fungal disasters:

■ **Do** sterilize your knife with alcohol between cuts.

■ **Do** treat each cutting with a 5 percent bleach solution (1 part bleach to 19 parts water) if you want an extra guard against fungi. If you plan to put the cuttings in a plastic propagating tent or enclosure, use chamomile tea instead of bleach solution. Dip the entire cutting for a few seconds to a minute.

■ **Don't** stick cuttings deeper than 1 inch or they may rot, and **don't** let leaves come in contact with the soil surface.

■ **Do** stick cuttings far enough apart so the leaves of adjacent plants don't touch.

■ **Don't** let the plastic you use to enclose the flat or pot touch the cuttings.

■ **Do** open the plastic on your propagating containers at least once a day—good circulation prevents fungal problems, while stagnant air encourages them.

■ **Do** check your cuttings daily for mildewed or dropped leaves. Remove dropped leaves and diseased cuttings as soon as you see them to keep fungi from spreading to healthy cuttings.

## ✿ Tips for Top Cuttings

Try these tips for best success with cuttings:

■ Never break off branch tips for cuttings by hand, and never scrape the bark with your fingernail to speed up rooting. The broken-off, ragged stem end will die back, inviting disease, and scraping off bark with a fingernail bruises plant tissues. Instead, always use a small, sharp knife to collect and prepare cuttings.

■ If you're taking cuttings of virus-prone perennials, sterilize your knife between plants by dipping it in skim milk. Research has shown that the milk prevents the spread of viruses.

■ If you need cuttings but have missed your plants' first flush of growth, you can trick plants like yarrows into creating a second flush by cutting the plants back almost to the ground. Take cuttings from the new growth.

■ Make your cuttings 3 to 6 inches long, unless the stock plant is small. Be sure to get at least two nodes (leaf-stem joints). Non-flowering shoots are best. Remove flowers and flower buds from unrooted cuttings.

■ To prevent cuttings from drying out as you collect them, place them in a plastic bag as soon as you cut them. Keep the bagged cuttings at a moderate temperature by placing each bagful in a covered foam ice chest—without the ice. To gently cushion each bag of cuttings, blow air into the bag and seal it like a balloon to keep the cuttings from being crushed.

■ To keep cuttings fresh if you have to travel with them, stick them in a raw potato. Slice the potato in half lengthwise, lay the cuttings along one half with the cut ends inside, and put the other half over them like a sandwich. Hold the halves together with rubber bands.

■ Plant large numbers of cuttings in wooden or plastic flats; use pots or homemade propagation containers for small quantities.

■ Keep the soil warm to encourage root formation and to discourage rot. Place containers of cuttings on a propagation mat (a rubber mat with heating cables, available from garden centers and garden-supply catalogs), on a board over a radiator, or on top of your refrigerator.

■ Use willow water to encourage your cuttings to root. The active ingredient in many commercial rooting preparations is a synthetic version of indolabutyric acid (IBA), a natural plant hormone. You can use the real thing by mixing up a batch of willow water. See "Rooting Hormones" on page 101 for directions on making and using willow water.

■ Home water softeners use salts that are harmful to plants. Be sure to use unsoftened water or rainwater.

■ Try a germinating-grain rooting stimulant. Place 1 cup of untreated wheat or barley seeds (available at health food stores) in a 1-quart, widemouthed jar and cover with water. The next day, cover the mouth of the jar with an 8-inch square of cheesecloth and secure with a rubber band. Turn the jar upside down to drain. Rinse and drain the seeds with warm water several times, removing broken seeds. Place the jar in a warm place and rinse the seeds several times a day until the majority have begun to sprout. Take your cuttings to be rooted and swirl the cut ends through the sprouted grain just before planting. Use a pencil or knife to make a narrow trench in the rooting medium before pushing the cuttings through to avoid rubbing off the sprouted-grain stimulant.

■ Don't tug on cuttings once they're in their rooting medium. Instead, check the bottom of the container to see if roots are visible.

Ventilate and water if necessary. Once roots appear, gradually harden off the cuttings. The new plants are best left in place until fall and then planted in the garden or in a pot.

## LEAF CUTTINGS

Some plants with thick or fleshy leaves can produce roots and shoots directly from leaf pieces. This is a popular propagation method for houseplants such as African violets and snake plants.

Take cuttings any time of year. Use healthy leaves that are young but fully expanded. Thoroughly water the parent plant a day or so before collecting cuttings. Fill a container with moist propagation medium.

Cut snake plant and streptocarpus leaves into 2-inch-long pieces. Plant the pieces right-side up, about 1 inch deep. Peperomias and African violets are reproduced by leaf-petiole cuttings. Detach a leaf along with 1½ to 2 inches of its petiole. Plant vertically or at a slight angle, so the petiole is buried up to the leaf blade. After planting, water the cuttings to settle them in the soil.

If excessive condensation occurs, ventilate the cuttings. When new leaves appear in six to eight weeks, gradually harden them off. Sever plantlets from the parent leaf if it has not already withered away; transfer rooted plants to pots.

## ROOT CUTTINGS

Root cuttings are a reliable way to propagate plants with thick, fleshy roots. Slice off pencil-thick roots, and cut them into 2-inch pieces. Use a diagonal cut at the bottom of each piece so that you'll know which end is up. (They won't grow if you plant them upside down.) Pot up root cuttings in pots or cell packs filled with sterile, porous potting medium, such as half seed-starting mix and half perlite. Keep the cuttings barely moist, put them in a cold frame

or an unheated room, and give them bottom heat, if possible.

These plants propagate well from cuttings of their thick, fleshy roots. Dig deep to lift the mother plant, then cut roots into 2-inch pieces for propagating.

  Adam's-needle (*Yucca filamentosa*)
  Baby's-breath (*Gypsophila paniculata*)
  Bear's-breeches (*Acanthus* spp.)
  Bugloss (*Anchusa* spp.)
  Butterfly weed (*Asclepias tuberosa*)
  Common bleeding heart (*Dicentra spectabilis*)
  Cranesbills (*Geranium* spp.)
  Mulleins (*Verbascum* spp.)
  Oriental poppy (*Papaver orientale*)
  Perennial salvias (*Salvia* spp.)

If you have a cold frame, unheated room, or greenhouse, you can also propagate perennials from root cuttings. The best perennials for root cuttings have fleshy roots, like Japanese anemone (*Anemone* × *hybrida*), grape leaf anemone (*A. vitifolia*), snowdrop anemone

 **Soilless Mix for Rooting**

This soilless mix is fine for rooting cuttings, but you will need to move the newly rooted plants to a richer mix as soon as they show any sign of growth.

Combine 1 part peat moss or vermiculite with 1 part perlite or sterilized sand in a clean plastic garbage bag and mix thoroughly. Work in a small amount of water by kneading the closed plastic bag. Continue adding water and kneading until the mix is evenly moist. Place the mix in a flat for cuttings or seal and store in a cool, dark place. If you are propagating acid-loving plants like rhododendron, be sure to use peat moss rather than vermiculite.

(*A. sylvestris*), bleeding hearts (*Dicentra* spp.), cranesbills (*Geranium* spp.), garden phlox (*Phlox paniculata*), great coneflower (*Rudbeckia maxima*), ligularias (*Ligularia* spp.), and Siberian bugloss (*Brunnera macrophylla*). Take root cuttings in the fall or winter when plants are dormant, grow them in the greenhouse or cold frame, and plant them out in a nursery bed when they are growing strongly.

# LAYERING

Layering is a way of propagating plants by encouraging sections of stems to sprout new roots, which are cut from the mother plant and planted. This simple method produces good-sized new plants in a relatively short time.

## SIMPLE LAYERING

Simple layering involves bending a low-growing branch to the ground and burying several inches of stem. It is used to propagate many types of vines and woody plants, including grapes and magnolias.

Spring is the best time to start simple layers. Choose flexible, vigorous one-year-old shoots about as thick as a pencil.

Thoroughly water the soil around the plant.

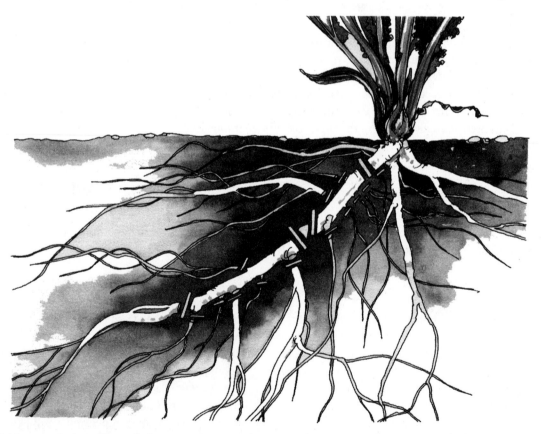

**Making root cuttings.** Choose fleshy, mature, tan roots for root cuttings. Use a sterile propagating knife to cut 1½-inch-long segments of root. Start at the bottom of the root and cut up. Make a slanted cut at the bottom of the root cutting and a straight cut across the top so that you'll be able to plant it right-side up.

The next day, bend a shoot down to the soil. Measure back 9 to 12 inches from the tip of the shoot, and mark the spot where that point on the stem touches the ground. Release the shoot, and dig a 4-inch hole at the marked point. The hole should have one side sloping toward the parent plant. Work in several handfuls of finished compost.

Remove leaves and sideshoots along the chosen stem from 6 to 15 inches behind the stem tip. Wound the stem by making a shallow 2-inch-long cut at a point about 9 inches behind the tip. Insert a toothpick or small pebble in the cut to keep it open. Dust the cut with rooting hormone. Bend the stem down into the hole, and use a wire pin to keep the wounded area in contact with the soil. Stake the stem tip if it doesn't stay upright by itself. Cover the pinned stem with soil and water thoroughly.

Keep the layered area moist and weeded. The stem may root by fall; check by uncovering the stem, removing the wire pin, and tugging lightly. If the stem feels firmly anchored, it has rooted. Sever it from the parent plant, but leave it in place until spring. Then pot it up or transplant it. If the stem is not well rooted, replace the soil and wait a year before checking again for roots.

## TIP LAYERING

Shoot tips of certain plants such

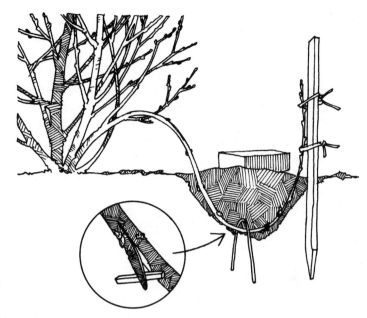

**Simple layering.** Use a piece of wire, bent into a hairpin shape, to hold the wounded stem in the trench. A brick over the buried stem helps to retain moisture.

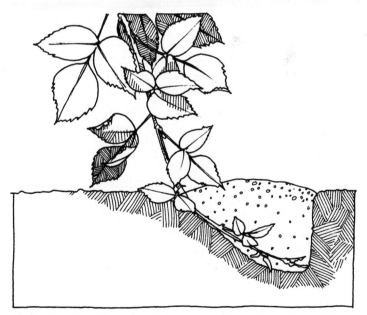

**Tip layering.** Keep the soil moist to promote rooting. Sever the rooted layer from the parent plant in early fall; wait at least a few weeks before moving the new plant.

as black and purple raspberries root when they touch the ground. Plant tip layers in late summer, using the ends of the current season's growth. Make sure you use healthy, vigorous canes. Prepare a hole as you would for simple layers; judge the placement of the hole by the tip of the stem.

Bend the stem tip down to the prepared planting hole. Lay the cane against the sloping side and place the tip against the farthest edge of the hole. Replace the soil, and water well.

By early fall, shoots will appear and roots will have formed; cut the original cane where it enters the soil. In mid-fall or the following spring, carefully dig up the rooted tip, and plant it in its new position.

## AIR LAYERING

Air layering is similar to simple layering, but the stem is covered with long-fibered (unmilled) sphagnum moss rather than soil. You can air-layer upright stems of trees, shrubs, and indoor plants such as philodendrons.

Outdoors, start air layers in early fall with young wood, or in spring with the previous season's growth. Indoors, air layers can be done any time, but it's best to start when plants begin growing actively in spring.

---

 ### Let Your Plants Layer

Layering takes advantage of the natural tendency that many plants have to sprout roots along their stems. Try this technique to multiply herbs and shrubs or to regenerate a leggy houseplant.

Simple layering is one technique that really lives up to its name. You can propagate many of your favorites anytime during the growing season with this easy trick: Merely bend a low branch to the ground and scoop a handful of soil over a short section of the stem, patting it down and weighting it with a stone if the branch is inclined to spring upward.

The herb garden is a good place to start experimenting. Many herbs, including absinthe, anise hyssop, artemisias, bee balm, clary sage, culinary sage, lemon balm, rosemary, scented geraniums, and thymes of all types, are especially easy to propagate just by scuffing a bit of soil over a low stem. The perennial border, too, is full of likely candidates, such as candytuft (*Iberis* spp.); catmint (*Nepeta* × *faassenii*); chrysanthemums; goldenrods (*Solidago* spp.); perennial asters (*Asters* spp.); sweet William (*Dianthus barbatus*); thread-leaved coreopsis (*Coreopsis verticillata*), including the popular 'Moonbeam'; and periwinkle (*Vinca major* and *V. minor*). Vines such as English ivy, honeysuckle, jasmine (*Jasminum* spp.), trumpet vine (*Campsis radicans*), and Virginia creeper (*Parthenocissus quinquefolia*) are also gratifyingly easy to propagate.

Herbs, perennials, and vines will usually root within several weeks, depending on the species. Even some woody shrubs can be propagated with this no-fuss method, though it may take a year or even two before they're ready to transplant. Try your hand with barberries (*Berberis* spp.), border forsythia (*Forsythia* × *intermedia*), rhododendrons and azaleas (*Rhododendron* spp.), rose-of-Sharon (*Hibiscus syriacus*), common lilac (*Syringa vulgaris*), pussy willows, willows (*Salix* spp.), viburnums, and weigelas (*Weigela* spp.). But don't limit yourself to these suggestions—experiment with whatever you like.

---

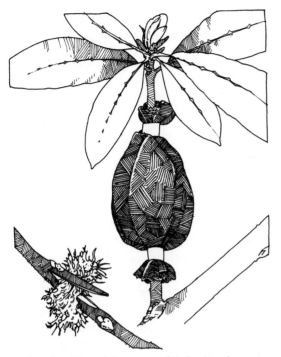

**Air layering.** Wound the stem and tuck a bit of moss into the wound. Wrap the remainder around the stem, and cover with plastic. If the moss looks dry during rooting, open the plastic, moisten the moss, and reseal.

Soak the sphagnum moss in water for a few hours or overnight. Before using, wring the excess water out of the moss, so it is moist but not dripping wet.

Start with a healthy, vigorous stem. Decide where you want the roots of the new plant to be, anywhere from 6 to 18 inches behind the tip. Remove all leaves and sideshoots for 3 inches on either side of that point. Wound the stem by making a shallow 2-inch-long cut into it. Dust the wounded area with rooting hormone. Wrap the ball of moist sphagnum moss around the wound and tie it with string. Next, cover the moss ball with a piece of clear plastic about 6 inches square. For indoor plants, tie the plastic at both ends with string or twist ties. Use waterproof tape to secure the ends on outdoor air layers; make sure the ends are completely sealed. For outdoor plants, also cover the plastic wrap with foil or black plastic and tie or tape it to the stem; this will keep the layered area from getting too hot in the sun.

Indoor plants can produce roots in a few months; outdoor plants may take one or two growing seasons. You'll be able to see the roots growing in the moss. Cut off the top of the plant below the new roots and remove the plastic. Soak the root ball for three to four hours, pot it up, and place it in a sheltered spot for a few days. Let outdoor plants grow in their pots for a few months before planting them out.

# Chapter 7

# PESTS AND DISEASES

No one wants pests in their yard and garden. Yet at one time or another, we've all had to deal with a disease that ruins beautiful foliage or with insects that eat holes in our favorite crop.

There's no denying that, at times, insects and diseases can be vexing, if not downright defeating. It's equally true that most gardeners invest a great deal of time, energy, and money battling bugs and blights.

What organic gardeners learn from the struggle is that there are no real good guys and bad guys and there's no real battle to fight. The true key to pest control is knowledge—understanding the interconnections between the diverse life forms in your garden and how you can manage your garden to tip the scales in your favor without causing damaging side effects. In this chapter, you'll learn how to make an organic pest management (OPM) program for your own garden. OPM programs combine organic soil building, proper plant care, and preventive pest control to create a garden environment where even organically acceptable pesticides are used as a last resort.

## PEST PROBLEMS

Basic organic gardening practices are an important part of organic pest management. These practices bring your yard and garden into natural balance. The goal is to create a stable system where there are no huge population explosions of pests, but rather a diverse ecosystem where pest populations are regulated naturally. If you take good care of your soil and plants, your garden will be healthier and have fewer problems with insects, diseases, and weeds.

Healthy plants attract fewer insect pests, are less susceptible to diseases, and beat out weeds. Make soil building a priority. The more organic matter you add to your soil, the better. Have your soil tested, and correct any imbalances. Use organic fertilizers to keep your plants thriving while you work to improve your soil. See Chapters 2 and 3 for more information on soil care and fertilizing.

Good garden sanitation is another prerequisite for a healthy garden. Remove and dispose of garden waste. Every pulled weed represents thousands of seeds that won't take root. Each disease-spotted leaf you remove represents untold numbers of disease spores that won't find their way onto next year's crop.

Don't spread problems with your hands, feet, or tools. Clean your tools regularly—always after working with diseased plants. Do a fall cleaning of all your garden tools and equipment every year, and you'll reduce the number of problems the following season. Disinfect stakes, plastic mulch, and the like before storing them for the winter.

### MAKE AN OPM PLAN

An organic pest management program starts with a plan. Planning ahead will allow you to make full use of preventive control measures and to have the tools and materials you'll need to fight problems if they arise. Your pest control measures will include cultural, biological, and physical controls, and, as a last resort, organically acceptable chemical controls.

The first step in developing your own specific OPM plan is identifying the problems that you've had in the past or that are common in your area. Make a list of these problems. If you don't know what causes them, try to find out. Then learn as much as you can about each one. By knowing how pests and diseases overwinter and when they attack your plants, you will be able to pick effective control methods.

Note the ways in which you could help to control each of the problems on your list. Also note what times during the pest's life cycle each control is effective. It may help to make a chart of the life cycle and control activities.

Once you have all your options in front of you, make a comprehensive plan. Start by noting what cultural controls are effective and when they need to be done. Then add the biological controls. Follow with the physical controls. If any supplies are needed, be sure to order them in advance.

Complete your plan by considering chemical control options. Certain problems like brown rot on fruit may require sulfur or copper fungicides. Decide on a spray schedule, and consider how you'll adjust it depending on weather conditions. During a prolonged wet period, which favors fungal growth, you may need extra sprays. In a dry year, you may never have to get out your sprayer. Be sure to order pesticides so you'll have them if needed; not all organically acceptable pesticides are readily available at garden centers.

# CULTURAL CONTROLS

Cultural controls are steps you can take as you plant and care for a garden that make the envi-

## Words to Know

**Organic Pest Management (OPM):** An approach to pest control that combines cultural, biological, physical, and certain chemical control measures to prevent problems or to keep them in check. Organically acceptable chemical controls are a last resort used only when all other methods aren't adequate.

**Integrated Pest Management (IPM):** A pest control philosophy that combines cultural, biological, and physical controls to supplement chemical (including synthetic) control measures to prevent or eliminate problems.

**Cultural controls:** Gardening practices that reduce pest problems, including keeping plants healthy, selecting well-adapted cultivars, and keeping the garden clean.

**Biological controls:** Pest control measures that use living organisms to fight pests and diseases, including releasing, attracting, and protecting natural insect predators and parasites, and using microbial sprays to control problems.

**Physical controls:** Control measures that prevent pests from reaching your plants or that remove them if they do. Barriers, traps, and handpicking are physical controls.

**Chemical controls:** Control methods that involve substances that kill pests. Organically acceptable chemical controls are naturally occurring minerals or plant products, and they tend to break down into harmless substances faster than synthetic pesticides. They do have toxic side effects and are used only as a last resort.

ronment less hospitable to pests. Some cultural controls work by benefiting the plant and making it better able to resist damage; others interfere with a pest's life cycle or behavior.

## CHOOSE RESISTANT PLANTS

You can make an important contribution to pest control by choosing insect- and disease-resistant cultivars and avoiding susceptible ones. Disease-resistant cultivars of apples, corn, tomatoes, and many other plants are available. Some new cultivars are bred specifically for disease resistance.

The resistance will be listed in catalog descriptions or perhaps as a series of letter codes in the cultivar name. If you can't find a cultivar resistant to a pest that is problematic in your area, choose cultivars that are well adapted to your local climate and soil conditions.

Keep in mind that older cultivars, selected for superior performance before the widespread use of synthetic pesticides, may offer some resistance to specific problems. These resistances may not be noted in catalog descriptions.

Certain physical characteristics of plants make

---

 **The Garden Detective**

All the planning in the world won't help if you don't keep a watchful eye out for problems. Make it a habit to walk through your garden at least once a week—daily is best—looking carefully at your plants, turning over leaves, and noting overall appearance.

Plant problems fall into three general categories: insects and animals, diseases, and cultural problems (water stress, heat or cold, nutrient imbalances). Symptoms caused by different problems may look remarkably similar. You need to investigate a number of possibilities and do some detective work:

1. Look at the entire plant and those around it. Is just one plant or an entire row affected? Is the whole plant affected, or just part of it? Does it seem to be random, or is there some distinct pattern, such as that only new growth is affected?

2. Check the undersides of leaves and the stems, flowers, and roots for insects, eggs, webs, or damage such as borer holes. Examine the affected areas with a hand lens, looking for tiny insects or fungal growth.

3. Collect sample insects and samples of damaged leaves for later identification. Put them in pill bottles or plastic bags.

4. Ask knowledgeable gardeners, garden center employees, or extension agents to help diagnose problems. There are also many good books available that can help you identify pests, diseases, and cultural problems. Some are arranged by plant type and list the common problems for each, which makes finding the answer easier.

5. Once you have identified the problem, find out as much as you can about it. Then develop a plan to control it.

6. Even if you can't diagnose the problem, don't despair. Give your plants the best care you can. Plants often recover when conditions improve. But keep an eye on the problem—if more plants develop the same symptoms, put your detective hat back on.

7. Keep notes on your program during the season. Make notes about what works and what doesn't, what controls you used, how much you used, and where. The more information you have, the better you'll be able to refine your plan for the next season.

them more or less attractive to pests. Corn cultivars with good husk cover are least damaged by corn earworms. Imported cabbageworms rarely trouble purple cabbage and broccoli.

## MAINTAIN HEALTHY PLANTS

Plants grown on fertile soils with adequate water tolerate insect attack better than plants suffering from nutrient deficiency, water stress, crowding, or low light levels. Healthy plants also mount their own chemical defenses to diseases and insects faster.

**Healthy Soil**  Healthy soils contain a complex community of soil organisms that are vital to plant health. Mycorrhizal fungi protect fine roots from infections and aid plants in taking up nutrients. Nitrogen-fixing bacteria live symbiotically with roots of legumes, beneficial fungi trap harmful nematodes, and many fungi and bacteria produce antibiotics that suppress pathogens. Nutrient deficiencies and imbalances make plants more attractive to pests. Conversely, overfertilizing with nitrogen can cause soft, lush growth, which is very attractive to sucking pests such as aphids.

**Proper Moisture**  Water-stressed plants are more attractive to pests and susceptible to diseases. For example, aphids and thrips are more likely to attack wilted plants, while wet, waterlogged soil encourages soilborne diseases. Plants usually grow best when moisture is maintained at a constant level. Most plants need about 1 inch of water per week from rain and/or irrigation while they are actively growing. Learn your plant's specific likes and dislikes. Some plants have critical times during their development when sufficient water is crucial.

Be sure to water effectively. Apply water to the soil, below mulch if possible. Avoid routinely wetting leaves because water helps spread many leaf diseases and may burn leaves in full sun. Water thoroughly: A long, slow soak every

few days is much better than a short sprinkle every day. For more information on effective watering methods, see "Watering Your Garden" on page 180.

**Mulches**  Mulching saves water, controls weeds, and may add organic matter. It provides pest control by acting as a barrier, preventing

**Trellising.** Trellises can be great space savers for climbing and vining crops such as cucumbers, tomatoes, peas, and beans. Trellising also reduces disease problems because it keeps fruit off the ground and increases air circulation, thus preventing rot. Trim the foliage from the bases of trellised plants to allow air movement and to cut off corridors for crawling insects.

## Diagnosing Tree Disorders

People unintentionally cause almost as many plant problems as insects and diseases do. Selecting a tree well suited to the site is the best way to prevent frustrating, costly, and fatal plant disorders.

If illness does befall your favorite tree, don't assume that blight or bugs are to blame, even if such pests are evident—they may only be taking advantage of a plant weakened by environmental conditions. Here are some factors to consider:

**Growth habits:** Know a tree's growth habit before you buy. How high and wide will it be? Will its branches extend into power lines, inviting inexpert or untimely pruning by utility companies? If a tree's branches extend 25 feet from the trunk, its supporting roots reach out that far into the surrounding soil. Other plants within its radius will compete for nutrients and water. More aggressive plants often win this battle, while losers grow slowly, have poor appearance, and produce few fruits. Trees with surface roots will destroy sidewalks or invade sewer and water lines within that radius, too.

**Construction:** Many home buyers ask that large trees on a lot be saved during construction. However, few trees can withstand the rigors of construction— changing grades and drainage, topsoil removal, and soil compaction around roots.

To preserve trees on a new homesite, keep equipment away from trees by erecting fences beyond the drip line before construction begins. For help in preserving trees close to the site, consult a tree specialist.

**Trees versus lawn:** Healthy trees and healthy lawn grass do not necessarily go hand in hand.

Lawn mowers often bump and scrape a tree's bark just above ground level; the blades chop into roots rising from the lawn. Shallow watering—soaking only the top 2 inches of soil—can cause trees to develop droughtlike symptoms, including small, yellowing leaves, early leaf drop, slow growth, and brittle twigs.

Keep grass out of the area covered by the tree's fully leafed branch spread by planting shade-tolerant groundcovers that don't need mowing. During droughts, use a root irrigator to water trees deeply every two weeks.

**Salt damage:** Ocean spray and road salt, as well as animal urine, can injure plants. Salts can accumulate on leaves, stems, and buds or build to toxic levels around the roots. Over time, salt burn weakens the entire plant and causes droughtlike symptoms.

Use barriers to protect plants near roads and sidewalks from salt, grow salt-tolerant species, and use water to flush salts from the soil. If visiting dogs are a problem, put up a fence or ask owners to curb their pets.

**Air pollution:** Motor-vehicle exhaust and industrial emissions affect plants as well as people. Symptoms may result from a sudden excess of pollutants in the air or long-term exposure. Grow tolerant species where pollution is a problem, and avoid planting in sites that receive direct, regular exposure to exhaust.

**Girdling roots:** Sometimes a root wraps around another root or even the entire trunk and gradually strangles the tree as it grows. A girdling root looks like a thick coil wrapped around the trunk at ground level. Carefully remove girdling roots with a saw, axe, or chisel. If this girdling occurs underground, it may not be evident until it's too late.

soilborne problems from reaching plants, or providing a home for beneficial insects. You can mulch with a variety of organic or inorganic materials. A deep straw mulch in the potato patch can help prevent damage caused by Colorado potato beetles. Reflective aluminum mulch confuses aphids and prevents them from landing on your plants. For more information on what materials to use and how and when to apply them, see Chapter 2.

**Spacing and Training** Proper spacing, staking, and pruning can reduce pest problems. Crowded plants are weak and spindly and are more prone to disease and insect problems. Staking keeps plants from coming in contact with soilborne diseases, prevents them from being stepped on or damaged, and increases air movement. Pruning plants increases air movement and makes it easier to spot insects before they become a major problem. Leafy crops can be their own living mulch and suppress weeds if spaced so that the plants just touch at maturity.

## KEEP THE GARDEN CLEAN

Garden sanitation is a basic principle of organic pest management. Don't bring diseased or infested plants into your garden, and promptly remove any pest-ridden plant material from the garden.

**Don't Bring In Problems** Check all new plants for signs of insects, disease, or hitchhiking weeds. Thoroughly inspect leaves, buds, bark, and, if possible, roots. Discard, reject, or treat infested plants. Choose certified disease-free plants and seeds when possible. Don't buy grass or cover-crop seeds contaminated with weed seeds, don't let weeds or garden plants go to seed, and avoid hay or other mulches that contain weed seed.

**Handle Plants Carefully** Stay out of the garden when it's wet because disease organisms spread easily on the film of water on wet leaves. Don't step on or bend plants when you work around them. Use mowers and trimmers with care: Any wound provides an entry for disease.

**Don't Spread Problems** Wash your tools, boots, and clothes at the end of every work session. Even if you don't notice disease, you may spread it as you work. If you do touch a diseased plant, sanitize your tools and wash your hands before moving on. Dip or swab with a 10 percent bleach solution (1 part bleach to 9 parts water), and allow to air dry. If you use the bleach solution on metal, be sure to wipe it with a little oil after it dries to prevent rust. Also sanitize plastic mulch and stakes before reusing them. Carry a plastic bag with you to put seed-bearing weeds and sick plants into.

**Clean Up Pest-Damaged Plants** Pull up diseased plants or prune off damage. Burn them, put them in sealed containers for disposal with household trash, put them in the center of a hot compost pile, or feed them to animals. Picking up and destroying dropped fruit weekly is an effective way to reduce infestations of apple maggots, currant fruit flies, codling moths, and plum curculios.

**Clean Up Crop Residues** Good sanitation includes cleaning up all crop residues promptly. Compost them well or turn them under. Cultivating crop residues into the soil after harvest kills pests, including corn earworms, European corn borers, and corn rootworms.

## TIME YOUR PLANTING

Seeds planted before the soil has warmed up in the spring are more susceptible to disease. Learn the soil temperature that each crop requires to germinate, and use a soil thermometer to determine proper planting time.

Some pests have only one to two generations per year. You can reduce damage by planning planting or harvesting times to avoid peak pest populations. For example, plant radishes to mature before the first generation of cabbage root maggots appear, or delay setting out your cabbage-family plants until after the first generation of cabbage root maggots has passed.

## ROTATE CROPS

Crop rotation is the practice of shifting the locations of crops within the garden each season so the same crop does not grow in the same place year after year. This technique helps manage soil fertility and helps avoid or reduce problems with soilborne diseases and some soil-dwelling insects, such as corn rootworms.

**Nutrient Balance**  Plants affect the soil in different ways. To keep soil nutrients balanced, avoid planting the same type of crop (leafy, fruiting, root, or legume) in the same place two years in a row.

Leafy and fruiting crops (such as lettuce, cabbage, corn, and tomatoes) are heavy feeders and rapidly use up nitrogen. Root vegetables and herbs are light feeders. Peas, beans, and other legumes add nitrogen to the soil but need lots of phosphorus. Follow a soil-building crop with a heavy-feeding crop, and follow a heavy feeder with a root crop or another soil builder to balance the supplies of nutrients in the soil.

**Disease and Pest Prevention**  Many diseases and pests are host-specific: They attack only a certain plant or family of plants. Although it may be difficult in a small garden, it's best to avoid planting the same plants—or plants in the same family—in the same location in your garden year after year. For more information ands tips on rotating plant families in the vegetable garden, see the table "Rotating Vegetable Families" on page 201.

Green manure crops can be included in a rotation plan to discourage specific types of pests and to improve soil. For example, beetle grubs thrive among most vegetables, but not in soil planted in buckwheat or clover. A season of either crop can greatly reduce grub populations and at the same time increase the soil's organic matter content.

Lengthy rotations are sometimes necessary to control chronic soilborne problems. Bean anthracnose fungus can persist in soil for up to three years, so a four-year rotation is needed to keep the disease at bay. The same holds true for such fungal disease as Fusarium wilt and Verticillium wilt. A few problems, such as club root, persist in the soil for even longer, so rotation is less useful for controlling them.

## TRY COMPANION PLANTING

Mixing marigolds and herbs in the vegetable garden to confuse or repel plant pests is a well-known example of the practice of companion planting. Hundreds of examples of plant companions are recorded in garden lore. Modern research substantiates the effectiveness of some companion plants in repelling pests or attracting pest predators and parasites. However, the mechanisms that cause a plant to repel or attract pests remain largely unverified, and many companion planting practices continue to combine folklore and fact.

"Evidence" from scientific studies and gardeners' experimentation indicates several possible benefits from companion planting:

■ Masking or hiding a crop from pests

■ Producing odors that confuse and deter pests

■ Serving as trap crops that draw pest insects away from other plants

■ Acting as "nurse plants" that provide breeding grounds for beneficial insects

■ Providing food to sustain beneficial insects as they search for pests

■ Creating a habitat for beneficial insects

It's interesting to find scientific justification for companion planting, and it's fun to try your

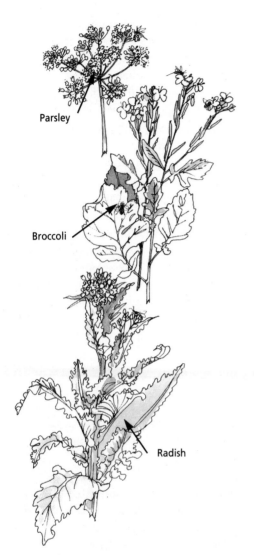

Parsley

Broccoli

Radish

**Good companions.** Crop plants such as parsley, broccoli, and radishes will attract beneficial insects if allowed to flower. (Parsley, a biennial, bears flowers the second year after planting.) Be sure to plant two crops—one for you and one for the beneficials.

own companion planting experiments. Try the following combinations in your garden:

- Plant basil among your tomatoes to control tomato hornworms.
- Combine thyme or tomatoes with cabbage plantings to control flea beetles, cabbage maggots, white cabbage butterflies, and imported cabbageworms.
- Sow catnip by eggplant to deter flea beetles.
- Set onions in rows with carrots to control rust flies and some nematodes.
- Grow horseradish with potatoes to repel Colorado potato beetles.
- Grow radishes or nasturtiums with your cucumbers for cucumber beetle control.
- Alternate double rows of corn with double rows of snap beans or soybeans to enhance the growth of the corn.
- Interplant peanuts with corn or squash to increase the yields of both crops.
- Plant spinach, lettuce, or Chinese cabbage at the base of trellised peas, where they benefit from the shade and the wind protection.
- Grow tomatoes, parsley, or basil with asparagus to help control asparagus beetles.

Nasturtiums also deter whiteflies and squash bugs, but they are more often used as a trap crop for aphids, which prefer nasturtiums to other crops. Planting a ring of them around apple trees limits woolly aphid damage to the trees (although the nasturtiums won't look great).

# BIOLOGICAL CONTROLS

Using living organisms—beneficial insects and animals, parasitic nematodes, and microbial pesticides—to control pests is called biological control. Biological control is the essence of a balanced ecosystem. A good OPM plan takes the fullest advantage of the beneficial species that are naturally present and supplements them with purchased biological controls.

Conserving and attracting native beneficial insects, birds, and animals is one of the best and most economical ways for gardeners to control pests. In a well-balanced garden, thousands of benefical species do most of the work of suppressing pests for you. Learn to identify your helpers and find out what they like. Attract them and encourage them to stay by providing food and nesting sites.

## TAKE A LOOK AT BENEFICIAL INSECTS

Our insect allies far outnumber the insect pests in our yards and gardens. Bees, flies, and some moths pollinate flowers; predatory insects eat pest insects; parasitic insects lay their eggs inside pests, eventually killing them; dung beetles, flies, and others break down decaying material; and many species of insects are food for birds and other beneficial animals.

**Bees** These are called the "spark plugs" of agriculture because of their importance in pollinating crops. All bees gather and feed on nectar and pollen, which distinguishes them from wasps, hornets, and other members of the order *Hymenoptera*. As they forage for food, bees transfer stray grains of pollen from flower to flower and pollinate the blooms. Different kinds of bees favor different flowers, and some are better pollinators than others. Of the nearly 5,000 species in North America, several hundred are vital to the pollination of cultivated crops. Many others are crucial to wild plants.

**Parasitic Wasps** Most species belong to one of three main families: chalcids, braconids, and ichneumonids. They range from pencil-point-sized *Trichogramma* wasps to huge black ichneumonid wasps. Parasitic wasps inject their

---

 **Repel with Smell**

Experiments demonstrate that night-flying moths (parents of many destructive cutworms and caterpillars) approach flowers by flying upwind. If netting is placed over flowers, the moths will still land and feed, indicating that they react to flower odor. However, moths won't land on colored flowers that don't have noticeable aroma. Can masking odors from plants such as marigolds work, too? If pests can't smell your prize plants, or if the scent isn't right, maybe they'll go elsewhere.

Common sources of repellent or masking fragrances include the following plants:

**Marigolds:** Plant them as thickly as you can in a vegetable garden, but keep in mind that unscented marigolds won't work for this trick. French marigolds (*Tagetes patula*) offer a second benefit—their roots emit a substance that repels nematodes in the immediate area.

**Mints:** Cabbage pests and aphids dislike catnip and some other members of this fragrant family. Since mints can grow out of control, set potted mints around your garden, or plant in areas where growth can be controlled.

**Rue:** Oils from the leaves of rue (*Ruta graveolens*) give some people a poison-ivy-like rash, so use this low-growing plant with care. However, what annoys people also deters Japanese beetles. Grow rue as a garden border, or scatter leaf clippings near beetle-infested crops.

**Sweet basil:** Interplant *Ocimum basilicum* in vegetable or flower gardens, or chop and scatter the leaves to repel aphids, mosquitoes, and mites. It also acts as a fungicide and slows the growth of milkweed bugs.

**Tansy:** Used as a mulch, tansy (*Tanacetum vulgare*) may cause cucumber beetles, Japanese beetles, ants, and squash bugs to go elsewhere for a meal. It attracts imported cabbageworms, however, limiting its appeal as a repellent.

eggs inside host insects; the larvae grow by absorbing nourishment through their skins. Commercial insectaries sell several parasitic wasp species for control of whiteflies, aphids, and some pest caterpillars.

**Yellow Jackets** Most people fear yellow jackets and hornets, but these insects are excellent pest predators. They dive into foliage and carry off flies, caterpillars, and other larvae to feed to their brood. So don't destroy the gray paper nests of these insects unless they are in a place frequented by people or pets, or unless a family member is allergic to insect stings.

**Lady Beetles** This family of small to medium, shiny, hard, hemispherical beetles includes more than 3,000 species that feed on small, soft pests such as aphids, mealybugs, and spider mites. Both adults and larvae eat pests. Most larvae have tapering bodies with several short, branching spines on each segment; they resemble miniature alligators. Convergent lady beetles (*Hippodamia convergens*) are collected from their mass overwintering sites and sold to gardeners, but they usually fly away after release unless confined in a greenhouse.

**Ground Beetles** These swift-footed, medium to large, blue-black beetles hide under stones or boards during the day. By night they prey on cabbage root maggots, cutworms, snail and slug eggs, and other pests; some climb trees to capture armyworms or tent caterpillars. Large ground beetle populations build up in orchards with undisturbed groundcovers and in gardens under stone pathways or in semipermanent mulched beds.

**Rove Beetles** These small to medium, elongated insects with short, stubby top wings look like earwigs without pincers. Many species are decomposers of manure and plant material; others are important predators of pests such as root maggots that spend part of their life in the soil.

**Other Beetles** Other beneficial beetles

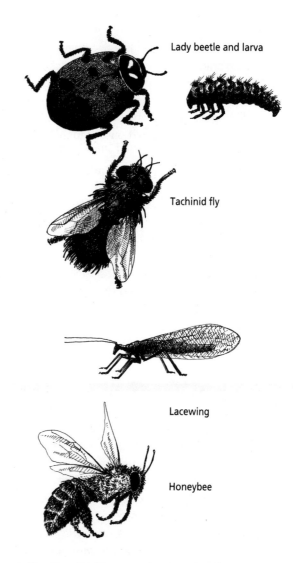

Lady beetle and larva

Tachinid fly

Lacewing

Honeybee

**Insect allies.** Beneficial insects such as lacewings, honeybees, lady beetles, and tachinid flies are at the heart of a good OPM plan and are the best and most economical way for gardeners to control pests.

include hister beetles, tiger beetles, and fireflies (really beetles). Both larvae and adults of these beetles eat insect larvae, slugs, and snails.

**Tachinid Flies** These large, bristly, dark gray flies place their eggs or larvae on cutworms, caterpillars, corn borers, stinkbugs, and other pests. Tachinid flies are important natural suppressors of tent caterpillars or armyworms.

**Syrphid Flies**  These black-and-yellow or black-and-white striped flies (also called flower or hover flies) are often mistaken for bees or yellow jackets. They lay their eggs in aphid colonies; the larvae feed on the aphids. Don't mistake the larvae—unattractive gray or translucent sluglike maggots—for small slugs.

**Aphid Midges**  Aphid midge larvae are tiny orange maggots that are voracious aphid predators. The aphid midge is available from commercial insectaries for use in the garden, greenhouse, and yard.

**Dragonflies**  Often called "darning needles," the dragonflies and their smaller cousins, the damselflies, scoop up mosquitoes, gnats, and midges, cramming their mouths with prey as they dart in zigzag patterns around marshes and ponds.

**Lacewings**  The brown or green alligator-like larvae of several species of native lacewings prey upon a variety of small insects, including aphids, scale insects, small caterpillars, and thrips. Adult lacewings are delicate, $\frac{1}{2}$- to 1-inch green or brown insects with large, transparent wings marked with a characteristic fine network of veins. They lay pale green oval eggs, each at the tip of a long, fine stalk, along the midrib of lettuce leaves or other garden plants. Lacewings are produced commercially for release in home gardens.

**True Bugs**  True bug is the scientifically correct common name for a group of insects. This group includes several pest species, but there are many predatory bugs that attack soft-bodied insects such as aphids, beetle larvae, small caterpillars, pear psylla, and thrips. Assassin bugs, ambush bugs, damsel bugs, minute pirate bugs, and spined soldier bugs are valuable wild predators in farm systems.

## ENCOURAGING BENEFICIALS

Attracting and conserving natural enemies of insect pests is an important part of managing your garden organically. The best way to protect beneficial insects is to avoid using toxic sprays or dusts in the garden. Even botanical insecticides kill beneficial species, so use them only when absolutely necessary to preserve a crop—and then only on the plants being attacked. Be careful when you handpick or spray pest insects, or you may end up killing beneficial insects by mistake. While many beneficials are too small to be seen with the unaided eye, be sure you can identify the larger common beneficials. For illustrations of lacewings, tachinid flies, and lady beetles, see the illustration on page 119.

You can make your yard and garden a haven

---

### ❀ Beneficial Borders

At the Rodale Institute Research Center in Kutztown, Pennsylvania, researchers have studied beneficial insect habitats. They recommend planting the following plants in and around your garden beds and borders to attract and nurture beneficial insects:

Buckwheat (*Fagopyrum esculentum*)

Caraway (*Carum carvi*)

Common tansy (*Tanacetum vulgare*)

Crimson clover (*Trifolium incarnatum*)

Dill (*Anethum graveolens*)

Fennel (*Foeniculum vulgare*)

Hardy marguerite (*Anthemis tinctoria* 'Kelwayi')

Lemon-scented marigold (*Tagetes tenuifolia* 'Lemon Gem')

Spearmint (*Mentha spicata*)

White clover (*Trifolium repens*)

'White Sensation' cosmos (*Cosmos bipinnatus* 'White Sensation') for beneficials by taking simple steps to provide them with food, water, and shelter. The idea of gardening to *attract* insects may seem odd, but in the case of beneficial insects, this companion planting technique can really pay off. Although some beneficials feed on pests, host plants provide food and shelter during some or all of their life cycle.

Beneficial insects have short mouthparts. They can't reach deeply into flowers for food. Plants with numerous small flowers, containing easy-to-reach pollen and nectar, provide the necessary high-protein and high-sugar meals

that maintain beneficial insect populations.

Help beneficial insects get a jump on early spring aphid activity by planting gazanias, calendulas, or other small-flowered plants that will grow in your area despite early-season cool weather. Beneficial insects need a series of blossoms to sustain them from spring until fall.

Herbs such as fennel, dill, anise, and coriander are carrot-family members that produce broad clusters of small flowers attractive to beneficials. Grow these culinary items near your vegetables to keep parasitic wasps nearby. Composite flowers such as sunflowers, zinnias, and

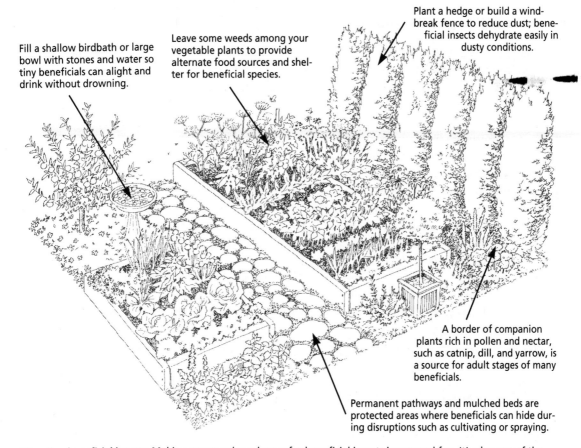

Fill a shallow birdbath or large bowl with stones and water so tiny beneficials can alight and drink without drowning.

Leave some weeds among your vegetable plants to provide alternate food sources and shelter for beneficial species.

Plant a hedge or build a windbreak fence to reduce dust; beneficial insects dehydrate easily in dusty conditions.

A border of companion plants rich in pollen and nectar, such as catnip, dill, and yarrow, is a source for adult stages of many beneficials.

Permanent pathways and mulched beds are protected areas where beneficials can hide during disruptions such as cultivating or spraying.

**Attracting beneficial insects.** Making your garden a haven for beneficial insects is easy and fun. It's also one of the cheapest and most environmentally sound ways to help prevent insect pests from getting the upper hand on your food crops and ornamentals.

asters also attract beneficials and have a longer season of bloom than carrot-family herbs.

Use this list of plants and the beneficials they attract to lure such insects to your garden:

Angelica (*Angelica archangelica*); lady beetles, lacewings

Baby-blue-eyes (*Nemophila menziesii*); syrphid flies

Candytuft (*Iberis* spp.); syrphid flies

Evening primrose (*Oenothera biennis*); ground beetles

Goldenrod (*Solidago* spp.); lady beetles,

predaceous beetles, parasitic wasps

Morning-glory (*Ipomoea purpurea*); lady beetles

Yarrow (*Achillea* spp.); bees, parasitic wasps, hover flies

## BUYING BENEFICIAL INSECTS

Before ordering beneficial insects, make sure you identify the target pest because most predators or parasites attack only a particular species or group of pests. Find out as much as you can by reading or talking to suppliers before buying beneficials. You'll find a summary of commercially available beneficials listed in "Beneficial Bugs to Buy" on the opposite page.

Once you receive your order, don't open the package unprepared. There may be insects loose inside the container. Read the directions on the label for handling and releasing: Every species is unique and must be treated differently.

Shipping and being confined in packaging is stressful for insects. Release the beneficials in your garden or greenhouse as soon as you can after they arrive. If you can't release the insects right away, keep them cool (usually 45° to 50°F). The door shelf of a refrigerator is suitable for storing most species. Don't keep them in the packaging for more than 24 hours.

Get a good look at the beneficials before releasing them so that you'll be able to recognize them in the garden. You don't want to kill them by mistake later on, thinking them to be pests. A magnifying glass is useful for seeing tiny parasitic wasps and predatory mites. Release some of the insects directly on or near the infested plants; distribute the remainder as evenly as possible throughout the rest of the surrounding area.

Once you have let out your hired killers, give them time to become established; it usually takes two to five weeks before there is an obvious effect on the pests. The key to remember is

### All-Star Spiders and Mites

Cars, cigarettes, and high-fat diets kill far more people every year than U.S. spiders have in a whole century. Yet more people panic at the sight of a spider than at more legitimate threats.

It's unfortunate that so many people are scared of spiders because they are some of the best pest predators around. We are most familiar with spiders that spin webs, but there are many other kinds. Some spin thick silk funnels, some hide in burrows and snatch insects that wander too close, while others leap on their prey using a silk thread as a dragline.

Mites are other predators worth having around. Predatory mites are extremely small. Many native species are found in trees, shrubs, and surface litter. Phytoseiid mites control many kinds of plant-feeding mites, such as spider mites, rust mites, and cyclamen mites. Some also prey on thrips and other small pests. There are many families of soil-dwelling mites that eat nematodes, insect eggs, fungus gnat larvae, or decaying organic matter.

# Beneficial Bugs to Buy

Many species of beneficial insects and mites are now available from commercial insectaries. The following list includes those that are effective for release in home greenhouses or gardens.

| Beneficial Species | Pests Controlled | Notes and Tips |
|---|---|---|
| **INSECTS** | | |
| **Aphid midge** (*Aphidoletes aphidimyza*) | Aphids, many species | Release 3–5 pupae per plant; 2 releases may provide better results. Good in greenhouses, shade trees, orchards, gardens, rose bushes. |
| **Braconid wasp** (*Aphidius matricariae*) | Green peach and apple aphids | Buy the minimum order for a garden. Plant parsley-family flowers to provide a food source. |
| **Convergent lady beetle** (*Hippodamia convergens*) | Aphids | Release minimum order in greenhouses with screened vents; will hibernate in cool greenhouses. |
| **Lacewings** (*Chrysoperla carnea, Chrysoperla rufilabrus*) | Any small, soft pests including aphids, thrips | Shipped as eggs; distribute widely through garden; apply 1–3 eggs per plant. |
| **Mealybug destroyer** (*Cryptolaemus montrouzieri*) | Mealybugs | Use in greenhouses or cage on houseplants; use 2–5 per plant. Nymphs look like mealybugs. |
| **Minute pirate bug** (*Orius tristicolor*) | Thrips, mites | Release 1–3 per plant. Plant pollen-rich flowers to entice them to stay in your garden. |
| **Spined soldier bug** (*Podisus maculiventris*) | Colorado potato beetle, Mexican bean beetle | Try releases of 5 per square yard; similar in appearance to stink bugs. |
| **NON-INSECTS** | | |
| **Predatory mite** (*Geolaelaps=Hypoaspis* spp.) | Fungus gnats, thrips | Release a minimum order to establish population early in season; good in greenhouses or on houseplants or ornamentals. |
| **Predatory mite** (*Phytoseiulus persimilis*) | Spider mites | Release 2–5 per plant, once, in greenhouses or on strawberries or houseplants; survive best in moderate temperatures (65°–75°F). |
| **Western predatory mite** (*Metaseiulus occidentalis*) | European red mite | Release 50–100 mites per tree to establish population, 1,000 per tree to control outbreaks; also useful on strawberries. |

that biological controls provide a long-term solution to pest problems, not a quick fix.

## IDENTIFYING BENEFICIAL ANIMALS

Menacing their friends with a shovel while shouting threats is not a common quirk of gardeners. But even mild-mannered folks get violent when they find bats, snakes, spiders, or skunks in their yards. However, these animals really are a gardener's friends because they eat insects, rodents, and other garden pests.

These helpful animals have gotten bad press over the years. A lot of people blame the wrong animal for damage. Skunks are often blamed for raccoon damage, moles for mouse damage, and so on. It's hard to tell the difference, so don't be too quick to condemn animals you don't like.

**Birds** Birds are most gardeners' favorite visitors, with their cheerful songs, sprightly manners, and colorful plumage. But birds are also among nature's most efficient insect predators, making them valuable garden allies. In an afternoon, one diminutive house wren can snatch up more than 500 insect eggs, beetles, and grubs. Given a nest of tent caterpillars, a Baltimore oriole will wolf down as many as 17 of the pests per minute. More than 60 percent of the chickadee's winter diet is aphid eggs. And the swallow lives up to its name by consuming massive quantities of flying insects—by one count, more than 1,000 leafhoppers in 12 hours.

Unless your property is completely bare, at least some birds will visit with no special encouragement from you. Far more birds, however, will come to your yard and garden if you take steps to provide their four basic requirements: food, water, cover, and a safe place in which to raise a family. Robins, nuthatches, hummingbirds, titmice, bluebirds, mockingbirds, cardinals, and various sparrows are among the most common garden visitors.

**Bats** With the exception of Batman, bats are reviled. They supposedly tangle in long hair, suck blood, and spread rabies. This is largely nonsense. Bats have no interest in human hair, and North American bats eat bugs and sometimes fruit, but no blood.

As for rabies, scientists once blamed bats for much of the spread of the disease but have since decided that was an overreaction. Only about 1 percent of bats get the disease themselves, and far fewer pass it on to humans. In 30 years of record keeping, only 12 to 15 cases of human rabies have been traced to bats. Most of these incidents could have been avoided: The victim was not attacked by a swooping bat, but instead picked up a diseased bat flapping around on the ground. To avoid a bite, don't handle bats

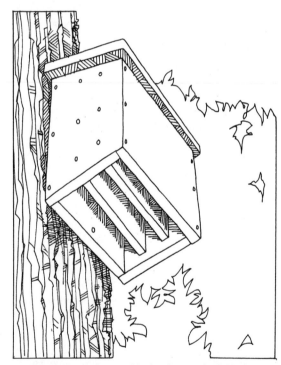

**Bat house.** From the outside, bat houses look like bird houses, but instead of using a door in the front, bats fly in and out through the bottom. They cling to the partitions inside to roost.

bare-handed. If you must move them, use a shovel.

Healthy bats perform astonishing feats in the air, catching insects with their wings. The little brown bat, a common U.S. species, eats moths, caddis flies, midges, beetles, and mosquitoes. Big colonies of bats, like the Mexican free-tails that cluster in groups of 20 million, can catch 100,000 pounds of bugs in a night.

One way to attract bats is to put up a bat house, a wooden box like a flattened birdhouse with an entrance slot in the bottom. You can buy bat houses or make your own. Make the entrance slot of your homemade bat house ¾ inch wide. Scribe grooves in the inside back wall about ¹⁄₁₆ inch deep and ½ inch apart so the bats can hang on. Fasten it 15 to 20 feet above the ground on the east or southeast side of a building. Then be patient. If there are many roosts available in the neighborhood, bats may take several years to move into yours.

**Snakes**  Of the 115 species of snakes in North America, only 4 kinds are poisonous: rattlesnakes, copperheads, coral snakes, and cottonmouths, also called water moccasins. Most of the snakes that find their way to a backyard will bite only if handled or stepped on, and even then the bite is harmless. In fact, garden pests, especially insects and rodents, are the real prey of snakes.

Beneficial backyard snakes include the common garter snake, eastern ribbon snake, western terrestrial garter snake, green or grass snake, and brown snake, all of which eat slugs, snails, and insects. The corn snake, black rat snake, and milk snake eat mice and rats. Most of these beneficial snakes are beautiful, too.

How can you tell whether a snake is poisonous? Rattlers, copperheads, and cottonmouths are all thick-bodied snakes with large, triangular heads. A rattlesnake will rattle a warning if threatened. The position of the bands on the

red, black, and yellow coral snake tells its story: "Red next to yellow kills a fellow."

If you don't like the idea of snakes patrolling your garden, take a few simple precautions. First, don't mulch your plots. Mulch provides shelter and attracts mice, a favored food. Keep your yard cleaned up and stack wood away from the house: Cordwood, junk, brush piles, and other debris will attract snakes to your yard. So will dog food or cat food set outdoors and left unattended.

**Skunks**  Around the beginning of the twentieth century, hops growers in New York State pushed for regulations protecting, of all things, the skunk. The growers claimed that skunks were controlling the dreaded hop grub. Modern gardeners have been less enthusiastic, since in addition to spraying, skunks dig holes in lawns. Actually, the skunks are digging for grubs of Japanese beetles and other pests.

Skunk texts state that the animals take alarm at menaces within 25 feet and that they can spray accurately at 12 to 15 feet. Yet skunks seem inclined to mind their own business and ignore all but loud, blatant menaces like cars and charging dogs.

The bigger concern with skunks is rabies. They're the number one carriers of the disease, followed by raccoons. Stay away from skunks that seem disoriented or too bold, and have your pets vaccinated.

**Toads**  Like ladybugs and earthworms, toads are humble heroes in the garden. One toad will eat 10,000 to 20,000 insects a year (that's 50 to 100 every night from spring until fall hibernation). Toads clean up slugs, flies, grubs, wood lice, cutworms, grasshoppers, and anything else that's smaller (and slower) than they are. And unlike many part-time garden allies, toads won't do an about-face and head for your vegetables and flowers as dessert.

To encourage toads to make your garden

Plastic bucket

Ceramic pot

**Give a toad a home.** To make a toad house out of a plastic bucket, turn it upside down and cut a toad-sized archway at the base. Put the shelter in a moist place out of the sun, and throw a little soil up around the sides to keep it anchored. Broken ceramic flower pots can be used in the same way.

their home, provide shelter and water, and, above all, use only the least-toxic organic pesticides. Toads like to live in places that are fairly light, humid, and out of the wind; you might find them in a rock garden or an old stone wall. Make your own shelters by digging shallow depressions in the garden (just a few inches deep) and loosely covering them with boards. (Leave the toad room to get in!) A plant saucer

or ground-level birdbath will provide water for your toads. Set it near rocks or plants where the toads can take shelter from predators. Once a toad has found your garden, it may live there for decades. Remember, too, that toads, like frogs, lay their eggs in ponds. Adding a water garden to your yard may provide a breeding ground for future generations of toads.

## BIOLOGICAL SPRAYS AND DUSTS

Biological insecticides kill insect pests without harming the environment. While they may not work as quickly as some chemical sprays and dusts do, they are effective, with virtually no harmful side effects.

**Microbial Insecticides** Microbial insecticides cause pests to get sick. Just like people, insects sometimes get diseases caused by bacteria, fungi, viruses, and other microorganisms. Microbial insecticides make use of these often highly specific insect diseases.

BT (*Bacillus thuringiensis*) bacteria produce crystals and spores that paralyze the digestive tract of certain insect larvae. BT products are nontoxic to mammals, are specific to the target pest, do not harm beneficial insects, and may be used right up to harvest. There are several BT varieties. BTK (*B.t.* var. *kurstaki*) controls cabbage looper, cabbageworm, tomato hornworm, fruitworms, European corn borer, and similar larvae. BTSD (*B.t.* var. *san diego*) controls small larvae of the Colorado potato beetle. BTI (*B.t.* var. *israelensis*) controls mosquitoes, black flies, and fungus gnats.

Milky disease (*Bacillus popilliae* and *B. lentimorbus*) infects the grubs of the Japanese beetle and its close relatives. The disease will persist in the soil for many years.

*Nosema locustae* provides long-term control of grasshoppers. About half the grasshoppers that eat the bait containing the organisms will die within three to four weeks. Surviving grasshoppers will infect the following year's generations.

**Beneficial Nematodes**   Some nematodes parasitize larvae and grubs. They attack an insect and release bacteria that paralyze and kill the insect within 2 to 4 days. The nematode then feeds on the dead insect and reproduces rapidly. About 10 to 20 days later, huge numbers of nematodes leave the dead insect in search of new victims. Their larvae can survive for long periods in the soil, but for the greatest effect you need to release more each year. Because nematodes perish in sunlight or dry places, they are most useful against pests in soil or hidden locations. Use a syringe or an oil can to inject nematodes into borer holes.

Some interesting new insecticides make use of toxins produced by naturally occurring organisms. Avermectins are derived from the antibiotics made by a common soil bacterium, *Streptomyces avermitilis*. Thuringiensin is derived from the BT toxins, which seem to have very low toxicity to animals but are toxic to

some degree to a wide range of insects and mites—including beneficial ones. More research is needed to determine the side effects that new pesticides like these may have and whether they have a place in organic pest control.

**Other Controls**   Biological fungicides and herbicides are currently being researched and tested. Here's what you may soon be hearing about:

**Microbial fungicides:** Certain harmless fungi can be used to exclude disease-causing organisms. Binab T, a mixture of beneficial fungi, is painted on fresh tree wounds to prevent decay. Development of these highly specific fungicides is an active area of research.

**Biological herbicides:** Researchers are looking for specific insects that eat, and microbial diseases that kill, problem weeds. Watch for these products in the future.

# PHYSICAL CONTROLS

Physical controls either keep pests from reaching your plants or remove pests from plants. These controls include old-fashioned hand-weeding and modern insect traps.

## KEEP OUT PESTS WITH BARRIERS

Barriers are among the most effective ways to prevent pest damage because they stop the pests from reaching the crop in the first place. Deny larger animal pests access to your garden riches with fences, barriers, repellents, and scare tactics.

**Floating Row Covers**   Floating row covers of spunbonded polypropylene material were introduced to improve plant growth and extend the growing season. They have proven to be excellent barriers to such insect pests as carrot rust flies, cabbage maggots, flea beetles, and Mexican bean beetles. They also stop many pests whose feeding habits transmit plant diseases. Row covers also help to frustrate some

---

 **BT Rule of Thumb**

When is the best time to apply *Bacillus thuringiensis* (BT) to pest-infested plants? "Wait until the caterpillars are just big enough to eat a hole through a leaf," says Linda Gilkeson, Ph.D., the IPM Coordinator for the British Columbia Ministry of Environment. "If you spray when they're teeny, they probably won't eat enough BT to kill themselves. But if they're able to bite through the leaf, they're more likely to ingest enough to kill them. Also, you won't have to be super careful to spray the underside of every single leaf, because the pests will be chewing both sides anyway."

small animals and birds.

Cover newly seeded beds or pest-free transplants with row covers, leaving plenty of slack in the material to allow for growth. Be sure to bury the edges in the soil or seal them in some other way. Otherwise, pests will sneak in and thrive in the protected environment.

You can leave row covers over some crops, such as carrots or onions, all season. Uncover other crops, such as beans or cabbage, once the plants are well grown or the generation of pests is past. Plants such as squash that require pollination by insects must be either uncovered when they start to flower or hand-pollinated. In a hot climate you may have to remove covers to prevent excessive heat buildup.

**Fences and Netting**  These barriers help keep out animals and birds who want to make a meal of your garden. See "Using Fencing" on page 146 for specific ways to frustrate hungry moochers.

**Cutworm Collars**  These collars fit around transplant stems to protect them from nocturnal cutworm raids. To make collars, cut strips of lightweight cardboard about 8 inches × 2½ inches, overlap the ends to make a tube, and fasten with tape. Or cut sections of cardboard tube to similar dimensions. When transplanting, slip a collar over each plant and press it into the soil around the stem so about half of the collar is below the soil line.

**Root Fly Barriers**  Tar-paper squares are an old-fashioned and effective barrier to cabbage root flies, preventing them from laying their eggs around the roots of cabbage-family plants.

Cut tar paper into 6- to 8-inch squares and make a small X-shaped cut in the center of each. Slide the square over the plant and flat against the soil, press the center flaps firmly around the stem, and anchor the square with pebbles.

**Tree Bands**  Tree bands are effective against pests that can't fly, such as snails, slugs, ants,

and gypsy moth caterpillars. Some prevent pests from crossing; others actually trap pests.

Make cloth tree bands from strips of heavy cotton cloth or burlap about 15 inches wide, and long enough to form a generous overlap when they are wrapped around the trunk. Tie the band to the trunk with a string around the middle of the cloth, then pull the top section down over the lower half to make a dead end for creatures climbing up the tree. Check daily and destroy any pests trapped in the material.

Make corrugated cardboard tree bands by wrapping long strips around the trunk several times, with exposed ridges facing in, and tying snugly with string. These bands attract codling-moth caterpillars looking for a sheltered place to spin their cocoons. Check for and destroy cocoons weekly.

**Sticky Tree Bands**  When pests try to cross sticky bands, they get caught on them and eventually die. Paint a 3-inch band of sticky compound all the way around the trunk of mature trees, reapplying as needed. Younger trees may be damaged by the compound, so for them, wrap a strip of fabric tightly around the trunk and cover that with a strip of plastic wrap. Apply the sticky compound to the plastic wrap. When the barrier loses effectiveness, replace the plastic.

**Copper Barriers**  Strips of copper sheet metal make an excellent and permanent barrier against slugs and snails. Fasten them around the trunks of trees and shrubs, wrap them around legs or edges of greenhouse benches, or use them to edge garden beds. Be sure that there are no alternate routes over the strips for slugs to get to the plants: Pull or cut back leaning or overhanging weeds and plants.

To install a copper barrier around a garden bed, press the edge of a 3- to 4-inch-wide strip about 1 inch into the soil around the entire perimeter of the bed. Bend the top edge out-

## Homemade Barriers

There's no limit to the ingenious devices you can buy or make that will protect your plants from pests. Barriers are great organic controls. They are simple to use and quite effective, and they generally pose no hazard to you or the environment. Try these techniques to keep pests from harming your plants.

**Tuck in row covers:** Floating row covers made of super-light spunbonded polypropylene are popular among gardeners. These inexpensive, gauzy barriers keep pests off plants while allowing light and moisture to pass through. And they're easy to use: You just drape the fabric over your crops and tuck in the edges. Weighting down the edges with rocks is not quite good enough, though. Even the smallest opening between the soil and row cover will be found and exploited by pests. So seal your row covers by pushing the edges of the fabric into the soil, then patting the dirt down. (The soil in the bed to be covered should be moist, but not wet.) Water plants after the cover is installed.

**Hang 'em high:** After a heavy rain, row covers can mat down and ruin plants. Here's how to make a simple support system for covering small seedlings and keeping out pests:

1. Cut several 5-foot lengths of medium-gauge wire. (This assumes your garden beds are about 4 feet wide. Use less or more wire for narrower or wider beds.)

2. Make wire arches over the bed by sticking the ends of the pieces of wire into each side of the bed. Position the arches about 2 feet apart.

3. Pound an 18-inch-long stake into the ground at each end of your planting row.

4. Tie string to the stakes, and extend it along the row over the tops of the arches.

You can make a similar support system with wire coat hangers, and save yourself the cost of the wire. Here's how:

1. Bend several wire coat hangers by pulling outward at the top and bottom of each to form a diamond shape. Straighten the hooks.

2. Pound an 18-inch-long stake into the ground at each end of your planting row.

3. Tie twine to one of the stakes, then thread the hanger hoops bottom-side up onto the twine. Tie the opposite end of the twine to the other stake.

4. Space the suspended hanger hoops at equal intervals along the row, and push the straightened hooks into the ground.

5. Lay the row cover over the hoops and anchor the sides with soil.

**Pull on the panty hose:** Wrapping cantaloupes and other melons in "socks" made of old panty hose is an old and reliable pest-protection trick. You can use panty hose to keep bugs off almost any vegetable crop.

If you have a small corn patch, you can cover every ear. Panty hose works great on crops such as cabbages, cauliflower, cucumbers, and squash because as they grow, the material expands right along with them.

To make a plant protector, cut a section from the leg of old nylons or panty hose and sew or tie off one end. Then slip this nylon sack over the vegetable or fruit, pull it tight, and tie the other end shut.

ward at a right angle to form a ½-inch lip. Eliminate slugs from inside the barrier by using slug traps and by leaving the soil bare as long as possible.

**Dehydrating Dust Barriers**  Sharp dusts such as a layer of cinders or diatomaceous earth (DE) scratch insects and cause them to die from dehydration. Dusts also act as repellents, although a hungry slug will cross a dust barrier. Dusts work best when dry; renew after a rain.

To deter cabbage root maggots from laying eggs, spread a 6-inch circle of wood ashes, talc, DE, or lime around the stem.

Paint a thick slurry made from ¼ pound DE, 1 teaspoon soap, and water on tree bark to repel ants and to deter adult borers from laying their eggs in the bark.

## REMOVAL

Removing insects or diseased plants is often an effective way to prevent problems from getting worse. For some pests, it's the only control method needed.

**Weeds**  Hand-pulling and hoeing weeds are effective physical controls. Be especially vigilant in not allowing weeds in or near your garden to set seed. Tilling and mowing can help, but don't till perennial weeds that re-grow from small sections of root. For more information on discouraging weeds, see "Controlling Weeds" on page 164.

**Insects**  Handpicking insects is an effective, though rather tedious, way to control light or moderate infestations of large, easy-to-see caterpillars, such as tomato hornworms or cabbage loopers. Dig cutworms out of their daytime hiding places at the base of plants. Pick and destroy leaves with leafminer mines. Scrape gypsy moths' egg masses off tree trunks. Pry newly hatched corn earworms out of the tips of corn ears before they can get very far into the cob.

Shaking pests from plants is a variation of handpicking and works especially well for heavy beetles, such as Japanese or Colorado potato beetles and plum curculios. Shake or beat them off the foliage onto a sheet of plastic, then pour them into a pail of soapy water.

A strong spray of water can physically injure aphids and knock them off plants. Spray plants in early morning or late afternoon to avoid scorching the leaves. If you have problems with diseases that thrive in wet conditions, you may want to choose another control method.

**Diseases**  Pulling up diseased plants or pruning off diseased shoots and disposing of them can be a good control method. Remove diseased weeds near the garden, too. Some plant diseases rely on alternate hosts for part of their life cycle. Removing the alternate hosts within a certain distance of your garden can reduce or eliminate disease problems.

Dispose of diseased material by placing it in the center of a hot compost pile, burying it, burning it, or putting it in sealed containers for disposal with household trash. See Chapter 3 for directions for making a hot compost pile.

## TRAPS

Traps are used to help control insect and animal pests. They generally consist of one or more attractive components or lures (usually a color, odor, or shape) and a trapping component (usually sticky glue, a liquid, or a cage). Traps are used in one of two ways: to catch so many individuals that the local population is too low to do significant crop damage, or to monitor the emergence or arrival of a pest so that other controls can be timed to have the most impact.

When using traps to control pests directly, judge their effectiveness by the reduction in plant damage, not just by the number of dead insects in the trap. If damage does not decrease, try other controls. Monitoring traps are useful for timing release of beneficial insects, such as

## Controlling Slugs and Snails

Slugs and garden snails have an appetite for so many fruits, vegetables, and ornamentals that they are among the most damaging home garden pests. They need moist surroundings and will hibernate during dry periods. They hide under rocks, garden debris, and mulches during the day. At night, they emerge and chew large, ragged holes in leaves. Damage usually is worst in spring, when soil is moist and plants are young. These pests are managed most effectively by using a wide variety of controls. To control slugs and snails, follow these guidelines:

■ Create a diverse garden ecosystem to encourage biological controls. Ants, beetle grubs, earwigs, flies, birds, snakes, toads, and turtles prey on slugs.

■ Armed with a flashlight, handpick slugs and snails from plants at night and drop them into a bucket of soapy water.

■ Set out boards or inverted clay flowerpots as traps. Check the traps daily and kill the slugs or snails that may be hidden there.

■ Sprinkle dry soil or diatomaceous earth around the stem bases of your plants.

■ Make a slug-proof barrier around garden beds by edging them with copper-based strips. See "Copper Barriers" on page 128 for directions.

■ Attract slugs and snails with any fermenting or yeasty liquid. See "Food Lures" on page 132 for directions.

■ Put sandpaper collars around your plants. Cut circles from sheets of sandpaper, or simply recycle used sandpaper discs from orbital sanders. Cut a slit to the center of each circle, and slip the collars around the stems, laying them on the ground.

Slug eggs in soil

Slug

Snail

**Slugs and snails.** Mulches and plants with low-growing leaves, like these hostas, provide shady hiding places for slugs and snails. They rasp large holes in leaves and stems and leave a characteristic shiny slime trail. There are a variety of controls for these pests, including handpicking, barriers, and traps.

*Trichogramma* wasps, or for timing a spray application to hit the peak pest population.

**Colored Sticky Traps**  Colored sticky traps are useful to control or monitor a variety of species. Bright blue traps are suitable for monitoring flower thrips. White traps attract tarnished plant bugs, but they also attract beneficial flies, so should be used only early in the season. Yellowish orange traps lure carrot rust flies. Yellow sticky traps are effective controls for whiteflies, fungus gnats, and imported cabbageworms. However, they work only as monitors for thrips and aphids.

**Apple Maggot Traps**  Red spheres covered with sticky glue attract female apple maggot flies and are often the only control necessary in a home orchard. Starting in mid-June, hang one trap in a dwarf tree and up to six traps in a full-sized tree, renewing the glue every two weeks. Some research shows that attaching an apple-scented lure to the trap increases its attractiveness, but not necessarily to the target pest— other related species may gum up the trap instead.

**Cherry Fruit Fly Traps**  Yellow sticky traps catch cherry fruit flies if a small bottle of equal parts water and household ammonia or a commercial apple maggot lure is hung up with the trap. Hang one trap in each tree or four traps in a small orchard, and renew the sticky glue and the ammonia bait as necessary.

**Yellow Water Traps**  Fill a bright yellow pan or tray with water to which a small amount of liquid soap has been added to attract and drown aphids. These traps are effective monitors but not controls. They also attract tiny beneficials; remove the traps if this happens.

**Traps with Pheromone Lures**  Pheromones are chemical cues that insects use to communicate with others of their species. Sex pheromones are wafted into the air by females to attract males, who follow the direction of the odor until they find a mate. Synthetic pheromones are available in long-lasting lures and are widely used in sticky traps to monitor pest populations, especially the various species of moths that attack fruit trees. When enough pheromone traps are used, they can control the population by trapping so many males that a significant portion of the females go unmated and don't lay eggs.

Commercial lures are long-lasting, and many are available in small quantities for home gardeners; these can be used in commercial traps or incorporated into homemade traps. Set out traps about two to three weeks before the target pest is expected to emerge; one trap is usually enough for a home orchard or garden. Check the traps daily or weekly; follow package directions.

Pheromones can also be used without traps to control pests. When large numbers of pheromone lures are put out, the air becomes saturated with aroma and males can't locate females to mate. Twist ties impregnated with pheromones are available for controlling oriental fruit moths and other pests.

**Food Lures**  Japanese beetles are attracted to a fermenting mush of mashed fruit and sugar water or wine, with some yeast to speed fermentation. See "Homemade Traps and Controls" on the opposite page for instructions for making food lure traps for these pesky insects. Japanese beetle traps are most effective if used over a wide area of a community and in conjunction with other controls.

Slugs and snails are attracted to stale beer, spoiled yogurt, or a mixture of yeast and water. Set out the bait in saucers or tuna cans, buried with the lip of the container level with the soil surface, so the pests fall in and drown. Put a cover with holes in it on the trap to keep rain from diluting the bait and to keep large animals from drinking it.

## Homemade Traps and Controls

Here are a few simple pest traps you can make:

**Sticky traps:** You can make sticky traps from wood, cardboard, or stiff plastic. Paint the base with a coat of primer and two coats of bright yellow or medium blue paint. Coat with a sticky compound using a paintbrush, or spread it on with a knife. Use stiff adhesives like Tanglefoot for large insects and thinner glues such as Stiky Stuff or STP oil treatment for small insects. Scrape off insects and recoat as needed. Plastic balls can be painted red to make apple maggot traps. Plastic soda bottles make good cherry fruit fly traps—paint the shoulders of the bottle yellow and fill the bottle with lure.

**Traps to use with pheromone lures:** You can make a simple trap from a 1-quart plastic ice-cream or yogurt container. Cut three large holes in the upper half of the sides. Paint the lid, or line it with cardboard to shade the lure. Tape a commercial lure to the inside of the lid. Fasten the trap to a sturdy stake. Fill the bottom half of the container with soapy water and snap on the lid, holding the lure.

**Japanese beetle traps:** Cut the necks off 1-gallon plastic jugs and fill one-third full with fermenting mixtures of water, sugar, crushed fruit, and yeast. Strain out the beetles regularly, and reuse the mixture.

**Wireworm traps:** Cut fresh potatoes in half and cut out the eyes. Poke a stick into each piece of potato to use as a handle. Early in the season, bury the traps 4 to 6 inches deep in the garden or flower bed, before seeds or tubers are planted, to attract wireworms. Every day, pull out the potatoes, using the sticks as handles, and shake off the wireworms into a bucket of soapy water. Reuse the same potato for a while, then replace with a new one. Use one potato trap for every square yard of soil.

**Wireworm spray:** Crush wireworms and add some water to make a bug-juice liquid. Strain and spray on affected crops.

**Cutworm bait:** Mix 1 pint of hardwood sawdust (not cedar or pine) with 1 pint of wheat bran and 1 quart of molasses. Slowly add cupfuls of water until the sawdust and bran are moist and all ingredients are well mixed. Spread a handful of bait around each transplant or sprinkle evenly on long rows of corn seedlings. Molasses attracts the cutworms to the sawdust and bran, which cakes on their bodies and prevents them from burrowing into the soil for protection from sun or birds. Destroy any cutworms you see on the ground each morning, and renew the bait after heavy rains. To increase the bait's effectiveness during the first few nights, add ½ cup of pyrethrum or rotenone, or 2 to 4 tablespoons of *Bacillus thuringiensis* (BT).

**Cutworm repellent:** Sprinkle a mixture of chopped wormwood leaves (*Artemisia* spp.) and sharp sand in a wide circle around the base of each plant.

**Cutworm collars:** Cut 2-inch-long sections from a paper towel tube or toilet paper tube. Slip one section over each small seedling and press the collar lightly into the soil. Or cut a strip of lightweight cardboard, curve it around the base of the seedling, and fasten the ends with a paper clip. Make the collar 2 to 3 inches tall and about 2 inches in diameter.

**Beetle brush-off:** Hold a large bucket under potato and tomato plants, and jostle the plants as you move down the row to release Colorado potato beetles. Once the bucket is full, fill it with soapy water to destroy the beetles.

**Food Traps** Control onion maggots by planting sprouted or shriveled onions between rows of onion seeds in early spring. The onion maggot flies lay their eggs in the soil nearby, and the maggots burrow into the trap onions. About two weeks after the trap onions sprout, pull and destroy them to prevent the next generation of flies from developing.

Reduce the number of wireworms in the soil before you plant—use fresh potato traps as described in "Homemade Traps and Controls" on page 133.

**Trap Crops** Plants that are more attractive to certain pests than the crop you want to protect are useful as trap crops. For example, dill or lovage lures tomato hornworms away from tomatoes, and early squash traps pickleworms before late melons are set out. Pull and destroy trap plants as soon as they are infested, or the pests may reproduce on the crop and thus provide a larger pest population.

## SOIL SOLARIZATION

Soil solarization is an effective way to control many soilborne problems. Covering the soil with clear plastic for one to two months can generate high enough temperatures in the top 6 to 12 inches of soil to kill pest insects, nematodes, weed seeds, and many disease organisms. This process has proven valuable for home gardeners because soilborne pests, particularly nematodes, accumulate in crops grown in the same place year after year. The beneficial effects seem to last for several seasons. The illustration on the oppposite page shows how to prepare a bed for solarizing.

# CHEMICAL CONTROLS

Chemical controls are your last resort, after a combination of cultural, biological, and physical controls have proved inadequate. In some cases,

one to two well-timed applications of an insecticide while the first generation of a pest is just emerging can reduce the problem to such an extent that no further applications are needed. Careful timing of applications helps make the best use of pesticides and can reduce overall use. Remember that these planned applications are only part of your complete management plan. In conjunction with cultural, biological, and physical controls, they bring down pests or diseases to acceptable levels.

Some organic pesticides are much less toxic than others to nontarget organisms. Always choose the least toxic but most effective method available. Botanical insecticides and copper and sulfur fungicides vary in their effectiveness against different pests. Choose the one best suited to each problem. For detailed information on specific chemical controls, see "Insecticides"on this page and "Fungicides" on page 139.

Botanical pesticides and naturally occurring minerals break down into more harmless compounds in a relatively short time. But remember: Some of them are very toxic to you and to other organisms at the time they are applied. Use them sparingly or as a last resort. Wear protective clothing, a face mask, and gloves when handling them. See "Pesticide Safety" on page 137 for more information on safety.

## INSECTICIDES

Insecticides kill insects. They're a quick and seemingly simple solution for pest problems in houses, office buildings, restaurants, farm fields, and backyard gardens. However, organic gardeners prefer to use control techniques that are less toxic and less environmentally damaging whenever possible for managing insect pests. Even botanical poisons—organically acceptable insecticides—pose environmental risks and should be used only when all other control methods fail.

The first step in controlling an insect problem is to identify the pest and learn about its life cycle. By identifying the times when the pest is most susceptible and how and where it lives, you can plan the best controls.

If you decide to apply an insecticide, always follow the appropriate safety precautions. The list of natural insecticides has grown long enough to be confusing even to experienced gardeners. Knowing how these substances work may help you decide when to use them, if at all.

The following list is arranged from least to most toxic. For maximum effect, be sure to spray both the upper and lower surfaces of the leaves. When using commercial products, follow the directions on the label. Do not mix pesticide products together or add activators or boosters unless the label directs you to do so.

**Pheromones** Pheromones are hormonelike chemicals produced and emitted by insects and other animals to communicate with other members of their species. They are highly specific and can attract insects from great distances. Pheromone products are available for many pests, including peachtree borers, codling moths, corn earworms, cabbage loopers, apple maggots, and Japanese beetles.

Traps baited with pheromones are used to keep track of specific pest populations. Small capsules containing pheromones are placed inside cardboard traps coated with a sticky material. The species attracted to the pheromone flies into the trap and gets caught in the glue. Gardeners and orchardists may also be able to control certain pests by hanging large numbers of traps. Pheromone lures without traps confuse pests and keep them from finding food or mates.

**Growth Regulators** Insect growth regulators (IGRs) are chemical mimics of insect hormones. IGRs disrupt feeding, development, or reproduction of a specific insect, and they present little risk to nontarget species. They are

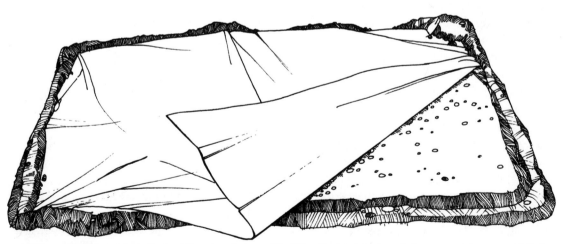

**Solarizing soil.** Midsummer is the best time to solarize soil to kill soilborne insects and disease organisms, especially in the North. Cultivate and remove crop residues from the soil, rake it smooth, and water it if it is dry. Dig a trench several inches deep around the bed, and spread thin (1 to 4 mils), clear plastic film over the bed. Press the plastic into close contact with the soil, and seal the edges by filling the trench with soil. Leave in place for one to two months, then remove the plastic.

currently available for controlling aphids, whiteflies, fleas, and fungus gnats. IGRs are synthetic compounds. While they appear to be free of side effects, more research is needed to determine what place they have in organic pest control.

**Insecticidal Oils** Petroleum and plant oils have long been used to kill eggs and immature stages of insects. Oils block the insect's supply of oxygen and are especially effective because they spread well over surfaces. Oils may also poison or repel some insects. They break down quickly and are more toxic to pests than to beneficial insects.

Dormant oils are heavy petroleum oils that can be sprayed on dormant orchard trees and ornamental plants to control overwintering stages of mites, scales, aphids, and other insects. Spray a 1 to 3 percent oil-and-water mixture when the air temperature is above 40°F. Certain plants such as Japanese maple are very sensitive and can be severely damaged by dormant oil. It also removes the blue "bloom" from blue spruce. Before spraying the whole plant, spray a small area and see if yellowing occurs.

Summer oils, also called superior or supreme oils, are lighter petroleum oils that contain fewer of the impurities that make dormant oils toxic to plants. Spray up to a 2 percent mixture of summer oil and water even on fully leafed plants as long as the air temperature is below 85°F and the plants are not drought- or heat-stressed. Summer oil controls aphids, spider mites, scales, psylla, mealybugs, and some caterpillars. It is slightly toxic to mammals and is registered for ornamental and greenhouse use. Oils may cause leaf damage to some plants under certain conditions. Spray a small area and wait a few days. If the plants are unharmed, spray thoroughly.

Vegetable oils provide similar control. Mix 1 cup of cooking oil with 1 tablespoon of liquid

soap. Use 2½ teaspoons per cup of water to spray.

**Diatomaceous Earth** Diatomaceous earth (DE) is a nontoxic mineral product mined from fossilized shell remains of an algae known as diatoms. This fine powder has microscopic sharp edges that pierce soft-bodied insects and cause them to dehydrate.

Apply natural-grade DE as a dust, preferably after a light rain so that it will stick better. Or to spray DE, mix 1 ounce of DE with ¼ teaspoon liquid soap and add 1 gallon of water. To protect trees and shrubs from caterpillar attack, paint a thicker mix on their trunks.

**Insecticidal Soaps** Insecticidal soaps are specially formulated solutions of fatty acids that kill insect pests such as aphids, mites, and whiteflies. Insecticidal soap is a contact insecticide that paralyzes insects, which then die of starvation. Spray plants every two to three days for two weeks for bad infestations. Mix with soft water. Soaps may damage plants if applied too strongly or if plants are drought- or heat-stressed. Soaps break down within one to two weeks.

Many organic gardeners use 1 to 3 teaspoons of household soap (not detergent) per gallon of water as a garden insecticide.

**Sulfur** You can use sulfur to control mites and chiggers. Sulfur is gentle on large predaceous insects but will kill tiny parasitic wasps.

**Neem Oil** Neem oil is extracted from the neem tree, *Azadirachta indica,* native to India. The oil is extracted from seed kernels, leaves, bark, flowers, and wood. Neem oil is a broad-spectrum insect poison, repellent, and feeding deterrent. It also stops or disrupts insect growth and sterilizes some species. Research is ongoing, but neem oil appears to be easy on beneficials and of very low toxicity to mammals.

Neem oil solution can be used as a spray to control many insects and as a soil drench to control soil stages of pests. Spray when the leaves will remain wet for as long as possible.

**Pyrethrins** Pyrethrins are derived from the flowers of pyrethrum daisies (*Chrysanthemum cinerariifolium* and *C. coccineum*). The dried flowers are finely ground to make an insecticidal dust. Pyrethrins are extracted from the dust and used in sprayable solutions. Pyrethrins attack an insect's central nervous system, providing the rapid knockdown that gives many gardeners a satisfying feeling of revenge. At low doses, however, insects may detoxify the chemical and recover. The addition of synthetic synergists, like piperonyl butoxide (PBO), prevents insects from detoxifying insecticides. Synergists may be toxic themselves, so you may wish to avoid products with them. Pesticide manufacturers have also created synthetic pyrethrin-like insecticides called pyrethroids. Check labels to be sure you're getting a plant-derived, organically acceptable product.

Pyrethrins are effective against a broad spectrum of pest insects, including flies, mosquitoes, and chewing and sucking insect pests. You can apply them up to one day before harvest because they break down rapidly in heat and light. Pyrethrins are moderately toxic to mammals and highly toxic to fish. Don't apply them around ponds or waterways.

Pyrethrins are available in many commercial dusts and sprays, some of which also contain soap and/or other natural insecticides. Apply pyrethrins in the early evening. Two applications two hours apart may provide better pest control.

**Rotenone** Rotenone is prepared from the roots of various South American legumes in the genus *Lonchocarpus*. Rotenone is a nonselective,

## ✿ Pesticide Safety

Some natural pesticides are very toxic, and any control can be damaging if not used properly. Even organically acceptable pesticides like rotenone and sulfur can harm your health or be caustic to your skin and eyes. Keep the following points in mind:

■ Keep all pesticides in original containers with product name and instructions. Read the label. Those marked "Danger" are super toxic, "Warning" very toxic, and "Caution" moderately or mildly toxic.

■ Store pesticides tightly closed, away from food, and out of reach of children.

■ Mix and apply exactly according to directions. Measure carefully, and keep a set of measures just for mixing pesticides.

■ Wear protective clothing when mixing, applying, and cleaning up. This may include a long-sleeved shirt and pants, rubber boots, rubber or other waterproof gloves, goggles, and a dust mask or respirator. Read the label for requirements.

■ Wash clothing, skin, containers, and sprayers thoroughly when cleaning up. Launder your clothing after each day of spraying, or discard heavily contaminated clothing. If possible, pre-rinse the clothes by hosing them off outdoors. Wash protective clothing separately from the rest of your family's laundry. Fill the washer with hot water and add ½ cup heavy-duty laundry detergent and ½ cup chlorine bleach. Rinse for two full warm cycles and hang outside to dry. Before doing normal laundry, run the washer through one cycle with water only.

■ Stay out of treated areas until spray is dry or dust has settled.

slow-acting nerve poison that paralyzes insects after they eat it. It is highly toxic to most beetles and other insects with chewing mouthparts. Use it to control flea beetles, aphids, Colorado potato beetles, cucumber beetles, and whiteflies. Rotenone is highly toxic to fish, birds, and pigs. It breaks down when exposed to air, sunlight, and water, losing its effect on insects in a week. Like pyrethrin products, some rotenone formulations may contain synthetic additives such as PBO. Rotenone is considered relatively nontoxic to humans, but some people are allergic to it. Wear a face mask and rubber gloves when using it, and choose a liquid formulation. Avoid using it around lakes and waterways.

Rotenone powder can be used for dusting or mixed with water to make a sprayable solution. It is also available mixed with other insecticides and/or fungicides as an all-purpose garden pesticide. One application should provide control. Reapply after one week if needed.

**Ryania** The South American shrub *Ryania speciosa* yields the insecticidal alkaloid ryanodyne. It is a contact and stomach poison that paralyzes insects, preventing them from feeding. It is a nonselective insecticide, but it is most toxic to the immature, wormlike stages of moths and butterflies and is easy on beneficial insects. Use it to control codling moths, cabbageworms, Japanese beetles, and Mexican bean beetles. Ryania is more stable in light and air than pyrethrins or rotenone. However,

---

 **Home-Brewed Pest Controls**

Organic gardeners have long relied on homemade sprays that are relatively safe to use and easy to prepare. Results from these "home remedies" aren't guaranteed, so monitor the plants after treating them. Here are some you may want to concoct:

**Bug juice:** Collect ½ cup of a specific pest and mash well. Mix with 2 cups of water, and strain. Mix ¼ cup of this bug juice and a few drops of soap with 2 cups of water, and spray. Don't make yourself sick, too! Use nonfood utensils and wear plastic gloves.

**Garlic oil:** Finely chop 10 to 15 garlic cloves and soak in 1 pint of mineral oil for 24 hours. Strain and spray as is, or dilute with water and add a few drops of soap.

**Hot-pepper spray:** Blend ½ cup of hot peppers with 2 cups of water. Strain and spray. Caution: Hot peppers burn skin and eyes.

**Killer cooking oil:** Combine 1 tablespoon of dishwashing liquid with 1 cup of vegetable oil.

Add 1 to 2½ teaspoons of the oil/detergent mix to 1 cup of water and spray on infested plants once every seven days.

**Firewater:** Mix two to four jalapeño, serrano, or habanero peppers, three cloves of garlic, and 1 quart of water in a blender, or chop the peppers and garlic and let them steep in a quart jar of water set in the sun for several days. Strain through cheesecloth. Spray as needed; repeat after rain.

**Alcohol spray:** Combine 1 to 2 cups of rubbing alcohol (isopropyl alcohol) with 1 quart of water. Test spray a small area on one plant. Wait a day to check for damage before spraying entire plants. Or add between ½ and 1 cup of rubbing alcohol to 1 quart of insecticidal soap or horticultural oil sprays to increase their effectiveness.

**Alcohol plant rub:** Soak a cotton ball in 70 percent rubbing alcohol solution to wipe scales off plants.

it is very water-soluble and is rapidly diluted by dew and rain. Ryania is moderately toxic to mammals.

Ryania powder is applied as a dust or dissolved in water as a spray. Two applications ten days apart should control most pests.

**Sabadilla** Sabadilla comes from the seeds of a South American lilylike plant, *Schoeno-caulon officinale*. Sabadilla is composed of a group of alkaloids. It is toxic to bees but easy on most other beneficials. Sabadilla is moderately toxic to mammals and irritates mucous membranes. Human poisoning symptoms include sneezing, retching, muscle spasms, and depressed heart rate and circulation, and they are slow to disappear. Sabadilla is used as a last-resort insecticide for hard-to-kill pests like squash bugs and thrips. Apply sabadilla dust to plants directly or mixed with water as a spray. Always wear protective clothing and equipment when applying sabadilla.

**Nicotine** Tobacco has been used as an insecticide since the late 1600s. Nicotine is the active ingredient in tobacco. It is extremely toxic to insects and humans. It is absorbed by plant leaves and remains toxic for several weeks, so use it on young plants and don't use it the last month before harvest. Nicotine is poisonous if swallowed or if it comes in contact with your skin. Always wear protective clothing and equipment when applying nicotine.

Tobacco dust is about 0.5 percent nicotine and is applied in its dry form. Nicotine sulfate, extracted from tobacco leaves, is diluted and used as a spray. Nicotine is effective against soil pests, like root aphids, and against many leaf-chewing insects.

## FUNGICIDES

Fungicide use dates back to the late 1800s, when sulfur was used to kill fungi and other disease-causing organisms on both plants and peo-ple. Organic gardeners use certain organic fungicides to help control disease problems, but they are a method of last resort.

Fungicides can be classified as protectants or

 **The Way to Spray**

Finding the right dust or spray for your pest-ridden plants is only the first step in pest control. The next step is actually applying the substance exactly where it's needed. For best results, choose an application method suited to the substance you are applying and to the size of the job. Here are some practical guidelines.

■ For small jobs, use a hand-held trigger sprayer. Keep one sprayer for nonpoisonous liquid sprays, like those made from soap, garlic, peppers, or kelp, and label a separate sprayer for biological or botanical pesticides. Remember to wear rubber gloves while applying biological or botanical controls.

■ For larger spray jobs, select a pressure sprayer that you can pressurize manually through pumping. Choose a sprayer large enough to handle the area you want to cover without frequent refilling. The more times you must refill the spray reservoir, the more often you will be exposed to the spray. Carefully clean and dry the nozzle and any filters after each use.

■ When spreading nonpoisonous dust, such as diatomaceous earth, punch small holes in the sides and bottom of a paper bag, place a cup of the dust inside, and shake it over the areas you want to treat. Or place the dust in an old sock, tie the end closed, and beat the sock above the plants with a stick or broom handle. Use caution, and wear protective gear to avoid inhaling dusts.

eradicants. A protectant fungicide stops disease organisms from infecting a plant. Eradicant fungicides can destroy disease organisms or inhibit their development after initial infection. Virtually all fungicides used by organic gardeners are protectants with little or no eradicant action. They must be applied before infection occurs and before symptoms appear. For example, once blackspot appears on roses, no amount of spraying will remove it.

Applying fungicides on a regular basis is often recommended to prevent disease. To use protectant fungicides efficiently, keep records of the disease problems that occur in your garden, or ask fellow gardeners what diseases to expect in your area and when to expect them. By learning about diseases common to your area, you can reduce fungicide use, spraying or dusting only during the seasons and weather conditions when infection is likely to occur.

Few fungicides are available to organic gardeners, and their drawbacks often outweigh their benefits. Rather than relying on fungicides, discourage diseases from developing by using preventive cultural practices and by keeping the garden clean. Choose less-susceptible or resistant cultivars of plants whenever possible. Accept some level of disease symptoms as tolerable, rather than striving for a 100 percent disease-free garden. For more about steps you can take to prevent and limit disease problems, see "Pest Problems" on page 110.

If you decide to apply a fungicide, select the least toxic substance that will prevent or control the problem. Always take appropriate safety precautions when applying fungicides.

The following listing of fungicides is arranged from least to most toxic.

**Microbial Fungicides**  These fungicides contain benign organisms that establish themselves on or in plants and prevent disease-producing organisms from gaining a foothold. For example, Binab T, a mixture of beneficial fungi, is painted on fresh tree wounds to prevent decay.

**Barriers**  A thorough spray of vegetable or light horticultural oil coats plant surfaces, acting as a barrier to infection. Oils seem to help prevent fungal rusts and mildews. For application rates, see "Insecticides" on page 134.

Antitranspirants such as Wilt-Pruf, designed to prevent leaves from losing moisture, may also prevent powdery mildew. Follow label directions, and don't treat heat- or drought-stressed plants.

**Plant Products**  Garlic appears to be a fungicide as well as an insecticide. Mix five to ten cloves with 1 pint of water in a blender, strain, and spray on plants. Horsetail (*Equisetum arvense*) infusion sprayed on plants may help prevent fungal diseases. For more information on making homemade sprays, see "Home-Brewed Pest Controls" on page 138.

Some research indicates that a compost tea spray may have possibilities for combating disease. Fungicides based on natural vitamins and amino acids also are being developed.

**Baking Soda**  Baking soda (sodium bicarbonate) prevents fungal spores from establishing themselves on plants and may even prevent established fungi from continuing to develop. While baking soda alone is effective, adding oil improves results. In tests on a variety of vegetables—including squash, cucumbers, melons, pumpkins, and tomatoes—a simple solution of baking soda, water, and horticultural oil was found to control powdery mildew, leaf blight, gummy stem, anthracnose, leaf spot, and even early blight on tomatoes.

To make your own "plant bicarb," mix 2 to 3 teaspoons of baking soda with 1 gallon of water, along with 2 or 3 tablespoons of SunSpray Ultrafine Oil (available from garden centers and mail-order suppliers). The oil helps the spray stick to the leaves, and it cleanses pathogens from the feeding parts of aphids that might dine on the infected leaves and then transmit the disease to other plants.

Use the spray as soon as you see any signs of fungal infection on a plant. Apply it once every five to seven days, making sure to cover the undersides of leaves. Continue the treatment as long as any signs of infection persist.

**Sulfur**   Direct contact with sulfur prevents the development of disease organisms. However, it also damages important soil microorganisms and beneficial insects and is moderately toxic to mammals, including humans. Apply sulfur sparingly, and always take appropriate safety precautions.

Both a plain spray mix of elemental sulfur and mixtures of sulfur with other substances are effective preventive fungicides. Powdered sulfur is almost insoluble in water. Wettable sulfur has been finely ground with a wetting agent and is easier to use. Liquid sulfur is the easiest to dissolve. Sulfur also can be applied as a dust or as a fumigant.

Adding lime to sulfur increases its effectiveness as a fungicide. Lime allows the sulfur to penetrate leaves and kill recently germinated disease spores. However, lime sulfur sprays are more likely to damage plant tissue than are plain sulfur sprays.

At temperatures above 85°F, sulfur becomes highly phytotoxic and will injure plants. Combining sulfur and oil also causes damage to growing plants, though a combination of oil and lime sulfur is safe to use on dormant trees.

**Copper**   Copper is a powerful, nonspecific fungicide that kills disease organisms. It damages beneficial soil microorganisms and beneficial insects and is more toxic to plants than sulfur is. Copper sulfate has been used as an herbicide to control annual weeds. Repeated applications of any copper product will stunt

plants. Copper sulfate is classified as very toxic to humans. Organic gardeners often choose to avoid copper fungicides when possible because of their negative effects on nonpest species.

Copper is available as a powder or liquid. Fixed-copper fungicides are available from organic suppliers as dusts or sprayable solutions. Bordeaux mixture is a combination of hydrated lime and copper sulfate that can be applied as a dust or spray. Bordeaux mixture is a strong fungicide. To prevent leaf damage, spray only when it will dry rapidly. On edibles, use it at half the rate recommended for ornamentals.

# ANIMAL PESTS

Four-footed creatures and birds can cause more damage than insects in many suburban and rural gardens. They may ruin your garden or landscape overnight, eating anything from apples to zinnias. Most animal pests feed at night, so you may have to scout for signs such as destroyed plants, tracks, tunnels, or excrement to figure out who the culprits are.

Follow these guidelines for coping with animal pests:

■ Identify the pest. Tracks are often a good clue to the pest's identity. Learn scientific names, because most mammals have more than one common name. Read books on wildlife. Perhaps you'll find an easy control solution, based on the animal's habit.

■ Assess the damage. If it's only cosmetic, you may decide your plants can tolerate it. If the damage threatens harvest or plant health, control is necessary. If damage is limited to one plant type, consider dropping it from your landscape or garden plants.

■ Determine the best way to prevent or control damage. Combining several tactics may be most effective. Fences and barriers are two of the best control methods. If fencing is impractical, you can use humane traps to catch pests and then release them in a natural habitat at least 1 mile from your property. Homemade or commercial repellents can give inconsistent results, so use them experimentally. Scare tactics such as scarecrows and models of predator animals may frighten pest animals and birds. Flooding tunnels, trapping, and shooting require killing the pests. It's up to you to decide if the damage is severe enough to warrant these methods.

## DEER

Deer have a taste for a wide range of garden and landscape plants. A few deer are a gentle nuisance; during a hard winter, a large herd will eat almost every plant in sight. Deer are nocturnal, but they may be active at any time.

 **Look, Don't Touch**

While we may wish that solving animal pest problems was as easy as posting a "Look, Don't Touch" sign, we should heed the warning ourselves when dealing with animal pests. Wild animals are unpredictable, so keep your distance. They may bite or scratch and, in doing so, can transmit serious diseases such as rabies. Any warm-blooded animal can carry rabies, a virus that affects the nervous system. Rabies is a threat in varying degrees throughout the United States and Canada. Among common garden animal pests, raccoons and skunks are most likely to be infected. It's best never to try to move close to or touch wild animals in your garden. And if you're planning to catch animal pests in live traps, be sure you've planned a safe way to transport and release the animals *before* you set out the baited traps.

Watch for deer tracks or deer droppings in your yard.

**Fences** Electric fencing is the most effective way to keep deer out, but it may not be practical for the home garden. A six-strand, high-voltage electric fence, with the wires spaced 10 inches apart and the bottom one 8 inches off the ground, is an effective deterrent. But it is an impractical choice for many small-scale growers because of the high cost and complex installation. For small areas, snow fencing may be effective.

Another alternative is to build a fence that is simply too high for a deer to jump over. The absolute minimum height for a jump-proof, nonelectric deer fence is 8 feet. Standard woven-wire farm fencing comes 4 feet tall, so it's a common practice to stack one course on top of another to create an 8-foot fence. This method is neither inexpensive nor easy.

An easier approach is to erect two fences, 3 or 4 feet high and spaced 3 feet apart, of welded-wire or snow fencing. Deer seldom jump a fence when they can see another fence or obstacle just on the other side. If you already have a fence around your garden and deer become a problem, add a 3-foot nonelectric or a 2-foot, single-strand electric fence 3 feet outside the existing one.

**Barriers** If deer are damaging a few select trees or shrubs, encircle the plants with 4-foot-high cages made from galvanized hardware cloth, positioned several feet away from the plants.

**Repellents** For minor deer-damage problems, repellents may be effective. Buy soap bars in bulk, and hang them from strings in trees. Or nail each bar to a 4-foot stake and drive the stakes at 15-foot intervals along the perimeter of the area.

Some gardeners report that human hair is an effective repellent. Ask your hairdresser or barber to save hair for you to collect each week. Put a handful of hair in a net or mesh bag (you can use squares of cheesecloth to make bags), and hang bags 3 feet above the ground and 3 feet apart.

Farmers and foresters repel deer by spraying trees or crops with an egg-water mixture. Mix 5 eggs with 5 quarts of water for enough solution to treat ¼ acre. Spray plants thoroughly. You may need to repeat application after a rain. Commercial repellents are available at garden centers. Be sure to ask whether a product contains only organic ingredients. You may have to experiment to find one that offers good control.

Experiment with homemade repellents by mixing blood meal, bonemeal, exotic animal manure, hot sauce, or garlic oil with water. Recipes for concocting these repellents differ, and results are variable. Saturate rags or string with the mixtures, and place them around areas that need protection. Be mindful, though, that under the pressure of a scarce food supply, deer will learn to tolerate repellents and will even use them as guides to choice food sources.

## GROUND SQUIRRELS AND CHIPMUNKS

Ground squirrels and chipmunks are burrowing rodents that eat seeds, nuts, fruits, roots, bulbs, and other foods. They are similar to each other, and both are closely related to squirrels. They tunnel in soil and uproot newly planted bulbs, plants, and seeds. Ground-squirrel burrows run horizontally; chipmunk burrows run almost vertically.

**Traps** Bait live traps with peanut butter, oats, or nut meats. Check traps daily.

**Habitat Modification** Ground squirrels and chipmunks prefer to scout for enemies from the protection of their burrow entrance. Try establishing a tall groundcover to block the view at ground level.

**Other Methods** Place screen or hardware cloth over plants, or insert it in the soil around bulbs and seeds. Try spraying repellents on bulbs and seeds. Domestic cats are effective predators.

## MICE AND VOLES

Mice and voles look alike and cause similar damage, but they are only distantly related. They are active at all times of day, year-round. They eat almost any green vegetation, including tubers and bulbs. When unable to find other foods, mice and voles will eat the bark and roots of fruit trees. They can do severe damage to young apple trees.

**Barriers** Sink cylinders of wire mesh or ¼-inch hardware cloth several inches into the soil around the bases of trees.

**Traps and Baits** Some orchardists place snap traps baited with peanut butter, nut meats, or rolled oats along mouse runways to catch and kill them. A bait of vitamin D is available. It causes a fatal calcium imbalance in mice.

**Other Methods** Repellents such as those described for deer may control damage. You can also modify the habitat to discourage mice and voles by removing vegetative cover around trees and shrub trunks.

## MOLES

In some ways, moles are a gardener's allies. They aerate soil and eat insects, including many plant pests. However, they also eat earthworms. Their tunnels can be an annoyance in gardens and under your lawn. Mice and other small animals also may use the tunnels and eat the plants that moles have left behind.

**Traps** Harpoon traps placed along main runs will kill the moles as they travel through their tunnels.

**Barriers** To prevent moles from invading an area, dig a trench about 6 inches wide and 2 feet deep. Fill it with stones or dried, compact material such as crushed shells. Cover the material with a thin layer of soil.

**Habitat Modification**  In lawns, soil-dwelling insects such as Japanese beetle grubs may be the moles' main food source. If you're patient, you can solve your mole (and your grub) problem by applying milky disease spores, a biological control agent, to your lawn. However, if you have a healthy organic soil, the moles may still feed on earthworms once the grubs are gone.

**Other Methods**  You can flood mole tunnels and kill the moles with a shovel as they come to the surface to escape the water. Repellents such as those used to control deer may be effective. Unfortunately, repellents often merely divert the moles to an area unprotected by repellents.

## POCKET GOPHERS

These thick-bodied rodents tunnel through soil, eating bulbs, tubers, roots, seeds, and woody plants. Fan- or crescent-shaped mounds of soil at tunnel entrances are signs of pocket-gopher activity.

**Fences and Barriers**  Exclude gophers from your yard with an underground fence. Bury a strip of hardware cloth so that it extends 2 feet below and 2 feet above the soil surface around your garden or around individual trees. A border of oleander plants may repel gophers.

**Flooding**  You can kill pocket gophers as you would moles, by flooding them out of their tunnels.

## RABBITS

Rabbits can damage vegetables, flowers, and trees at any time of year in any setting. Their favorite vegetables are beans, beet tops, carrots, lettuce, and peas. They also eat spring tulip shoots, tree bark, and buds and stems of woody plants.

**Fences**  The best way to keep rabbits out of a garden is to erect a chicken-wire fence. Be sure the mesh is 1 inch or smaller so that young rabbits can't get through. You'll find instructions for constructing this in "Chicken-Wire Garden Fence" on page 148.

**Barriers**  Erect cylinders made of ¼-inch hardware cloth around young trees or valuable plants. The cages should be 1½ to 2 feet high, or higher if you live in an area with deep snowfall, and should be sunk 2 to 3 inches below the soil surface. Position them 1 to 2 inches away from the tree trunks. Commercial tree guards are also available.

**Other Methods**  Repellents such as those used for deer may be effective. Commercial inflatable snakes may scare rabbits from your garden.

## RACCOONS

Raccoons prefer a meal of fresh crayfish but will settle for a nighttime feast in your sweet corn patch. Signs that they have dined include broken stalks, shredded husks, scattered kernels, and gnawed cob ends.

**Habitat Modification**  Electric fencing is the best way to prevent raccoon damage, but it may be impractical or too expensive for home gardens. Try lighting the garden at night or planting squash among the corn—the prickly foliage may deter the raccoons.

**Barriers**  Protect small plantings by wrapping ears at top and bottom with strong tape. Loop the tape around the tip, then around the stalk, then around the base of each ear. This prevents raccoons from pulling the ears off the plants. Or try covering each ear with a paper bag secured with a rubber band.

## WOODCHUCKS

Woodchucks, or groundhogs, are large, lumbering animals found in the northeast United

States and Canada. You are most likely to see woodchucks in the early morning or late afternoon, munching on a variety of green vegetation. Woodchucks hibernate during the winter. They're most likely to be a pest in early spring, eating young plants in your gardens.

**Fences**   A sturdy chicken-wire fence with a chicken-wire-lined trench will keep out woodchucks. See "Chicken-Wire Garden Fence" on page 148 for instructions for constructing one of these deterrents.

**Barriers**   Some gardeners protect their young plants from woodchucks by covering them with plastic or floating row covers.

## OTHER ANIMAL PESTS

A few animal pests usually cause only minor damage to gardens or are only pests in a limited area of the country.

**Armadillos**   These animals spend most of the day in burrows, coming out at dusk to begin the night's work of digging for food and building burrows. Their diet includes insects, worms, slugs, crayfish, carrion, and eggs. They sometimes root for food in gardens or lawns. Armadillos cannot tolerate cold weather, so their range is limited to the southern United States.

A garden fence is the best protection against armadillos. You also can trap them with live traps or box traps.

**Prairie Dogs**   Prairie dogs can be garden pests in the western United States. They will eat most green plants. If they are a problem in your landscape, control them with the same tactics described in "Ground Squirrels and Chipmunks" on page 143 and in "Pocket Gophers" on the opposite page.

**Skunks**   Skunks eat a wide range of foods. They will dig holes in your lawn while foraging and may eat garden plants. Skunks can be a real problem when challenged or surprised by curious pets or unwary gardeners.

Keep skunks out of the garden by fencing it. You can try controlling them indirectly by treat-

 **Raccoon Cures**

You'll probably never see a raccoon in your garden, since they're shyer than woodchucks and more strictly nocturnal. But you may find their footprints! Here are some steps you can take to keep them at bay:

**Make a moat:** Encircle your corn or melon patch with a 3-foot-wide "moat" made by laying black plastic or mesh fencing on the ground. A raccoon's feet are hairless, sensitive, and plantigrade, which means that the entire bottom of the foot touches the ground when it walks. The animal doesn't like to tread on unusual surfaces.

**Make a raccoon night-light:** Put a blinking or rotating light in the garden at night. Like other nocturnal animals, raccoons have an extra set of light-gathering cells in their eyes. Flashing light is unsettling to them.

**Irritate them:** Plant a scratchy vine crop such as winter squash or pumpkins around and among your corn to irritate and discourage the masked raiders.

**Surround your crops:** Sprinkle hydrated lime in a 4- to 5-inch-wide band around your corn crop when it ripens.

**Cover your ears:** Wrap individual corn ears in paper bags, foil, or plastic, and secure the covering with a rubber band.

**Let your fence top flop:** If you use a chicken-wire fence, don't attach the top 1 foot of wire to the posts. When a coon tries to climb up, the loose portion will bend backward and keep the animal from making it over the top.

ing your lawn with milky disease spores to kill grubs that skunks like to feed on.

## BIRD PESTS

To the gardener, birds are both friends and foes. Though they eat insect pests, many birds also consume entire fruits or vegetables or pick at your produce, leaving damage that invites disease and spoils your harvest.

In general, birds feed most heavily in the morning and again in late afternoon. Schedule your control tactics to coincide with feeding times. Many birds have a preference for certain crops. Damage may be seasonal, depending on harvest time of their favorite foods.

You can control bird damage through habitat management, physical controls, or chemical controls. For any method, it is important to identify the bird. Effective controls may not be effective for all species. Also, you don't want to mistakenly scare or repel beneficial birds.

Try these steps to change the garden environment to discourage pesky birds:

■ Eliminate standing water. Birds need a source of drinking water, and a source near your garden makes it more attractive.

■ Plant alternate food sources to distract birds from your crop.

■ In orchards, prune to open the canopy, since birds prefer sheltered areas.

■ In orchards, allow a cover crop to grow about 9 inches tall. The growth will be too high for birds, who watch for enemies on the ground while foraging.

You can also use a variety of physical control devices to prevent birds from reaching your crops. The most effective way is to cover bushes and trees with lightweight plastic netting and to cover crop rows with floating row covers. You can also use a variety of commercial or homemade devices to frighten birds away from your crops. See "Give Birds a Fright" on the opposite page for suggestions.

# USING FENCING

The size and type of fence to use depends largely on the kind of animal you're trying to stave off. A simple 2-foot-high chicken-wire fence will discourage rabbits, but a more formidable barrier is necessary to deal with such garden burglars as deer, raccoons, or woodchucks.

Cost and appearance are also important considerations. A solid or picket-style wooden fence is attractive but is expensive and difficult to

---

 **The Woodchuck War**

Woodchucks can devastate a whole crop of beans and frustrate you to tears by taking one or two nibbles out of each and every butternut squash on the vine. Here are some hints for discouraging them:

**Blow their cover:** "Landscape" the areas directly around woodchuck burrows by removing all brush, tall weeds and grasses, and other forms of protective cover. Replace the plants with onions and garlic, which repel woodchucks.

**Put out the "unwelcome mat":** If you have a dog, give your pet a small scrap of carpet remnant (sold inexpensively at carpet stores) to sleep on for a week or two. Then place the canine-scented unwelcome mat among plants favored by woodchucks and give your pet a new carpet bed, also destined for the garden. Swap the beds every few weeks, keeping the rotation going for the whole season.

**Make them hot under the collar:** Sprinkle cayenne pepper in and around woodchuck burrows and among the crops they like best.

# Give Birds a Fright

Birds can be a mild nuisance or a major pest in home gardens. Some of the birds likely to raid your gardens are the American robin, blackbird, blue jay, cedar waxwing, common starling, grackle, gray catbird, house finch, oriole, sparrow, and warbler. Try some of these tactics to scare them away from your garden:

**Fool them into thinking their enemies are present:** Try placing inflatable, solid, or silhouetted likenesses of snakes, hawks, or owls strategically around your garden to discourage both birds and small mammals. They'll be most effective if you occasionally reposition them so that they appear to move about the garden. Kites and balloons that startle birds by moving in the breeze and mimicking predators are also available.

**Frighten them with unusual noises:** Try putting up a humming line or fastening aluminum pie plates to stakes with strings in and around your garden. Leaving a radio on at night in the garden can scare away some pests. Blinking lights may work, too.

**Annoy them with obstacles:** Coat surfaces near the garden where they might roost with Bird Tanglefoot. And don't forget two tried-and-true methods: making a scarecrow and keeping a domestic cat or dog on your property.

**Scare them with snakes:** Cut an old green garden hose into snakelike lengths 4 or 5 feet long. Wrap yellow, red, black, or brown plastic tape around the hose at intervals to simulate stripes. Hang the snakes in fruit trees, or place them in plain view among garden rows.

**Menace them with Mylar:** Tie helium-filled Mylar party balloons to tomato stakes and fence posts around the garden. These reflective

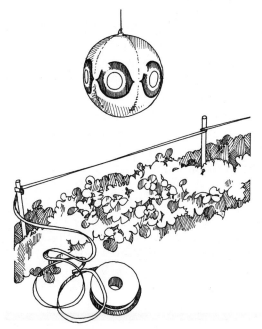

**Scare devices.** Hang "scare-eye" and hawklike balloons and kites that mimic bird predators in large plantings. Use four to eight balloons per acre in orchards or in small fruit or sweet corn plantings.

A humming line works well in a strawberry patch or vegetable garden. The line, made of very thin nylon, vibrates in even the slightest breeze. The movement creates humming noises inaudible to us but readily heard and avoided by birds.

inflatables are often left for the taking after special occasions. Most businesses that sell them will refill deflated balloons for little or no charge.

**Terrorize them with tape:** Stretch a length of audio-cassette tape tightly between stakes placed at either end of a row of plants. The humming noise created by the tape vibrating in the wind can scare off birds.

install. Wooden fences also tend to shade the perimeter of the garden and require regular maintenance. Wire fencing and electric fencing cost less but are by no means inexpensive, particularly if you're fencing in a large area.

You may be able to forego fencing in your entire garden or orchard by erecting barriers around only those beds or crops most vulnerable to animal pests. A fenced plot for corn and melons is a good idea for raccoon problems. You'll find more information about making barriers, as well as suggestions for using traps and repellents, earlier in this chapter.

## CHICKEN-WIRE GARDEN FENCE

A simple 3-foot-high chicken-wire fence and a subterranean chicken-wire barrier can protect

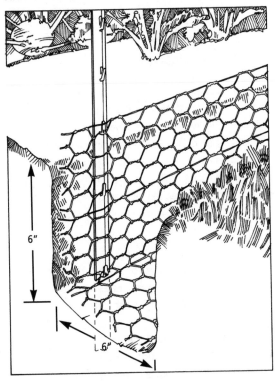

**Chicken-wire-lined trench.** A 6-inch trench lined with chicken wire provides protection against animals that try to burrow underground to get into the garden.

your garden from nearly all small and medium-sized animals, including the burrowing types.

Chicken wire comes in a variety of widths and mesh sizes and is generally sold in 50-foot rolls. The 1-inch mesh is best for excluding animal pests.

The first step in building a fence is to decide where you want it to run. Mark the corners with small stakes and measure the perimeter. You will need two lengths of 1-inch-mesh chicken wire, one 3 feet wide for the fence itself, and another 1 foot (or more) wide to line an underground trench; or use one length wide enough to do both.

You'll also need one 5-foot post for each corner, additional posts for long sections, and one post for each side of the gate(s). Steel T-posts are inexpensive, can be driven into the ground with a hammer or sledge, and come with clips for attaching the fencing. Rot-resistant wooden posts such as locust provide excellent support, but you'll need a post-hole digger to set them.

### ✿ Easy Movable Fencing

Here's an easy way to make a temporary, portable fence to protect individual beds or crops from animal pests:

1. Cut several 4- or 5-foot lengths of 1-inch-mesh chicken wire (available at hardware stores).

2. Attach a metal or fiberglass post to each end of each chicken-wire panel. Allow an extra foot or so of the post to extend past the bottom of the fencing, so that the posts can be pushed into the ground.

3. Use the panels to surround susceptible crops such as young broccoli or lettuce plants. When they're no longer needed, take the panels down and store them flat.

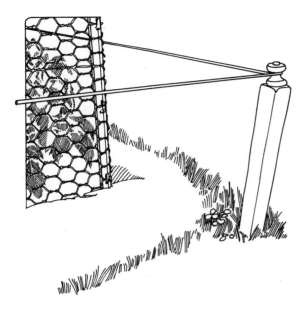

**Animal-proof fence.** Adding a low, single-strand electric fence just outside a nonelectric fence should put an end to problems with virtually any animal pest except deer. Set up the electric fence 6 inches outside the chicken-wire fence, with the wire 4 to 6 inches off the ground.

Also, nailing or stapling fencing to dense wood can be difficult.

Stretch string between the small stakes to mark the fencing line. Dig a trench 6 inches deep and at least 6 inches wide along the outside of the string. Line the trench with the 1-foot-wide chicken wire bent into the shape of an L, so that the wire covers the bottom of the trench as well as the side nearest the fence. Be sure the wire extends an inch or so above ground level.

Set the posts 2 feet deep along the marked fence line. Stretch the 3-foot-wide chicken wire between the posts, and attach it to them. The fencing should overlap the chicken wire lining the trench by 2 or 3 inches. Use wire to fasten the two layers together. (If you use one wider length of chicken wire, you save this last step.) Then refill the trench with soil.

If woodchucks are a serious problem, make the wire-lined trench a foot or more deep and up to 3 feet wide. If you're trying to keep gophers out, dig the trench 2 feet deep and 6 inches wide, line it with ¼-inch-mesh hardware cloth, and/or fill it with coarse gravel.

Raccoons are good climbers. To foil them, don't attach the topmost 1 foot of fencing to the posts. When the burglars clamber up, the loose section will flop backward and keep the raccoons from climbing over the top.

If pests continue to raid your garden despite the chicken-wire barrier, you can add a single-strand electric animal-proof fence, as shown in the illustration on this page.

Most garden supply stores sell easy-to-install electric fence kits, including a plug-in or battery-powered charger, 100 feet of wire, and plastic posts. Or check mail-order gardening catalogs, which carry a variety of electric fence products designed for the home gardener.

 **Make a Fabric Fence**

Floating row covers, which are widely used as season extenders and insect barriers, also serve as an effective "fence" against animal pests. Simply laying the lightweight polypropylene material, such as Reemay, over crops seems to keep four-legged pests from finding the munchies underneath. Floating row covers keep rabbits and woodchucks away. They make no effort to dig under the fabric or to push it aside.

Reemay and products like it come in a variety of widths and are sold in rolls (usually 25 feet or more) at garden centers. To install the cover, just lay the fabric directly on top of a row or bed of plants, and anchor the edges with boards or soil.

# Troubleshooting Vegetable and Fruit Pests

While the most troublesome pests of home gardens vary from region to region in North America, there are some well-recognized pests that plague gardens in most of the country. Use this table to identify the insects and other related pests that are damaging your fruit and vegetable crops and to find out what your control options are.

| Pest | Description and Control |
|------|-------------------------|

### APHIDS

These tiny, pear-shaped insects attack most edible crops. They suck plant sap, causing distorted foliage and dropped leaves. They excrete "honeydew," which supports the growth of sooty mold.

**Control:** Avoid feeding too much nitrogen, as fleshy growth attracts aphids. Spray plants with a strong stream of water to knock aphids off. Release beneficial insects such as lacewings or aphid midges. Spray severe infestations with soap or oil.

### APPLE MAGGOTS AND CODDLING MOTHS

Apple maggot flies are $1/4$" flies with yellow legs and transparent wings that are patterned with dark crosswise bands. Larvae are white maggots that tunnel through apples, blueberries, and plums. Codling moth adults are gray-brown moths with a $3/4$" wingspan; larvae are pink or creamy white caterpillars with brown heads that tunnel through apple, apricot, cherry, peach, pear, and plum fruits to center.

**Control:** To limit apple maggot damage, collect and destroy dropped fruit daily until September, twice a month in fall. Hang apple maggot traps in trees from mid-June until harvest (1 per dwarf tree, 6 per full-sized tree). Plant clover ground cover to attract predatory beetles. Grow late-maturing cultivars. To control codling moths, scrape loose bark in early spring to remove overwintering cocoons, and then spray dormant oil. Grow cover crops to attract native parasites and predators. Use pheromone traps to determine main flight period for moths, then release parasitic *Trichogramma* wasps to attack eggs. Trap larvae in tree bands and destroy daily. In areas with severe infestations, spray ryania when 75% of petals have fallen, followed by 3 sprays at 1–2 week intervals.

| **Pest** | **Description and Control** |
| --- | --- |

## CABBAGE LOOPER AND IMPORTED CABBAGEWORM

Cabbage looper adults are gray moths; larvae are smooth green caterpillars with 2 lengthwise white lines. Imported cabbageworm adults are white butterflies; larvae are velvety green caterpillars. Larvae chew large holes in leaves of cabbage-family and other plants, which may kill plants.

**Control:** Cover plants with row covers. Handpick. Spray BTK. Spray pyrethrins, ryania, or sabadilla for severe infestations.

## COLORADO POTATO BEETLE

Adults are yellowish orange, $\frac{1}{3}$" beetles with black stripes on wing covers, black spots on thorax. Larvae are small, dark orange, humpbacked grubs. Eggs are bright yellow ovals found in clusters on leaf undersides. Both adults and larvae chew leaves of tomato-family plants.

**Control:** In spring, shake adults from plants onto ground cloth in early morning. Dump beetles into soapy water. Attract native predators and parasites with pollen and nectar flowers. Mulch plants with deep straw layer. Cover plants with floating row covers until midseason. Release 2–5 spined soldier bugs per square yard of plants. Apply parasitic nematodes to soil to attack larvae. Apply double-strength sprays of BTSD on larvae. Spray weekly with pyrethrins, rotenone, ryania, or neem.

## CORN EARWORM AND EUROPEAN CORN BORER

Corn earworm (tomato fruitworm) adults are tan moths; larvae are 1"–2" caterpillars of various colors. European corn borer adults are brown moths; larvae are small beige caterpillars. Larvae feed on corn silks and burrow into ears; may damage many other vegetables.

**Control:** Destroy infested crop debris. Apply BTK.

*(continued)*

# Troubleshooting Vegetable and Fruit Pests – Continued

| Pest | Description and Control |
|------|------------------------|

### CUCUMBER BEETLES

Cucumber beetle adults are $\frac{1}{4}$" yellowish beetles with black spots or lengthwise stripes; larvae are small whitish grubs. Beetles chew flowers and leaves of squash-family and other plants. Larvae feed on corn or squash-family roots. Larvae and adults spread mosaic virus and bacterial wilt.

**Control:** Destroy infested crop residues. Treat soil with parasitic nematodes. Use row covers. Spray adults with pyrethrins or rotenone.

### CUTWORMS

Adults are brown or gray moths. Larvae are fat, greasy gray or dull brown caterpillars with shiny heads. At night, caterpillars feed on stems of vegetable and flower seedlings and transplants near the soil line, severing them or completely consuming small seedlings.

**Control:** Put collars made of paper, cardboard, or plastic around transplant stems at planting, anchoring each collar half above and half below soil. A week before setting out plants, scatter moist bran mixed with BTK and molasses over surface of beds. Apply parasitic nematodes to soil. Dig around base of damaged transplants in the morning and destroy larvae hiding below soil surface. Set out transplants later in season to avoid damage.

### FLEA BEETLE

Adults are tiny dark beetles that jump like fleas; larvae are tiny white grubs. Adults chew numerous small, round holes in leaves of many crops; larvae feed on roots. Plants may be stunted or killed. Adults may spread virus diseases.

**Control:** Delay planting to avoid peak populations. Cover seedlings with row cover. Treat soil with parasitic nematodes. Spray with neem, pyrethrins, or sabadilla.

| Pest | Description and Control |
|------|-------------------------|

## HORNWORMS

Adults are large, gray moths; larvae are green caterpillars up to $4\frac{1}{2}$", with a red or black horn on the tail. Larvae eat leaves, stems and fruit of nightshade-family plants.

**Control:** Handpick caterpillars from foliage. Attract native parasitic wasps. Spray BTK while caterpillars are still small.

## JAPANESE BEETLES

Adults are metallic blue-green, $\frac{1}{2}$" beetles with bronze wing covers; larvae are fat, dirty white grubs with brown heads. Adults eat flowers and skeletonize leaves of a broad range of plants. Larvae feed on roots of lawn grasses and garden plants.

**Control:** In early morning, shake beetles from plants onto ground sheets and destroy. Cover plants with floating row covers. Apply milky disease (Bacillus popilliae) or parasitic nematodes to sod to kill larvae. Attract native species of parasitic wasps and flies. Organize a community-wide trapping program to reduce adult beetle population. Spray plants attacked by beetles with ryania or rotenone.

## LEAF HOPPERS

Adults are wedge-shaped, slender insects that jump rapidly into flight when disturbed. Nymphs are pale, wingless, and similar to adults and hop rapidly when disturbed. Adults and nymphs suck juices from most fruit and vegetable crops. Their toxic saliva distorts and stunts plants. Fruit may be spotted with drops of excrement and honeydew.

**Control:** Wash nymphs from plants with stiff spray of water. Attract natural enemies (predatory flies and bugs, parasitic wasps). Spray with insecticidal soap, pyrethrins, rotenone, or sabadilla.

*(continued)*

# Troubleshooting Vegetable and Fruit Pests – Continued

| Pest | Description and Control |
|------|------------------------|

### MEXICAN BEAN BEETLE

Adults are $\frac{1}{4}$" long, yellowish brown, with 16 black spots. Larvae are yellowish orange. Both skeletonize bean leaves, chew pods, and may eventually kill plants.

**Control:** Plant beans early to avoid the main beetle population. Cover young plants with row covers. Handpick daily. Release spined solder bugs or parasitic wasps. Spray severe infestations with pyrethrins, sabadilla, or neem.

### ORIENTAL FRUIT MOTH

Adults are small, dark gray moths. Larvae are white to pinkish gray, $\frac{1}{2}$" caterpillars with a brown head. In spring, young larvae bore into green twigs of peach, almond, cherry, apple, pear, or other fruits causing twig wilting and dieback; later generations bore into fruits.

**Control:** Where possible, plant early-bearing peach and apricot cultivars that are harvested before midsummer. To destroy overwintering larvae, cultivate soil 4" deep around trees in early spring. Attract native parasitic wasps and flies with flowering cover crops. Disrupt mating with pheromone patches applied to lower limbs of trees (1 patch per 4 trees). Spray summer oil to kill eggs and larvae; spray ryania as last resort.

### PEACH TREE BORERS

Adults are blue-black, $1\frac{1}{4}$" wasplike moths with narrow translucent wings; larvae are white caterpillars with a dark brown head. Larvae bore beneath bark of peach trees at the base and into main roots near the surface. Also occasionally attack plum, prune, cherry, apricot, and nectarine trees.

**Control:** Maintain vigorous trees, and avoid mechanical injury to trunks. Beginning in late summer and into fall, inspect tree trunks from 1' or so above ground level to a few inches below ground level, digging away soil to expose the trunk area below the ground surface. Kill borers in exposed burrows by inserting a sharpened wire. In fall and spring, cultivate soil around trunk base to expose and destroy larvae and pupae. Attract native parasitic wasps and predators.

| Pest | Description and Control |
|------|------------------------|

## PLUM CURCULIO

Adults are brownish gray, ¼" beetles, with warty, hard wing covers and prominent snout; larvae are plump white grubs with brown heads. Adult curculios feed on petals, buds, and young fruit; females make a crescent-shaped cut in fruit skin to deposit an egg, scarring fruit. Newly hatched larvae feed inside the fruit. Susceptible fruits include plums, apples, peaches, cherries, and apricots.

**Control:** Twice daily throughout growing season, knock beetles out of trees onto a ground cloth by hitting branches with padded stick; gather and destroy beetles. Every other day, pick up and destroy all fallen fruit. In areas where severe infestations occur, check developing fruit for egg scars twice a week. When first fruit scars appear, apply a botanical pesticide containing pyrethrins, ryania, and rotenone, such as Triple Plus; repeat in 7–10 days. Do not use a botanical pesticide before petals drop—it kills beneficial pollinators.

## SLUGS AND SNAILS

Adults are soft-bodied, wormlike animals. Slugs have no shells, and snails have coiled shells. Measuring ⅛"–1", both slugs and snails leave a characteristic trail of mucus wherever they crawl. Both slugs and snails rasp large holes in foliage, stems, and bulbs. They feast on any tender plant or shrub and may demolish seedlings.

**Control:** Wrap copper strips around trunks of trees or shrubs, or use copper flashing as edging for garden beds. Trap under flower pots or boards. Attract them with pieces of raw potato or cabbage leaves set out in the garden; collect and destroy every morning. Trap in shallow pans of beer or fermenting liquids, buried with container lip flush to soil surface. To encourage predatory ground and rove beetles, maintain permanent walkways of clover, sod, or stone mulch. Protect seedlings with wide bands of cinders, wood ashes, or diatomaceous earth, renewed frequently.

*(continued)*

## Troubleshooting Vegetable and Fruit Pests – Continued

| Pest | Description and Control |
|------|------------------------|

### SPIDER MITES

Adults are minute, 8-legged mites with fine hairs on body; most species spin fine webs. Nymphs are similar, smaller than adults. Adults and nymphs suck plant juices from many food crops, ornamentals, and fruit trees. Early damage appears as yellow-specked area on leaf undersides. Leaves may drop and fruit may be stunted. Webs may cover leaves and growing tips.

**Control:** Spray fruit trees with dormant oil to kill overwintering eggs. In garden or greenhouse, rinse plants with water, and mist daily to suppress reproduction of mites. Release predatory mites *Metaseiulus occidentalis* on fruit trees, *Phytoseiulus persimilis* or similar species on vegetables, strawberries, and flowers. Spray insecticidal soap, pyrethrins, or neem; as last resort spray abamectins or rotenone.

### SQUASH BUG

Adults are brownish-black, flat-backed, $\frac{1}{2}$" bugs. Nymphs are whitish green or gray when young, darkening as they mature, similar in shape to adults. Eggs are shiny yellow to brown ellipses, found in groups on leaf undersides. Both adults and nymphs suck plant juices of all squash-family crops, causing leaves and shoots to blacken and die back.

**Control:** Maintain vigorous plant growth. Handpick all stages from undersides of leaves. Support vines off the ground on trellises. Attract native parasitic flies with pollen and nectar plants. Cover plants with floating row covers (hand pollinate flowers). Spray rotenone or sabadilla.

### TARNISHED PLANT BUGS

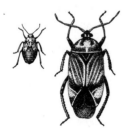

Adults are oval, light green to brown, mottled $\frac{1}{4}$" bugs. Nymphs are yellow-green, wingless, similar to adults. Adults and nymphs suck plant juices of most flowers, fruits, and vegetables, causing shoot and fruit distortion, bud drop, wilting, stunting, and dieback.

**Control:** Cover plants with floating row covers. Attract native predators with ground covers and pollen plants. Try releases of minute pirate bugs. Spray rotenone or sabadilla as last resort.

# Troubleshooting Fruit and Vegetable Diseases

Home gardeners often have few options when it comes to fighting plant diseases. This table will help you decide what type of disease problem you have, and it offers some general suggestions to prevent recurrence of that problem. In some cases, there are some organically acceptable fungicides that can help prevent the spread of a disease.

| Disease | Symptoms | Controls |
|---|---|---|
| Alternaria blight | Infected leaves develop brown to black spots that enlarge and develop concentric rings like a target. Heavily blighted leaves dry up and die. Sunken spots appear on fruits and tubers. Affects many vegetables and fruit trees. Known as early blight on nightshade family crops. | Plant resistant cultivars. Soak seeds in a disinfecting solution before planting. Dispose of infected annual crops; use a 3-year rotation. |
| Anthracnose | Infected fruits and pods develop small, dark, sunken spots. Pinkish spore masses appear in the center of the spots in wet weather. Tomatoes, cucumbers, melons, and beans are often affected. Also a problem on raspberries and gooseberries, where symptoms appear as gray spots surround by red or purple margins on canes and leaves; sideshoots may wilt and entire canes may die. | Plant resistant cultivars. Using disease-free seeds and rotating crops may help prevent the problem. For cane plants, apply lime-sulfur spray just as leaf buds break in the spring. Remove and destroy severely infected plants. |
| Bacterial leafspot | Appears as small, dark spots on fruit tree leaves; centers dry and drop out, leaving shot-holes. Small, sunken dark spots or cracks form on fruit. On cabbage-family crops, small brown or purple spots appear on leaves; leaves eventually turn yellow and die. Affects apricot, peach, plum, and cabbage-family crops. | Spray copper on fruit trees when buds open until temperatures reach 85°–90°F in wet weather; check with supplier, as some types burn leaves. Limit high-nitrogen fertilizers. Destroy infected vegetable plants. Use a 3-year crop rotation to reduce problems. |

*(continued)*

# Troubleshooting Fruit and Vegetable Diseases – Continued

| Disease | Symptoms | Controls |
| --- | --- | --- |
| Brown rot | Flowers and new growth on infected trees wilt and decay. Developing or mature fruits show soft, brown spots that enlarge rapidly and may grow gray mold. Affects apricot, peach, and plum trees. | Remove and destroy dried fruit. Cultivate soil just before bloom. Cut out infected twigs. Spray sulfur during summer and lime-sulfur when trees are dormant. |
| Canker, perennial | Infection causes sunken, oozing cankers to form on trunk or twigs. May cause wilting or death of branches or trees. Affects apricot, cherry, peach, and plum trees. | Avoid mechanical injury: The fungus enters through wounds. Cut out cankers, and paint wounds with a 1:1 mix of lime-sulfur and white latex paint. |
| Club root | Infected cabbage-family plants wilt during the heat of the day; older leaves turn yellow and drop. Roots are distorted and swollen. | Select resistant cultivars, buy uninfected transplants, and rotate crops. |
| Downy mildew | A white to purple downy growth forms on the underside of leaves and along stems. Affects many fruit and vegetable crops. | Buy disease-free seeds and plants, follow a 3-year rotation, and remove and dispose of infected plants. On perennials such as grapes, remove and destroy badly infected leaves. Try sprays of bordeaux mix or other copper-based fungicides to reduce the spread of the disease. |
| Fireblight | Young, tender shoots on infected trees die back suddenly. Leaves turn brown or singed-looking and remain on the twig. Areas of bark may become water-soaked and ooze. Affects apple, pear, and quince trees. | Select resistant cultivars. Cut off blighted twigs at least 12" below decay on a dry day. Sanitize pruning tools between cuts. Limit high-nitrogen fertilizers. |
| Late blight | First symptom is water-soaked spots on lower leaves. Downy white growth appears on leaf undersides. In wet weather, plants will rot and die. Affects nightshade-family crops. | Dispose of all infected plants and tubers, presoak seeds in a disinfecting solution, and plant resistant cultivars. Sprays of bordeaux mix can help control outbreaks during wet weather. |

| Disease | Symptoms | Controls |
|---------|----------|----------|
| Mosaic | A viral disease that causes mottled green and yellow foliage or veins. Leaves may be wrinkled or curled; growth may be stunted. Attacks beans, tomatoes, and many other crops. | Plant resistant cultivars. Mosaic is spread by insects, especially aphids and leafhoppers. Keep insects away from crops by covering them with floating row covers. Remove and destroy infected plants. |
| Powdery mildew | Mildew forms a white to grayish powdery growth, usually on the upper surfaces of leaves. Leaves of severely infected plants turn brown and shrivel. Fruit ripens prematurely and has poor texture and flavor. Infects melons, cucumbers, apples, grapes, and many other crops. | Plant resistant cultivars whenever possible. Prune or stake plants to improve air circulation. Dispose of infected plants. Applying a 0.5 percent solution of baking soda (1 teaspoon baking soda in 1 quart water) may help to control the disease. Apply sulfur weekly to prevent infection of susceptible plants. |
| Rust | Infected plants develop reddish brown powdery spots on leaves and stems. Leaves turn yellow and growth is stunted. Different species of rust fungi infect apples, asparagus, beans, brambles, carrots, corn, onions, and other crops. | Provide good air circulation around plants. Remove and destroy seriously affected plants or plant parts. Starting early in the season, dust plants with sulfur to prevent infection or keep mild infections from spreading. For bramble fruits, immediately destroy any infected plants and replant with resistant cultivars. |
| Wilt, Fusarium and Verticillium | Infected plants wilt and may turn yellow. Leaves may drop prematurely; severely infected plants may die. Affects a wide range of fruits and vegetables, especially tomatoes, peppers, melons, strawberries, peaches, and cherries. | Select resistant cultivars when available. Crop rotation does not control these diseases well because so many crops are susceptible. Soil solarization before planting may help. |

# Chapter 8

# SEASONAL CARE

After the planning and planting come the watering, weeding, and tending. While we all realize that gardening is work, it's nice to know that there are ways to make that work more pleasurable so we can spend more time enjoying our gardens rather than taking care of them. Of course, low-maintenance gardens start with proper planning. For a complete discussion on garden planning, see Chapter 1.

Good garden care requires the proper tools. Tools not only help you get the job done, but the right tools—used properly—will save time and effort on your part. Next on the garden-care list is weed control. Weeds can drive the most peaceful gardener to herbicidal thoughts. But we'll tell you how to keep weeds from becoming a problem in your garden—and how to control those that do appear—without resorting to dangerous chemicals.

Mulch plays another important role in the garden—it will save you time watering your plants and fighting pests. Along with mulching, you need to know the best ways to feed, stake, trellis, and water your plants. And if you feel as though all this work gets crammed into a very short time span, read on to discover ways to extend the season to get the absolute most from your garden.

## CHOOSING TOOLS

The notion that a tool is nothing more than a device for doing work stops at the garden gate.

Anyone who has worked garden soil with a well-balanced fork or rake, sliced weeds effortlessly with a skillfully sharpened hoe, or pruned effortlessly with a good, sharp pair of shears knows that a high-quality tool not only gets the job done but also adds pleasure to the doing. Little wonder that gardeners come to think of their most effective tools as friends.

## HAND TOOLS

Whenever it's practical, use hand tools rather than power tools. Power tools are expensive and contribute to both our air and noise pollution problems. If you keep them sharp, good-quality hand tools will make your garden work go quickly and easily.

**Hoes**  You can use hoes to lay out rows, dig furrows, cultivate around plants to loosen the soil and kill weeds, create hills and raised beds, break up clods, and prepare bare spots in lawns for reseeding.

The standard American pattern hoe is a long-handled tool that allows you to work without too much bending. It has a broad, straight blade, a little larger than 6 inches wide and 4 inches deep. However, many gardeners prefer a nursery hoe, which is lighter and has a 2- to 3-inch-deep blade.

Use an oscillating hoe to slice weeds just below the soil surface. It cuts on both the push and the pull stroke. On modern variations, often called "hula" or action hoes, the slicing blade moves back and forth to cut while being pulled or pushed.

Narrow hoe blades utilize your arm power more efficiently than wider blades. The hoe handle should be at least 4½ feet long so you can work without bending over and straining your lower back muscles. In general, when working with hoes, try to remain standing upright and run the hoe blade below and parallel to the soil surface. Keep your hoe sharp so it will cut through weeds rather than yanking them out.

**Shovels**  A standard American long-handled shovel is good for mixing cement and for scooping up soil, gravel, and sand. You can also use it

to pry rocks and root clumps from the soil. You can use a shovel to dig rounded planting holes, but a garden fork or a spade generally works better for most digging.

The standard shovel handle is about 4 feet. The shovel handle should come to shoulder height or higher. Shovels should also have a turned edge or footrest on the shoulders of the blade to protect your feet when you step on the tool.

**Spades**  Spades have a flat, rather than scooped, blade with squared edges. With a spade, you can cut easily through sod and create

**Basic tools for gardeners.** Hand tools form the basis of a garden tool collection. If they are carefully chosen to suit the kind of gardening you do and are kept in good shape, hand tools will make your garden work go smoothly.

straight edges in soil. Use a spade for digging planting holes, prying up rocks, dividing and moving perennials, cutting unwanted tree and shrub roots, tamping sod, and digging trenches.

A spade handle is generally shorter than a shovel handle, usually ranging from 28 to 32 inches. Like shovels, spades should have a turned edge or footrest on the shoulders of the blade.

**Forks** Spading forks cut into soil, usually more easily than solid-bladed tools can. A spading fork is handy for mixing materials into the soil and for harvesting potatoes, carrots, and other root crops. The tines of a standard spading fork are broad and flat; those of the English cultivating fork are thinner and square. The English version is better for cultivating and aerating soil. Remember that forks are used to loosen soil, not to lift it. Use a pitchfork (three tines) or a straw fork (five or six tines) for picking up, turning, and scattering hay mulch, leaf mold, and light compost materials.

The standard handle length for a spading fork is 28 inches. Very tall gardeners may prefer a 32-inch handle. Short gardeners, including children, should use a border fork, which has shorter tines and handle.

**Trowels** A garden trowel is a miniature version of a shovel. Use it to dig planting holes for small plants and bulbs, for transplanting seedlings, or for weeding beds and borders.

Some trowels are made from forged steel and fitted with hardwood handles; good ones are also available in unbreakable one-piece cast aluminum. Trowels come with a variety of blade widths and lengths. Choose one that feels comfortable in your hand.

**Rakes** Rakes generally fall into one of two categories: garden rakes and leaf rakes. Garden

---

 **Buying Tools**

The first rule of tool buying is to avoid cheap tools at all costs. They are poorly designed and constructed, they don't do the job well, and they break easily. Also, don't buy cheap tools for children; they won't learn to love gardening if the first tools they use don't work well. Here are some other tips on tool buying:

■ The best wood for the handle of a shovel and all long-handled garden tools is North American white ash, which is strong, light, and resilient. Hickory is stronger but heavier It is better suited for hammers and other short-handled tools.

■ Examine the lines (rings) in a wooden handle; they should run straight down the entire length of the handle, with no knots. Avoid tools with painted handles; the paint often hides cheap wood.

■ The attachment of the metal part of the tool to its handle affects durability. Buy tools with solid-socket or solid-strapped construction, forged from a single bar of steel that completely envelops the handle, thus protecting it and adding strength.

■ If you buy a one-piece cast-aluminum trowel, select one with a plastic sleeve over the handle to prevent your hands from blackening from contact with the aluminum. This will also provide a more comfortable grip.

■ A rotary tiller is an important investment. Borrow or rent various models to test before buying one. Wheeled tillers are always easier to operate than those without wheels, and large wheels provide more maneuverability than small ones. Look for heavy, heat-treated carbon-steel blades.

rakes are essential for leveling ground, creating raised beds, killing emerging weeds, gathering debris from rows, covering furrows, thinning seedlings, working materials shallowly into the soil, erasing footprints, and spreading mulch. Garden rakes come in many widths, with long or short teeth that are widely or closely spaced. The handle should be long (4½ to 5 feet) and the head should be heavy enough to bite into the soil easily. If you have rocky soil, choose a rake with widely spaced teeth.

Lawn or leaf rakes, also called fan rakes, are good for gathering up leaves, grass clippings, weeds, and other debris and for dislodging thatch from the lawn. Metal lawn rakes last longest and are the springiest, although many gardeners prefer the action and feel of bamboo tines, and some prefer plastic or rubber.

**Pruning Tools** There are two types of pruning shears: the anvil type, with a straight blade that closes down onto an anvil or plate, and the bypass type, which cuts like scissors. Anvil pruners are often easier to use, requiring less hand pressure to make a cut. Bypass shears make a cleaner cut, can work in tighter spaces, and can cut flush against a tree trunk or branch (anvil pruners leave a short stump). Most models of either type will cut hardwood branches up to ½ inch in diameter.

Lopping shears, also called loppers, are heavy-duty pruners with long handles. Both anvil and bypass loppers can cut branches up to 2 inches in diameter. Hedge shears have long blades and relatively short handles. They can cut branches up to ½ inch thick. Pruning saws cut through most branches that are too thick for shears.

**Push Mowers** Push mowers have several revolving blades that move against a single fixed blade, producing a neat trim. They do a fine job, cutting evenly and quietly. For those with small, level lawns, the push mower is the ideal lawn-cutting instrument. It is inexpensive, not difficult to push, nonpolluting, and quiet, and it produces a neat-looking lawn.

## POWER TOOLS

In some cases, you may need the extra power of engine-driven equipment. It's tempting to use these machines on a regular basis because they get the job done quickly. Keep in mind, though, that handwork can be part of the pleasure and relaxation of gardening. If you routinely use power tools to speed through garden chores, you'll miss the opportunity to observe the growth of your plants and to watch for the beginning of disease or insect problems.

**Power Mowers** Gas-powered rotary mowers have a single blade that revolves at a high speed, literally ripping the tops off grass plants. Unlike push mowers, power mowers can handle rough terrain and knock down high weeds. Mulching mowers blow finely cut grass pieces back into the lawn, building up soil organic matter while removing the need to rake or bag clippings.

**Tillers** Rotary tillers can make short work of turning and churning garden soil, breaking new ground, cultivating, aerating, weeding, and mixing materials into the soil. The rotary tiller is a gasoline-powered machine equipped with steel blades that rotate on a central spindle.

 **Use Sled Power**

Rescue that plastic sledding disk from the garage, attach a long rope to one side, and use it to slide loads of mulch or compost to where you want them. A plastic sled is also good for hauling plants that you're transplanting from one part of the garden or yard to another.

**Chipper/Shredders** After a lawn mower and a rotary tiller, the favorite large power tool of gardeners is often a chipper/shredder. This machine, powered with gasoline or electricity, reduces leaves, pruned branches, and plant debris to beautiful mulch or compost material. Shredders are better for chopping up weeds and other soft plant material; chippers can handle heavier, woody materials.

## TOOL CARE

After making the considerable investment in good-quality tools, it is wise to spend some time to keep them in good shape.

**Routine Care** Clean, dry, and put away all hand tools after each use. Keep a large plastic kitchen spoon handy to knock dirt off metal blades. Don't use a trowel or other metal tool,

since you could damage the blades of both tools. A 5-gallon bucket of sharp builder's sand in the tool shed or garage is useful for cleaning tools. Dip the metal blade of each tool into the sand and plunge it up and down a few times to work off any clinging soil. Use a wire brush to remove any rust that may have formed. Keep power equipment in good repair and properly adjusted.

**Handles** Regularly varnish and sand wooden handles to maintain their resilience and good looks. If you buy a good-quality tool second-hand and it has a weather-beaten handle, refresh it with several coats of varnish, sanding between each coat. You can repair split handles temporarily with tape and glue, but replace broken handles as soon as possible.

**Sharpening** Sharp-bladed hand tools will perform efficiently and with ease only if you keep them sharp. Take the time to study the angle of the bevels on all your tools, then sharpen each, as needed, to keep the proper bevel. If you have tools that are especially difficult to sharpen, take them to a professional for sharpening.

**Winter Care** At the end of the season, polish all metal parts of hand tools with steel wool, oil them to prevent rust, and store them in a dry place. Lubricate all tools that have moving parts. This is also a good time to take hard-to-sharpen tools to the sharpening shop.

# CONTROLLING WEEDS

Fast, tough, and common—that's all it takes to earn a plant the name of weed. But any plant growing in the wrong place—especially if it's growing there in abundance—is a weed. Maple tree seedlings that sprout between the lettuce and radishes are weeds. So is the Bermuda grass that keeps invading your perennial beds from the lawn.

---

 **Easy Machine Maintenance**

Here are some things you should keep in mind as you winterize your machinery:

1. Clean off all dust, dirt, matted grass, and excess grease.

2. Look for loose or missing screws, bolts, or nuts; replace if necessary.

3. Disconnect the spark plug wire, and check the blades or tines of your machine. If necessary, sharpen and oil the blades or tines before replacing them.

4. If your machine has a 4-cycle engine, change the oil.

5. Clean and oil the air filter, following the manufacturer's directions.

6. To clean out the fuel line, drain out all gasoline and then run the engine until it stops.

7. Remove, clean, and replace the spark plug.

# Types of Weeds

L ike flowers, there are annual, biennial, and perennial weeds. Each group poses its own control problems, so you need to know which group they fall into. Here's a rundown:

**Annual Weeds:** Annual weeds, like lamb's quarters, wild mustard, pigweed, purslane, and ragweed, live only one season. But they produce thousands of seeds, guaranteeing success through sheer strength of numbers. Control them by pulling them before they flower and set seed.

**Biennial Weeds:** Biennial weeds, like Queen-Anne's-lace, form a rosette of leaves their first season. The following year, they flower, set seed, and die. Control them by removing their rosettes the first season, or pull the weeds the second season, before they set their seed.

**Perennial Weeds:** Perennial weeds include dandelion, Canada thistle, bindweed, dock, wild onions, ground ivy, plantain, pokeweed, and wood sorrel. Some of the worst perennial weeds are grasses, including crabgrass and quackgrass. They live for years, set seed, have deep, persistent root systems, and often have creeping stems; so a single plant can send up offspring all over the garden. The same is true for woody weeds like poison ivy. To control these difficult weeds, dig carefully to remove as much of the root system as possible. Then pull up the plants that grow from the pieces you've missed.

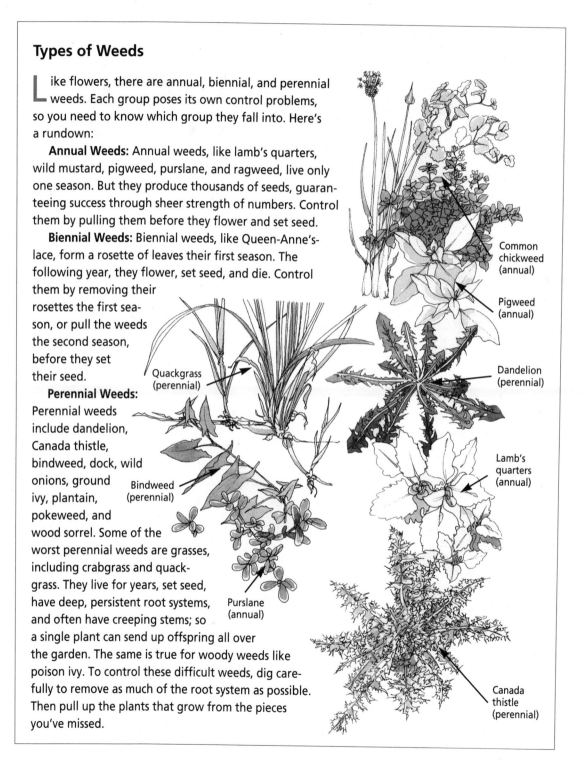

Common chickweed (annual)

Pigweed (annual)

Dandelion (perennial)

Lamb's quarters (annual)

Quackgrass (perennial)

Bindweed (perennial)

Purslane (annual)

Canada thistle (perennial)

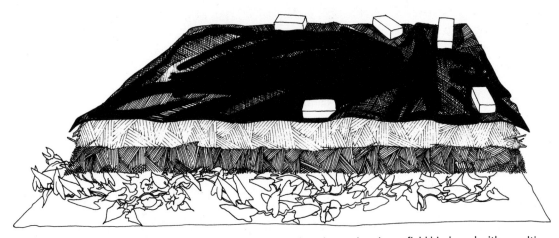

**Mulching perennial weeds.** Wipe out stubborn perennial weeds such as poison ivy or field bindweed with a multi-layered mulch treatment. Spread lime or rock fertilizers if needed, then put down compost or manure. Next, spread a thick layer of organic mulch such as hay, wood chips, or shredded leaves. Top the mulch with an opaque, impenetrable cover: Black plastic, old carpeting, or a 6-inch-thick layer of newspaper works well. Leave the mulch and heavy cover in place for the season. The following spring, remove the cover and mulch, and check in the soil for weed roots. If the roots aren't dead yet, re-cover the area. Two years under this kind of cover will kill virtually any weed.

The bigger your weeds get, the more difficult they are to control. Get into the habit of a once-a-week weed patrol to cut your weed problem down to size. Using the right tools and techniques also will help to make weeding a manageable—maybe even enjoyable—task.

## HAND WEEDING

Hand-pulling weeds is simple and effective. It's good for small areas and young or annual weeds such as purslane and lamb's quarters. Using your hands allows you to weed with precision, an important skill when sorting the weeds from the seedlings. For notorious spreaders like ground ivy, the only choice for control is to patiently hand-pull the tops and sift through the soil to remove as many roots as you can find.

Short-handled tools such as dandelion forks (sometimes known as asparagus knives), pronged cultivators, and mattocks are good for large, stubborn weeds, especially in close quarters such as among perennials. Use these tools to pry up tough perennial weeds. Hand weeders come in all shapes, and everybody has a favorite. If one type feels awkward, try another.

A hoe is the best tool for weeding larger areas quickly and cleanly. Use it to rid the vegetable garden of weeds that spring up between rows. When you hoe, slice or scrape just below the soil surface to sever weed tops from roots. Don't chop into the soil—you'll just bring up more weed seeds to germinate. Keep the hoe blade sharp. Hoeing kills most annual weeds, but many perennial weeds, such as dandelions, will grow back from their roots. Dig out these roots with a garden fork or spade.

## USING MULCH

One of the best low-effort ways to beat weeds is to block their access to light and air by mulching bare soil areas. A 3- to 4-inch layer of mulch smothers out many weeds, and weeds that manage to poke through are easier to pull.

Black plastic mulch can practically eliminate

weeding in the vegetable garden. Cut slits for plants and water to penetrate. Remove the plastic at the end of the growing season to let the soil breathe. You can use biodegradable materials, such as newspaper or corrugated cardboard, to temporarily suppress weeds, tilling them into the soil at the end of the season. See "Mulching Your Garden" on this page for more information on organic and black plastic mulches.

A living mulch of a low-growing grass or legume crop seeded between rows of plants in your vegetable garden can keep down weeds and improve soil organic matter content at the same time. See "Using Green Manure" on page 36 for suggestions on planting living mulches in your garden.

Even tough perennial weeds will succumb eventually to a thick layer of mulch. The illustration on the opposite page shows how to layer on mulches to solve tough weed problems.

Just as weeds compete with your garden and landscape plants for water, food, and growing space, your plants use the same method to crowd out weeds. As your plants grow, they will shade the ground, reducing weed germination and growth. Space vegetable and flower plants closely in beds to decrease the time until the leaves form an effective light-blocking canopy.

Reduce weed growth in your lawn by setting your lawn mower blade a notch or two higher. Taller grass is generally healthier and lets less light reach the soil.

## USING HERBICIDES

In some cases, fatty-acid-based herbicides such as Safer SharpShooter can help control weeds. These herbicides provide effective spot control for annual weeds, but perennial weeds will spring up anew from the unharmed roots. Some organic gardeners have traditionally relied on vinegar or salt to kill weeds. However, these substances will affect soil balance and can harm your gar-

den plants as well. Only use them in areas where you don't want *any* plants to grow, such as between cracks in a patio.

# MULCHING YOUR GARDEN

Every organic gardener should be a mulch expert. Mulching is one of the best ways to fight weeds. It also improves your garden's appearance, reduces water loss, and protects soil from compaction and erosion. If you use an organic mulch, the icing on the cake is improved soil quality as the mulch decays.

There are two basic kinds of mulch: organic and inorganic. Organic mulches include formerly living material such as wood chips, shredded bark, chopped leaves, straw, grass clippings, compost, sawdust, pine needles, and even paper. (See "Best Organic Mulches" on page 172 for more information.) Inorganic mulches include gravel, stones, black plastic, and geotextiles (landscape fabrics).

Both types discourage weeds, but organic mulches also improve the soil as they decompose. Inorganic mulches don't break down and enrich the soil, but under certain circumstances they're the mulch of choice. For example, black plastic warms the soil and radiates heat during the night, keeping heat-loving vegetables such as eggplant and tomatoes cozy and vigorous.

## USING ORGANIC MULCHES

There are two cardinal rules for using organic mulches to combat weeds: First, be sure to lay the mulch down on soil that is already weeded, and second, lay down a thick enough layer to discourage new weeds from coming up through it. It can take a 4- to 6-inch layer of mulch to completely discourage weeds, although a 2- to 3-inch layer is usually enough in shady spots where weeds aren't as troublesome as they are in full sun.

## ❀ Weeding Wisely

Weeding is a fact of life in the garden. It will be easier and more effective if you start weeding as soon as you see a problem and then continue to monitor for any new weeds. Control is much more difficult if you let the weeds take over the garden and then try to bring the situation under control in one marathon weeding session.

Here are some surefire ways to minimize your weeding chores:

■ Mulch your garden. Mulch not only suppresses weed germination and growth, it also makes those weeds that do turn up easier to pull, since the soil stays soft and moist beneath the mulch.

■ Spread several sheets of newspaper under an organic mulch such as wood chips to provide added insurance against weeds.

■ Get out the whole weed the first time. A lot of weeds can spread from a tiny piece of root or stem left in the ground, and taprooted weeds like dandelions grow back if you don't take out the whole taproot.

■ Get them while they're young. Small weeds are easy to pull or hoe, and you avoid the possibility of having them set seed and sow future weed problems. Become familiar with the seedling stage of the common weeds in your garden, and show them no mercy.

■ Don't bring potential weed problems (like uncomposted manure, which may carry weed seeds, and seed-rich hay) into the garden. Always specify weed-free straw or hay if you use them in your garden.

■ Don't compost mature weed seed heads. A really hot compost pile will kill weed seeds, but you can't guarantee that the seeds will be in the hottest part of the pile or that your pile will get hot enough. It's better to throw them out than to spread weeds along with your compost.

■ Use vertical barriers, such as wood or metal edgings, between lawn and garden areas to prevent grass from infiltrating.

■ Be a good housekeeper in the garden. Pull weeds before they set seed. Police nearby areas, not just the garden; they may be reservoirs of weed seeds just waiting to blow into your freshly prepared seedbed.

■ Let the sun's heat weed your vegetable garden by solarizing the soil. Covering bare soil tightly with clear plastic for several weeks can kill weed seeds in the top few inches of the soil. For details on this technique, which also helps reduce soilborne diseases and pests, see "Soil Solarization" on page 134.

■ After preparing garden soil for planting, let it set for seven to ten days. Then slice off newly emerged weeds with a hoe, taking care to disturb the soil surface as little as possible. If you have time, wait another week and weed again. This tactic puts a considerable dent in the reservoir of surface weed seed that could germinate and cause problems later in the season.

Even if you use these preventive tactics, you'll have weeds. There are weed seeds, roots, and crowns already in your soil. Birds, wind, and even pets can bring in weed seeds from outside. But only five to ten minutes a day can keep weeds in a mulched perennial garden under control, even if the garden is fairly large. The key to effective weeding is persistence. A year-round weeding program saves time and labor in the long run. Weed in winter, when the soil tends to be damp and weed seedlings are vulnerable, as well as throughout the growing season.

The best organic mulch is compost, a mixture of decomposed organic materials. For directions on making compost, see Chapter 3.

You can purchase bags of decorative wood chips or shredded bark from the local garden center to mulch your flower garden and shrub borders. A less expensive source of wood chips might be your tree-care company or the utility company. They may be willing to sell you a truckload of chips at a nominal price. Many communities are also chipping yard debris or composting grass clippings and fall leaves, then offering the result back to the community for free or for a small charge.

If you have a lot of trees on your property, shredding the fallen leaves creates a nutrient-rich mulch for free. You can use a leaf-shredding machine, but you don't really need a special machine to shred leaves—a lawn mower with a bagger will collect leaves and cut them into the perfect size for mulching.

You can spread a wood chip or shredded leaf mulch anywhere on your property, but it looks especially attractive in flower beds and shrub borders. Of course, it's right at home in a woodland or shade garden. Wood chips aren't a great idea for vegetable and annual flower beds, though, since you'll be digging these beds every year and the chips will get in the way.

Grass clippings are another readily available mulch, but they aren't particularly attractive. Some people pile the nitrogen-rich clippings under shrubs or on flower beds, but they are more appropriate on vegetable beds, where appearance is less critical. Your vegetables will thank you for the nitrogen boost!

Another great mulch for the vegetable garden is straw, salt hay, or weed-free hay. It looks good and has most of the benefits of mulches: retaining soil moisture, keeping down weeds, and adding organic matter to the soil when it breaks down. But be sure the hay you use is weed- and seed-free, or you'll just be making trouble for your garden. And don't pull hay or straw up to the stems of vegetables or the trunks of fruit trees, or you'll be inviting slug and rodent damage.

## USING PLASTIC MULCH

Mulching a vegetable garden with sheets of black plastic film can do wonders. The plastic heats up in the sun, warming the soil and radiating heat during the night, effectively creating a microclimate about 3°F warmer than an unmulched garden. Because the plastic film remains warm and dry, it protects the fruits of vining crops such as strawberries, melons, and cucumbers from rotting and keeps them clean. And of course, the mulch prevents weed growth and retains soil moisture.

In raised bed gardens, lay down a sheet of plastic over the entire bed. Bury it at the edges or weigh the plastic down with rocks. Then punch holes in it for the plants. A bulb planter makes quick work of hole cutting. Sow seeds or plant transplants in the holes. You should be able to reuse the plastic for several years if you take it up and store it over winter.

Because water can't permeate the plastic, the mulch retains soil moisture but can also keep rainwater from soaking the planting bed. That means you'll have to water the garden yourself, with a drip irrigation system or soaker hoses placed beneath the plastic. The simplest method is to shove the end of the hose through a hole in the plastic and turn it on.

Don't use black plastic as a mulch under shrubs. Although it keeps out weeds and can be camouflaged with decorative mulch, black plastic destroys the shrubs' long-term health. Because water and air cannot penetrate the plastic, roots grow very close to the soil surface—sometimes right beneath the plastic—seeking moisture and oxygen. The shallow roots suffer from lack of oxygen and moisture and from extremes of heat and cold. Eventually the plants decline and die. Stick to organic mulches such as shredded leaves, bark, wood chips, or compost under your trees and shrubs.

Unlike black plastic, geotextiles—or landscape fabrics—let air and water through to the soil beneath while keeping weeds from coming up. But geotextiles have some of the same drawbacks as black plastic. If exposed to light, they degrade, so you have to cover them with a second mulch (they're ugly, so you'd want to, anyway). Some studies have found that shrub roots may grow up into the geotextile mulch, creating real problems if you want to remove it. And weeds that germinate in the mulch on top of the geotextile can send roots down into the fabric, tearing it when you pull them out.

# FEEDING YOUR PLANTS

Plants make their own food through the process of photosynthesis, but gardeners play an important supporting role by making sure that all the necessary raw materials are available. Organic gardeners do this primarily by enriching their soil with a wide variety of organic materials. Feeding your plants with organic fertilizers can also help to provide them with optimum nutrition.

Organic gardeners use fertilizers like seasonings: They add the finishing touch that brings out the very best in plants. Because an organically managed soil is biologically active and rich in nutrients, organic gardeners don't need to pour on fertilizers to get good plant performance.

 ## More on Mulch

When you're getting ready to mulch your garden, keep these tips in mind:

■ Don't mulch near slug-susceptible plants. In damp climates, organic mulches can harbor slugs and snails, which will munch on any nearby plants.

■ If you're using low-nitrogen mulches such as wood chips or sawdust, fertilize first with a high-nitrogen product such as cottonseed meal, blood meal, or chicken manure. These boost soil nitrogen levels, which are depleted when low-nitrogen mulches decay.

■ In spring, pull organic mulches away from perennials and bulbs to speed up soil warming.

■ Keep mulch about 1 inch away from flower and vegetable crowns and stems to prevent rot.

■ Don't let mulch touch the trunks and stems of trees and shrubs. It retains moisture,

inviting bark rot and diseases such as canker. Layer about 3 inches at the drip line of the tree and taper it down to about a 1/2-inch-thick layer near the trunk.

■ Apply thin, fine particles such as compost or finely shredded bark about 2 inches deep around plants. Large chunks of bark or rock can be applied about 4 inches deep. The larger spaces between the chunks allow more air and light in, so a thicker layer is needed for weed control.

■ Mulch with plants. A thick covering of plants in the garden, where foliage shades the ground and there are no bare spots, helps retain water, protects the soil, and keeps down weeds. When the garden dies down in fall, apply a winter mulch to protect the plants. In spring, the foliage will once again take over as a living mulch.

## CHEMICAL VERSUS ORGANIC

Many organic materials serve as both fertilizers and soil conditioners—they feed both soils and plants. This is one of the most important differences between a chemical approach and an organic approach toward soil care and fertilizing. Soluble chemical fertilizers contain mineral salts that are readily available for uptake by plant roots. However, these salts do not provide a food source for soil microorganisms and earthworms, and they will even repel earthworms because they acidify the soil. Over time, soils treated only with synthetic chemical fertilizers will have decreased organic matter and altered biological activity. And as soil structure declines and water-holding capacity diminishes, a greater proportion of the soluble chemical fertilizers applied will leach through the soil. This results in ever-increasing amounts of chemicals needed to feed the plants.

Most chemical fertilizers are synthesized from nonrenewable resources, such as coal and natural gas. Others are made by treating rock minerals with acids to make them more soluble. Fortunately, there are more and more truly organic fertilizers coming on the market. These products are made from natural plant and animal materials or from mined rock minerals. However, there are no national standards regulating the content of organic fertilizers. Read labels to be sure that commercial fertilizers labeled "organic" contain only safe, natural ingredients. Look for products labeled "natural organic," "slow release," and "low analysis." Be wary of products labeled organic that have an NPK (nitrogen-phosphorus-potassium) ratio that adds up to more than 15 (one labeled 10-10-10, for example).

## USING ORGANIC FERTILIZERS

If you're a gardener who's making the switch from chemical to organic fertilizers, you may be afraid that using organic materials will be more complicated and less convenient than using premixed chemical fertilizers. Not so! Commercially formulated organic fertilizer blends can be just as convenient and effective as blended synthetic fertilizers. You don't need to custom-feed your plants unless it's an activity you enjoy. So while some experts spread a little blood meal around their tomatoes at planting, then some bonemeal just when the blossoms are about to pop, most gardeners are satisfied to make one or two applications of general-purpose organic fertilizer throughout the garden.

If you want to try a plant-specific approach to fertilizing, you can use a variety of specialty organic fertilizers that are available from mail-order supply companies or at many well-stocked garden centers. For example, you can use blood meal, chicken-feather meal, or fish meal as a nitrogen source. Bonemeal is a good source of phosphorus, and kelp and greensand are organic sources of potassium.

**Dry Organic Fertilizers**   Dry organic fertilizers can be made from a single material, such as rock phosphate or kelp, or can be a blend of many ingredients. Almost all organic fertilizers provide a broad array of nutrients, but blends are specially formulated to provide balanced amounts of nitrogen, potassium, and phosphorus, as well as micronutrients. There are several commercial blends, but you can make your own general-purpose fertilizer by mixing individual amendments, as suggested in "Mix and Match" on page 173.

The most common way to apply dry fertilizer is to broadcast it and then hoe or rake it into the top 4 to 6 inches of soil. You can add small amounts of fertilizer to planting holes or rows as you plant your seeds or transplants. Unlike dry synthetic fertilizers, most organic fertilizers are nonburning and will not harm the delicate roots of your seedlings.

# Best Organic Mulches

These are the best organic mulches for gardens. All of them will biodegrade over time, adding humus to the soil. They provide mulch's other benefits as well—retaining moisture and suppressing weeds. Shredded leaves, compost, and pine needles are the most attractive, while newspaper and straw are most readily available (of course, leaves are abundant in fall). Grass clippings will give your plants a nitrogen boost, but they break down fast and are best used to supplement more stable mulches in areas where appearance is not so important.

| Material | Primary Benefits | When to Apply | How to Apply |
|---|---|---|---|
| Compost | Adds humus. Suppresses weeds. Fertilizes. Warms soil. | At planting time and as needed throughout the season. | Spread 1" or more as a top-dressing around plants. |
| Grass clippings | Add nitrogen and humus. | At planting time and as needed thoughout the season. | Apply a 1"–4" layer around plants. May burn plants if placed too close to stems. |
| Leaves, shredded | Add humus. Suppress weeds well. Modulate soil temperature. | At planting time and as winter cover. | Apply in 3" layers; best if chopped and composted. |
| Newspaper | Suppresses weeds well. Retains moisture. | At planting time. | Lay down whole sections of the paper and anchor with soil or cover with more attractive mulches like wood chips. |
| Pine needles | Attractive. Suppress weeds well. Some control of fungal diseases. | At planting time and as winter cover. | Apply in 2"–4" layers. Needles tend to acidify soil; don't use around non-acid-loving plants. |
| Straw | Adds humus. Suppresses weeds well. Cools soil. | At planting time and as winter cover. | Lay down 8" layers around but not touching plants. May tie up nitrogen in soil; oat straw best. |
| Wood or bark chips, shredded | Attractive. Suppress weeds well. Cool soil and retain water. | At planting time and as needed throughout the season. | Best to compost before using. Apply in 1"–2" layer. |

During the growing season, boost plant growth by side-dressing dry fertilizers in crop rows or around the drip line of trees or shrubs. It's best to work side-dressings into the top inch of the soil.

**Liquid Organic Fertilizers**  Use liquid fertilizers to give your plants a light nutrient boost or snack every month—or even every two weeks—during the growing season. Simply mix a tankful of foliar spray, and spray all your plants at the same time.

Plants can absorb liquid fertilizers both through their roots and through leaf pores. Foliar feeding can supply nutrients when they are lacking or unavailable in the soil, or when roots are stressed. It is especially effective for giving fast-growing plants like vegetables an extra boost during the growing season. Compost tea and seaweed extract are two common examples of organic foliar fertilizers.

Some foliar fertilizers such as kelp are rich in micronutrients and growth hormones. These foliar sprays also appear to act as catalysts, increasing nutrient uptake by plants. You can make your own liquid fertilizer by brewing up compost or manure in water. See "Tea Time for Your Plants" on page 177.

With flowering and fruiting plants, foliar sprays are most useful during critical periods (such as after transplanting or during fruit set) or during periods of drought or extreme temperatures. For leaf crops, some suppliers recommend biweekly spraying.

When using liquid fertilizers, always follow label instructions for proper dilution and application methods. You can use a surfactant, such as coconut oil or a mild soap (1/4 teaspoon per gallon of spray), to ensure better coverage of the leaves. Otherwise the spray may bead up on the foliage and you won't get maximum benefit. Measure the surfactant carefully: If you use too much, it may damage plants. A slightly acidic spray mixture is most effective, so check your spray's pH. Use small amounts of vinegar to lower pH or baking soda to raise it. Aim for a pH of 6.0 to 6.5.

Any sprayer or mister will work, from hand-trigger units to knapsack sprayers. Set your sprayer to emit as fine a spray as possible. Never use a sprayer that has been used to apply herbicides.

The best times to spray are early morning
*(continued on page 177)*

 **Mix and Match**

If you want to mix your own general-purpose organic fertilizer, try combining individual amendments in the amounts shown here. Just pick one ingredient from each section. Because these amendments may vary in the amount of the nutrients they contain, this method won't give you a mixture with a precise NPK ratio. The ratio will be approximately between 1-2-1 and 4-6-3, with additional insoluble phosphorus and potash. The blend will provide a balanced supply of nutrients that will be steadily available to plants and encourage soil microorganisms to thrive.

**Nitrogen (N)**

2 parts blood meal
3 parts fish meal

**Phosphorus (P)**

3 parts bonemeal
6 parts rock phosphate or colloidal phosphate

**Potassium (K)**

1 part kelp meal
6 parts greensand

## Organic Fertilizer Primer

You don't have to be an expert to feed your plants with organic materials—you just need to understand which materials supply which nutrients and how they can be of most help to your garden. Here's a lineup of organic fertilizers and how best to use them.

| Organic Fertilizer | Nutrients Supplied | Rate of Application | Uses and Comments |
|---|---|---|---|
| Blood meal; dried blood | Blood meal: 15% nitrogen, 1.3% phosphorus, 0.7% potassium. Dried blood: 12% nitrogen, 3% phosphorus, 0% potassium. | Up to 3 lb. per 100 sq. ft. (more will burn plants). | Source of readily available nitrogen. Add to compost pile to speed decomposition. Repels deer and rabbits. Lasts 3–4 months. |
| Bonemeal | 3% nitrogen, 20% phosphorus, 0% potassium, 24–30% calcium. | Up to 5 lb. per 100 sq. ft. | Good source of phosphorus. Raises pH. Best on fruit trees, bulbs, and flowers. Lasts 6–12 months. |
| Compost (commercial) | 1% nitrogen, 1% phosphorus, 1% potassium. | Up to 20 lb. per 100 sq. ft. | Excellent source of organic matter. Improves soil structure. |
| Cottonseed meal | 6% nitrogen, 2–3% phosphorus, 2% potassium. | 2–5 lb. per 100 sq. ft. Trees: Apply 2–4 cups around drip line for each in. of trunk diameter. | Acidifies soil; use on crops that prefer low pH, such as azaleas and blueberries. Lasts 4–6 months. |
| Fish emulsion | 4% nitrogen, 4% phosphorus, 1% potassium. | Dilute 20:1 water to emulsion. | Apply as a foliar spray. Also sold as fish solubles. |
| Fish meal | 10% nitrogen, 4–6% phosphorus, 0% potassium. | Up to 5 lb. per 100 sq. ft. | Use in early spring, at transplanting, and any time plants need a boost. Lasts 6–8 months. |
| Granite dust | 0% nitrogen, 0% phosphorus, 3–5% potassium, 67% silica; 19 trace minerals. | Up to 10 lb. per 100 sq. ft. | Very slowly available. Lasts up to 10 years. Improves soil structure. Use mica-rich type only. Also sold as granite meal or crushed granite. |

| Organic Fertilizer | Nutrients Supplied | Rate of Application | Uses and Comments |
|---|---|---|---|
| Greensand | 0% nitrogen, 1% phosphorus, 5–7% potassium, 50% silica, 18–23% iron oxide; 22 trace minerals. | Up to 10 lb. per 100 sq. ft. | Slowly available. Lasts up to 10 years. Loosens clay soils. Apply in fall for benefits next season. Also sold as glauconite. |
| Guano, bat | 8% nitrogen, 4% phosphorus, 2% potassium average, but varies widely; 24 trace minerals. | Up to 5 lb. per 100 sq. ft; 2 T. per pint of potting soil; 1 lb. per 5 gal. water for manure tea. | Caves protect guano from leaching, so nutrients are conserved. |
| Guano, bird | 13% nitrogen, 8% phosphorus, 2% potassium; 11 trace minerals. | 3 lb. per 100 sq. ft. Fruit trees: 3–6 oz. per in. of trunk diameter. Houseplants: 1–2 oz. per gal. of water. | Especially good for roses, bulbs, azaleas, and houseplants. Also sold as Plantjoy. |
| Gypsum (calcium sulfate) | 23–57% calcium, 17.7% sulfur. | Up to 4 lb. per 100 sq. ft. | Use when both calcium and sulfur are needed and soil pH is high. Sulfur will tie up excess magnesium. Helps loosen clay soils. |
| Hoof and horn meal | 14% nitrogen, 2% phosphorus, 0% potassium. | Up to 4 lb. per 100 sq. ft. | High nitrogen source. Odorous. Takes 4–6 weeks to start releasing nitrogen; lasts 12 months. |
| Kelp meal; liquid seaweed | 1% nitrogen, 0% phosphorus, 12% potassium; 33% trace minerals, including calcium, sodium, chlorine, and sulfur, and about 50 other minerals in trace amounts. | Meal: up to 1 lb. per 100 sq. ft. Liquid: Dilute 25:1 water to seaweed for transplanting and rooting cuttings; 40:1 as booster and for fruit crops. | Contains natural growth hormones, so use sparingly. Best source of trace minerals. Lasts 6–12 months. Also sold as Folia-Gro, Sea Life, Maxicrop, Norwegian Sea Weed, liquid kelp. |

*(continued)*

## Organic Fertilizer Primer – Continued

| Organic Fertilizer | Nutrients Supplied | Rate of Application | Uses and Comments |
|---|---|---|---|
| Langbeinite | 0% nitrogen, 0% phosphorus, 22% potassium, 22% sulfur, 11% magnesium. | Up to 1 lb. per 100 sq. ft. | Will not alter pH. Use when there is abundant calcium and sulfur. Magnesium and potassium are needed. Also sold as Sul-Po-Mag or K-Mag. |
| Manure, composted cow | 2% nitrogen, 1% phosphorus, 1% potassium. | 40 lb. per 50–100 sq. ft. as soil conditioner; 2 parts to 6–8 parts loam as potting mix. | Low level of nutrients and slow release makes it most valuable as a soil conditioner. |
| Phosphate, colloidal | 0% nitrogen, 18–22% phosphorus, 0% potassium, 27% calcium, 1.7% iron; silicas and 14 other trace minerals. | Up to 10 lb. per 100 sq. ft. | More effective than rock phosphate on neutral soils. Phosphorus availability higher than rock phosphate. Half the pH-raising value of ground limestone. Lasts 2–3 years. |
| Phosphate, rock | 0% nitrogen, 33% phosphorus, 0% potassium, 30% calcium, 2.8% iron, 10% silica; 10 other trace minerals. | Up to 10 lb. per 100 sq. ft. | Releases phosphorus best in acid soils below pH 6.2. Slower release than colloidal phosphate. Will slowly raise pH 1 point or more. Also sold as phosphate rock. |
| Wood ashes | 0% nitrogen, 0–7% phosphorus, 6–20% potassium, 20–53% calcium carbonate; trace minerals such as copper, zinc, manganese, iron, sodium, sulfur, and boron. | 1–2 lb. per 100 sq. ft. | Nutrient amounts highly variable. Minerals highest in young hardwoods. Will raise soil pH. Put on soil in spring, and dig under. Do not use near young stems or roots. Protect ashes from leaching in winter. Lasts 12 or more months. |

and early evening, when the liquids will be absorbed most quickly and won't burn foliage. Choose a cool, clear day.

Spray until the liquid drips off the leaves. Be sure to concentrate the spray on leaf undersides, where leaf pores are more likely to be open. You can also water in liquid fertilizers around the root zone. A drip irrigation system can carry liquid fertilizers to your plants. Kelp is a better product for this use; fish emulsion can clog the irrigation emitters.

# STAKING AND TRELLISING

Staking plants in the flower and vegetable garden is a job that busy gardeners sometimes overlook. In most cases, however, the time you spend staking will be amply rewarded by the improved health and appearance of your garden.

Vining plants virtually require stakes or other support. Top-heavy, single-stemmed flowers like delphiniums, lilies, and dahlias benefit from support. Left unstaked, they are apt to bend unattractively and may snap off during heavy storms. Staking also improves the appearance of plants with thin, floppy stems that flatten easily.

Choose stakes and supports that match the needs of the plant and of you as a gardener. They must be tall enough and strong enough to support the entire mature plant when wet or windblown, and they must be firmly inserted in the soil. A stake that breaks or tips over can cause more damage than using none at all. Take care not to damage roots when inserting a stake, and avoid tying the shoots too tightly to the stake. Install the supports as early in the growing season as possible so that the plants can be trained to them as they grow, not forced to fit them later on. When growing plants from seed, install the support before planting.

In the flower garden, choose supports that are as inconspicuous as possible. Thin, slightly

flexible stakes that bend with the plant are less conspicuous and may be better than heavier, rigid ones. In general, select stakes that stand about three-fourths of the height of the mature plant. Insert them close to or among the stems so that as the plant grows, the foliage will hide the supports. Choose colors and materials that blend with the plants. Bamboo stakes tinted green are available in a variety of sizes and are a good, inexpensive choice for many plants. You can also buy wood, metal, and plastic stakes and trellises, and a wide assortment of metal rings and support systems. Using green twine or plastic-covered wire is an inconspicuous way to fasten plants to their supports.

In the vegetable garden, sturdiness is more important than appearance. Staking vegetables

 **Tea Time for Your Plants**

Your perennials will find a bucket of manure tea or compost tea as refreshing as you find your morning cup, and it's just as easy to make. Put a shovelful of fresh or dried manure (or finished compost) in a burlap or cheesecloth bag. (You can also make your own bag using a big square of either fabric.) Tie the top closed, and sink the sack in a large bucket or barrel of water. Cover the container, and steep the "tea" for one to seven days. (As with real tea, the longer it steeps, the stronger it gets.)

Use the tea full strength as a liquid fertilizer around your plants, or dilute it and use it to give plants a boost when you water. You can also use manure or compost tea with drip irrigation systems if you filter it through cheesecloth or old panty hose first so it doesn't clog the tubes. Manure and compost tea are both great for foliar feeding.

like tomatoes, peppers, and beans makes them easier to cultivate and harvest. It increases yields by preventing contamination with soilborne diseases and allowing for more plants in a given area. Choose tall, sturdy stakes or cages that can support the plant even when it is heavy with

## Standard Staking Methods

Here are four ways to stake plants in the garden. Be sure to match the staking method to each plant's growth habit:

**Individual stakes:** Sink stake firmly near the stem when plant is 6 to 8 inches high. A loose figure-eight tie connects stem to stake securely yet maintains the plant's natural form and prevents damage to the stalk. As the plant grows, add ties every 8 to 10 inches. Two closely spaced plants can be tied to one stake if it is placed between them. Top-heavy flowers like this delphinium need stakes almost as tall as the mature plant.

**Twiggy brush:** For plants such as peas, coreopsis, and baby's-breath, try lengths of sturdy, twiggy brush or branches. Cut the brush to the final height of the plants, and push it 6 inches into the ground between the plants.

**Wire ring supports:** Bushy plants with heavy flowers, like peonies, can be grown in a wire ring. The foliage will hide the ring as the plants grow. The natural form of the plant is enhanced, not disrupted.

**Stakes and strings:** Insert four stakes into the corners of the bed when shoots are a few inches high. Tie string (or wire) from stake to stake to form a box about 6 to 8 inches off the ground. Add strings as needed. Run additional strings across the bed or weave them back and forth to keep plants from falling inside the bed.

Twiggy brush

Individual stake

Wire ring

fruit, and insert stakes firmly into the ground. Use narrow strips torn from rags or bands cut from stockings to gently fasten plants to supports. See Chapter 9 for more information on staking vegetable crops.

Perennial vines such as roses and grapes are commonly grown on trellises or on wires between sturdy posts. For more information

on training fruit, see Chapter 10.

Trees and tall shrubs are commonly staked temporarily at planting to help hold them upright until their roots become established. Fruit trees on dwarfing rootstocks may need to be permanently staked. For more information on staking trees, see Chapter 13.

---

##  Support Your Vegetables

Vegetables such as tomatoes, peppers, and beans need sturdy support in the garden. Try these methods to keep plants growing strong:

### Lifetime Cages

The same welded steel mesh that gives reinforced concrete its strength is just the thing for making vegetable cages that will last a lifetime. You can buy it at just about any building supply center. Figure on buying at least 16 feet—enough for two cages.

The only tools you need are a small pair of bolt cutters to cut the heavy wire and a good pair of pliers. Be sure to wear work gloves to avoid cuts and blisters.

Lay the mesh strip flat on the ground. Measure an 8-foot piece by counting off 16 sections of the mesh (each section of mesh is 5¼ inches × 6 inches). In the middle of the 16th section, cut each cross wire in the middle. You'll use those loose ends later to fasten the cage together.

Next, trim off the bottom horizontal wire to create a row of 5-inch tines along the base of the cage. Now gently bend the prepared mesh section into a circle. Pull the clipped ends together, and use your pliers to twist them around each other to form the cage.

Set the cage upright around the plant, and

push the tines into the ground to anchor it. Even high winds and bumper crops have a hard time toppling these cages. At the end of the season, clear off old vines and store the cages for winter, or leave the cages standing and have them double as compost bins.

### Drying-Rack Trellis

For a simple trellis, set up an old wooden clothes-drying rack, lay it on its side in the garden, and set your tomatoes between the rungs, which will stand about 3 feet high. As the plants grow larger, they will be supported by the rungs, and the fruit will ripen well above the ground.

### Custom Stakes

Tying up tomatoes and other vegetable plants is easy with custom-made stakes. First, take a ¾-inch × 1½-inch stake and make saw cuts about ½ inch deep and about 1 foot apart, staggering them on either side. Next, cut strips of panty hose ⅜-inch × 10 inches, and tie knots at each end. Put the stake in the ground, then put one end of a strip in one of the slots, using the knot as an anchor. Loop the strip around the tomato stem in a figure-eight pattern and secure it in another slot on the other side of the stake.

# WATERING YOUR GARDEN

At one time or another, most of us have run into a water shortage. We couldn't wash our cars, water our lawns and gardens, or let the children play in the sprinkler. It lasted maybe a few weeks; then it rained and life returned to normal. Or so it seemed. Running on empty is becoming a way of life in state after state in the United States and in a growing number of countries around the world.

Another problem is water quality. In coastal areas with shallow water tables, for example, heavy pumping of groundwater allows salt water to seep into wells. In heavily agricultural areas, pesticides and fertilizers are tainting both surface and groundwater supplies.

While we can't as individuals change patterns of water use in commercial agriculture, we can all take steps to reduce water usage in our homes and yards.

So how do you go about conserving water *and* watering your garden at the same time? One answer is drip irrigation. A drip irrigation system delivers water directly to the root zone of plants, without the waste of evaporation or runoff. Coupled with basic conservation techniques such as using mulch, selecting plants that require less water, and limiting lawn area, drip irrigation can help conserve water while ensuring a healthy garden.

## CONSERVING WATER IN THE GARDEN

With a little planning, it's possible to have good gardens, a beautiful lawn, and landscaping that need very little supplemental watering. The first step, of course, is to increase the water-holding capacity of your soil by adding organic matter. In deep, rich soil protected by mulch, plants find it much easier to develop the strong, deep root systems necessary to find water during dry periods. Cultivating the soil between row crops

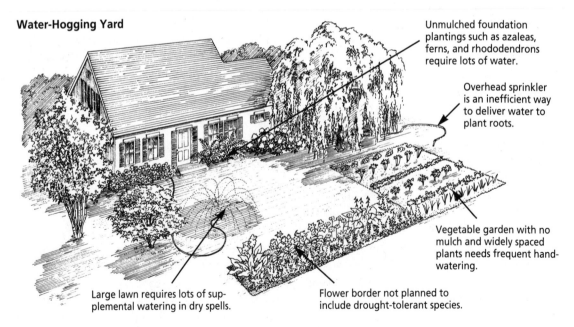

**Water-Hogging Yard**

Unmulched foundation plantings such as azaleas, ferns, and rhododendrons require lots of water.

Overhead sprinkler is an inefficient way to deliver water to plant roots.

Vegetable garden with no mulch and widely spaced plants needs frequent hand-watering.

Large lawn requires lots of supplemental watering in dry spells.

Flower border not planned to include drought-tolerant species.

**Is your yard a water hog?** Dull and unimaginative, the typical American yard is a water hog. Conventional sprinklers waste water needed by thirsty plants.

also helps water filter into the soil. For more information on soil improvement, see Chapter 2.

There are many other things you can do to reduce watering needs without sacrificing the beauty or pleasure of your yard and gardens:

■ Mulch trees, shrubs, and other plants with up to 3 inches of mulch. See "Mulching Your Garden" on page 167 for suggestions on materials to use.

■ Water less frequently, but water deeply, making sure to soak the root zone rather than the whole yard.

■ Select native plants that require less water.

■ In arid climates, follow the principles of Xeriscaping in planning and maintaining your yard. A Xeriscape (from the Greek *xeros,* meaning dry) is a water-saving garden designed for a dry region. Many municipal and state water departments publish low-cost or free guides for the beginning Xeriscaper. Check your library, bookstore, or the government listings in your phone book to read more about planning a Xeriscape. Publications on this topic are available from the National Xeriscape Council, P.O. Box 163172, Austin, TX 78751-3172.

■ Limit the size of your lawn. Replace lawn with groundcovers, mulches, and shade trees to help you and your yard keep cool.

■ Add a walkway, deck, or patio to help reduce water consumption while adding more enjoyment to your yard.

## USING DRIP IRRIGATION

For those situations in which you have to water, always strive for the most efficient method. When you water with the hose or an overhead sprinkler, some water is immediately lost to evaporation from plant surfaces, through surface run-off, or by falling in areas that don't need water, such as a street or walkway.

A more efficient method is a custom-designed drip irrigation system that will water all or any

**Water-Conserving Yard**

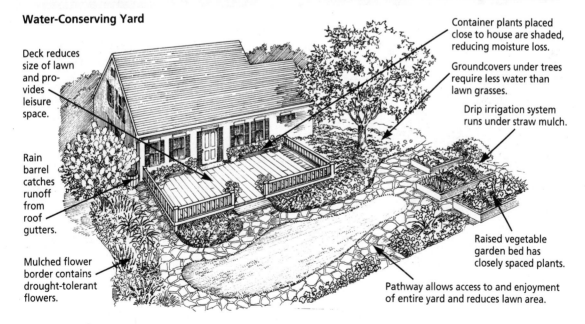

Deck reduces size of lawn and provides leisure space.

Rain barrel catches runoff from roof gutters.

Mulched flower border contains drought-tolerant flowers.

Container plants placed close to house are shaded, reducing moisture loss.

Groundcovers under trees require less water than lawn grasses.

Drip irrigation system runs under straw mulch.

Raised vegetable garden bed has closely spaced plants.

Pathway allows access to and enjoyment of entire yard and reduces lawn area.

**Conserve water.** With a little advance planning and thoughtful plant selection, any yard can be transformed into a water-efficient Eden that is as pleasing to the eye as it is friendly to the environment.

part of your landscape. Also called "trickle" or "weep" irrigation, drip systems are as beneficial for dryland gardeners as for those in the northern, eastern, and southern parts of the country. The water savings and increased plant growth in your garden will more than make up for the cost and effort involved in the design and installation of a drip irrigation system.

A drip irrigation system delivers water directly to a plant's root zone, where it seeps slowly into the soil one drop at a time. Almost no water is lost through surface runoff or evaporation, and soil particles have plenty of opportunity to absorb and hold water for plants. It also means very few nutrients leach down beyond the reach of plant roots. Furthermore, since drip irrigation delivers water directly to the plants you want to grow, less is wasted on weeds. The soil surface between plants also remains drier, which dis-

courages weed seeds from sprouting. All these benefits add up to the fact that drip irrigation systems can save a great deal of water—and money in terms of reduced water bills. Studies show that well-designed drip systems use at least 30 percent, and in some cases 50 percent, less water than other methods of watering such as sprinkling.

For busy gardeners, the main benefit of installing a drip irrigation system is the savings of both time and effort. Drip systems eliminate the need to drag hoses and sprinklers around. For systems that use a timer, gardeners need only spend a few seconds to turn the system on; the timer automatically turns it off.

Plants watered with drip systems grow more quickly and are more productive, because they have all the water they need and their growth isn't slowed by water stress. (This is especially

**Drip irrigation.** For large beds, use a drip system, which delivers water through spaghetti tubes directly to the base of each plant.

**Soaker hoses.** For small beds, soaker hoses are great, releasing water slowly and evenly to the whole bed. Cover the hoses with mulch to conserve moisture.

true when drip irrigation is used in conjunction with mulch.) These systems also keep water off the foliage, which helps prevent some foliage diseases such as powdery mildew.

**Designing a System**  The first decision to make in designing a drip irrigation system is what you want to water. Do you want a system only for your vegetable garden or for your entire landscape? Topography is also a consideration: If your garden is hilly, you'll probably need to use emitters that compensate for pressure changes in the line.

You can design your own system, but most companies that sell drip irrigation equipment will design systems for you if provided with a scale drawing of your garden, information on what you're growing, your soil type, and garden topography. Their design will come complete with a list of parts and spacing for emitters. Whatever method you choose, start by making a fairly accurate drawing of your garden to determine how many feet of tubing you'll need.

Plants can become "addicted" to drip irrigation, because roots will concentrate in the area where the water is available. When designing a drip system to carry water along the rows of a vegetable garden or to the roots of a prized rhododendron, it's important that the water be spread uniformly throughout the irrigated area so root growth will be uniform. For example, if you are irrigating larger plants such as trees and shrubs, place emitters on two or more sides of each plant to encourage roots to grow out in all directions rather than clustering on one side. Using your system for frequent, short waterings, rather than long, slow ones, is a bad idea for the same reason; the water doesn't have a chance to spread far in the soil, and consequently the roots form a tight, ball-like mass around the emitters.

**Soaker Hoses**  Soaker hoses are another type of drip irrigation system that provides many of the advantages of emitter drip systems at a fraction of their cost. Some ooze water over their entire length; others spurt water through tiny holes. When using soaker hoses with holes, be sure to face the holes downward so the water doesn't squirt up in the air like a sprinkler. Systems using these hoses need no assembly; it's easy to lay out the hoses between small plants and along narrow rows.

Soakers save water, reduce loss through evaporation, and keep leaves dry. However, since water emerges evenly along the length of the hose, water delivery can't be directed as precisely as with an emitter system. Soaker hoses can be used for short runs (100 to 200 feet) over flat surfaces. They're useful for crops such as carrots that are closely spaced.

Also known as dew hoses, soaker hoses can be made of canvas, various types of plastic, or rubber. Hoses made of rigid plastics or rubber can be hard to lay flat and difficult to bend around corners. Plastic and rubber soakers are resistant to fungal attack and seldom develop leaks at couplings or seams, so they can be left in the beds for long periods of time without deterioration. In contrast, canvas hoses are susceptible to mold and mildew and should be drained and dried after each use.

# EXTENDING THE SEASON

Gardeners can't control the weather, but they can work around it. Many gardeners have discovered ways to make their wish for a longer gardening season come true, using materials as simple as a plastic milk jug or as grand as a greenhouse.

Starting seeds indoors in pots or flats is a type of season extension that any gardener with a sunny window can try. For full information on indoor seed starting, see Chapter 4. Protecting young plants from cold temperatures outdoors in a cold frame or under row covers is a tried-and-true technique for extending the season.

Season extenders are materials or structures used to keep the air and soil around plants warmer. There are many different types of season extenders you can make or buy. Backyard gardeners have used cold frames, cloches, hot-caps, and row covers for many years. Even commercial vegetable growers use season extenders to lengthen short growing seasons and get an earlier and larger crop to market.

## COLD FRAMES

The best-known season extender is the cold frame. This type of structure, usually made of wood with a transparent glass or plastic top, relies on solar energy to warm the air and soil. Most have slanting sash "roofs," with the high end toward the north, so the sun's rays strike the glass at about a 90-degree angle, and water and snow slide off the lids easily. A lid with a slope of 35 to 45 degrees catches the most sunlight year-round. Glass window sashes are most often used to cover frames, but you can substitute fiberglass, Plexiglas, or heavyweight polyethylene.

Gardeners most commonly use cold frames in early spring for starting or hardening off seedlings destined for the garden. However, there are many other uses for cold frames. A moist, shady frame provides a good start to fall crops in the dry heat of summer; in winter, the same frame offers a spot for cold-treating spring bulbs for forcing. Some models are also useful for rooting cuttings of woody plants or perennials.

Hotbeds are cold frames with an auxiliary heat source. Manure, compost, a heating cable, or some other heating source maintains warm temperatures in the frame.

There are two types of frames to consider: permanent and portable. Permanent models are built over foundations that are either dug into the ground or constructed on the surface.

Aboveground models provide less frost protection than ones built over a dug foundation, but both provide more reliable protection from the cold than portable frames. Permanent frames are generally sturdier and last longer.

Portable frames, which are basically bottomless boxes with clear lids, function in much the same way as permanent frames. In the vegetable garden, portable frames can extend the season for spring or fall crops such as lettuce or spinach, or keep frost off late-ripening crops.

## CLOCHES

Cloches are small plant coverings that trap the sun's warmth, raising the air temperature around an individual plant or a small group of plants. You can buy commercial cloches or make your own. See the illustration on the opposite page.

## ROW COVERS

A row cover is a versatile season extender that you can use to protect rows, small garden areas, or the whole garden from frost or cold temperatures. Row covers are sheets of transparent plastic or fabric. They are made of permeable and impermeable plastic, slitted plastic, or spun, bonded, or woven fabric and are available in many widths. Row covers can provide from 2° to 7°F frost protection at night; during the day, temperatures under row covers can be 5° to 30°F higher than the surrounding air. Using row covers in spring and fall can add a month or more of growing time to most garden seasons.

Plastic row covers keep air temperatures warmer during the day and night than other row cover fabrics. You will need to vent them on warm days and close them back up at night. Slitted plastic row covers don't require venting. Colored or shaded plastic covers are available for southern gardeners. The coloring blocks out some of the sunlight, reducing the heat inside the tunnel.

Suspend plastic row covers over the row with metal, plastic, wire, or wooden hoops to prevent injuring plants. Anchor row cover edges securely in place with soil, boards, pipes, or similar material.

Floating row covers made of spun-bonded synthetic fabric can be laid right on plants and soil. They provide only a few degrees' frost protection. Loosely cover the row or garden area. Allow enough slack for four to six weeks of plant growth. Secure the row cover edges with soil, pipes, or boards.

Season extenders such as cloches and row covers are most effective if you prewarm the garden soil before planting. Seeds will not germinate and transplants will suffer in cold soil, even if the air temperature is high enough. To warm the soil, put the season extender in place one to two weeks prior to planting, or cover soil with clear or black plastic several weeks before planting.

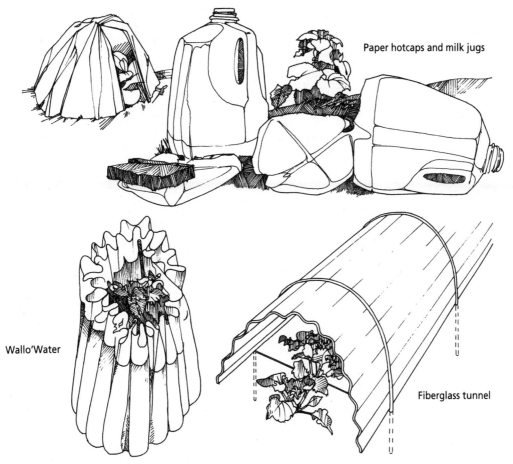

Paper hotcaps and milk jugs

Wallo'Water

Fiberglass tunnel

**Cloches in the garden.** Several types of cloches are available for season extension. Commercial products include paraffin-treated paper hotcaps and Wallo'Water; the latter surrounds plants with an upright ring of narrow plastic tubes filled with water. For a homemade cloche, cut along three sides of the bottom of a plastic milk jug. Or create a tunnel cloche out of 4-foot-long translucent corrugated fiberglass. Small cloches heat up quickly on sunny days, so remove cloches or tip them up during good weather so you don't "cook" your plants.

# PLANT SELECTION AND CARE GUIDE

# Chapter 9

# VEGETABLE GARDENS

Fresh-picked sweet corn, tomatoes, and snap peas are a taste treat you can get only from your backyard vegetable garden. The quality and flavor of fresh vegetables will reward you from early in the growing season until late fall. And when you garden organically, you know that your harvest is free of potentially harmful chemical residues.

Although the plants grown in vegetable gardens are a diverse group from many different plant families, they share broad general cultural requirements. Most will thrive in well-drained soil with a pH of 6.5 to 7.0. Some will tolerate frost; others will tolerate some shade. You should have little trouble growing vegetables successfully if you pick an appropriate site, prepare the soil well, and keep your growing crops weeded and watered.

This chapter will serve as your guide to planning, preparing, and tending your vegetable plot through the seasons.

Vegetable gardens are ideal sites for putting organic soil improvement and pest management techniques into practice. Since you're working the soil each year, you'll have lots of opportunities to add organic matter and soil amendments that help keep the soil naturally balanced.

As you make your yearly plan for planting and caring for your garden, you can incorporate techniques such as crop rotation, soil enrichment, and other cultural pest prevention methods. And there's a broad range of organically acceptable pest control methods and products for vegetable crops. See "Putting It All Togeth-

er" on the opposite page for a guide to where to find information on these topics in other chapters of this book.

## PLANNING YOUR GARDEN

Planning your garden can be as much fun as planting it. When you plan a garden, you'll balance all your hopes and wishes for the crops you'd like to harvest against your local growing conditions, as well as the space you have available to plant. Planning involves choosing a site (unless you already have an established garden), deciding on a garden style, selecting crops and cultivars, and mapping your garden.

### SITE SELECTION

Somewhere in your yard, there is a good place for a vegetable garden. The ideal site has these characteristics:

**Full or almost full sun:** In warm climates, some vegetables can get by on six hours of direct sunshine each day, while a full day of sun is needed in cool climates. The best sites for vegetable gardens usually are on the south or west side of a house, where sunshine is most abundant. If part of the site you select is too shady for planting, put your compost pile there.

**Good drainage:** A slight slope is good for vegetable gardens. The soil will get well soaked by rain or irrigation water, and excess will run off. Avoid low places where water accumulates.

**Limited competition from nearby trees:** Tree roots take up huge amounts of water. Leave as much space as possible between large trees and your vegetable garden.

**Easy access to water:** If you can't get a hose or irrigation line to a prospective garden site, don't plant vegetables there. No matter what your local climate is, you'll most likely have to provide supplemental water at some point in the growing season, or your harvest will suffer.

**Accessibility:** Organic gardens need large amounts of mulch, plus periodic infusions of other bulky materials such as well-rotted manure or rock fertilizers. If you have a large garden, you should be able to drive a truck up to its edge for easy unloading. In narrow city lots, the garden access path should be wide enough for a cart or wheelbarrow.

Once you find a site that has these characteristics, double-check for hidden problems. For example, don't locate your garden over septic-tank field lines, buried utility cables, or water lines.

## GARDEN LAYOUT

Once you've decided on a site, think about the type of vegetable garden you want. Possible layouts range from traditional row plantings to intensive raised beds and container gardens.

**Row Planting** A row garden, in which vegetables are planted in parallel lines, is easy to organize and plant. However, it's not as space-efficient as more intensive methods, such as raised beds. You may spend more time weeding unless you mulch heavily and early between rows. Also, you'll get less yield per area than you would from an intensively planted garden. Row planting is quick and efficient for large plantings of crops such as beans or corn.

You can enhance the appearance and productivity of a row garden by making a raised bed along the front edge and planting it with herbs and flowers. "Sod Strips Save Work" on page 192 describes an easy way to start a row garden.

**Beds** Productivity, efficient use of space, less weeding, and shading the soil are all benefits of intensively planted beds. Beds are raised planting areas, generally with carefully enriched soil, so they can be planted intensively. While they require more initial time to prepare, they save time on weeding or mulching later in the season. Because they're more space-efficient, you'll also get higher yields per area than from a traditional row garden.

Beds for vegetables should be no more than 4 feet wide so you can easily reach the center of the bed to plant, weed, and harvest. See "Raised Bed Gardening" on page 40 for directions on making raised beds. The illustration on page 194 shows interesting ways to adapt beds to your needs.

**Spot Gardens** If your yard is small, with no

 **Putting It All Together**

Vegetable gardeners will find helpful information throughout this book for fine-tuning their gardens. Here's a summary of other entries to refer to for additional information:

**Preparing the soil:** Chapter 2 offers detailed instructions for evaluating and improving garden soil. Chapter 3 offers information on making and using compost.

**Planting:** For more information on starting and planting vegetable seeds, see Chapters 4 and 5. Chapter 7 offers suggestions on planting flowers and herbs among your vegetables to help attract beneficial insects or repel pests.

**Care during the season:** Chapter 8 offers advice on how to get the most from your garden tools and instructions on controlling weeds and feeding, staking, trellising, and watering plants.

suitable space for a separate vegetable garden, look for sunny spots where you can fit small plantings of your favorite crops. Plant a small bed of salad greens and herbs near your kitchen door for easy access when preparing meals. Tuck vegetables into flower beds. You can dress up crops that aren't ornamental, such as tomatoes, by underplanting them with annuals such as nasturtiums and marigolds. For ideas on incorporating vegetables into your landscape, see "A Gallery of Edibles" on page 16.

**Containers** You may not be able to grow all your favorite vegetables in containers, but many dwarf cultivars of vegetables grow well in pots or planters. Garden catalogs include dwarf tomato, cucumber, pepper, and even squash cultivars suitable for container growing. Vegetables that are naturally small, such as loose-head lettuce,

scallions, and many herbs, such as basil, also grow nicely in containers.

## CROP CHOICES

Generally, vegetables can be divided into cool-weather, warm-weather, and hot-weather crops. "Some Like It Hot" on page 196 lists popular vegetables in these categories.

Consider the length of your growing season (the period of time between the last frost in spring and the first one in fall), seasonal rainfall patterns, and other environmental factors when choosing vegetables. There are many new fast-maturing and heat- or cold-tolerant cultivars that make it easier for northern gardeners to grow hot-weather crops such as melons and for Southern gardeners to be able to enjoy cool-loving crops such as spinach. See "Making the

---

 **Making the Right Choices**

Seed catalogs and seed racks present a dazzling array of choices for the vegetable gardener. They all look tasty and beautiful in the pictures, but here's how to choose:

■ If you're a beginning gardener, talk with other gardeners and your local extension agent. Ask what vegetables grow best in your area, and start with those crops. Most extension service offices will also provide lists of recommended cultivars.

■ Seek out catalogs and plant lists offered by seed companies that specialize in regionally adapted selections.

■ Match cultivars to your garden's characteristics and problems. Look for cultivars that are resistant to disease organisms that may be widespread in your area, such as VF tomato cultivars—which are resistant to *Verticillium* and *Fusarium* fungi.

■ If you buy seeds by the packet, take note of how many seeds you're getting. Seed quantity per packet varies widely. Some packets of new or special cultivars may contain fewer than 20 seeds.

■ When buying transplants at local garden centers, always check the plants for disease and insect problems.

■ Ask whether the transplants you're buying have been hardened off yet. If the salesperson doesn't know what you're talking about, take the hint, and buy your transplants from a more knowledgeable supplier.

■ Remember, with transplants, larger size doesn't always mean better quality. Look for stocky transplants with uniform green leaves. Don't buy transplants that are already flowering—they won't survive the shock of transplanting as well as younger plants will.

Right Choices" on the opposite page for more ideas on how to make good crop and cultivar choices for your garden.

Have some fun when you choose plants for your vegetable garden as well. Make some of your selections for beauty as well as flavor. Beans with purple or variegated pods are easy to spot for picking and lovely to behold, for example. Look through catalogs and try some of the heirloom or other unusual cultivars they offer.

## GARDEN MAPPING

As you fill out seed order forms, it's wise to map planned locations for your crops. Otherwise, you may end up with far too little or too much seed. Depending on the size of your garden, you may need to make a formal plan drawn to scale.

Consider these points as you figure out your planting needs and fill in your map:

■ Are you growing just enough of a crop for fresh eating, or will you be preserving some of your harvest? For some crops, it takes surprisingly little seed to produce enough to feed a family. You can refer to seed catalogs or check individual vegetable entries for information on how much to plant.

■ Are you planning to rotate crops? Changing the position of plants in different crop families from year to year can help reduce any pest problems.

■ Are you going to plant crops in spring and again later in the season for a fall harvest? Order seed for both plantings at the same time.

For more ideas to help you create your own garden map and plan, see Chapter 1.

# PREPARING THE SOIL

Since most vegetables are fast-growing annuals, they need garden soil that provides a wide range of plant nutrients and loose soil that plant roots

can penetrate easily. In an organic vegetable garden, soil with high organic-matter content and biological activity is paramount in importance. Every year when you harvest vegetables, you're

 **Small Garden Strategies**

If your appetite for fresh vegetables is bigger than the space you have to grow them in, try these ways to coax the most produce from the least space:

■ Emphasize vertical crops that grow up rather than out: trellised snow peas, shell peas, pole beans, and cucumbers.

■ Interplant fast-maturing salad crops (lettuce, radishes, spinach, and beets) together in 2-foot-square blocks. Succession-plant every two weeks in early spring and early fall.

■ Avoid overplanting any single vegetable. Summer squash is the number one offender when it comes to rampant overproduction. Two plants each of zucchini, yellow-neck, and a novelty summer squash will yield plenty.

■ Choose medium- and small-fruited cultivars of tomatoes and peppers. The smaller the fruits, the more the plants tend to produce. Beefsteak tomatoes and big bell peppers produce comparatively few fruits per plant.

■ Experiment with unusual vegetables that are naturally compact—such as kohlrabi, bok choy, and oriental eggplant. Experiment with dwarf cultivars of larger vegetables.

■ Maintain permanent clumps of perpetual vegetables such as chives, hardy scallions, and perennial herbs. Even a small garden should always have something to offer.

carting off part of the reservoir of nutrients that was in your vegetable garden soil. To keep the soil in balance, you need to replace those nutrients. Look for every opportunity to incorporate different forms of organic matter into your soil.

## ASSESSING YOUR SOIL

If you're starting a new vegetable garden or switching from conventional to organic methods (or if you've just been disappointed with past yields or crop quality), start by testing your soil. Soil acidity or alkalinity, which is measured as soil pH, can affect plant performance. Most vegetables prefer soil with a pH of 6.5 to 7.0. Overall soil fertility also will influence yield, especially for heavy-feeding crops such as broc-

coli and tomatoes. A soil test will reveal soil pH as well as any nutrient imbalances. "Investigating the Soil" on page 26 explains how to collect a soil sample and have it tested, as well as more about pH and nutrient requirements of plants.

## CREATING NEW GARDENS

If you're just starting out, you'll probably be tilling under sod, or possibly bare ground, to start your garden. Using a rotary tiller may be the only practical way to work up the soil in a large garden. But whether you're working with a machine or digging by hand, use care. Don't work the soil when it's too wet or too dry; that would have detrimental effects on soil structure and quality. "Sod Strips Save Work" on the

 **Sod Strips Save Work**

When transforming a plot of lawn into a vegetable garden, try cultivating strips or beds in the sod. You'll only have to contend with weeds in the beds. Plus, you'll have excellent erosion control and no mud between the rows, which makes picking easier and more enjoyable. Follow these suggestions:

**Tilling the bed:** Overlap your tilling so that the finished bed is 1½ to 2 times the cutting width of your tiller. Start out with a slow wheel speed and shallow tilling depth. Gradually increase speed and depth as the sod becomes more and more workable. Make the beds as long or as short as you want, but space the beds about 3 feet apart. Depending on how tough the sod and your tiller are, you may have to retill in a week or two or hand-dig stubborn grass clumps to make a proper seedbed.

**Weed control:** You can control weeds easily in the rows with a wheel-hoe cultivator or hand

hoe or by hand-weeding. What about weeds along the outside edges of the beds? Just mow them down with your lawn mower when you mow the grassy areas between the beds. You'll be rewarded with a ready supply of grass clippings for compost or mulch.

**Caution:** Before mowing, be sure to pick up all of the larger rocks that your tiller brought to the surface. Rocks will quickly dull and chip your mower blade, and they're downright dangerous to people, pets, and property when your mower kicks them up and hurls them through the air.

Once your garden is finished for the season, sow a green manure crop, such as buckwheat, clover, or ryegrass, in the beds. The following spring, till the strips that were in sod. It's crop rotation made easy! Or let your sod strips be permanent pathways. Over time, as the soil in the tilled strips improves, they naturally evolve into raised beds.

opposite page explains a simple method for creating a new garden in a lawn area.

If you're ambitious, a great way to start a vegetable garden is by double digging the soil. This process thoroughly loosens the soil so that it will retain more water and air, have better drainage, and be easier for roots to penetrate. For step-by-step instructions, see "Double Digging" on page 40.

Depending on the results of your soil tests, you may need to work in lime to correct pH, or rock fertilizers to correct deficiencies, as you dig your garden. In any case, it's always wise to incorporate organic matter as you work.

## ENRICHING THE SOIL

If you're an experienced gardener with an established garden site, you can take steps to replenish soil nutrients and organic matter as soon as you harvest and clear out your garden in the fall. Sow seed of a green manure crop in your garden, or cover the soil with a thick layer of organic mulch. Both green manures and mulches protect the soil from erosion and improve organic matter content. In the spring, you'll be ready to push back or incorporate the mulch or green manure and start planting.

If you don't plant a green manure crop, spread compost or well-rotted manure over your garden in spring and work it into the soil. You can add as much as a 6-inch layer of organic material, if you're fortunate enough to have that much on hand. The best time to do this is a few weeks before planting, if your soil is dry enough to be worked. You can cultivate with a rotary tiller or by hand, using a turning fork and rake. Never cultivate extremely wet soil, or you will be compacting it instead of aerating it. Be conservative when you work the soil. While some cultivation is necessary to prepare seedbeds and to open up the soil for root growth, excess cultivation is harmful. It introduces large

amounts of oxygen into the soil, which can speed the breakdown of soil organic matter. And if soil is too wet or too dry, cultivating it can ruin soil structure.

Other opportunities for improving your soil will crop up at planting time, when you add compost or other growth boosters in planting rows or holes, and during the growing season, as you mulch your developing plants.

# PLANTING YOUR CROPS

Planting season can be the busiest time of year for the vegetable gardener. Some careful planning is in order. To help you remember what you have planted and how well cultivars perform in your garden, keep written records. Fill in planting dates on your garden map as the season progresses. Later, make notes of harvest dates. If you would like to keep more detailed records, try keeping a garden journal, or set up a vegetable garden data file on index cards. With good records, you can discover many details about the unique climate in your garden, such as when soil warms up in spring, when problem insects emerge, and when space becomes available for replanting.

## GETTING SET TO PLANT

Once the soil is prepared, lay out your garden paths. Then rake loose soil from the pathways into the raised rows or beds. As soon as possible, mulch the pathways with leaves, straw, or another biodegradable mulch. Lay mulch thickly to keep down weeds. If you live in a region that has frequent, heavy rain, place boards down the pathways so you'll have a dry place to walk.

You can prepare planting beds and rows as much as several weeks before planting. However, if you plan to leave more than three weeks between preparation and planting, mulch the soil so it won't crust over or compact.

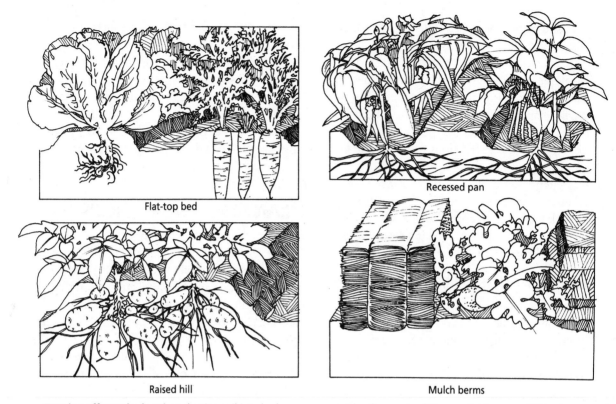

Flat-top bed

Recessed pan

Raised hill

Mulch berms

**Topping off your beds.** When shaping soil into beds or rows, consider the needs of the vegetables you will be planting. Flat-top beds are best for small-seeded crops that need lots of water, such as lettuce and other leafy greens, carrots, and cabbage-family plants. Use raised hills or rows when planting crops that may be prone to foliar diseases, such as cantaloupes, cucumbers, potatoes, corn, and squash. Recessed pans help slow evaporation of soil moisture; use in hot climates for crops such as beans, okra, and eggplant. Put up mulch berms made of hay bales or layers of soil and mulch alongside beds in arid climates to retain soil moisture and protect plants from drying winds.

**Plant Arrangement** There are practically no limits to the ways you can arrange plants in a vegetable garden. In a traditional row garden, you'll probably plant crops such as tomatoes and summer squash in single rows of single species. If you have raised rows or raised beds, you can interplant—mix different types of crops in one area—and use a variety of spacing patterns to maximize the number of plants in a given area. See the illustration on this page and the illustration on the opposite page for ideas on planning the layout of your garden crops.

**Planting Combinations** Frequently you can

practice succession cropping—growing two vegetable crops in the same space in the same growing season. You'll plant one early crop, harvest it, and then plant a warm- or hot-season crop afterward. To avoid depleting the soil, make sure one crop is a nitrogen-fixing legume, and the other a light feeder. All vegetables used for succession cropping should mature quickly. For example, in a cool climate, plant garden peas in spring, and follow them with cucumber or summer squash. Or after harvesting your early crop of spinach, plant bush beans. In warm climates, try lettuce followed by field

Single rows        Trellised plants        Matrix planting        Zigzag planting

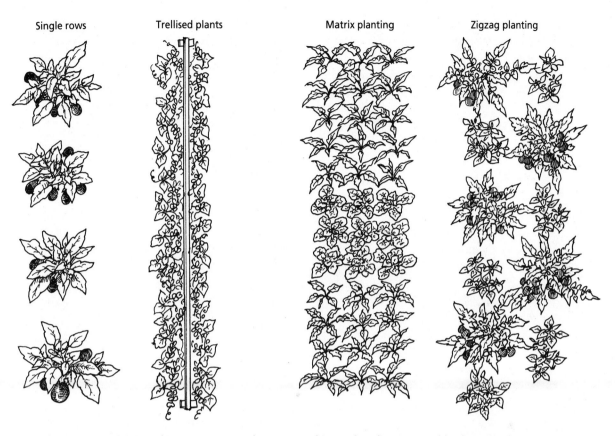

**Spacing and interplanting.** There are many good ways to combine and configure vegetable plants. Single rows are good for upright bushy plants and those that need good air circulation such as tomatoes and summer squash. Use double rows for trellised plants such as pole beans and cucumbers and for compact bushes such as snap beans and potatoes. Matrix planting is good for interplanting leafy greens such as lettuce and spinach and root crops such as carrots and onions. A zigzag arrangement works well for interplanting vegetables and flowers.

peas, or plant pole beans and then a late crop of turnips after the bean harvest.

## SEEDS AND TRANSPLANTS

Some vegetable crops grow best when seeded directly in place. Other crops benefit from being coddled indoors during the seedling stage and then grow robustly after transplanting.

**Direct-Seeding** You can plant many kinds of vegetable seeds directly into prepared soil. But even when you follow seed-spacing directions given on the seed packet, direct-seeded crops often germinate too well or not well enough. When germination is excellent, thin plants ruthlessly because crowded vegetable plants will not mature properly. When direct-seeding any vegetable, set some seeds aside so you can go back in two weeks and replant vacant spaces in the row or bed.

Soil temperature and moisture play important roles in germination of vegetable seeds. Very few vegetable seeds will sprout in cold soil. High soil temperatures also inhibit germination. Also, be sure to plant seeds at the recommended planting depth, and firm the soil with your fingers or a hand tool after planting to ensure good contact of seed and soil.

**Starting Seeds Indoors** To get a head start on the growing season or escape poor outdoor germination conditions, many gardeners start seeds indoors. Tomatoes, peppers, eggplant, cabbage, broccoli, cauliflower, brussels sprouts, onions, and celery are almost always handled this way. Cold-climate gardeners might add lettuce and members of the squash family to this list.

Keep in mind that most vegetable seedlings need sun to grow well. A sunny windowsill is adequate for vegetable seedlings, but natural sun plus supplemental artificial light is best. Also remember that vegetables started indoors receive very little exposure to stress factors present outdoors, such as wind, fluctuating temperatures, and intense sunlight. One week before you plan to transplant, begin hardening off vegetable plants by exposing them to these natural elements. Move them to a protected place outdoors, or put them in a cold frame.

If temperatures are erratic or windy weather is expected, use cloches to protect tender seedlings from injury for two to three weeks after transplanting. Remove cloches when the plants begin to grow vigorously—a sign that soil temperature has reached a favorable range and roots have become established. See the illustration on page 185 for examples of good cloches for vegetable transplants.

In late summer, sun and heat can sap moisture from the new transplants of your fall crops faster than the roots can replenish it. Protect seedlings and transplants with shade covers instead of cloches. You can cover plants with cardboard boxes or flowerpots on sunny days for one week after transplanting, or you can cover them with a tent made of muslin or some other light-colored cloth.

## Some Like It Hot

Because vegetables differ so much in their preferred growing temperatures, planting the vegetable garden isn't a one-day job. Be prepared to spend several days over the course of early spring to early summer planting vegetable seeds and plants. You'll plant cool-weather crops a few weeks before the last spring frost. Set out warm-weather crops just after the last spring frost. Hot-weather crops cannot tolerate frost or cold soil. Unless you can protect them with a portable cold frame or row covers, plant them at least three weeks after the last spring frost. In warm climates, plant cool-weather crops again in early fall so that they grow during the fall and winter. Here is a guide to the temperature preferences of 30 common garden vegetables:

| Cool | Warm | Hot |
|------|------|-----|
| Beets | Cantaloupes | Eggplant |
| Broccoli | Carrots | Field peas |
| Cabbage | Chard | Lima beans |
| Cauliflower | Corn | Okra |
| Celery | Cucumbers | Peanuts |
| Garden peas | Peppers | Shell beans |
| Lettuce | Potatoes | Sweet |
| Onions | Pumpkins | potatoes |
| Radishes | Snap beans | Watermelons |
| Spinach | Squash | |
| Turnips | Tomatoes | |

# CARE DURING THE SEASON

After the rush of planting, there's a lull while most of your crops are growing, flowering, and setting fruit. But regular plant care is important if you want to reap a good harvest later in the season. Get in the habit of taking regular garden walks in order to thin crops, pull weeds, and check for signs of insect and disease problems.

## WEEDING

Start weed control early and keep at it throughout the season. Remove all weeds within 1 foot of your plants, or they will compete with the vegetables for water and nutrients. If you use a hoe or hand cultivator, be careful not to injure crop roots.

Some vegetables benefit from extra soil hilled up around the base of the plant. When hoeing around young corn, potatoes, tomatoes, and squash, scatter loose soil from between rows over the root zones of the plants. Once the garden soil has warmed (in late spring or early summer), mulch around your plants to suppress weeds and cut down on moisture loss. If you have areas where weeds have been a problem in the past, use a double mulch of newspapers covered with organic material such as leaves, straw, grass clippings, or shredded bark.

Another solution to weed problems is to cover beds with a sheet of black plastic. The plastic can help warm up cold soil, and it is a very effective barrier to weeds. If you do use black plastic, buy the thickest sheets you can find, and use them over and over again. Don't leave the plastic in place in the garden any longer than necessary, since exposure to sunlight will quickly degrade it. As soon as you remove the crop, rinse off and store plastic sheeting in a cool place. See "Mulching Your Garden" on page 167 for more information about using black plastic.

## WATERING

In the vegetable garden, some supplemental water is invariably needed, especially from midsummer to early fall. Most vegetables need ½ to 1 inch of water each week, and nature rarely provides water in such regular amounts. Dry weather can strengthen some vegetable plants by forcing them to develop deep roots that can seek out moisture. However, the quality of other crops suffers when plants get too little water. Tomatoes and melons need plenty of water early in the season when they're initiating foliage and fruit. However, as the fruit ripens, its quality often improves if dry conditions prevail. The opposite is true of lettuce, cabbage, and other leafy greens, which need more water as they approach maturity.

**When to Water**   How can you tell when your crops really need supplemental water? Leaves that droop at midday are a warning sign. If leaves wilt in midday and still look wilted the following morning, the plants are suffering. Provide water before soil becomes this dry.

If you don't water in time and the soil dries out completely, replenish soil moisture gradually, over a period of three days. If you soak dry

---

 **Strategies for Weed Control**

Over a period of years, you can effectively reduce the number of weed seeds present in your vegetable garden. Here's how:

■ Mulch heavily and continuously to deprive weed seeds of sunlight.

■ Remove all weeds before they produce seeds.

■ Plant windbreaks along any side of the garden that borders on woods or wild meadows. Shrubs and trees can help filter out weed seeds carried by the wind.

■ Grow rye as a winter cover crop. Rye residue suppresses weed germination and growth.

■ Solarize soil to kill weed seeds in the top 3 inches of prepared beds.

soil quickly, your drought-stressed crops will suddenly take up large amounts of water. The abrupt change may cause tomatoes, melons, carrots, cabbage, and other vegetables to literally split their sides, ruining your crop.

**Watering Methods** Watering by hand, using a spray nozzle on the end of a hose, is practical in a small garden but can be time-consuming in a large one. Sprinklers are easier to use but aren't water efficient. Some of the water from a sprinkler may fall on areas that don't need watering; and on a sunny day, some water evaporates and never reaches your plants' roots. Using sprinklers can saturate foliage, leading to conditions that favor some diseases, especially in humid climates. The one situation in which watering with a sprinkler may be the best option is when you have newly seeded beds, which need to be kept moist gently and evenly.

In terms of both water usage and economy of labor, the best way to water a vegetable garden is to use a drip irrigation system. You can buy several different types, including versatile systems that "weep" water into soil via porous tubing or pipes. These systems are most efficient when you install them between soil and mulch and use them at low pressure. Water seeps slowly into the soil, and there is very little surface evaporation. See "Watering Your Garden" on page 180 for more information on drip irrigation systems.

Many gardeners make their own irrigation lines by punching holes into short lengths of garden hose or plastic pipe. You can also drip water to your vegetables by punching small holes in the bottoms of plastic milk jugs, filling the jugs with water, and placing them over the roots of thirsty plants.

Irrigation pipes do not take the place of a handy garden hose—you need both. Buy a two-headed splitter at the hardware store, and screw it onto the faucet you use for the vegetable garden. Keep the irrigation system connected to one side, leaving the other available for hand-watering or other uses.

## STAKING

Many vegetables need stakes or trellises to keep them off the ground. Without support, the leaves and fruits of garden peas, tomatoes, pole beans, and some cucumbers and peppers easily become diseased. Also, many of these crops are easier to harvest when they're supported because the fruits are more accessible. You'll find many handy tips for staking and supporting crops in the individual vegetable entries later in this chapter.

## FERTILIZING

Keeping your soil naturally balanced with a good organic-matter content will go a long way toward meeting the nutrient needs of your crops. Crops that mature quickly (in less than 50 days) seldom need supplemental fertilizer when growing in a healthy soil, especially if they're mulched. But vegetables that mature slowly (over an extended period) often benefit from a booster feeding in midsummer.

Plan to fertilize tomatoes, peppers, and corn just as they reach their reproductive stage of growth. Sprinkle cottonseed meal or a blended organic fertilizer beneath the plants just before a rain. Or rake back the mulch, spread a ½-inch layer of compost or rotted manure over the soil, and then put the mulch back in place. When growing plants in containers, feed them a liquid fertilizer such as manure tea every two to three weeks throughout the season. You can also use manure tea to feed vegetables grown in the ground. For instructions on making and using manure tea, see "Tea Time for Your Plants" on page 177.

Foliar fertilizing—spraying liquid fertilizer on plant leaves—is another option for mid-season fertilization. Kelp-based foliar fertilizers contain nutrients, enzymes, and acids that tend to enhance vegetables' efforts at reproduction. They're most effective when plants are already getting a good supply of nutrients through their roots. Use foliar fertilizers as a mid-season tonic for tomatoes, pole beans, and other vegetables that produce over a long period.

## POLLINATION

You'll harvest leafy greens, carrots, and members of the cabbage family long before they flower. But with most other vegetables, the harvest is a fruit—the end result of pollinated blossoms. A spell of unusually hot weather can cause flowers or pollen grains to develop improperly.

Conversely, a long, wet, cloudy spell can stop insects from pollinating. Either condition can leave you with few tomatoes, melons, or peppers, or with ears of corn with sparse, widely spaced kernels. The blossom ends of cucumbers and summer squash become wrinkled and misshapen when pollination is inadequate.

To prevent such problems, place like vegetables together so the plants can share the pollen they produce. Two exceptions here are hot and sweet peppers, and super-sweet and regular hybrid corn: Separate these by at least 25 feet to limit the amount of cross-pollination that takes place, or your harvest may not be true to type.

Tomatoes, corn, and beans are pollinated primarily by wind, though honeybees and other

---

 **Pest Control Primer**

Insects are a natural part of the organic garden. But don't allow them to wreak havoc. When insects threaten to remove more than 20 percent of the leaves on any vegetable plant or are known to carry viral diseases, it is time for you to intervene. In most cases, once you've identified the pest that's damaging your crop, you'll be able to control it by implementing one of the following five treatments:

■ Handpick or gather the insects with a net or hand-held vacuum. As you gather them, put the bugs in a container filled with very hot water or alcohol. Set the container in the sun until the bugs die.

■ Spraying insecticidal soap is effective against aphids on leafy greens, thrips on tomatoes, and several other small, soft-bodied pests.

■ Use floating row covers as a barrier to problem insects. Row covers are particularly useful in protecting young squash, cucumber, and melon plants from insects. Remember to

remove the cover when the plants begin to flower. You can also wrap row covers around the outside of tomato cages to discourage disease-carrying aphids and leafhoppers.

■ BT (*Bacillus thuringiensis*) gives excellent control of leaf-eating caterpillars. It is often indispensable when you're growing members of the cabbage family, which have many such pests, and when hornworms are numerous enough to seriously damage tomatoes. A special strain—BTSD (*B.t.* var. *san diego*)—is available that is effective against the most common enemy of potatoes, the larvae of Colorado potato beetles.

■ As a last resort, sabadilla, a powder made from the seeds of a tropical lily, gives excellent control of hard-backed bugs such as squash bugs, harlequin bugs, and adult Mexican bean beetles. Sabadilla's toxicity is lower than that of other plant-derived pesticides, such as rotenone and pyrethrins, but it is toxic to honeybees.

insects provide a little help transporting pollen about the plants. The presence of pollinating insects is crucial for squash, cucumbers, and melons. Plant flowers near these crops to lure bees in the right direction. You'll find more suggestions for helping with pollination in the individual vegetable entries later in this chapter.

## PEST AND DISEASE MANAGEMENT

Pests and diseases of vegetable crops include insects, fungi, bacteria, and viruses, as well as larger animals such as raccoons and deer. Fortunately for organic gardeners, there are ever-increasing numbers of vegetable cultivars that are genetically resistant to insects and diseases. If you know that a pest or disease has been a problem in your garden, seek out and plant a resistant cultivar whenever possible.

Prevention can go a long way toward solving insect and disease problems in the vegetable garden. An important part of your continuing care for your garden is to practice the principles of organic pest management. It's important to realize that a weed-free or insect-free environment is not a natural one. If your garden is a diverse miniature world, with vigorous plants nourished by a well-balanced soil and an active population of native beneficial insects and microorganisms, you'll likely experience few serious pest problems. See "Pest Control Primer" on page 199 for a brief overview of insect controls for the vegetable garden; for more complete information on organic pest management, see Chapter 7.

**Animal Pests** Rabbits, woodchucks, deer, and other animals can wreak havoc in a vegetable garden. A sturdy fence is often the best solution. For tips on keeping problem animals away from your plants, see "Animal Pests" on page 141.

**Diseases** Vegetable crop diseases are less threatening in home gardens than they are in farm fields, where crops are grown in monoculture. When many different plants are present, diseases that require specific host plants have a hard time gaining a firm foothold. Plus, a healthy, naturally balanced soil contains many beneficial microorganisms capable of controlling those that are likely to cause trouble.

Two of the best techniques for combating disease problems in the vegetable garden are rotating crops and solarizing the soil. Rotate crops by planting them in different places in the garden from one year to the next. When you plant the same vegetable continually in the same spot, disease organisms that feed on that plant flourish. When crops change from year to year, the disease organisms don't have a host plant and will not build up large populations. "Rotating Vegetable Families" on the opposite page presents many helpful suggestions for planning crop rotation in your garden.

Where diseases, weeds, soil-dwelling insects, or root knot nematodes seriously interfere with plant health, you can often get good control by subjecting the soil to extreme temperatures. Leave the soil openly exposed for a few weeks in the middle of winter. In the hottest part of summer, solarization can kill most weed seeds, insects, and disease organisms present in the top 4 inches of soil. See "Soil Solarization" on page 134 for step-by-step instructions.

# HARVEST AND STORAGE

As a general rule, harvest your vegetables early and often. Many common vegetables, such as broccoli, garden peas, lettuce, and corn, are harvested when they are at a specific and short-lived state of immaturity. Also be prompt when harvesting crops that mature fully on the plant, such as tomatoes, peppers, melons, and shell beans. Vegetable plants tend to decline after they have produced viable seeds. Prompt harvesting prolongs the productive lifespan of many vegetables. See "Vegetable Harvest and Storage" on page 202 and the individual vegetable entries later in this chapter for tips on when to harvest specific crops.

Use "Days to Maturity" listed on seed packets as a general guide to estimate when vegetables will be ready to pick. Bear in mind that climatic factors such as temperature and day length can radically alter how long it takes for vegetables to mature. Vegetables planted in spring, when days are becoming progressively longer and warmer, may mature faster than expected. Those grown in the waning days of autumn may mature two to three weeks behind schedule.

In summer, harvest vegetables mid-morning, after the dew has dried but before the heat of

*(continued on page 204)*

## Rotating Vegetable Families

Susceptibility to pests and diseases runs in plant families. Leave at least two, and preferably three or more, years between the times you plant members of the same crop family in an area of your garden. When planning your rotations, keep in mind that some crops are heavy feeders, taking up large amounts of nutrients as they grow, while others are light feeders. Balance plantings of heavy feeders with soil-restoring legumes or green manure crops. Here are the seven family groups most often planted in vegetable gardens, plus ideas for rotating them.

| Family Name | Common Crops | Rotation Relations |
| --- | --- | --- |
| Cruciferae | Broccoli, brussels sprouts, cabbage, cauliflower, kale, radishes, turnips | High level of soil maintenance required for good root health. Heavy feeders. Precede with legumes; follow with open cultivation and compost. |
| Cucurbitaceae | Cucumbers, melons, squash, pumpkins, watermelons | For improved weed and insect control, precede with winter rye or wheat. Follow with legumes. |
| Gramineae | Wheat, oats, rye, corn | Plant before tomato- or squash-family crops to control weeds and to improve soil's ability to handle water. |
| Leguminosae | Beans, peas, clovers, vetches | Beneficial to soil and have few pest problems. Rotate alternately with all other garden crops whenever possible. |
| Liliaceae | Onions, garlic | Rotate with legumes, but avoid planting in soil that contains undecomposed organic matter. |
| Solanaceae | Eggplant, peppers, potatoes, tomatoes | Heavy feeders with many fungal enemies. Precede with cereal grain or grass; follow with legumes. |
| Umbelliferae | Carrots, parsley, dill, fennel, coriander | Moderate feeders. Precede with any other plant family, but condition soil with compost before planting. Follow with legumes or heavy mulch. |

# Vegetable Harvest and Storage

Your refrigerator is one of your best storage options. If you have two available, set one at a cold temperature (32° to 40°F) and the other at a cool temperature (45° to 50°F). In a refrigerator set for normal operation, the temperature in the center storage section is usually between 38° and 42°F. The temperature just below the freezing unit is lower—often 30° to 35°F. The bottom of the cabinet is somewhat warmer than the center. Check temperatures in different parts of your refrigerator.

Your basement is another possible storage place. Temperatures in most heated or air-conditioned basements will usually be 65°F or higher in summer and 60°F or lower in winter. Create partitions to vary the temperature and humidity. You can use outdoor air, dirt floors, or wet sacks to vary the temperature and humidity needs. Unheated basements, if well ventilated, can provide good storage conditions for some vegetables.

This listing gives you the facts on when and how to harvest your vegetables for maximum flavor and how to store them properly to maintain freshness and taste:

## COLD, MOIST
### (32° to 40°F, 90 to 95% relative humidity)

**Asparagus:** Harvest by snapping 10- to 12-inch spears off at ground level. Store in plastic bags in refrigerator for up to one week. Freeze or can any surplus.

**Beans, lima:** Harvest when pods have filled. For tender limas, harvest when a bit immature; for "meaty" limas, harvest when mature. Store shelled limas in perforated plastic bags in the refrigerator for about one week. Surplus limas can be canned or frozen.

**Beets:** Begin harvest when beet is 1 inch in diameter. Tender tops make excellent greens. Main harvest is when beets are 2 to 3 inches across. Harvest spring-planted beets before hot weather; fall beets, before the first light freeze. For storage, wash roots, trim tops to ½ inch, place in perforated plastic bags, and store in the refrigerator or cold, moist cellar for two to four months.

**Broccoli:** Harvest terminal head while florets are still tight and of good green color. Smaller side heads will develop. Store in perforated plastic bags for up to one week in the refrigerator. Freeze any surplus.

**Cabbage:** Harvest when heads are solid. Store cabbage in the refrigerator, cold cellar, or outdoor pit for up to two months.

**Carrots:** Harvest spring crops before hot weather; fall ones, before the first light freeze. For storage, wash roots, trim tops to $1/2$ inch, and place in perforated plastic bags. Store in the refrigerator or cold, moist cellar for two to four months.

**Cauliflower:** Tie outer leaves above the head when curd diameter reaches 1 to 2 inches (except purple types). Heads will be ready for harvest in about two weeks. Cauliflower may be stored in perforated plastic bags in the refrigerator for up to two weeks. Freeze any surplus.

## COOL, MOIST
### (45° to 50°F, 80 to 90% relative humidity)

**Beans, snap:** Pods will be most tender when seeds inside are one-fourth normal size. They become fibrous as the beans mature. Store up to one week in perforated plastic bags in the warm part of refrigerator. Can or freeze surplus.

**Cucumbers:** Harvest cucumbers when they are about $1 1/2$ to $2 1/2$ inches in diameter and 5 to 8 inches long. Pickling cucumbers will be more blocky and not as long as slicers. Store slicing cucumbers up to one week in plastic bags in the warm part of the refrigerator. Cool pickling cucumbers quickly in ice water; keep up to two days in a plastic bag in the refrigerator.

**Eggplant:** Harvest when fruits are nearly full grown but color is still bright. Keep in warm part of the refrigerator for about one week.

**Peppers, sweet:** Harvest when fruits are firm and full-sized. For red fruits, leave fruits on the plant until ripe. Store in the warm part of refrigerator in plastic bags for two to three weeks.

**Squash, summer:** Harvest when fruits are young and tender. Skin should be easily penetrated with the thumbnail. Store for up to one week in perforated plastic bags in the refrigerator. Surplus can be frozen.

## COOL, DRY
### (45°to 55°F, 50 to 60% relative humidity)

**Onions, dry:** Harvest when the tops have fallen over and the necks have shriveled. Remove tops, place in shallow boxes or mesh bags, and cure in an open garage or barn for three to four weeks. Store in mesh bags in a cool place. Keep ventilated during humid, muggy weather.

**Peppers, hot:** Pull plants late in the season and hang to dry in the sun or a warm place. Store in a dry, cool place, such as a basement.

## WARM, DRY
### (55° to 60°F, 60 to 70% relative humidity)

**Pumpkins; Squash, winter:** Harvest when skin is hard and the colors darken. Harvest before frost. Cut the fruits from the vine with a portion of stem attached. Store spread out on shelves so air can circulate.

## WARM, MOIST
### (55°–60°F, 80–85% relative humidity)

**Tomatoes:** Ripe tomatoes will keep for a week at 55° to 60°F. Harvest green, mature tomatoes before frost, and keep at 55° to 70°F; for faster ripening, keep at 65° to 70°F. Mature green fruits should approach normal size and have a whitish green skin color. Keep them three to five weeks by wrapping each tomato in newspaper. Inspect for ripeness each week.

---

**Text source:** Arthur E. Gaus and Henry DiCarlo, "Vegetable Harvest and Storage," *Grounds for Gardening: A Horticultural Guide,* University of Missouri–Columbia.

midday. Wait for a mild, cloudy day to dig your potatoes, carrots, and other root crops so they won't be exposed to the sun. To make sure your homegrown vegetables are as nutritious as they

---

**Try to Remember**

Try to keep a year's worth of garden records in your head, and your memory may fail you. Write it down! Here's what to do:

**List crop rotations:** Changing the placement of crops within your garden each year is one way to outwit pests and fungi that attack certain plant families. Using a chart to record exactly where you planted each crop last year will give you a visual reference for planning this year's crop placement. This chart will help you make sure that you don't plant crops from the same family in the same spot year after year, making them more vulnerable to disease.

**Maintain soil records:** Knowing when you applied fertilizers and amendments and what kinds and amounts you applied is important in avoiding mineral imbalances in the soil. Lack of nutrients can limit plant growth, and excesses of certain nutrients can also have detrimental effects. See "Feeding Your Plants" on page 170 to learn more about fertilizers.

**Keep a weather diary:** Environmental disorders, such as water stress, sometimes cause symptoms that look very much like symptoms caused by insects or diseases. If you have data on weather conditions to refer to, it will help you make a better judgment about the underlying cause of the symptoms you see.

**Use comparison records:** Include jottings of how well your plants resisted heat and pests and also how well they were received on the dining room table!

can be, harvest and eat them on the same day whenever possible.

Refrigerate vegetables that have a high water content as soon as you pick them. These include leafy greens, all members of the cabbage family, cucumbers, celery, beets, carrots, snap beans, and corn. An exception is tomatoes—they ripen best at room temperature.

Some vegetables, notably potatoes, bulb onions, winter squash, peanuts, and sweet potatoes, require a curing period to enhance their keeping qualities. See the individual entries on these vegetables later in this chapter for information on the best curing and storage conditions.

Bumper crops of all vegetables may be canned, dried, or frozen for future use. Use only your best vegetables for long-term storage, and choose a storage method appropriate for your climate. For example, you can pull cherry tomato plants and hang them upside down until the fruits dry in arid climates, but not in humid climates. In cold climates, you can mulch carrots heavily to prevent them from freezing and dig them during the winter. In warm climates, carrots left in the ground will be subject to prolonged insect damage.

# OFF-SEASON

After you harvest a crop in your vegetable garden, either turn under or pull up the remaining plant debris. Many garden pests overwinter in the skeletons of vegetable plants. If you suspect that plant remains harbor insect pests or disease organisms, put them in sealed containers for disposal with your trash, or compost them in a hot (at least 160°F) compost pile.

As garden space becomes vacant in late summer and fall, cultivate empty spaces and allow birds to gather grubs and other larvae hidden in the soil. If several weeks will pass before the first hard freeze is expected, consider planting a green manure crop such as crimson clover, rye, or annual ryegrass. See "Using Green Manure" on page 36 or instructions on seeding these crops.

Another rite of fall is collecting leaves, which can be used as a winter mulch over garden soil or as the basis for a large winter compost heap. As you collect the leaves, shred and wet them thoroughly to promote leaching and rapid decomposition. You can also till shredded leaves directly into your garden soil.

# VEGETABLE CROP GUIDE

Good site selection and proper soil care are the two most important steps you can take to ensure a great vegetable harvest. Knowing how to handle your crops at planting time and how

to care for them through the season is icing on the cake. Use the guidelines and tips in this crop-by-crop guide to popular vegetables to ensure a bumper harvest every time.

# Asparagus

Asparagus officinalis (Liliaceae)

**Site:** At least ½ day of sun; protection from strong winds.
**Soil:** Evenly moist, well-drained, light, sandy loam that is rich in organic matter; pH of 6.5–7.5.
**How much to plant:** 20–40 plants per person.
**Spacing:** 1½'–2' between plants in rows 3'–4' apart.
**Seasons to bearing:** Begin harvesting after 2–3 seasons of growth.

Asparagus is hardy in Zones 2 through 9. It thrives in any area with winter ground freezes

---

 **Crops That Wait for You**

Few things are more frustrating than planting a beautiful garden and then not being able to keep up with the harvest. Leave your sugar snap peas on the vine for a few too many days, and you might just as well till them under as a green manure crop.

Fortunately, there are a host of forgiving crops that will more or less wait for you. They include onions, leeks, potatoes, garlic, many herbs, kale, beets, popcorn, sunflowers, hot peppers (for drying), horseradish, pumpkins, winter squash, and carrots. You can measure the harvest period for these crops in weeks or even months.

To keep your harvest from hitting all at once, stagger plantings. Make a new sowing every ten days to two weeks. Mix early, mid-season, and late cultivars. Some vegetables, like bok choy and other oriental greens, can

be harvested through Thanksgiving.

Never have time to pick all of your fresh snap or shell beans at their prime? Relax. Plant cultivars meant for drying, and enjoy hearty, homegrown bean dishes throughout winter.

You can pick leeks young and small or wait the full 90 to 120 days until they mature. Leeks have excellent freeze tolerance. When protected by mulch, they can be harvested well into winter. In mild-winter areas where hard freezes are few and far between, winter is the best time to grow collards, spinach, turnips, carrots, and onions.

In all climates, be prepared to protect overwintering vegetables from cosmetic damage by covering them with an old blanket during periods of harsh weather. Or you can try growing cold-hardy vegetables such as spinach and kale under plastic tunnels during the winter months.

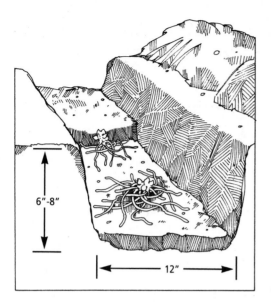

**Planting asparagus.** Dig 12-inch-wide planting trenches 6 to 8 inches deep and 4 feet apart. Set the crowns with their tentacle-like roots draped over small mounds of soil or compost 1½ to 2 feet apart in the trenches; top with 2 inches of soil. Plant seedlings the same way, but pinch off any branches covered by soil. In two weeks, add another 2 inches of soil. Continue adding soil every two weeks until the soil is slightly mounded above surface level to allow for settling.

6"-8"

12"

or a dry season to provide a dormant period each year. Asparagus does best in full sun and deep, well-drained soil. Select a permanent location carefully, since plants will produce for 20 years or more. Dig out all weeds and add plenty of compost to the soil before planting. Asparagus requires high levels of nitrogen, phosphorus, and potassium. Do a soil test, and add amendments as necessary. If your soil is heavy or poorly drained, plant asparagus in raised beds.

Plant one-year-old crowns from a reputable nursery that sells fresh, firm, disease-free roots, or start your plants from seed. Soak seeds or crowns in compost tea for five minutes before planting to reduce disease problems.

Most seed-grown asparagus plants eventually out-produce those started from crowns. Growing from seed also allows you to eliminate female plants. A bed of all male plants can produce as much as 30 percent more spears than a mixed bed of male and female plants. Plants grown from seed will flower their first summer. When the tiny flowers appear, observe them with a magnifying glass. Female flowers have well-developed, three-lobed pistils; male blossoms are larger and longer than females. Weed out all female plants. The following spring, transplant the males to the permanent bed.

Harvesting new plantings too soon can stress plants and make them more susceptible to pest problems. Harvest for two weeks the second season, four weeks the third season, and up to eight weeks thereafter.

Mulch with a high-nitrogen compost each spring before spears emerge, and again in fall. Leave winter-killed foliage, along with straw or other light mulch, on the bed to provide winter protection. Remove and destroy the foliage before new growth appears in the spring; it can harbor diseases and pest eggs. Over the years, the crowns will push closer to the soil surface, resulting in smaller and less-tender spears. To remedy this, mound 6 inches of soil over the rows each spring.

# Bean

*Phaseolus* spp. (Leguminosae)

**Site:** Needs at least ½ day of sun.
**Soil:** Prefers a light, sandy soil with good drainage; pH of 5.5–6.8.
**How much to plant:** Bush beans: 10–15 plants per person. Pole beans: 3–5 hills per person.
**Spacing:** Bush beans: 4"–6" between plants in rows 1½'–3' apart. Pole beans: 6"–9" between plants in rows 3'–4' apart.
**Days to maturity:** Bush beans: 48–60 days. Pole beans: 62–68 days.

**Staking methods.** Staking pole and runner beans helps produce a clean, high-yielding crop in a small space. Use a single stake for a string-and-stake trellis. A bean "tee-pee" can be a great place for kids to play.

Beans thrive in most soil. Work in plenty of low-nitrogen compost before planting to loosen the soil. For a healthy, trouble-free crop, plant beans after soil has warmed. Optimum soil temperature for germination is 80°F. At soil temperatures be-low 60°F, most bean cultivars germinate poorly and are more susceptible to pests and root rot. Choose light, well-drained soil for early plantings, if possible, and cover beans with a row cover or clear plastic until they emerge. If you use clear plastic, be sure to remove it as soon as the seeds germinate to avoid "cooking" the seedlings.

Beans do best when soil pH is between 5.5 and 6.8. They don't require high soil fertility. In fact, a high nitrogen level will delay maturity. Spray young plants with seaweed extract to prevent micronutrient deficiencies and to improve overall plant health.

Soak seed in compost tea for 25 minutes before planting to help prevent disease and speed germination. Treat seed with an inoculant labeled for the type of bean you are planting before sowing to promote nitrogen fixation. Be sure to buy fresh inoculant each year, or check the date on the package for viability.

To avoid spreading diseases, don't touch plants when foliage is wet. Compost plants after harvest. Prevent problems by not planting beans in the same location more often than every three years.

# Beet

*Beta vulgaris* (Chenopodiaceae)

**Site:** Full sun, but will tolerate partial shade.
**Soil:** Prefers a light, sandy loam; pH of 6.0–7.5.
**How much to plant:** 5'–10' of row per person.
**Spacing:** 4"–6" between plants in rows 12"–20" apart.
**Days to maturity:** 46–70 days.

Beets grow best in deep, well-drained soil with a pH between 6.0 and 7.5. Beets are cool-season plants and will tolerate temperatures as low as 40°F. However, plants will bolt, or go to flower prematurely, if exposed to two to three weeks of temperatures below 50°F after the first true leaves have formed. Beets grow poorly

---

above 75°F and are best grown as a spring or fall crop. Keep soil moist but not soggy, since rapid and uninterrupted growth produces the best roots. Prevent problems by not planting beets in the same location more often than every three years.

# Cabbage

*Brassica oleracea* Capitata group (Cruciferae)

**Site:** Full sun.
**Soil:** Rich, sandy loam; pH of 6.0–6.8.
**How much to plant:** 5–10 plants per person.
**Spacing:** 15″–24″ between plants in rows 2′–3′ apart.
**Days to maturity:** 62–120 days from transplanting.

---

 **Culture Clues: Cabbage**

Heat and improper watering are two factors that can foil your cabbages. Here are some other growing tips:

■ Cool weather brings out the flavor in maturing cabbages.

■ Wide spacings produce bigger heads, but young, small cabbages are tastier. To get both, space plants 6 inches apart, and harvest every other one before maturity. Stagger plantings at two-week intervals for a longer harvest.

■ Water evenly to prevent cracking of heads. Don't get foliage wet during cool weather or periods of high humidity. Cut back on water as cabbages mature.

■ Carefully hand-weed around roots; apply a thick mulch to keep soil moist and cool.

■ If leaves start to yellow, provide a mid-season nitrogen boost with manure tea.

■ Harvest firm heads with a sharp knife. Leave stalks and roots in place to produce small cabbages.

---

Plant cabbages in full sun in a site with fertile, well-drained soil and a pH between 6.0 and 6.8. If you have a choice of sites, spring plantings do best in lighter, sandier soils, while fall plantings do better in soils that contain more clay. Plants grow best at temperatures between 40° and 75°F.

Cabbages are biennial, and transplants exposed to cool temperatures (35° to 45°F) for ten or more days may bolt. High temperatures also cause bolting.

These plants have very shallow roots, so be sure to keep the top few inches of soil from drying out. Fluctuations in soil moisture after the heads have formed may cause them to split. Mulching helps to balance and conserve moisture. Most cabbage diseases need free water to spread, so don't water with overhead sprinklers.

To avoid problems, don't plant cabbages where members of the cabbage family (broccoli, cauliflower, brussels sprouts, or kale) have grown for at least three years. Also, avoid areas with cabbage family weeds, such as wild mustard. Destroy all crop residues, including roots, after you harvest.

If you start your own plants, soak the seed in 122°F water for 25 minutes before planting to eliminate seed-borne diseases. (Be aware that this treatment can damage seed viability; for more information, see "Pretreating Seeds" on page 54.) Once your seeds have germinated, grow seedlings at 60°F to keep them short and stocky.

Cabbages are heavy feeders and are susceptible to several nutrient deficiencies, including boron, calcium, phosphorus, and potassium.

# Carrot

*Daucus carota* var. *sativus* (Umbelliferae)

**Site:** Full sun to light shade.
**Soil:** Deep, loose, moist, and well aerated; pH of 5.5–6.8.

**How much to plant:** 5'–10' of row, or 30 plants, per person.
**Spacing:** 3"–4" between plants in rows 16"–30" apart.
**Days to maturity:** 50–95 days from seed to harvest.

Carrots grow best in deeply worked, loose soils with a pH between 5.5 and 6.8. No other vegetable is as sensitive to poor soil structure. Misshapen carrots result more often from lumpy or compacted soil than from any pest problem. Carrots do well in raised beds. Work in a generous amount of compost or well-rotted manure before planting. Cultivars with short roots will tolerate shallow or poor soil better than long, thin cultivars.

Carrots grow best when temperatures are between 60° and 70°F. They grow poorly above 75°F but will tolerate temperatures as low as 45°F. Most cultivars grow short roots at high temperatures and longer, more pointed roots at lower temperatures.

Abundant water is necessary for good root development. It is especially important to give emerging seedlings an edge against weeds. Keep soil evenly moist but not saturated.

To prevent problems with diseases and insects, do not plant carrots where carrots or parsley has grown for three years.

Carrots require moderate to high levels of potassium and phosphorus, but only a moderate level of nitrogen, so avoid high-nitrogen fertilizers. Carrots are very sensitive to salt injury and do poorly in soils with high sodium levels.

# Corn

*Zea mays* var. *rugosa* (Gramineae)

**Site:** Full sun; needs wind for pollination.
**Soil:** Rich, well-drained loam with pH of 5.5–6.8; evenly moist but not wet.
**How much to plant:** 15–40 plants per person.
**Spacing:** 8"–12" apart in rows 30"–42" apart.
**Days to maturity:** 65–90 days from seed to harvest.

Corn does best in a rich, sandy, or well-worked soil with a pH between 5.5 and 6.8. Prepare soil

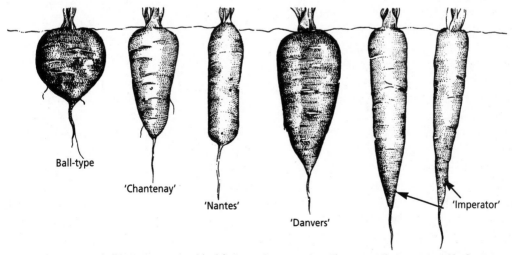

Ball-type

'Chantenay'

'Nantes'

'Danvers'

'Imperator'

**Carrot shapes.** Compact ball-type carrots are ideal for container growing. The stout 'Chantenay' and hefty 'Danvers' are good for heavy soils. Slender 'Nantes' and long, thin 'Imperator' are best suited for deep, loose soils.

by working in a generous amount of compost. Side-dress plants with alfalfa meal when they are 1 foot high and again when silk first shows at the ends of the ears. Spraying plants with seaweed extract or compost tea periodically also improves your harvest and prevents deficiencies.

Plant corn seed only after the soil is at least 60°F, or 75°F for supersweets. Seed planted in cooler soil is prone to many problems. To help speed soil warming, cover soil with clear plastic at least two weeks before planting. After planting, use row covers for about a month to give seedlings a boost.

Corn needs at least 1 inch of water a week. Keep soil moist but not soggy. Mulch plants to conserve moisture and to cut down on weeds.

Plant corn in blocks rather than long single rows to ensure good pollination. To prevent problems, do not plant corn where it has grown in the past two years. After harvest, cut or mow stalks and let them dry. Then turn them under or collect and compost them. Destroy any diseased or infested material.

---

 **Culture Clues: Corn**

Root disturbance and lack of nutrients both can hamper your corn crop. Keep these points in mind as well:

■ If you start corn indoors, use peat pots to avoid disturbing the roots at transplanting time.

■ To promote pollination, plant the same cultivar in blocks, or hand-pollinate.

■ Remove unwanted seedlings by cutting them off at soil level.

■ Cultivate thoroughly around the stalks for the first month of growth. After that, control weeds by applying mulch (to avoid damaging the shallow roots).

■ To avoid cross-pollination, keep different corn cultivars 400 yards apart or more, or plant so that they tassel two weeks apart.

■ Corn is a heavy feeder, especially on nitrogen. It thrives where earth-enriching crops like beans or clover have grown the previous year.

■ For early plantings, sow seeds 1 inch deep; in the hot weather of midsummer, sow 4 inches deep.

■ Three weeks after corn silks appear, pull back part of the husk and pierce a kernel with your thumbnail. If "milk" spurts out, the sweet corn is ripe. A completely dry silk or a yellow or faded green sheath means the ear is past its prime.

# Cucumber

*Cucumis sativus* (Cucurbitaceae)

---

**Site:** Full sun, or full morning sun and less than 3 hours of afternoon shade.

**Soil:** Well-drained sand or clay loam with pH of 6.0–6.8.

**How much to plant:** For eating fresh: 1 plant per person; for pickling: 5 plants per person.

**Spacing:** Grow trellised plants 6"–10" apart, or grow in hills spaced 4'–6' apart.

**Days to Maturity:** 55–70 days from seed, depending on the cultivar.

---

Cucumber seeds need 60°F soil to germinate, so wait until weather is warm to plant. Make a second planting four to five weeks after the first so you will have fruit all season. Cover plants with floating row covers to protect them from insects and late cold snaps. Remove row covers when plants begin to flower so insects can pollinate the blossoms, or you will not get any fruit.

Cucumbers do best in well-drained, loose-textured soils with lots of organic matter. They will grow in soils with a pH between 5.5 and

6.8, but they prefer a pH above 6.0. Plants need lots of water, but don't let soil become saturated. Prevent disease problems by keeping leaves dry. Mulch cucumbers to help conserve water; black plastic is a good choice for central and northern areas, but in extremely warm areas it can warm the soil too much. Organic mulches are good, too, but may provide shelter for pests like squash bugs. Foil mulches help prevent aphid problems. If rotting fruit is a problem, raise fruits off the ground by placing scraps of wood under them.

Rotate crops so that no member of the cucurbit family (squash, melon, and cucumber) is grown in the same place more often than every four years.

**Caution:** Cucumber leaves are easily burned by insecticidal soap and copper sprays. Use the most dilute spray recommended and use sparingly. Do not spray plants in direct sun or if temperatures are above 80°F, and don't spray drought-stressed plants.

# Eggplant

*Solanum melongena* var. *esculentum*
(Solanaceae)

**Site:** Full sun.
**Soil:** Moderately fertile, well-drained loam; pH of 6.0–6.8.
**How much to plant:** 2–3 plants per person.
**Spacing:** 20"–24" apart each way.
**Days to maturity:** 60–100 days from transplanting.

Eggplants do best in full sun and well-drained, fertile soil with lots of organic matter. They prefer a pH between 6.0 and 6.8 but will tolerate a pH as low as 5.5. Eggplants need a high level of nitrogen and moderate levels of phosphorus and potassium. Have the soil tested, and correct any deficiencies. They grow best at temperatures between 70° and 85°F, and poorly above 95° or below 65°F.

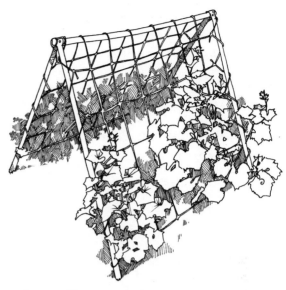

**A-frame trellis.** To save garden space, grow cucumbers on a vertical structure such as this A-frame trellis. Such supports produce healthier, cleaner fruits by keeping the crop off the ground and allowing for air circulation.

Eggplants need lots of water. Keep the soil evenly moist, and never let it dry out. They do well in mulched, raised beds with drip irrigation. Black plastic mulch is a good choice because it warms the soil.

Purchase stocky, insect- and disease-free plants, or start your own from seed indoors. Eggplant seeds germinate best between 80° and 90°F. Once seedlings are up, they grow best at 70°F. Do not plant out before average daily temperatures have reached 65° to 70°F. Protect transplants from wind, and water new transplants well with seaweed extract or compost tea to give them a good start. Spray plants with seaweed extract with 1 teaspoon of Epsom salts added per gallon when the first flowers open to improve fruit set.

Eggplants are susceptible to many of the same problems, pests, and diseases as tomatoes, including flower drop or misshapen fruit due to extreme temperatures, flea beetles, Colorado potato beetles, aphids, hornworms, mites, Verticillium and Fusarium wilts, tobacco mosaic virus, and anthracnose fruit rot.

# Lettuce

*Lactuca sativa* (Compositae)

**Site:** Tolerates partial shade; thrives in light shade in summer; does well in humid spots.
**Soil:** Loamy soil that is well drained and moderately rich; needs constant moisture; pH of 6.0–6.8.

 **Culture Clues: Lettuce**

Avoiding high heat and root disturbance will help deliver a good lettuce crop. Here are some other good tips to remember:

■ To help prevent disease, water on sunny mornings, so the leaves will dry by evening.

■ After a good watering, apply a thick layer of mulch to conserve moisture, suffocate weeds around the easily damaged roots, and keep lettuce leaves clean.

■ Lettuce needs plenty of nitrogen. To promote quick growth, side-dress with manure tea or fish emulsion once or twice during the growing season.

■ Just before bolting, lettuce plants start to elongate and form a bitter sap. To keep this from happening, pinch off the top center of the plant.

■ Lettuce is crispest if picked in the morning. Watch your crop closely, as mature plants decline quickly. To test the firmness of head-forming types, press down gently on lettuce hearts with the back of your hand; don't pinch them, as this can bruise the hearts. Use a sharp knife to cut heads below the lowest leaves, or pull plants out by the roots.

**How much to plant:** Plant 15–20 leaf lettuce plants or 7 head lettuce plants per person.
**Spacing:** Leaf lettuce: 6"–12" between plants in traditional rows 1'–3' apart, or in intensive beds with 6"–9" between plants. Head lettuce: 8"–14" between plants in traditional rows 1'–3' apart.
**Days to maturity:** Leaf lettuce: 40 days from seed to harvest. Head lettuce: 70 days from seed to harvest, or 20–35 days from transplanting to harvest.

Lettuce grows best in rich, loose soil with a pH between 6.0 and 6.8. It likes full sun, but in hot weather it does better with light shade in the heat of the day. Lettuce needs to grow rapidly and without interruption. Provide plenty of nitrogen in both quicker-release forms, such as blood meal or soybean meal, and slower-release forms, such as compost or alfalfa meal. Spray the plants with compost tea and/or seaweed extract every other week to give them an extra boost. Spraying with compost tea may also help prevent some fungal disease problems.

Lettuce grows best at temperatures between 60° and 65°F. Most lettuce cultivars grow poorly above 75°F but will tolerate temperatures as low as 45°F. Plants exposed to high temperatures will bolt. Prevent bolting by providing plants with partial shade in the heat of the summer, harvesting promptly, and planting bolt-resistant cultivars.

To grow tender, trouble-free lettuce, keep the soil moist but not soggy, and do not allow the soil to dry out. Unlike most vegetables, lettuce responds well to having its foliage sprinkled with water. Plant in raised beds to improve drainage. To help prevent disease problems, do not plant lettuce in soil where it has been grown within the last three years.

# Melon

Melon, *Cucumis melo* and
Watermelon, *Citrullus lanatus* (Cucurbitaceae)

**Site:** Full sun.
**Soil:** Moderately rich, well-drained soil with a pH of 6.0–6.8.
**How much to plant:** 1–2 plants per person.
**Spacing:** 8"–12" apart in rows 6'–10' apart or 2 plants per hill, with the hills spaced 2'–3' apart.
**Days to maturity:** 75–90 days from seed, depending on cultivar.

Melon seeds need 60°F soil to germinate. In northern areas, start plants indoors two to three weeks before the last frost date and transplant outside once weather is warm. Melons need sun and warmth—90°F is ideal. Melons are especially vulnerable to pests and cool temperatures when young. Plants exposed to temperatures below 50°F can be permanently injured and fail to set fruit. Cover plants with floating row covers or clear plastic tunnels as soon as they are set out. If temperatures exceed 90°F inside the tun-

---

 **Cultivate Some Cole Crops**

Cabbage, broccoli, and their less-common cousins such as kale and brussels sprouts all belong to the same family of vegetables—Cruciferae. In fact, they're all different forms of the same species, *Brassica oleracea.* All are grown like cabbage and are cool-weather crops that are good for planting in spring and fall.

**Broccoli:** Grown for its crisp green heads of flower buds. Prevent problems by planting the following improved cultivars: 'Green Dwarf #36', 'Emperor', and 'Mariner' are black rot–tolerant; 'Premium Crop' is resistant to Fusarium wilt; 'Citation', 'Emperor', 'Esquire', 'Green Dwarf #36', 'Hi-Caliber', and 'Mariner' are tolerant of downy mildew; and 'De Cicco' is tolerant of flea beetles.

Transplants exposed to cool temperatures (35° to 45°F) for ten days or more may form tiny, useless flower heads prematurely. High temperatures can cause similar tiny head formation. Broccoli grows best at temperatures between 45° and 75°F. Harvest heads when buds are still tight and dark green or dusky violet, except for 'Romanesco', which should be yellow-green.

**Brussels sprouts:** One of the hardiest members of the cabbage family, they can tolerate lower pH (5.5 to 6.8) than any of the other brassicas. But they are less tolerant of heat. In warmer climates grow sprouts in soil with a high clay content if you have a choice, and shade the soil around roots. Harvest sprouts when they are 1 inch in diameter or smaller and still tight. Twist them off gently, starting at the base.

**Cauliflower:** Grown for its dense, white heads of flower buds. Prevent problems by planting the following cultivars: 'Alpha Paloma' and 'White Rock' are tolerant of cabbage root maggots; 'Super Snowball A' tolerates flea beetles better than most cultivars.

Cauliflower is fussier about temperatures than the other brassicas. Plants only tolerate a low of 45°F and grow poorly above 75°F. Transplants exposed to cool temperatures (35° to 45°F) for ten days or more may form tiny, unusable flower heads. High temperatures can cause the same problem. Cauliflower's optimum temperature range is 60° to 65°F.

**Kale:** Grown for its crinkly, blue-green leaves. It is a very hardy member of the cabbage family, tolerating temperatures below 40°F. Frost improves its taste. It is less tolerant of heat than other members of the cabbage family. In warmer climates, grow kale in soil with high clay content if possible, and shade soil around roots.

nels, vent them with a 6-inch cut in the plastic directly over each plant. Remove covers when melons flower so insects can pollinate the blossoms, or you will not get any fruit. In the fall, temperatures below 50°F cause cold stress and rapid wilting. Cover plants on cool nights.

Melons perform best in well-drained, loose-textured soils with lots of organic matter. They prefer a pH between 6.0 and 6.8 but can tolerate a pH as high as 7.6. Melons are shallow-rooted and may wilt on hot, dry days even when they are not diseased. Keep them well watered, but do not let the soil become saturated. Wet soil can cause stems to rot at soil level. Overwatering or uneven watering can cause fruit to split. Potassium deficiency can also cause split fruit.

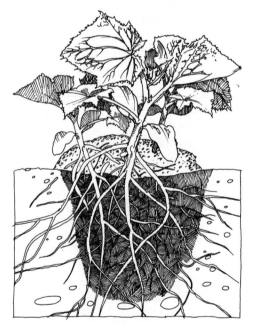

**Hill planting.** Raised mounds or "hills" provide warm soil and good drainage for your melons. Even in good garden soil, work an extra shovelful of compost or well-aged manure into each 1-foot-high, 2- to 3-foot-wide hill just before planting. Or to really baby your crop, dig a 1-foot-deep hole, fill it with compost or aged manure, and build the planting hill on top.

Prevent disease problems by keeping the leaves dry. Water carefully or use drip irrigation. Mulch melons to help conserve water: Black plastic is a good choice for central and northern areas, but in extremely warm areas it can warm the soil too much. Organic mulches are good, too, but also provide shelter for pests like squash bugs.

**Caution:** Melon leaves are easily burned by insecticidal soap and copper sprays. Use the most dilute spray recommended and apply sparingly. Do not spray plants in direct sun or if temperatures are above 80°F, and don't spray drought-stressed plants.

# Onion

*Allium cepa* and other species (Liliaceae)

**Site:** At least ½ day of sun.
**Soil:** Richly organic, well-drained loam with pH of 6.0–6.5; constantly moist, but not wet.
**How much to plant:** About 40 plants per person.
**Spacing:** 1"–4" between plants in rows 1'–2' apart.
**Days to maturity:** Varies with cultivar and method; 100–160 days from seed to harvest. Green onions: Harvest in 45 days from transplants or sets. Bulb onions: Harvest in 90 days from transplants or sets.

Onions grow best in full sun and deep, fertile, well-drained soil with lots of organic matter. Work in a generous amount of compost before planting. Onions need high levels of nitrogen and potassium and a moderate to high level of phosphorus, so do a soil test and amend soil as needed before planting. Onions grow well in raised beds or ridges, especially if soil is clayey.

Onions grow best between 55° and 75°F and will tolerate temperatures as low as 45° and as high as 85°F. They prefer cool temperatures early in their growth and warm temperatures near maturity.

Keep the soil moist since onions have shallow roots, but don't allow soil to become saturated

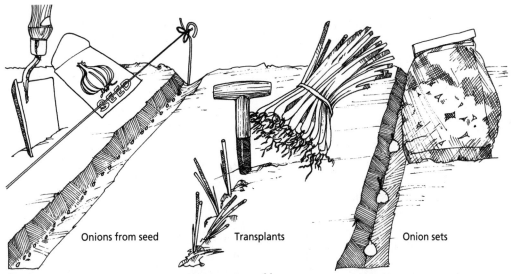

Onions from seed          Transplants          Onion sets

**Onion-planting methods.** Outdoors, sow seeds thickly about $\frac{1}{2}$ inch deep, mixing in radish seeds to mark the planted area and to lure any root maggots away from the onions and to the radishes. If planting in rows instead of raised beds, space the rows about $2\frac{1}{2}$ feet apart. Thin seedlings to 1 inch apart, and thin again in four weeks to 6 inches apart. At the same time, pull the soil back a little to expose the tops and sides of the bulbs; this will induce them to develop. Space transplants or sets 2 inches deep and 4 to 6 inches apart. Use the closer spacing if you plan to harvest some young plants at about five weeks as green onions. A pound of sets, which should be planted carefully with the stem-end up, is enough for a 50-foot row.

##  Culture Clues: Onions

Onions don't like too much heat early in their growth or too much nitrogen. For better onion bulbs, keep these hints in mind:

■ Sets are easier to plant than seeds or transplants. They mature earlier and are less susceptible to disease. Unfortunately, cultivar selection is limited for sets.

■ Look for $\frac{1}{2}$-inch-diameter sets. Larger ones often go to seed before producing decent-sized bulbs, and anything smaller may not grow well.

■ Weed beds well, using a sharp hoe to cut off weeds at soil level. Pulling weeds can damage onions' shallow roots.

■ Once soil has warmed, mulch plants to discourage weeds and conserve soil moisture.

■ Dry conditions cause bulbs to split. Water when necessary to provide at least 1 inch of water each week. Keep in mind that transplants require more water than sets do.

■ New growth from the center will stop when bulbs start forming.

■ To harvest, use the back of a rake to horizontally bend over yellowed onion tops. A day or so later, when the tops turn brown, pull or dig the bulbs on a sunny day, and leave them to dry in the sun. Lay the tops of one row over the bulbs of another to help prevent sunscald. When the outer skins are dry, wipe off any soil and remove the tops. Store in a cool, dry place; hang them in mesh bags or braids in an airy area.

because onions are susceptible to several root rot diseases. Mulching onions with composted leaves or straw is highly recommended to maintain soil organic content, help prevent disease, and keep down weeds. Wait until soil warms to apply mulch.

To help prevent populations of disease organisms from building up in the soil, avoid planting onions where onion-family members have been grown during the previous three years. In general, white onions are more prone to problems than yellow or red ones.

You can grow onions from seeds, transplants, or sets. Discard any diseased sets or transplants. Transplants are seedlings started in the current growing season and sold in bunches. Sets are immature bulbs grown the previous year. Soak sets, roots, or seeds in compost tea for 15 minutes before planting to help prevent disease. Dust the roots of sets and plants with bonemeal after soaking and before planting to give them a good start.

Onion bulb formation is controlled by day length, so selecting suitable cultivars for your area is crucial. In the North choose "long-day" cultivars, and in the South choose "short-day" cultivars.

Allow tops to fall over naturally, then pull

bulbs and let them air-cure for two weeks. After curing, sort out damaged bulbs and those with thick necks and put aside for immediate use. Store others at temperatures just above 32°F.

# Pea

*Pisum sativum* (Leguminosae)

**Site:** Full sun; will grow in partial shade.
**Soil:** Well-drained soil with high organic matter is best; pH of 5.5–6.8.
**How much to plant:** 40 plants per person.
**Spacing:** Bush types: 2' between rows. Climbing types: 3' between rows. Both types: 2"–3" between plants.
**Days to maturity:** 56–75 days from seed to harvest.

Peas grow well in almost any soil but do best in soil with lots of organic matter and a pH between 5.5 and 6.8. A 1-inch layer of compost worked well into the soil before planting will provide sufficient nutrients for a good crop.

Peas are a cool-season, moisture-loving crop. They grow best between 60° and 75°F; they do poorly at temperatures above 75°F but will tolerate temperatures as low as 45°F. Pea foliage can withstand a light frost, but pods and flowers will be damaged unless they are covered.

Most disease problems in peas can be avoided with proper culture. Do not plant in wet soils. Plant in raised beds, and add plenty of compost to loosen the soil. Rapid germination is essential to avoid root rot problems. Choose lighter soils for earliest plantings if you have a choice, and keep soil moist but not wet. Avoid touching plants when they are wet. Dispose of vines after harvest and till soil to reduce future problems. Plant peas where no peas or beans have grown for at least three years.

Soak seed in compost tea for 15 minutes or as long as overnight to help prevent disease and speed germination. To promote nitrogen fixa-

 **Pick Perfect Peas**

Pea pods are ready to pick about three weeks after blossoms appear. A daily harvest encourages more pods. For best results, eat peas immediately after harvest. Pick shell and snap peas when plump and bright green. Snow pea pods should be almost flat, barely showing developing seeds. Cut pods from vines with scissors or pinch them off with your thumbnail.

tion, treat seed with an inoculant labeled for garden peas before planting. Be sure to buy fresh inoculant each year, or check the date on the package for viability.

Peas are susceptible to certain micronutrient deficiencies. Spray young plants with seaweed extract every two weeks to help prevent deficiencies and boost production.

# Pepper

*Capsicum annuum* var. *annuum* (Solanaceae)

**Site:** Full sun.
**Soil:** Sandy loam, or any good, well-drained soil with a pH of 6.0–6.8.
**How much to plant:** 3–4 plants per person.
**Spacing:** Plant on 1½' centers.
**Days to maturity:** 65–80 days from transplanting.

Peppers require deeply worked, well-drained soil with lots of organic matter. They do best at a pH between 6.0 and 6.8 but tolerate pH as low as 5.5. Peppers require a moderate to high level of nitrogen and moderate levels of phosphorus, potassium, and calcium. Have the soil tested and amend as needed before planting. Peppers grow best between 65° and 80°F. Temperatures above 85°F or below 60°F can cause blossoms to drop without setting fruit.

Peppers tolerate drought, but they do best in soil that is evenly moist but not soggy. Plant in raised beds to improve drainage, if needed. Stake peppers to keep fruit from touching the ground, and use mulch to control weeds and prevent soil-borne diseases from splashing up on the fruit.

Do not plant peppers where tomatoes, potatoes, eggplants, or peppers have been planted within the past three to five years. Also, try to plan your planting scheme to separate these crops in the garden. Compost or till under all plant residues at the end of the season, and till the soil to reduce overwintering pests.

Purchase sturdy, insect- and disease-free plants, or start your own from seed indoors. Soak seed in a 10 percent bleach solution (1 part bleach to 9 parts water) for ten minutes, and rinse in clean water before planting to reduce seed-borne diseases. Pepper seeds germinate best

 **Culture Clues: Peppers**

Peppers can be finicky. They may not yield well if watering or temperatures fluctuate too much. Here are some other strategies for better peppers:

■ When buying transplants, look for strong stems and dark green leaves. Pass up ones with blossoms or fruit because such plants won't produce well.

■ Spread a thick but light mulch, such as straw or grass clippings, around plants. Water deeply during dry spells to encourage deep root development. Lack of water can produce bitter-tasting peppers.

■ To avoid damaging roots, gently hand-pull weeds.

■ Temperatures over 90°F often cause blossoms to drop and plants to wilt. To avoid this, plant so that taller plants will shade peppers during the hottest hours. Peppers do like warm soil, though—at least 60°F.

■ Pale leaves and slow growth may indicate a need for liquid fertilizer, such as manure tea.

■ Most sweet and hot peppers are at their best when mature. Early in the season, however, harvest before peppers ripen to encourage the plant to keep bearing.

■ Always cut (don't pull) peppers from the plant.

■ When frost is predicted, pick all fruit, or pull up plants by the roots and hang them in a dry, cool place indoors until fruits ripen.

above 80°F. Once seedlings are up, they grow best at 70°F during the day and 60°F during the night. Wait until soil temperatures reach 65°F before setting out transplants. Spray transplants with an antitranspirant to help reduce disease problems, and water them with seaweed extract or compost tea to give them a good start. To improve fruit set, spray plants when the first flowers open with a mixture of 1 gallon of seaweed extract and 1 teaspoon of Epsom salts.

# Potato
*Solanum tuberosum* (Solanaceae)

**Site:** Full or nearly full sun, with good air circulation.
**Soil:** Any good garden soil that drains well; pH of 5.0–6.8.
**How much to plant:** 5–10 plants per person.
**Spacing:** Leave 1' between plants in rows 3' apart, or plant in raised beds on 1½' centers.
**Days to maturity:** 90–120 days, depending on cultivar and climate.

Potatoes require deeply worked, well-drained soil with lots of organic matter and a pH between 5.0 and 6.8. They need moderate to high levels of nitrogen, phosphorus, potassium, calcium, and sulfur. Have the soil tested and amend as needed before planting. Gypsum is a good source of calcium and sulfur for potatoes.

Keep soil moist but not soggy, and do not allow it to dry out. Alternating dry and wet soil can cause cracked or knobby tubers. Once tops begin to yellow near harvest, you can let the soil dry out without damaging tubers.

Do not plant potatoes where tomatoes, potatoes, eggplants, peppers, strawberries, or brambles have been planted within the past four to five years. Also, try to plan your planting scheme to separate these crops in the garden. Don't plant potatoes where sod or small grains were grown the previous year: Wireworms, a common sod pest, also feed on potato tubers. Compost or till under all plant residues at the end of the season. Tilling the soil helps prevent pests from overwintering.

Potatoes are usually grown from seed pota-

 **Culture Clues: Potatoes**

Potatoes can develop disease problems in heavy or waterlogged soils. They're also sensitive to weather conditions. For healthier potatoes, try the following tips:

■ Plant only certified disease-free seed potatoes. Cut these into pieces and cure by spreading them out in a bright, airy place for 24 hours, or until they are slightly dry and the cut areas have hardened.

■ In wet climates, dust seed potatoes with sulfur to help prevent rot.

■ Keep the developing tubers covered; when exposed to sunlight, tubers turn green and develop a mildly toxic substance called solanine.

■ Once plants flower, stop hilling up soil. Apply thick mulch to save water and fight weeds.

■ Keep the area evenly moist but not soggy. Take special care to keep plants well watered from six to ten weeks after planting, as tubers are starting to develop.

■ When flowers open, harvest "new" potatoes. Pull aside earth around the base of the plants, and gently pick tubers. Once foliage starts to wither and die back, tubers are full-grown. If the weather is not too warm or wet, tubers will keep in the ground for several weeks. Dig them up with a spading fork before the first frost. Nicked or bruised potatoes don't store well, so eat them first.

toes (tubers) or "buds" (tiny tissue-cultured tubers), but a few cultivars, such as 'Explorer' and 'Homestead Hybrid', are grown from true seeds. Prevent problems by planting only certi-fied disease-free tubers. Planting true seeds or buds also helps avoid many tuber-borne diseases.

Be sure to consider the end use of your pota-to crop when you select cultivars for planting—the texture of a cooked potato depends on its starch content. Higher starch content yields a drier, flakier texture. New potatoes of most cul-tivars are 90 percent water and only 7 percent starch. At maturity, most bakers contain 15 to 18 percent starch. However, cultivars used for potato chips and french fries contain as much as 22 percent starch.

Pre-condition tubers by storing them between 65° and 70°F for two weeks before planting to encourage rapid growth. Soak pieces in compost tea for several hours before planting to help pre-vent disease problems. Plant them out when soil is at least 40°F.

# Radish

*Raphanus sativus* (Cruciferae)

**Site:** Full sun or partial shade
**Soil:** Any soil; pH of 5.5–6.8.
**How much to plant:** A few feet of row per person per planting.
**Spacing:** 2" apart in rows 8"–18" apart.
**Days to maturity:** Spring types 21–35 days; winter types 55–60 days.

Radishes are annual and biennial vegetables grown for their crisp, peppery roots. Certain cultivars do not have fleshy roots but are grown for their crunchy seed pods. Some Daikon rad-ishes grow 2-foot roots.

Most radishes do best in cool, moist condi-tions. They need a pH between 5.5 and 6.8 and light, relatively rich soil. Plant radishes as soon as soil can be worked in spring. Make small

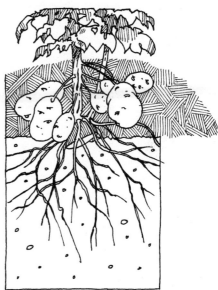

**Potato-planting methods.** To plant in hills (*top*), pile up a 3- to 4-foot-wide mound of soil 4 to 6 inches high. Space seed potatoes 6 inches apart near the center of the hill and bury with 4 to 5 inches of soil; continue cov-ering tubers as they develop. To mulch-plant (*bottom*), form hills in the fall with a 3- to 4-foot-thick mound of leaves. The next spring, plant the seed potatoes on top of the partially decomposed mound and cover them with 1 foot of straw or hay, adding more as the vines mature.

plantings weekly until early summer for a continuous supply of radishes. Temperatures between 50° and 65°F produce the best radishes; growth above 75°F is poor. Some cultivars of Daikon radishes are designed for summer planting and will flower without forming large roots if planted too early.

The secret to mild, tender radishes is rapid growth. Water heavily the first two weeks after they come up if soil is dry. A light application of compost is usually enough for a good radish

crop. Radishes will not tolerate soils high in salt.

Radishes are related to cabbage and suffer from many of the same problems. Since leaves are not harvested, more insect damage can be tolerated than in cabbage plants. See the Cabbage entry on page 208 for descriptions and controls. Prevent problems with Fusarium wilt by planting resistant cultivars such as 'Fancy Red', 'Fuego', 'Red Devil B', 'Red King', and 'Red Pak'.

# Spinach

*Spinacia oleracea* (Chenopodiaceae)

**Site:** Sun to partial shade; needs a cool, moist site.
**Soil:** Heavy, fertile loam that is moist but not soggy; pH of 6.0–7.0.
**How much to plant:** About 30 plants per person.
**Spacing:** 1'–3' between rows, 2"–6" between plants.
**Days to maturity:** 37–45 days from seed.

Grow spinach in well-drained soil with lots of organic matter and a pH between 6.0 and 7.0; it won't tolerate pH below 5.0. Spinach seed germinates best at soil temperatures between 45° and 75°F but will germinate as low as 35°F.

Mature spinach can survive temperatures of 20°F if gradually hardened off. However, prolonged exposure of young plants to temperatures below 45°F will cause bolting—production of a flower stalk—and plants will produce few, low-quality leaves. Temperatures above 75°F and long days also cause bolting. In warmer climates, plant spinach in filtered shade to extend its season into the warmer months.

Keep soil moist but not soggy. Do not allow it to dry out, or plants may bolt. Spread a thin layer of mulch around plants to conserve moisture, suppress weeds, and keep soil cool.

Soak seed in compost tea for 30 minutes before planting to speed germination and to help suppress soilborne diseases.

Spinach requires moderate levels of potassium

## Culture Clues: Spinach

Spinach needs cool conditions and moist soil for best growth. Here are several pointers for better spinach:

■ In warm climates, plant spinach in the shade of tall crops to help prevent bolting.

■ In warm weather, freeze the seeds for a few days, then moisten and refrigerate them for a few more days before sowing. Shade soil until the seeds germinate.

■ In many areas, spinach will grow in cold frames all winter.

■ Fertilize with manure tea or fish emulsion when plants have four true leaves; an early dose of nitrogen discourages bolting.

■ A light mulch of hay, straw, or grass clippings discourages weeds and helps retain moisture.

■ Cover with shade cloth if the temperature goes above 80°F.

■ Start harvesting when plants have at least six leaves that are 3 to 4 inches long. Carefully cutting the outside leaves will extend harvests, particularly with fall crops. Harvest the entire crop at the first sign of bolting by using a sharp knife to cut through the taproot just below the soil.

## Heat-Tolerant Greens

There are some greens that can take the heat and still produce a good crop. Collards are a traditional southern vegetable that can resist cold and grow well in cooler climates. Basella, also called Malabar spinach, is a vine that grows best when trellised. New Zealand spinach is not a true spinach but has a similar flavor. Swiss chard produces huge, mild-flavored leaves.

Swiss chard

Collards

New Zealand spinach

Basella

and phosphorus and a high level of nitrogen. It is also sensitive to low levels of calcium and boron. Have the soil tested and amend as necessary. Fast-acting sources of nitrogen, such as blood meal and soybean meal, are good fertilizers for spinach.

# Squash

*Cucurbita* spp. (Cucurbitaceae)

**Site:** Full or almost full sun.
**Soil:** Any good garden soil that drains well; pH of 6.0–6.8.
**How much to plant:** 2–4 plants per person.
**Spacing:** Bushy cultivars: in hills 2′–4′ apart. Vining types: in hills 3′–8′ apart.
**Days to maturity:** Summer squash: 45–50 days. Winter squash and pumpkins: 85–110 days.

**Identifying male and female flowers.** Squash plants need both male and female flowers to produce fruit. Male flowers, which appear about a week earlier than female flowers, do not have the swollen stems characteristic of female flowers.

Squash seeds need 60°F soil to germinate, so wait until warm weather to plant. Cover plants with floating row covers to protect them from insects and late cold snaps. Remove row covers when plants begin to flower so insects can pollinate the blossoms, or you will not get any fruit.

Squash perform best in well-drained, loose-textured soils with lots of organic matter. They will grow in soils with a pH between 5.5 and 6.8 but prefer a pH above 6.0. Squash need lots of water, but don't let the soil become saturated. Prevent disease problems by keeping the leaves dry. Mulch squash to help conserve water. Black plastic is a good choice for northern areas, but in extremely warm areas it can warm the soil too much. Organic mulches are good, too, but may provide shelter for pests like squash bugs. Foil mulches help prevent aphid problems. To prevent rot, support fruit on scraps of wood.

Rotate crops in your garden so that no member of the cucurbit family (cucumbers, melons, and squash) is grown in the same place more often than every four years.

**Caution:** Squash leaves are easily burned by insecticidal soap and copper sprays. Use the most dilute spray recommended and use sparingly. Do not spray plants in direct sun or if temperatures are above 80°F, and don't spray drought-stressed plants.

## Sweet Potato

*Ipomoea batatas* (Convolvulaceae)

**Site:** Full sun; afternoon shade in warm climates.
**Soil:** Loose soil with a pH of 5.5–6.5.
**How much to plant:** 2–4 plants per person.
**Spacing:** 12" apart in rows 3' apart; 18" apart each way in beds.
**Days to maturity:** 70–100 days.

Sweet potatoes prefer loose, well-drained soil with a pH between 5.5 and 6.5. They require moderate amounts of nitrogen and boron, a moderate to high level of phosphorus, and a high level of potassium. Have the soil tested and amend as necessary before planting. Sweet potatoes do well in raised beds. Work in lots of or-

---

 **Culture Clues: Squash**

Squash and other cucurbits love warm growing conditions and rich soil. Grow your best squash ever by following these guidelines:

■ Water seedlings thoroughly. Keep soil moist throughout the season. To avoid transmitting diseases to the plants, water the soil, not the foliage, and don't handle plants when they're wet.

■ Pull weeds until vines begin to lengthen, then apply thick hay, straw, or leaf mulch.

■ Apply compost tea or manure tea when the first fruits set.

■ When vines grow to 5 feet, pinch off the growing tips to encourage fruit-bearing sideshoots.

■ By midsummer, remove remaining flowers of winter squash to focus the plant's energy on the ripening crop.

■ To avoid rot, put a board or thick mulch under fruit.

■ During dry weather, harvest by using a sharp knife to cut fruit off the vine, leaving 3 to 4 inches of stem on the fruit. For summer squash, pick each fruit before the blossom drops off the tip, or the plant will quit producing. Before expected frost, pick ripe winter squash, and cover any unripe squash with heavy mulch. Don't store bruised or washed winter squash. Dry winter types (except acorn squash) in the sun until stems shrivel and turn gray. Store winter squash in a cool, dry area with temperatures of 45° to 50°F and with 65 to 70 percent humidity.

---

**Starting sweet-potato slips.** To grow your own slips, save a few tuberous roots from your last crop, or buy untreated ones; store-bought sweet potatoes are often waxed to prevent sprouting. Some six weeks before transplanting, place them in a box of moist sand, sawdust, or chopped leaves, and keep at 75° to 80°F. When shoots are 6 to 9 inches long, cut them off the tuberous root. Remove and dispose of the bottom inch from each slip, which sometimes harbors disease organisms.

ganic matter before planting. Avoid top-dressing after early summer, or root formation may be interrupted.

Keep soil moist, but not soggy, until the vines begin to spread. After that, water only if vines wilt. When the roots begin to enlarge in late summer, keep the soil moist until harvest. Mulch plants to suppress weeds and conserve moisture. Black plastic mulch will also warm the soil.

Plant sweet potatoes where they have not been grown for at least two years. After harvest, cut vines and let dry, then compost or till under to reduce disease buildup.

Purchase disease-free plants, or start your own

from healthy, overwintered roots. Plant out when nights stay above 60°F. Soak plant roots in compost tea for five minutes before planting to help reduce disease problems. Water well with a fish emulsion or fish-meal tea after planting to give the plants a good start.

Dig potatoes gently before the first frost, after foliage starts to yellow. Dry them for two to three hours in the garden. Use any damaged or diseased potatoes as soon as possible. Cure healthy potatoes for ten days in a humid place at 80° to 85°F. Gradually reduce temperature and store them in a humid room at 55° to 60°F.

# Tomato

*Lycopersicon esculentum* (Solanaceae)

**Site:** Full sun or full morning sun and less than 3 hours of afternoon shade.
**Soil:** Moderately fertile clay or sandy loam with good drainage and a pH of 6.0–6.8.
**How much to plant:** Warm climates: 2 plants per person; cool climates: 4 plants person.
**Spacing:** Staked tomatoes: $1\frac{1}{2}$'–2' apart. Unstaked, uncaged tomatoes: 3'–4' apart. Caged tomatoes: Space 2'-diameter cages 4' apart.
**Days to maturity:** 90–140 days from seed; 60–90 days from transplanting, depending on the cultivar.

Tomatoes require full sun and deep soil with a pH between 6.0 and 6.8. Work in plenty of compost before planting to add organic matter. Tomatoes require moderate levels of nitrogen and phosphorus and moderate to high levels of potassium and calcium. Tomatoes grow best between 75° and 90°F. Temperatures over 100°F can kill blossoms, while temperatures below 50°F can cause chilling injury.

Keep soil moist but not soggy, and do not allow it to dry out. Avoid wetting leaves when watering to help prevent diseases. Tomatoes do well in raised beds with drip irrigation and mulch. Black plastic is a good mulch in cool areas because it helps warm the soil as well as suppressing weeds and conserving water. Organic mulch helps keep the soil cooler in very warm areas while adding organic matter. Mulch also

**Pruning tomato plants.** Use your fingers to snap off suckers—the sprouts that grow between the main stem and the leaf axils. If you need scissors or pruning shears to do the job, you're waiting too long to prune.

 **Culture Clues: Tomatoes**

For all of the hints we have on growing tomatoes, we never know enough. Here are some important principles to remember for growing great tomatoes:

■ When planting, you can bury the stem horizontally in a shallow trench so that only top leaves show. (First, strip off leaves along the to-be-buried part of the stem.) Many claim that this produces high yields.

■ Sprawling plants may produce more, but they use a larger space and may encounter more pests.

■ Exposing young plants to nighttime temperatures below 55°F will prevent fruit from setting. Protect them with cloches.

■ Give plants at least 1 inch of water a week. A deep soaking is better than several light waterings. Avoid wetting the foliage.

■ A weekly dose of liquid seaweed increases health and yields. At flowering time, side-dress with compost. When small fruits appear, feed with manure tea.

■ Snapping off young suckers between the main stem and leaf axils encourages higher yields and earlier fruiting on staked plants. When the vine reaches the top of the stakes, pinch back the tip.

■ Once tomatoes start ripening, check vines almost daily. Cut or gently twist off fruits, supporting the vine at the same time.

■ At first sign of heavy frost, harvest all fruits. Green ones will eventually ripen in a warm place out of direct sunlight.

helps prevent disease by preventing the fruit from touching the ground or being splashed with soil containing disease-causing organisms.

Choose cultivars that are adapted to local growing conditions. Many of them are resistant to one or more problems. Resistant cultivars are usually denoted in seed catalogs as follows: F = Fusarium-resistant, V = Verticillium-resistant, T = tobacco mosaic virus–resistant, and N = nematode-resistant.

Do not plant tomatoes where tomatoes, potatoes, eggplants, or peppers have been planted within the past three to five years. Also, try to plan your planting scheme to separate these crops in the garden. Compost or till under all plant residues at the end of the season to reduce overwintering pests. After tilling, spread 2 to 4 pounds of blood meal or soybean meal per 100 square feet to encourage breakdown of plant material.

Purchase stocky, insect- and disease-free plants, or start your own from seed indoors. Soak seed in a 10 percent bleach solution (1 part bleach and 9 parts water) for ten minutes and rinse in clean water before planting to reduce seed-borne diseases. Tomato seeds germinate best between 75° and 90°F. Once seedlings are up, they grow best between 60° and 70°F. When plants are set out, add 1 cup each of bonemeal and kelp to each hole. Water the transplants thoroughly with fish emulsion or compost tea to give them a good start. Spray young plants with seaweed extract to help prevent transplant shock and nutrient deficiencies.

 ## Easy Unusual Vegetables

There's always room for a new crop in most vegetable gardens. If you're looking for new tastes and textures, try some of these uncommon—but easy-to-grow—vegetables.

■ **Arugula** (*Eruca vesicaria* subsp. *sativa*). Also known as rocket. A fast-growing annual with flavorful leaves. Sow seed in rich soil in early spring and autumn. Needs cool weather and lots of water. Add young leaves to salads and soup for a distinctive nutty, spicy flavor. Use the flowers as a garnish or in salads.

■ **Basella** (*Basella alba* and *B. a.* var. *rubra*). Also known as Malabar or summer spinach. A heat-tolerant, 6-foot perennial vine with thick, dark green leaves that can be harvested all season. Start plants indoors and transplant outdoors in rich soil after frost danger is past. Trellis to maximize garden space. Requires warm weather and plenty of moisture. Harvest sparingly until plants branch. Substitute the greens for spinach.

■ **Elephant garlic** (*Allium ampeloprasum*). A mild, garlic-flavored ½- to 1-pound bulb closely related to the leek. Prepare a deep bed with compost or aged manure. Plant cloves 8 inches apart in fall or late summer. Mulch well in the North. Harvest bulbs the following season when tops die back. Dry in shade and store in a cool, dark, dry place. Use cloves in cooked dishes and the greens for seasoning.

■ **Ground cherry** (*Physalis pruinosa*). Also known as dwarf Cape gooseberry. Low sprawling plants produce sweet, marble-sized, golden yellow fruit encased in a papery husk. Will self-sow. Start seed indoors or sow outdoors in rich soil after last spring frost. Harvest when the tan husks turn paper-thin. Add to vegetable and fruit salads for a sweet, exotic flavor. Makes delectable pies and jams. Freeze or dry to preserve.

■ **Hyacinth bean** (*Dolichos lablab*). An attractive vining legume with lavender flowers and deep burgundy pods on purple stems. Start seed indoors or direct-seed outdoors in rich soil after frost danger. Grow as you would pole lima beans or on trellises in the ornamental garden. Use flowers in salads and dips. Use the young pods like string beans or fresh in salads. Cook older beans as you would green shell beans.

■ **Sorrel, French** (*Rumex scutatus*). A hardy perennial with succulent, lemony leaves high in vitamin C. Start from seed or purchase plants. Plant in rich, well-drained soil in full sun or partial shade. Remove seed heads to prevent leaves from becoming bitter. Mix leaves with other greens for salads, or add them to soups or cooked dishes.

# Chapter 10

# FRUITS AND BERRIES

Nothing is as delicious as a mouthful of freshly picked fruit—be it a succulent, juicy peach; a tart, crisp apple; or luscious, tangy-sweet raspberries. And when that fruit comes from your own backyard, the taste is even better because you harvest your crop at the peak of perfection—you can say goodbye to the under- or over-ripe fruit found in most grocery stores. And you can grow the best-tasting cultivars, not necessarily the ones that are most attractive or ship best.

To get started, you need to determine what kinds of fruits you'd like to grow. Fruits commonly are subdivided into categories. *Tree fruits* are those that grow on trees, such as apples and peaches. *Small fruits* are either fruits that are small or fruits that are borne on small plants. Strawberries and blueberries are familiar small fruits. Some fruits, though, are difficult to place in a particular category. Mulberries and juneberries are examples of this: Both bear soft, small fruits, but they're produced on full-sized trees. Nuts are actually dry fruits with woody shells.

To develop fruit, most plants need to have their flowers pollinated. When flowers on a plant produce fruit after being dusted with their own pollen, that plant is self-pollinating. Strawberries are self-pollinating, so if you plant only one cultivar, you still get fruit. Flowers that need pollen from a plant of a different cultivar to develop fruit need cross-pollination. Apples, for example, require cross-pollination, so a 'McIntosh' tree needs a 'Golden Delicious' tree (or some other cultivar besides 'McIntosh')

nearby to supply pollen. By choosing the right cultivars, gardeners all over the country can enjoy fresh fruit, beginning in spring with strawberries and going through winter with the last of the apples that ripen in cold storage.

Don't overlook the ornamental value of fruit-bearing plants. A peach tree, for example, is transformed into a cloud of pink blossoms in spring. The crimson red color of blueberry leaves in fall rivals that of the sugar maple. And strawberries make an attractive edging.

This chapter will give you the basics on how to select, grow, and maintain fruits and berries. For information on pest and disease controls, see Chapter 7.

## GROWING FRUIT TREES

Fruit trees make great landscape plants, blooming abundantly in spring and trimmed with colorful fruit in summer and fall. But unlike strictly ornamental trees, their fruit is not only attractive but also a succulent edible treat. The flavor of tree-ripened apples, peaches, and other fruits is unmatched, and you'll appreciate the savings in your grocery bills. However, to reap good-quality fruit, you must commit to pruning, monitoring, and maintaining your trees.

### SELECTING FRUIT TREES

Before you buy, determine which fruit trees can survive and fruit in your climate. Northern gardeners should choose cultivars that will survive winter cold, blossom late enough to escape late-spring frosts, yet still set and mature fruit before the end of the growing season. Southern gardeners need cultivars that will tolerate intense summer heat and humidity. For organic gardeners, choosing disease-resistant trees is especially important. Check with local fruit growers or with your extension service office to see which cultivars have a good track record in your area. You should also do some independent research on your climate and consider your fruit needs.

Fruit trees need a dormant period during which temperatures are below 45°F. Trees that don't get sufficient winter chilling will not fruit properly. Low-chill cultivars flower and fruit with as little as half the usual cold requirement, stretching deciduous fruit production into Texas, northern Florida, and parts of California. Extra-hardy, high-chill cultivars for the far North require longer cold periods and flower a week later than most.

If winter temperatures in your area drop below −25°F, stick with the hardiest apple and pear cultivars; between −20° and 0°F, you can try most apples and pears, sour cherries, European plums, and apricots; if minimum temperatures stay above −5°F, you can consider sweet cherries, Japanese plums, nectarines, and peaches. If minimum temperatures in your area are above 45°F, be sure to select low-chill cultivars.

Freezing temperatures can kill fruit blossoms. If you live in an area with unpredictable spring weather and occasional late frosts, look for late-blooming or frost-tolerant cultivars, especially for apricots and plums.

In humid regions, select disease-resistant cultivars whenever possible. Diseases such as apple scab and brown rot are more troublesome in humid conditions.

If you are fond of baking, top your list with sour cherries and cooking apples, which make excellent pies. For canning, look for suitable cultivars of peaches, nectarines, and pears. For jellies, try apricots, plums, and quinces. If you're interested in fruit for fresh eating, think about how long the fruit will last in storage.

 **Words to Know**

**Standard:** A full-sized fruit tree, usually maturing to at least 20 feet in height.

**Dwarf and semidwarf:** Fruit trees grafted on size-controlling rootstocks. Dwarf trees often mature to 8 to 10 feet in height. Semidwarfs mature to 12 to 18 feet.

**Genetic dwarf:** A fruit tree that stays quite small without a dwarfing rootstock.

**Rootstock:** A cultivar onto which a fruiting cultivar is grafted. Rootstocks are selected for strong, healthy roots or for dwarfing effect.

**Whip:** A young tree, often the first-year growth from a graft or bud.

**Scaffolds:** The main structural branches on a fruit tree.

**Pome fruit:** Fruit that has a core containing many seeds, such as apples and pears.

**Stone fruit:** Fruit with a single hard pit, such as cherries, plums, and peaches.

**Low-chill:** Requiring fewer hours of cool temperatures to break dormancy.

**High-chill:** Requiring more hours of cool temperatures to break dormancy.

**Self-fruitful:** A tree that produces pollen that can pollinate its own flowers.

**Compatible cultivars:** Cultivars that can successfully cross-pollinate.

**Crotch:** The angle of emergence of a branch from the trunk.

**Suckers:** Shoots that sprout out of or near the base of a tree.

**Watersprouts:** Upright shoots that sprout from the trunk and main limbs of a tree.

Some apples stay good for months if kept cold, but soft fruits must be eaten within about one week or they will spoil.

Fruit trees come in shapes and sizes for every yard. Most home gardeners prefer dwarf or semidwarf trees, which fruit at a younger age and are easier to tend.

**Standards**  Standard fruit trees can reach 30 feet or taller, becoming small shade trees that can be underplanted with flowers or groundcovers. They are long-lived and hardy but can be more difficult to maintain and harvest.

**Grafted Semidwarfs**  Apples grafted on size-controlling rootstocks grow well. However, stone fruit trees grafted onto dwarfing rootstocks often are not long-lived. In just a few years, perhaps when the young tree is burdened with a heavy crop of fruit, the graft can unknit and the tree will die.

**Genetic Dwarfs**  Genetic dwarf or miniature trees are naturally compact trees grafted on standard-sized root systems. They reach about 7 feet and bear about one-fifth as much normal-sized fruit as a standard tree. Genetic dwarfs tend to be shorter-lived than standard trees and are not hardy in northern areas. They can be grown in planters and moved to a protected area where temperatures remain between 30°F and 45°F in winter, such as in an unheated storage room. Genetic dwarfs are ideal for the Pacific Northwest or the southern United States. In fact, in those areas they may be preferable to standard trees because they need less winter cold to flower.

Older genetic dwarf tree cultivars had poor-quality fruit, but modern types approach the flavor of their full-sized counterparts. However, none of the modern genetic dwarfs are disease-resistant. They need diligent thinning because foliage and fruit can become overcrowded.

##  Fruit Tree Catalog Shopping

If you can't find the kinds of fruit trees you want locally, turn to catalogs. Your best choice is a mail-order nursery that specializes in fruit trees, located in a climate similar to your own.

Most of the information you need to make the proper selection, such as chilling requirements and insect and disease resistance, should be listed in the catalog. However, you may have to call the nursery to find out what rootstock is used and make your own decision about its compatibility and potential in your area. Also, if the catalog doesn't list pollination requirements, inquire whether a particular cultivar is self-fruitful. If it's not, be sure to ask for names of compatible cultivars.

If you are looking for a specific cultivar or trying to locate mail-order sources that specialize in a certain type of fruit, you will find your answer in a book called *Fruit, Berry, and Nut Inventory*. This extensive listing of cultivar names is compiled by the Seed Savers Exchange. Check it out at your local library, or to buy a copy, contact:

Seed Saver Publications
Rural Route 3, Box 239, Decorah, IA 52101

If you do decide to buy trees at a local garden center, be wary of trees offered in containers. These trees may have been shipped to the garden center bareroot, had their roots trimmed to fit a container, and then were potted up just for the sake of appearance. This treatment will not help the tree grow any better, and the stress to the roots may actually set the tree back.

Pollination requirements are another important factor to consider when selecting trees. Most apples, pears, sweet cherries, and Japanese plums are not self-fruitful. You must plant a second compatible cultivar nearby to ensure good pollination and fruit set. Peaches, nectarines, tart cherries, and some European plums are self-fruitful. Some cultivars of apples, pears, sweet cherries, and European plums are somewhat self-fruitful, but they set better crops when cross-pollinated. Fruit tree entries later in this chapter provide details about pollination requirements.

## SITE SELECTION AND PLANTING

Plant fruit trees in a small traditional orchard, or intersperse them in borders, mixed beds, or a vegetable garden. You can even put a dwarf apple at the end of a foundation planting. Some will grow in lawns, but most perform better in a prepared bed.

Be certain the site you choose has the right growing conditions for fruit trees.

**Sunlight**   Even one or two hours of daily shade may make fruit smaller and less colorful. Envision the mature size of trees and shrubs close to your planned site. If their shadow will encroach on your fruit trees in years to come, you may want to select a different site, or remove the neighboring plants. Sour cherries tolerate a bit of shade better than other tree fruits do.

Shaded soil in early spring can be beneficial. A cool soil can delay flowering, perhaps until after late killing frosts.

**Soil**   Fruit trees need well-drained soil. Sandy soils can be too dry to produce a good crop of fruit. Wet, clayey soil encourages various root rots.

**Slope**   Plant near the top of a gentle slope if possible. Planting on a north-facing slope or about 15 feet from the north side of a building helps slow flowering in spring and protects blossoms from any late frosts. Planting on a south-facing slope can hasten flowering and lead to frost damage. Sheltered alcoves on the south side of a house protect tender trees. Planting in a frost pocket, as shown in the illustration on this page, can increase the risk of spring frost damage to flowers and young fruit.

**Wind**   Blustery winds in open areas or on hilltops can make training difficult, knock fruit off trees early, or topple trees. Staking will help

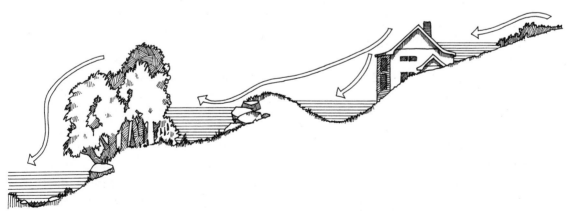

**Frost pockets.** In spring and fall, cold air sinks to the bottom of a slope, creating a frost pocket, a localized area of below-freezing temperature. Trees planted in frost pockets are more susceptible to frost damage. Buildings, small rises, and trees on a slope stop cold air flow but can create frost pockets on their uphill side.

trees resist the force of prevailing winds. Where wind is a problem, you can slow it by erecting a hedge or fence. However, don't box the tree in and stifle the breeze. Air circulation is helpful for reducing diseases.

**Spacing** The amount of room your trees will need depends on their mature height and width, how they are trained, their soil fertility level, and tree vigor. Give every tree plenty of space to grow without impinging on neighboring plants or spreading into shady areas. Small trees, such as dwarf peaches and nectarines, require only 12 feet between trees, while apple trees need 20 to 30 feet between trees.

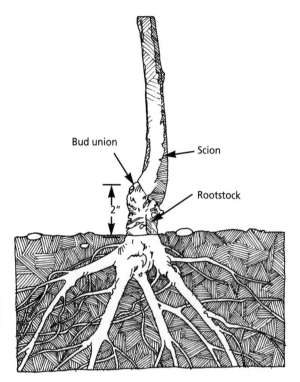

**Determining planting depth.** Plant a tree growing on standard roots at the same depth or slightly deeper than it grew at the nursery. If the tree is budded or grafted, set the bud union—the crooked area where the scion and rootstock join—2 inches above soil level. Scions can root if trees are set too deeply, and the trees can lose rootstock effects, including size control.

 **Try Something New**

If you like trying new fruits, there's an organization of like-minded gardeners who love to share their enthusiasm and experience with growing rare and native fruit. The organization is the North American Fruit Explorers (NAFEX). It publishes a quarterly magazine called *Pomona* and a handbook. For more information, write to:

NAFEX
Route 1, Box 84, Chapin, IL 62628

If your tastes run to tropical and subtropical fruits, you can learn more about how to grow your own by joining the California Rare Fruit Growers (CRFG). Members share information about growing subtropicals via a quarterly magazine called *The Fruit Gardener* and through a network of expert specialists. Despite the name, the organization isn't limited to California. For more information, write to:

CRFG, c/o Fullerton Arboretum
California State University
Fullerton, CA 92634

**Planting** To make the effort and expense of planting fruit trees worthwhile and to maximize yield and fruit quality, it pays to prepare the soil and plant them properly. See "Trees and Shrubs" on page 84 for complete information on getting your trees off to a healthy start.

Plant fruit trees while dormant in early spring, or in the fall where winters are quite mild. Fall planting gives roots a head start, because they continue to grow until the soil freezes. However, fall planting is risky in areas where the soil freezes, because the low temperatures may kill the newly grown roots.

Most nurseries stock bareroot fruit trees.

Plant the young trees as you would any bare-root tree. The illustration on the opposite page shows how to determine the proper depth to set a fruit tree at planting.

You may be able to speed a young tree's establishment by dipping the roots in powdered bonemeal before you plant. Also apply compost tea or manure tea at planting. Allow the tea to sit for several days before applying, or it may burn roots. See "Tea Time for Your Plants" on page 177 for instructions on making compost or manure tea.

# Caring for Fruit Trees

You can't, unfortunately, plant fruit trees and sit back and wait for them to produce. Fruit trees need your time and attention throughout the year in order to stay healthy and provide a bumper crop. You'll need to prune and train your trees, fertilize and mulch them, and protect them during the winter. Some trees may require hand-pollinating, while others need to have their fruit thinned. While there are few shortcuts to meeting these important demands, there are right and wrong ways to go about fulfilling them. Knowing the right way will save you time and frustration and give you the best possible fruit yield.

## PRUNING AND TRAINING

To grow top-quality fruit, and to have easy access for harvesting, you need to establish a sturdy and efficient branching framework. For home gardens, the two best training methods are open center and central leader. Both systems encourage the growth of branches with wide crotches that are less likely to split when burdened with a heavy fruit load.

It's important to establish the main branches while the tree is young. You'll then maintain tree shape of your bearing trees each year with touch-up pruning. Central leader trees produce more fruiting spurs, important for spur-type apple and pear cultivars. For nectarines, peaches, and Japanese plums, use open center training to maximize air circulation and sunlight penetration among the branches, which will help reduce disease. Illustrated instructions for central leader training are on page 232, and on page 233 for open center training.

Spread young branches so they will develop broad crotch angles. Use clothespins to hold branches out from the trunk, or insert notched boards in the crotch angle. Branches that aren't spread may develop a strip of bark called a bark inclusion in the crotch angle, making the crotch weaker and more likely to break.

In certain circumstances, it's best not to train. Some fruit trees, including apricots and pears, are particularly susceptible to disease, which can invade through pruning cuts or attack young growth that arises near the cuts. If disease is a problem in your area, you may want to limit pruning to general maintenance or renewal of fruiting wood. In the far North, keep training to a minimum, since new growth is more susceptible to winter injury. However, leave some young suckers on main scaffolds to act as renewal wood in case main branches are injured by cold.

Whether you train your trees or not, you should prune off shoots that emerge low on the trunk and any branches that cross and rub. Where one limb grows above and shades another, or when two branches of equal length and diameter arise at one fork, select one branch to keep and prune off the other. During the summer, remove suckers that sprout near the base, watersprouts that shoot out from the trunk or main limbs, and any dead or diseased wood.

When to prune varies with the tree type. You can prune apples and pears in early spring before the trees break dormancy. For stone

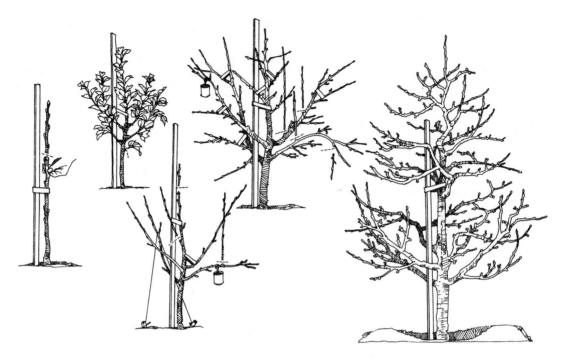

**Central leader training.** Follow these instructions for training a young fruit to a central leader form:

1. Head back a one-year-old whip to 2½ feet at planting.

2. In mid-June, select four branches that emerge in different directions and are spaced several inches apart along the trunk as scaffolds. The strongest-growing, uppermost shoot will be the central leader, which becomes the trunk.

3. For the following few years, repeat this process by heading back the central leader in early spring about 2 feet above the previous set of scaffolds. Then in June, select an additional layer of scaffolds. Choose branches that are at least 1½ feet above the last set of scaffolds. Scaffolds should spiral up the trunk so each branch will be in full sun.

4. Throughout the training process, spread young branches to ensure development of broad crotch angles.

fruits that are susceptible to cankers caused by disease organisms, wait until bud break, when they are less likely to be infected. Prune away dead and diseased branches on all kinds of fruit trees as the growing season continues. Stop pruning by the end of August in areas where winter injury is a concern. Late pruning can stimulate a flush of new growth that could be damaged when cold weather sets in.

## FERTILIZING

Even with thorough advance soil preparation, your fruit trees may need fertilizing. Nutrient consumption varies with tree type and age, soil, and growing conditions. For instance, you will have to fertilize a fruit tree growing in the lawn more frequently than if the soil around the tree is cleared and mulched. But don't simply fertilize on a set schedule. Overfertilizing can encourage soft new growth that is susceptible to disease attack and winter injury.

Monitor tree growth to determine when trees need fertilizing. Nonbearing apple trees should grow 1½ to 2 feet per year; those producing fruit average 8 to 12 inches. Mature peach trees should grow 1 to 1½ feet each

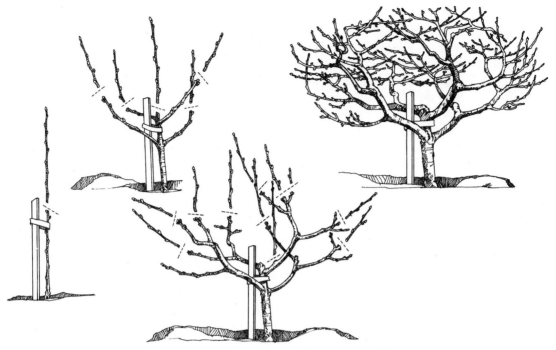

**Open center training.** Follow these steps to train a fruit tree to the open center form:

1. After planting, cut the whip back to 2 to 2½ feet and head back all side branches.
2. At the beginning of June, choose three scaffolds that emerge in different directions and are separated along the trunk by about 4 inches. Cut off all others.
3. In the third and fourth years, thin as lightly as you can to avoid delaying fruiting.
4. Once peach, nectarine, and Japanese plum trees begin to bear, they fruit only on year-old branches. To have plenty of fruiting wood, cut the scaffolds back to the same height every year, encouraging the growth of 1 to 1½ feet of new fruiting wood. Thin overly crowded or short and weak fruiting spurs.

year. If your trees seem to be lagging, have the nutrient levels in the leaves analyzed. Call your local extension office for information about leaf analysis.

Fertilize only in the spring. Spread materials on the soil surface in a circle around the trunk out to the edge of the leaf canopy. If the tree is growing in the lawn, make holes with a crowbar around the perimeter of the branches and drop fertilizer below the grass roots. Avoid high-nitrogen fertilizers. The best fertilizer for fruit trees is compost because it has a good balance of nutrients. Foliar seaweed sprays improve tree health, increase yields, and increase bud frost resistance. Spray trees when buds start to show color, when petals drop, and when fruit is ½ to 1 inch.

## MULCHING

Mulched trees will have access to more water and nutrients, especially if you use soil-enriching mulch such as compost or shredded leaves. Mulch also will keep down weeds that compete with trees for water and nutrients. It prevents excessive evaporation of soil moisture, a necessity around young or weak trees, in dry climates, and in sandy soils. In areas with fluctuating winter temperatures, mulch will eliminate damage from frost heaving. Mulch can keep the soil cooler in spring and delay flowering of early-spring bloomers such as apricots or peaches, hopefully beyond the threat of frost.

The drawback of mulching is that it can make heavy soils too wet and can harbor pests, especially mice and voles.

---

 **Restoring Old Trees**

If a fruit tree goes without regular care, it will become overgrown, minimally productive, and home to hoards of pests and diseases. Should you save the old tree or start over with a new one? If the tree has a lovely shape, vital position in your landscape, or sentimental value, it may be worth keeping. Here's how to restore it:

■ If the tree is suffering from diseases such as scab, black knot, or fire blight, begin a spray program to help lessen damage.

■ Remove dead and diseased branches.

■ Check for trunk or root rot and, in warm climates, nematodes.

■ Prune back any neighboring trees and shrubs that shade the fruit tree.

■ Take a leaf analysis for nutrient levels, and correct soil nutrient deficiencies. Use a foliar seaweed spray to restore tree vigor while the soil comes back into balance.

■ When the tree is reasonably healthy, you can begin to prune it into a productive shape. Gradually thin out unproductive branches to open the canopy to sunlight. To minimize watersprout and sucker regeneration, take no more than one-fourth to one-third of the new wood on the tree or on a particular branch any year.

---

Where mulch is warranted, apply a 3- to 6-inch layer of organic mulch in an area from 1 to 2 feet away from the trunk out to just beyond the branch tips. Fluff the mulch with a spading fork occasionally so it doesn't compact. Check the soil moisture level occasionally. If the soil is staying overly wet, rake the mulch back to prevent root rot. You also may want to push the mulch out from under the tree boughs during leaf fall if disease is a problem. Afterward, rake up the fallen leaves and respread the mulch.

## WATERING

Ideally, the soil around fruit trees should be evenly moist, neither dry nor waterlogged. Moisture is especially important to young trees and to trees bearing ripening crops. Thoroughly soak the root system of newly planted trees, and repeat whenever the soil becomes dry for the next few months.

After the tree is growing well, your watering schedule will depend on the weather and climate. If the weather has been dry, even during a midwinter warm spell, stick your little finger down in the soil around the drip line. If you do not feel moisture below the surface, water the tree thoroughly. A trickle irrigation system is ideal for watering fruit trees. In cold climates, stop watering by early fall to harden the plant for winter.

## WINTER PROTECTION

Protect your trees against winter sunscald, frost heaving, and pest damage, all of which can injure or kill fruit trees. Sunscald occurs when sun-warmed wood is killed by nighttime cold. The damaged area becomes dry, sunken, and attractive to borers and diseases. Prevent sunscald by wrapping the tree trunk with a white plastic tree guard or painting it up to the first (lowest) scaffold branch with white latex paint diluted 1:1 with water.

To minimize frost heaving—shifting of soil when it freezes and thaws—mulch *after* the soil freezes to keep it frozen. This is especially important for young trees, which can suffer extensive root damage due to frost heaving.

## FLOWER AND FRUIT CARE

Once your trees reach maturity, there are some extra activities involved in their seasonal care. Some trees may require hand-pollinating, others may need young fruit thinned, and all will have to be harvested.

**Hand-Pollinating** Early-flowering fruit trees can suffer partial to full crop loss if the weather is not mild when the tree is in bloom. If temperatures aren't high enough for insect activity, flowers won't be pollinated and fruit won't develop. If there's a cold spell when your trees are blooming, you can save your crop by hand-pollinating. Simply collect pollen from one tree by rubbing flowers gently with an artist's brush or cotton swab, and then brush the pollen onto the flowers of a compatible cultivar.

Be sure nights are frost-free if you plan to hand-pollinate. If you expect a late frost, you can cover small trees with plastic or spray them with a frost-protecting product. As a last resort, try sprinkling water on trees all night. Use care, as the weight of ice that forms on the trees can break branches.

**Thinning** Because fruit trees tend to be overburdened by young fruit, you should thin off the excess on all trees except those with cherry-size fruit. Without your intervention, the weight of the fruit may actually break limbs. The stress from the excessive fruit load may also reduce the number of flower buds the tree produces the next year. Disease problems such as brown rot can spread quickly among crowded fruits, ruining the crop before it ripens. In addition to avoiding problems, thinning lets you channel all the tree's resources into fewer but bigger and more beautiful fruit.

Thin when the fruit is young—the smaller the better. First clip or twist off all insect-damaged or deformed fruits. Then remove the smaller fruits. Leave only the biggest and best.

If you can't reach the upper limbs of large trees, tap the limbs with a padded pole to shake loose some of the extras. On small apple, nectarine, and peach trees with big fruit, thin fruit to 6 to 8 inches apart. Plums and apricots can be more closely spaced, about 3 to 5 inches apart.

Even after thinning, fruit may become heavy enough to tear a branch. For extra support, prop branches up with a forked stick. On central leader trees, you can secure branches to the central leader with a rope or with a chain covered with garden hose.

**Harvesting** Most fruit is ready to harvest when the green undercolor changes to yellow or the fruit softens and drops. Grasp the fruit in the palm of your hand and twist it off the stem carefully so you don't damage the branch. Handle the ripe fruit gently so it does not bruise.

## PESTS AND DISEASES

It's not easy to grow fruit trees using only organic pest control methods. Fruit is so succulent and tasty that it attracts a wide range of pests, from mites to deer. Watch your trees diligently for pests, and control them before they damage the tree or the fruit. See Chapter 7 for more detailed information on controlling pests and diseases.

# GROWING NUT TREES

Reliably long-lived, often gargantuan in size, and possessing many unique physical attributes, nut trees have become an important part of American culture. Grown since colonial times, nut trees are truly a multipurpose crop, provid-

# Nut Trees for Home Use

Besides producing a tasty crop, many nut trees are beautiful, long-lasting landscape specimens. You may want to try planting some of the nut trees described below in your home landscape.

| Plant Name | Cultural Requirements | Size and Zone | Comments |
| --- | --- | --- | --- |
| **Almond** (*Prunus amygdalus*) | Rich, well-drained soil. Blossoms cannot withstand late spring frosts. | Small (20'–30'); Zones 7–9 | Beautiful flowers, blooms very early, drought-tolerant; limited range. |
| **Butternut** (*Juglans cinerea*) | Prefers rich, deep soil, but will tolerate a range of conditions. | Medium (40'–70'); Zones 3–7 | Graceful; may be toxic to some plants; susceptible to disease; nuts stain pavement. |
| **Chestnut, Chinese** (*Castanea mollisima*) | Light, upland, sandy loam soil. | Small (10'–20'); Zones 5–8 | Ideal for small sites; prickly burrs surround nuts. Many Chinese-American crosses available. |
| **Chestnut, European** (*Castanea sativa*) | Rich, upland, loamy soil. | Large (50'–90'); Zones 5–8 | Long-lived, stately; prickly burrs surround nuts; needs a pollinator. Mostly grown from seed. |
| **Filbert, hazelnut** (*Corylus* spp.) | Rich, light, well-drained soil. | Small (10'–40'); Zones 2–8 | Crimson fall foliage; husks litter ground. Grow as a hedge, multi-stemmed bush, or small tree. |
| **Heartnut** (*Juglans ailantifolia* var. *cordiformis*) | Deep, rich soil. | Medium (30'–60'); Zones 5–8 | Light-colored bark, lacy foliage, fast-growing; may be toxic to some plants; nuts stain pavement. |
| **Hickory, shagbark and shellbark** (*Carya ovata* and *C. laciniosa*) | Rich, upland soil; tolerates a wide range of sites. | Large (60'–120'); Zones 3–8 | Stately, long-lived; husks litter ground. |
| **Pecan** (*Carya illinoinensis*) | Deep, rich, moist bottomland is required. | Large (70'–150'); Zones 6–9 | Stately, long-lived; husks litter ground. Grow strongly once established. |
| **Walnut, Eastern black** (*Juglans nigra*) | Rich, deep soil; tolerates a range of sites. | Large (60'–120'); Zones 4–8 | Lacy foliage, stately; may be toxic to some plants; nuts stain pavement. |
| **Walnut, Persian** (*Juglans regia*) | Rich, deep soil. | Large (50'–90'); Zones 5–9 | Stately, fast-growing; may be toxic to some plants; nuts stain pavement. |

ing shade, beauty, edible nuts, building materials, and wildlife habitats.

## SELECTING NUT TREES

People often ask whether they should plant cultivars or seedling nut trees. Named cultivars are produced vegetatively, usually by grafting or budding, yielding genetically identical clones. The advantage of grafted trees is that you know exactly what you are going to get with respect to hardiness, cracking quality, flavor, size, and other crop characteristics. Seeds, on the other hand, are always somewhat different genetically. This genetic diversity can make a stand of seedlings less susceptible to serious insect or disease problems than a stand of genetically identical cultivars.

Where high-quality nut production is of greatest importance, as with pecan or English walnut, stick to named cultivars where available. For trees such as black walnut and butternut, where timber value may be as important as the nut quality, plant a few grafted trees and use high-quality seedlings to fill out the rest of the planting. The resulting forest will be much healthier, and the cost of seedling trees is also a fraction of that of grafted ones.

## PLANTING AND CARE

These low-maintenance plants can adapt to a range of sites. They generally need very little extra care once they have been established. Keep in mind that many nut trees, including pecans and most black and English walnuts, need cross-pollination; be sure to plant more than one cultivar or seedling of each kind.

Chapters 5 and 8 include information on general care and maintenance of trees that also applies to nut tree culture.

Most nut trees have a deep anchoring taproot, making them a bit more difficult to establish than other trees. Whenever possible,

start with small, young trees; they will often adjust more quickly and begin growing sooner than larger trees. Make sure you dig the planting hole deep enough to accommodate the entire taproot.

Unlike fruit trees, most nut trees don't require special pruning techniques to produce good crops. Prune nut trees as you would any shade tree, removing dead, diseased, or crossing branches regularly. If you've planted grafted trees, be sure to prune off any suckers that may arise from the rootstock. For trees that are eventually intended for timber, keep side limbs pruned off to about 12 to 16 feet up the trunk.

Most nuts are best when they are gathered as soon as they become ripe. Remove the outer husk as soon as possible to prevent mold or darkening of the nut kernel. Store the husked nuts in their shells in a cool, dry, rodent-free area. Allow the nuts to cure (dry) for one to three months. After curing, most nuts will keep in the shell for at least a year.

# GROWING SMALL FRUIT

While tree fruits—apples, peaches, pears, plums, and so on—have similar cultural requirements,

---

 **Nuts for the North**

It's not always easy to find information about growing nut crops. If you're a nut fancier, you may want to join the Northern Nut Growers Association (NNGA), an international group of professionals and homeowners interested in growing hardy nuts. For more information, write to:

NNGA, c/o Tucker Hill
654 Beinholder Road, Etters, PA 17319

the small-fruit crops—blueberries, brambles, grapes, and strawberries—all require widely different care. Fortunately, they're all relatively easy to grow. In the pages that follow, you'll find details on how to plant, prune, train, and care for the most popular small-fruit crops.

# Blueberries

*Vaccinium* spp.
Ericaceae

Blueberries are among North America's few cultivated native fruits. They have become one of the most popular fruits for home gardeners for their ornamental value, pest resistance, and delicious berries. Only their soil requirements keep them from being more widely planted.

Northerners grow two species of blueberries: *Vaccinium corymbosum*, highbush, and *V. angustifolium*, lowbush. Southern gardeners tend to raise *V. ashei*, rabbiteye blueberry. All three bear delicious fruit on plants with beautiful white, urn-shaped flowers and bright fall color. Here's a rundown:

**Lowbush blueberries:** Although the fruit of the lowbush blueberry is small, many people consider its flavor superior to that of other blueberries. These extremely hardy plants are good choices for the North. They bear nearly a pint of fruit for each foot of row. Lowbush plants spread by layering and will quickly grow into a matted low hedge. Zones 2 to 6.

**Highbush blueberries:** Highbush are the most popular home-garden blueberries. Growing 6 to 12 feet or more in height, each bush may yield 5 to 20 pounds of large berries in mid- to late summer. Crosses between highbush and lowbush species have resulted in several hardy, large-fruiting plants. They grow between 1½ and 3 feet tall. Highbush blueberries vary in hardiness, but many cultivars grow well in the North if you plant them in a sheltered spot. Zones 3 to 8.

**Rabbiteye blueberries:** Rabbiteyes are ideal for warmer climates. They'll tolerate drier soils than highbush plants can, although they may need irrigation during dry spells. The plants grow rapidly and often reach full production in four to five years. They grow from 10 feet to more than 25 feet high and may yield up to 20 pounds of fruit per bush. Rabbiteyes do not grow well in areas that are completely frost-free, however, because they need a chilling period of a few weeks to break dormancy and set fruit. Zones 7 to 9.

## PLANTING AND CARE

Blueberries require full sun and well-drained, moisture-retentive, acidic soil with a pH of 4.0 to 5.0. Of the three species, highbush blueberries are the most finicky about soil. Blueberries generally grow well in soil enriched with acidic organic material, such as peat moss, composted pine needles or oak leaves, or compost made from pine, oak, or hemlock bark. Fertilize with acidic fertilizers, such as cottonseed meal or soybean meal. Blueberries enjoy a thick, organic mulch.

Most blueberries are not entirely self-pollinating. Plant at least two different cultivars near each other for adequate cross-pollination. Blueberries grow slowly and don't reach full production until they're six to eight years old, so get a head start with two- or three-year-old plants.

Like most bush fruits, blueberries benefit from pruning as they become older. Yearly pruning helps to encourage large fruits, maintains productivity, and lets sunshine into the bushes, which aids in ripening the berries. Late winter is the ideal time for pruning.

In general, both highbush and rabbiteye plants respond to the same type of pruning. For the first three to four years, prune only to make sure each bush is growing in a strong, upright

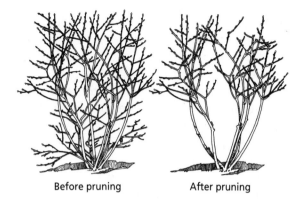

Before pruning        After pruning

**Pruning blueberries.** For rabbiteye blueberries and highbush plants in Zones 5 to 8, cut out a few of the thick older canes each year after the plants begin to produce well. Thin out branches that are crowding each other, and the twiggy ends of canes if they seem too thick. Cut back any plants that are growing too high to harvest conveniently. For highbush blueberries in Zones 3 and 4, simply thin out the twiggy ends of branches and cut out any wood that is broken or winter-damaged. For lowbush blueberries, cut up to half of the older canes to the ground each year, and harvest berries from the uncut stems. The next year, remove the stems you left the previous year and harvest fruit from the new stems.

shape. If the fruit buds are too numerous, remove some of them to get fewer but larger berries. (You can distinguish fruit buds on the dormant plants because they are fatter than leaf buds.) For information on pruning established plants, see the illustration on this page.

## HARVESTING

Blueberries ripen over a long season, and you don't need to pick them daily like strawberries. Different cultivars ripen to various shades of blue, so be careful not to pick them too early if you want the best flavor; taste them to determine when they're at their peak. Don't pull berries from the stem; instead, gently twist them off with your fingertips. If the berries don't come off with slight pressure, they're not ready

for harvest. Blueberries keep for several days after picking if you keep them cool and dry. They are also ideal for freezing.

## PREVENTING PROBLEMS

Although commercial growers encounter a variety of insects, home gardeners rarely have any problems. The blueberry maggot and cherry fruitworm are the most troublesome insects that are likely to appear. Reduce the chances of damage by cleaning up all the old fruit in a planting before winter.

Diseases are seldom a concern in the North but tend to be more common in the South. Botrytis tip blight kills new growth, and stem canker causes cracks in the canes. Cut away any growth that shows signs of abnormal appearance. Mummy berry makes the fruit rot and fall off. To prevent it, plant resistant cultivars, keep the berries picked, and clean up any dropped fruit. Viral diseases, such as stunt, are difficult to control and invariably result in the gradual deterioration of the plant. Buy from a reputable nursery to get disease-free plants.

Birds are unusually fond of blueberries. To

 **Pick Hands-Free**

It's faster and easier to pick blueberries with two hands. You can make a simple hands-free picking container from an empty can or a small plastic bucket. Use a can opener to make two triangular holes just under the can rim and tie a short loop of string through each hole. (On a bucket, thread string through the handle holes.) Then tie a 3-inch × 36-inch strip of cloth to each string loop. Tie the strips around your waist like apron strings, or tie them into a loop and hang the loop around your neck.

prevent damage, cover the bushes with tightly woven netting before the berries begin to ripen.

# Brambles

*Rubus* spp.
Rosaceae

Raspberries and blackberries are among the most delicious and desirable berries you can grow. They are frequently treated as gourmet fruit, but because they don't ship well, not because they are hard to grow.

Brambles can produce fruit for 10 to 25 years. It's important to choose cultivars that have the characteristics you want and that suit your climate. Here's a rundown:

**Raspberries:** There are two types of raspberries: summer-bearing and fall-bearing. In some areas of the country, their bearing seasons may overlap, so you can harvest raspberries from early summer until frost. Red and yellow cultivars are summer- or fall-bearers. Black and purple raspberries are all summer-bearers.

Red and yellow raspberries are the easiest raspberries to grow. Their fruit is both sweet and fragrant.

Black raspberries are not as winter-hardy as red ones, but tend to tolerate more summer heat. They also are more prone to viral and fungal diseases and have stiffer thorns. The berries are seedy but have a very intense flavor. They are good eaten fresh or in preserves.

Purple raspberries are hybrids resulting from crosses between reds and blacks. The canes are generally more winter-hardy than the black parents. They tend to be very spiny and productive with large, intensely flavored berries.

**Blackberries:** In general, blackberries are less winter-hardy than most raspberries. In northern areas, the roots may survive without protection, but the overwintering canes are often killed above the snow line. But because blackberries tend to be extremely vigorous, even a very short

portion of surviving cane will often produce a surprising amount of fruit.

Blackberries can be divided into three general groups: erect, semi-erect, and trailing.

The erect type has strong, upright canes that are usually thorny and don't require support. They tend to be more winter-hardy than the other types and produce large, sweet berries.

Semi-erect blackberries are thornless and more vigorous and productive than the erect type. Most of them grow better if supported. The fruit is tart and large. The plants bloom and mature later than the erect type.

Trailing blackberries, or dewberries, are the least winter-hardy. They need support, are early ripening, and have large wine-colored to black fruit of distinctively good flavor.

**Hybrids:** Raspberry-blackberry hybrids combine the characteristics of their parents. Most of them are very winter-tender. Some are thornless. The fruit resembles blackberries.

## PLANTING AND CARE

Plant brambles in a sunny site with good air circulation and well-drained soil. Start with disease-free stock, and plant in very early spring. Plant in hills or rows well away from wild or abandoned raspberries, which may carry diseases. Provide posts or a wire fence to support the canes.

Row spacing should be wide enough to allow sunlight and air to reach all plants and to allow you to walk or mow between the rows without damaging yourself or the plants. For home gardeners this means at least 5 feet between rows for raspberries and 7 feet for blackberries.

Some types of brambles produce suckers. Red and yellow raspberries spread 12 to 15 inches a year, so plant 1 to 2 feet apart, depending on how soon you want a solid hedgerow. Blacks and most purples don't sucker but form clusters of canes from their crowns. Plant them

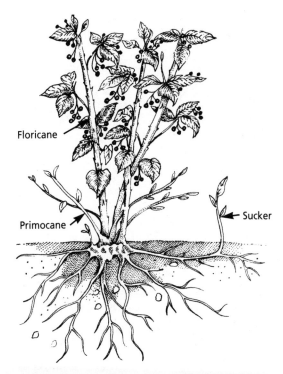

**Bramble plant.** Primocanes are new shoots that arise from the main plant or new suckers that rise from roots away from the main plant. On their second year they are called floricanes. Most brambles bear fruit only on flori-canes. Fall-bearing raspberries fruit on primocanes.

2½ to 3 feet apart. Blackberries sucker vigorously; space them 5 to 6 feet apart in rows.

Brambles are self-pollinating. Well-maintained plantings may fruit heavily for many years, but disease often appears as plants age. Plan on establishing a new raspberry bed every ten years (less if plants begin to decline).

## PRUNING AND TRAINING

For black, purple, and summer-bearing red raspberries, cut off all fruit-bearing canes at ground level as soon as harvest is over, or when growth begins in the spring. In late winter or early spring, thin out new canes that emerged the previous season; save the sturdiest ones and leave six canes per hill or 6-inch spacing between row-planted canes. Shorten lanky canes to 4 to 5 feet. Since black and purple raspberries fruit most heavily on side branches, induce side branching during the summer by pinching the growing tips of canes when they reach 2½ feet. The following late winter or early spring, shorten the side branches to about 1 foot.

For fall-bearing red raspberries, remove fruiting canes each summer as soon as the second fruiting is complete. Or sacrifice the second berry crop (which may be light anyway) and cut the entire planting to the ground as soon as leaves drop in the fall. Although this approach yields only one crop instead of two, it has several advantages. Pruning all canes to the ground eliminates winter injury to canes, results in vigorous new canes for next fall's crop, and cuts down on overwintering pests that will appear next spring.

On erect blackberries pinch the tips of 3-foot canes to force growth of lateral shoots. During the dormant season, shorten all lateral shoots to about 1½ feet. For both types of blackberry, cut away all fruiting canes right after harvest. In winter thin out canes, leaving three or four canes per clump for erect types and eight to twelve canes per clump for trailing types.

## TRELLISING

Though many brambles can be grown without a support system, all are best grown on a trellis. Trellising reduces disease problems, saves space, and speeds pruning and picking.

**V Trellis** Summer-bearing raspberries do well on a V trellis like the one illustrated on page 242. Construct it as follows:

1. Set a sturdy 4-inch post at each end of the row and about every 20 feet in between. Posts should be set at least 2 feet deep and extend 4 to 6 feet above ground.

2. Add a 2-inch × 4-inch cross arm, with

notches cut on each arm, to hold wires. The height of the cross arms will depend on how vigorous your brambles are. Try putting them about 3 feet high, and move them if necessary.

3. Cut two lengths of 12- or 14-gauge wire or synthetic baling twine a little longer than the trellis, and fasten the ends to either side of the endpost cross arms.

4. After pruning, put the wires in the outer notches, and arrange the canes outside the wire. Tie each cane individually to the wire. Or use two sets of wires on each side of the cross arm, and sandwich the canes between them. After harvest, move the wires to the inside notch to keep the new canes upright.

**Hedgerow Trellis** All types of bramble fruit do well when supported by a hedgerow-type trellising system like the one shown on the opposite page. To construct it:

1. Set a sturdy 4-inch post at each end of the row and about every 20 feet in between.

2. Hammer upward-slanting nails into both sides of each post 3 feet and 4 feet above the ground.

3. Cut four lengths of wire slightly longer than the trellis and twist the ends of the wires into a loop to fit over the end nail.

4. After pruning, lift the wires onto the nails to hold the canes upright between them. (Future pruning is easier if you can remove the wires, so don't staple them to the posts, just rest them on the nails.) Tuck new canes between the wires. A variation of this trellis uses 1-foot cross arms to hold the wires farther apart.

## HARVESTING

Brambles ripen in early summer. Red raspberries tend to ripen first, followed by black raspberries, and even later by blackberries. Berries do not keep ripening after harvesting. For best flavor and ease of picking, wait until they are fully ripe. Some raspberries offer a slight resistance to

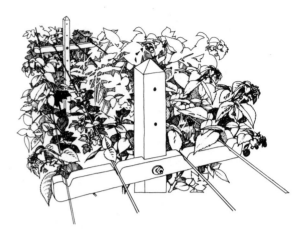

**V trellis.** This trellis bends the fruiting canes outward and lets the new primocanes grow straight and strong in the center without competition from the floricanes.

picking even when fully ripe. Let your taste tell you when to pick. Red raspberries vary in color at maturity from light to dark red. Some purple ones change from red to purple to almost black, with sugar levels increasing as the color darkens. Blackberries, though they also vary in color, are typically shiny black when not quite ripe and dull black when fully ripe. They come off the vines more easily when fully ripe.

Pick your berries as early in the morning as possible while they are cool. If the berries are wet, let them dry before picking. Handle them gently and place, don't drop, them into a shallow container. Refrigerate immediately.

It's easier to pick berries with both hands free. See "Pick Hands-Free" on page 239 for an easy-to-make picking container.

## PREVENTING PROBLEMS

Certain common garden pests attack brambles. Aphids can spread viruses. Japanese beetles feed on ripe fruit. Tarnished plant bugs feed on buds, blossoms, and berries. Keep surrounding areas weed-free to limit tarnished plant bugs. See Chapter 7 for more information on organic

**Hedgerow trellis.** This easy-to-build trellis system gives good support to any type of bramble.

control methods for pests and diseases.

Several viral diseases, which can drastically reduce yields, affect bramble crops. Raspberry mosaic stunts plants and causes yellow-blotched, puckered leaves. Blackberry sterility results in vigorous growing plants that produce only nubbins—tiny, crumbly, malformed berries—or none at all. Leaf curl causes dark green, tightly curled and malformed leaves. Since there is no cure for viral diseases, dig infected plants and dispose of them immediately.

To prevent problems with viral diseases, plant virus-resistant cultivars and purchase plants only from nurseries that sell virus-free tissue culture or certified bareroot plants. Remove all wild brambles within 500 to 1,000 feet, especially upwind, and keep aphids off your brambles because they spread viruses. Plant black raspberries away from red and yellow ones because blacks are more susceptible to viruses.

Several other diseases attack brambles, including anthracnose, powdery mildew, rust, wilts, and root rots. See "Troubleshooting Fruit and Vegetable Diseases" on page 157 for more on these problems.

Since fungi need warm temperatures and humid conditions to thrive, anything you do to keep the aboveground parts of the plants dry will be to your advantage. Select a planting site with good air circulation and drainage. Avoid overhead watering. Keep your rows narrow, and thin canes to recommended densities. Avoid excessive nitrogen. Trellis the canes for best air circulation. Keep the rows weed-free. Remove spent canes immediately after harvest. Collect and destroy all prunings. If fungal diseases have been a problem in previous years, apply lime-sulfur spray in the spring when the first leaves are ¼ to ½ inch long.

# Grapes

*Vitis* spp.
Vitaceae

Grapes make a wonderful treat straight from the vine, or preserved as jelly, juice, or wine. They thrive in full sun, with good drainage and protection from late frosts.

There are four main types of grapes grown in North America: European, or wine grapes (*Vitis vinifera*); American, such as 'Concord' (*V. labruscana*); hybrids between European and American; and muscadine (*V. rotundifolia*).

Vinifera (European) grapes produce most of the world's table grapes, wine, and raisins. They are not as hardy as their American cousins, are much more susceptible to disease, and require more work to harvest a satisfactory crop.

American grapes have a strong grape or "foxy" flavor and slipskins, which means that the berries can easily be squeezed out of the skins. Many good fresh-eating and juice grapes have been selected from the native species.

Plant breeders have crossed and recrossed vinifera and American species and created grapes to satisfy almost every taste and use. Many of them are as hardy as their American parent, to about –10°F, and have good disease resistance.

If you grow seedless cultivars, you probably won't get grapes as large as those on bunches for sale at the market. Commercial growers dip or spray clusters with synthetic growth regulators so they'll produce big berries.

If you live in the far South, you may only be able to grow muscadine grapes. They make good jelly and juice and a sweet wine.

American and hybrid grape cultivars can be grown on their own roots. Vinifera grape roots are very susceptible to phylloxera, a sucking insect native to the eastern and southern United States and now spread throughout the world. Choose vines grafted on American rootstocks. Certain American rootstock cultivars are also resistant to nematodes and the viral diseases they transmit.

## PLANTING AND CARE

Plant grapes in a sunny site with deep, well-drained, moderately fertile soil and good air circulation to promote disease resistance.

Plant dormant, one-year-old vines in the spring before their buds begin to swell and open. Soak roots in a pail of water with a handful of bonemeal for one to two hours before planting. Plant muscadines 15 to 20 feet apart in rows 10 feet apart; plant other types of grapes 8 feet apart in rows 8 feet apart.

Prune each vine back to leave two live buds before planting; also cut back long roots so they'll fit easily into the hole without bending. Leave 1 to 2 inches of trunk above ground and make a shallow basin around the vine to hold water. If you are planting grafted vines, be sure to keep the graft union above ground level.

## PRUNING AND TRAINING

There are many ways to train grapes. One of the most common methods for home gardeners is

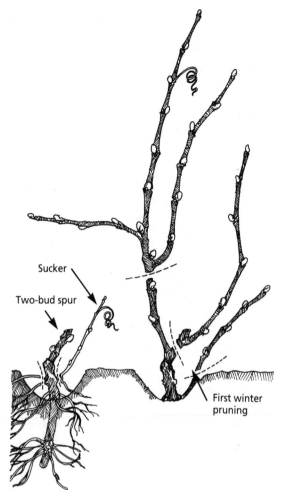

**Early pruning.** Prune newly purchased vines back to two buds before planting. The first winter, select the strongest, straightest shoot and cut it back to two buds. Prune off all other shoots. The vine will look very much like the little vine you planted the previous spring. See the illustration on the opposite page for second- and third-year pruning instructions.

cane pruning. If you are new to grapes, don't let talk about training and pruning scare you. Grapevines are very forgiving. You can train cane- and spur-pruned vines on an existing fence or wall. If you're planning to plant several vines, you'll probably need to build a trellis; the illustration on page 246 shows how.

No matter what training method you plan

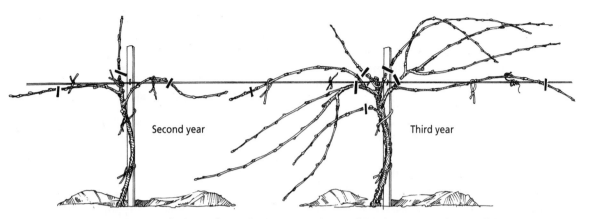

**Cane pruning.** During the second winter of growth, tie two sturdy, pencil-sized canes near the top of the trunk to the training wire. Rub off buds to leave buds spaced 4 to 5 inches apart. Shorten the canes so each has ten buds. The third winter, select a pencil-sized shoot from near the base of each of the previous season's canes or from the top of the trunk.

to use, all vines are treated the same until the second winter after planting.

**First Growing Season** During their first summer, the vines need to grow a strong root system. Use drip irrigation or a soaker hose, if needed, to keep the soil damp but not soggy. From mid-August on, water only if the leaves wilt so the vines will harden off for winter. Mulch or cultivate to control weeds.

You can let the vines sprawl on the ground the first year, or tie them loosely to a small stake to keep them out of harm's way.

**First Winter** Any time from midwinter on, select the strongest, straightest shoot and prune off all the others. Cut the chosen shoot back to two live buds. The result will look very much like the little vine you planted the previous spring. But remember, the first season is for growing roots. Go ahead and cut off all that top growth; you'll have a better plant in the long run. If cold injury is a problem in your area, wait until the buds start to swell so you can see which ones are alive. You may want to select two shoots rather than one as insurance against injury.

**Second Growing Season** If you haven't done so already, place a stake in the ground as close as possible to the vine. When new shoots are 6 to 12 inches long, select the sturdiest, most upright shoot and tie it loosely to the stake. Break off the remaining shoots with your fingers. As the shoot grows, tie it to the stake at 12-inch intervals to form a straight trunk.

When the shoot reaches the desired height, break off the small shoots that are growing above each leaf near the base of your trunk-to-be, but don't remove the leaves. Let the sideshoots grow on the five leaf nodes just below the vine head; cut the tip off the main shoot when it grows a few inches or so above the vine head. Prune off any suckers below the soil line as close to the trunk as possible.

If your vine doesn't reach the desired height by the end of the second season, it probably hasn't developed enough roots to produce the size plant you want. Cut the vine back to two buds, and let it try again the next summer.

**Fourth Growing Season** In the fourth growing season, vines are ready to bear a normal crop. For large table grapes, give vines 1 inch of water per week. In the fourth and subsequent winters, you may want to keep a few more buds on each cane for the next season. The vigor of a vine will tell you how many buds it can support. If your vine has many spindly shoots and little fruit, try leaving fewer total buds the next winter. If it has long, thick shoots and few clusters, leave more buds the next winter.

**Subsequent Growing Seasons** During the spring through mid-July, position shoots so light penetrates through the foliage. On short-trunk, trellised vines, tuck the shoots behind the catch wires above the training wire. If shoots reach the top of the trellis and hang down, they will shade the fruit and the canes where next year's flower buds are forming. Prune off the tips if they get too long. Pick off leaves and small shoots near fruit clusters to let in light. This is important because it promotes ripening

and discourages pests. You may want to remove or thin clusters to increase berry size or improve quality. If you have too heavy a crop, the fruit may be slow to ripen as well.

## WINTER PROTECTION

There are grape cultivars that will tolerate severe winter cold. You can grow cultivars beyond their normal northern limit by training trunks only 1 foot high and covering vines with mulch during the winter, or by bending whole vines over and burying or mulching them for the winter.

Once grape buds begin to swell in the spring, they become more frost-tender. All species are susceptible to frost damage at temperatures below 31°F. See "Growing Fruit Trees" on page 226 for more information on site selection and frost protection. Autumn frosts seldom cause damage because the high sugar content of

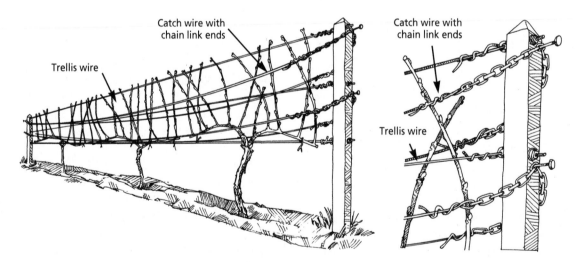

**A practical grape trellis.** Grape shoots will climb permanent trellis wires on their own, or they can be tucked through by hand during the season. Movable catch wires go around the trellis like a giant rubber band and keep shoots pointing up. Drop the catch wires to the nails below the vine heads when you prune each winter. Once growth starts and shoots are about 2 feet long, raise the catch wire to the nails above the vine head; as you lift it, the wire will pick up any shoots that are straying from the trellis. Raise the wire to the next set of nails as the shoots grow, or use a second catch wire.

the berries keeps them from freezing and the outer canopy protects both the foliage and fruit beneath it. If you live in an area with short seasons, plant an early-ripening cultivar.

## FERTILIZING

On most sites, careful soil preparation before planting eliminates the need for heavy fertilization. Mulch lightly with compost in late winter each year. Overfertilizing can cause vines to grow rampantly and produce little fruit. When in doubt, don't fertilize. Compost tea and dilute seaweed extract sprays are good general foliar fertilizers. For instructions on making compost tea, see "Tea Time for Your Plants" on page 177. If you suspect you have a specific nutrient problem, have a leaf analysis done; see "Other Tests" on page 29 for information.

## HARVESTING

Grapevines bear by their third or fourth growing season. Harvest when the fruit tastes ripe. Support the cluster with one hand and cut its stem with pruning shears. Handle clusters gently and lay them in a basket or flat. Harvest large quantities in the morning, small amounts any time of day. Move picked fruit to a cool, protected place as soon as possible.

## PREVENTING PROBLEMS

Grape berry moths lay eggs on flower clusters. The greenish or purplish larvae spin silver webs and feed on buds and flowers. Control grape berry moths with mating-disruption pheromone dispensers.

Many caterpillars can feed on grape leaves. Control by spraying BT (*Bacillus thuringiensis*). Japanese beetles are fond of grapes. A few won't hurt the vine, but complete defoliation will. See Chapter 7 for more information on controlling pests and diseases.

Prevention and good housekeeping are the best ways to avoid disease problems. Mulch or cultivation will help prevent spores from splashing up from the soil and infecting new growth. Keep the area under the vine weed-free to increase air movement and reduce disease problems. Fungal diseases thrive in dark, humid environments, so arrange shoots in the leaf canopy so some light falls on all foliage. Cut off any leaves that are shading clusters. Remove infected parts immediately, and collect prunings and fallen leaves and dispose of them.

Sulfur dust or spray helps prevent disease. If you've had past problems with disease, you may want to consider a regular preventive spray program. Coat all parts of the vines, including the undersides of leaves, before symptoms appear. Apply when canes are 6, 12, and 18 inches long, then every two weeks until four to six weeks before harvest.

# Strawberries

*Fragaria* × *ananassa, F. vesca*
Rosaceae

Strawberries are justly celebrated each spring in festivals all over America. Fresh strawberry shortcake, strawberry ice cream, strawberry pie, and even plain, red ripe strawberries are hard to beat. The plants are inexpensive, bear a full crop within a year of planting, and are relatively simple to grow.

Garden strawberry cultivars (*F.* × *ananassa*) are divided into three types: Junebearers, everbearers, and day-neutrals, which flower at different times in response to day length. Here's a rundown:

**Junebearers:** These bear fruit in June or July, or as early as April in Florida and California. They produce a single, large crop over three to four weeks. If you want to freeze lots of fruit at one time, plant Junebearers. There are early-, mid-, and late-season cultivars. Junebearers produce many runners and spread rapidly.

**Everbearers:** These produce a moderate crop in June, scattered berries in summer, and a small crop in late August. They are especially productive in northern areas with long summer days. The total harvest for everbearers is much less than the total harvest for Junebearers. Plant everbearers if you want berries for fresh eating all season. They produce fewer runners than Junebearers and so are easier to control.

**Day-neutrals:** These are unaffected by day length. They are extremely productive and bear fruit from June through frost in northern areas, or January through August in milder climates. Unfortunately, day-neutrals require pampering. They are fragile and sensitive to heat, drought, and weed competition. If you are willing to give them the care they need, they'll reward you with a generous supply of berries throughout the season from relatively few plants. Dayneutrals produce few runners, so they rarely get out of control.

**Alpine strawberries:** Alpine strawberries (*F. vesca*) are one of the parent species of the garden strawberry. They produce small, aromatic berries from early summer through frost. Alpines are grown from seed or divisions and produce no runners. They are care-free and make good ornamental edgings.

## PLANTING AND CARE

Plant strawberries in well-drained soil rich in organic matter. The ideal location is in full sun on high or sloping ground. Avoid frost-prone, low-lying areas.

To prevent diseases associated with overcrowding, allow a square foot of space for each plant. Choose one of three different planting systems: hill, matted row, or spaced runner. For a hill system, space plants 1 foot apart each way in double rows, with 2 to 3 feet between each double row. Remove every runner so plants channel their energy into producing large berries. Since plants are well spaced, the hill system minimizes diseases associated with crowding. For a matted-row system, space plants 1½ to 2 feet apart in rows 4 feet apart. Allow the runners and daughter plants to grow in all directions to form a wide, solid row. For the spaced-runner system, set plants closer than the matted row; remove all but a few runners. Pin down runner tips so daughter plants are about 8 inches apart in every direction.

Vigilant weed control is essential to prevent aggressive perennial weeds from out-competing shallow-rooted strawberry plants. It helps to lay down a thick mulch of straw around the plants during summer.

Even well-managed strawberries will decline after a few seasons. Start a fresh bed in a new site with new plants every few years. Renovate Junebearers each year right after harvest. Cut off and rake away leaves; dig out old, woody plants; and thin out remaining plants. Then fertilize and water.

## HARVESTING

Spring-planted Junebearers won't provide a harvest until a year after planting. Everbearers will produce a sizable late-summer crop, and dayneutrals will produce from midsummer through fall the year they're planted. Fall-planted berries will bear a full harvest the next growing season.

Harvest berries by pinching through the stem rather than pulling on the berry. Pick ripe berries every other day; always remove *all* ripe berries and any infected or malformed ones from the patch to prevent disease problems. During wet or humid weather, pick out diseased berries every day. Cull the moldy berries, wash your hands, and then pick the ripe berries. At the very least, carry a second basket or a plastic bag to put moldy or damaged berries in while you pick.

Strawberries need 1 inch of water per week

throughout the growing season. Drip irrigation works best; for information on installing a drip irrigation system, see "Using Drip Irrigation" on page 181.

After the ground has frozen, cover the plants with fresh straw, pine boughs, or spun-bonded fabric to protect them from alternate freezing and thawing, which can heave plants from the soil. (In climates where a snow cover remains through the winter, strawberries need no special winter mulch.) Pull the mulch away from the plants in early spring so the ground can warm up. Reapply fresh mulch around the plants to smother early weeds. Leave spun-bonded fabric on over winter and into spring for slightly earlier harvests. Remove it when flowers open so bees can pollinate the blossoms.

## PREVENTING PROBLEMS

Verticillium wilt and red stele infect strawberry plant roots. They are often carried in on new plants and made worse by heavy, wet soil. Remove and destroy infected plants. Replant new plants in a new location or choose resistant cultivars. Vegetables like tomatoes and potatoes are also infected by Verticillium wilt, so grow only resistant cultivars where these vegetables have grown in the last three years, and vice versa.

Gray mold rots the berries. Wet, humid weather and overcrowded beds with poor air circulation invite it. Keep rows narrow, thin out crowded plants, and remove moldy berries from the plants immediately to control gray mold.

Berries injured by the tarnished plant bug

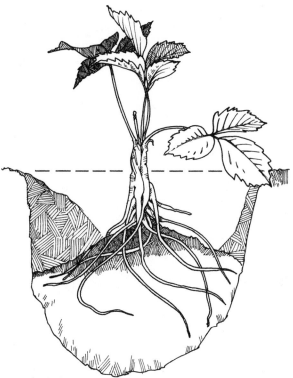

**Proper planting level.** It is important to spread out the roots of your new strawberries as you plant. Set the middle of the crown level with the soil surface.

don't grow or ripen properly, but remain small and woody or form hard, seedy tips. See Chapter 7 for more information on controlling pests and diseases. Birds love strawberries; cover plants with netting, and see "Animal Pests" on page 141 for other suggestions. Slugs can take a bite out of your ripe berries; "Controlling Slugs and Snails" on page 131 offers advice on how to get rid of these pests.

# Chapter 11

# HERB GARDENS

Herbs are among the easiest plants to grow in a garden—and the most useful. Perhaps best known for their role in cooking, where they add flavor to stews, soups, vinegars, jellies, relishes, and all types of recipes, herbs also have many other uses. They have been used medicinally and in cosmetics. In arts and crafts, they lend color and fragrance to potpourris, wreaths, and sachets. However you use herbs in your garden, you'll find that they offer fragrance, flavor, color, a sense of history—and more.

## YOUR HERB GARDEN

There are nearly as many ways to incorporate herbs into your garden as there are herbs to choose from. Traditionally, they have been grown in gardens devoted to herbs alone, but herbs can also add interest to annual or perennial plantings. It helps to be planful—make sure that your flower gardens won't begin to look bare as you harvest your herbs.

Herb growing can be as simple or as complicated as you choose to make it. Most herbs are easy to grow—they demand little and give a lot.

### PLANTING A KITCHEN GARDEN

It's a good idea to have a small herb garden easily accessible to the kitchen door so that you can snip a few herbs while cooking. To grow herbs successfully in a dooryard garden, be sure the soil has good drainage and the area is in sunlight for at least six hours per day.

A kitchen garden is the perfect place for thyme, parsley, marjoram, and oregano, as well as coriander (also called cilantro) if you like the flavor of the leaves. You might want to include several kinds of basils—sweet, small-leaved, and purple—since they have such different flavors. This is the place for French tarragon, too; it's not decorative enough for a flower border. Plan on keeping a rigorously controlled mint plant or two close at hand as well. Plant mint in tubs above ground or in bottomless sunken buckets to keep it from crowding out other plants.

Chervil, once started, will seed itself under a shrub, sticking to its spot for the rest of your life. Dill will also show up dependably every spring.

Chives and garlic chives are two more kitchen-garden favorites. Be sure to cut the dying blossom heads from the latter if you expect to grow anything other than garlic chives. This individual is as ruthless a colonizer as the mints, although it spreads only by seed, not by roots. Its umbels of white, starry flowers add beauty in the garden, and the flat leaves add interesting flavor when chopped and sprinkled on salads and soups.

### PLANTING IN VEGETABLE GARDENS

If you are going to grow herbs in quantity, you may want to grow them in rows or beds in your vegetable garden for ease of care and harvest. Plants such as oregano, savory, santolina, thyme, culinary sage, and lavender do best in well-drained soils to which lime and grit have been added. Place them on specially prepared ridges or in raised beds. Angelica can be settled into a wettish spot, and dill, coriander, parsley, French tarragon, mints, and basils will do well in well-drained soil rich in organic matter.

Herbs are often used as companion plants in the vegetable garden. According to folklore, in some cases backed by scientific studies, certain herbs can either aid or hinder vegetable growth.

 ## Herbs for the Flower Garden

Include herbs in your garden for their strong form, attractive foliage color, delightful fragrance, or culinary uses. Herbs are the ultimate hands-on plants—often you can appreciate their highly fragrant foliage only if you run your hands over it or brush against it.

Many herbs will thrive in a sunny mixed bed or border with average to rich, well-drained soil. The herbs listed here are showy enough to hold their own in any garden (plants are perennials unless otherwise noted):

Bee balm (*Monarda didyma*). Shaggy rose or pink blossoms; dried blossoms and foliage used for tea, fragrance, and herbal crafts.

Chamomile (*Chamaemelum nobile*). Low, spreading plant; sweet-scented, fine, ferny leaves; yellow button flowers.

Common foxglove (*Digitalis purpurea*). Biennial with tube-shaped pinkish purple or white flowers; used medicinally (with medical supervision).

Fennel (*Foeniculum vulgare*). Bluish green feathery leaves; yellow flowers; anise-scented; edible seeds, stems, and leaves.

Flax (*Linum usitatissimum*). Blue flowers; used medicinally.

Garden nasturtium (*Tropaeolum majus*). Annual with abundant flowers in shades of orange, yellow, and red; used in cooking and as a companion plant.

Garden sage (*Salvia officinalis*). Rough-textured oblong leaves; purple, green, gold, and tricolored cultivars; used as a seasoning.

Lavender (*Lavandula angustifolia*). Lavender or purple flowers; flowers and foliage used for fragrance and herbal crafts.

Mints (*Mentha* spp.). Fragrant but invasive; scents include apple, pineapple, peppermint; used to flavor tea and vegetables.

Pineapple sage (*Salvia elegans*). Red flowers attract butterflies; flavor drinks with pineapple-scented leaves.

Pot marigold (*Calendula officinalis*). Annual with bright orange or yellow daisylike flowers; used medicinally and in cooking.

Purple coneflower (*Echinacea purpurea*). Rosy purple daisies with high, bristly centers; used medicinally by Native Americans.

Rosemary (*Rosmarinus officinalis*). Bushy plant; narrow, gray-green, strongly scented leaves; excellent seasoning for meat.

Rue (*Ruta graveolens*). Rounded plants with blue-green, pungent foliage.

Salad burnet (*Poterium sanguisorba*). Rosette of blue-green, cucumber-flavored leaves.

Sweet marigold (*Tagetes lucida*). Single yellow flowers above anise-scented leaves.

Sweet woodruff (*Galium odoratum*). Low whorls of sweet-scented green leaves; airy, white flowers.

Tansy (*Tanacetum vulgare*). Fernlike leaves; clusters of small, yellow button flowers.

Yarrows (*Achillea* spp.). Yellow, white, red, or pink flowers; used medicinally and dried for herbal crafts.

Herbs also help deter pests. See "Companion Planting" on page 116 for more details.

## MIXING HERBS AND FLOWERS

Many herbs are suitable for a mixed border or bed—a flower garden that combines perennials, annuals, and shrubs. You may already have some herbs in your garden, although you think of them as flowers or foliage plants.

English lavender cultivars such as 'Hidcote' or 'Munstead' are always welcome among the flowers in beds or borders. Pure blue, silky flowers on delicate, wiry stems make blue flax (*Linum perenne*) a favorite in flower beds. Feverfew (*Chrysanthemum parthenium*) is another herb often used in mixed borders. Its lacy, bright green foliage sets off small, pure white, single or double daisies. Catmint (*Nepeta* spp.), with sprays of blue-lavender flowers, pungent, gray-green leaves, and tufted habit, is lovely with lilies and roses.

Many gray-leaved herbs, such as Russian sage (*Perovskia* spp.) with its silvery foliage and misty blue flowers, are useful for separating and blending colors in the garden. Even a culinary workhorse like dill can be used to fine effect in the mixed border. Its delicate, chartreuse flowers and lacy foliage add an airiness to any planting. See "Herbs for the Flower Garden" on page 251 for more suggestions.

## GROWING HERBS IN CONTAINERS

Herbs and containers are a happy combination, especially for a gardener short on space, time, or stamina. Maintenance chores—except for watering—are eliminated or much reduced. Even if your garden has plenty of space, a potted collection adds interest to a sunny porch, patio, or deck. An assortment of terra-cotta pots brimming with herbs used for cooking makes a charming—and useful—addition to a kitchen doorstep. Or try a sampler of mints in a wooden

**Growing herbs in containers.** Bottomless containers are a great way to control the outward creep of spreading herbs like mint. Or if you are growing frost-tender herbs like lemon verbena and rosemary, sink their pots into the garden soil in summer. Come fall, it's easy to lift the plant, pot and all, and bring it indoors.

half-barrel—the notorious perennial spreaders stay in control, will come back year after year, and are handy for brewing a pot of tea.

Some herbs are often grown—or at least overwintered—in containers because they aren't hardy and won't survive northern winters. These include rosemary (*Rosmarinus officinalis*), sweet bay (*Laurus nobilis*), myrtle (*Myrtus communis*), pineapple sage (*Salvia elegans*), and lemon verbena (*Aloysia triphylla*). See "Overwintering Tender Herbs" on page 255 for more information.

# GROWING HERBS

Herbs are generally undemanding plants. Given adequate light and good soil, they will produce well and suffer from few problems. Some herbs are perennials; others are annuals. Keep in mind that tender perennial herbs will behave like annuals in the northern states.

## GROWING ANNUAL HERBS

Common annual herbs are basil, chervil, coriander, dill, summer savory, and parsley, which is actually a biennial that is grown as an annual. More exotic annuals include safflower (*Carthamus tinctorius*), sweet wormwood (*Artemisia annua*), and sweet marigold (*Tagetes lucida*), a substitute for French tarragon. Sweet marjoram (*Origanum majorana*) is not hardy north of Zone 6, but it lives through the winter in the South.

Plant seeds for chervil, coriander, and dill outdoors where they are to grow, in spring or fall. These herbs are extremely difficult to transplant successfully. If you want a head start on outdoor planting, sow them in peat pots for minimum root disturbance at planting time. Sow sweet wormwood and Jerusalem oak outdoors in autumn.

Herb seedlings are often tiny and slower-growing than weeds, so it makes sense to start them indoors. Start basil, marigolds, marjoram, and summer savory indoors in flats or pots, and move them to the garden when no more cold weather is expected. Parsley takes so long to come up that you might be better off starting it indoors, too. Outdoors, you will be down on your knees every day trying to sort out the baby parsley plants from the weeds, which germinate quickly and will always have a head start.

## GROWING PERENNIAL HERBS

Perennial herbs can be grown from seed, but they take longer to germinate than the annuals. It's better to start out by buying young plants of perennial herbs such as mints, sages, and thymes. Once you've gotten started, increase your supply by dividing plants such as mint or by taking cuttings, which works well for rosemary and myrtle. For more on propagation techniques, see Chapter 6.

Many perennial herbs need no help once they're established. Sweet woodruff (*Galium odoratum*) will supply you with bushels of foliage for potpourri while it covers the ground.

Chamomile, chives, feverfew, garlic chives, lemon balm, and winter savory will self-sow eternally.

Horehound, oregano, and thyme usually sow some seedlings, but fennel and lovage seem to stay in one place. Some of the catmints (*Nepeta* spp.) self-sow; others don't.

You may prefer to propagate certain perennial herbs by means of cuttings because they are especially beautiful forms or cultivars. (Plants propagated from seed don't always resemble their parents, whereas those from cuttings do.) If you have a fine lavender such as 'Hidcote' and you would like to have more without pay-

### Herbs That Sow Themselves

Many herbs are so easy to grow that they'll practically plant themselves. You need to sow or transplant them into the garden the first year and then let a few of each kind go to seed. The seeds will fall and germinate the following spring. Some seedlings may pop up in the most unexpected places. Enjoy the informal effect, or transplant the young seedlings to where you want them to grow. Here are some dependable self-sowers:

Agrimony (*Agrimonia eupatoria*)
Borage (*Borago officinalis*)
Caraway (*Carum carvi*)
Chervil (*Anthriscus cerefolium*)
Coriander or cilantro (*Coriandrum sativum*)
Dill (*Anethum graveolens*)
Fennel (*Foeniculum vulgare*)
German chamomile (*Matricaria recutita*)
Lemon basil (*Ocimum basilicum* 'Citriodorum')
Roman chamomile (*Chamaemelum nobile*)
Sweet wormwood (*Artemisia annua*)

ing for more plants from the nursery, take 3- to 4-inch cuttings of the semi-hard tips and gently remove the lower leaves. Press the cuttings into a mixture of damp peat and sand in a light but not sunny spot, cover with a cloche or jar, and start yourself some new plants. You can also do this with thymes, taking cuttings from a silvery or variegated plant or any one that you especially like. Lemon verbena is sterile and must be propagated this way. Luckily, it roots readily.

French tarragon (*Artemisia dracunculus* var. *sativa*) must be purchased as a plant, since it never sets viable seed. The so-called Russian tarragon offered as seed has no culinary value.

When French tarragon is grown in sun or part sun and in light, well-watered but well-drained soil, it usually thrives and spreads enough to divide one plant into many each spring. It is hardy at least through Zone 5. However, if you do not succeed with it due to severe cold or high summer temperatures in your area, try the annual marigold from Mexico and South America called sweet marigold (*Tagetes lucida*). It makes an excellent substitute.

## CARING FOR HERBS

Like nearly all plants, herbs require well-drained soil. While most do best in full sun,

---

 **Herbs for Shady Gardens**

Although most herbs require a sunny site, there are herbs that will grow in shade. Some, like sweet woodruff, actually prefer shade. Others, such as thyme, will grow in partial shade, even though they prefer full sun. Their growth habit in the shade will simply be taller and more open. Provide these shade-loving and shade-tolerant herbs with loose, rich soil and plenty of moisture. The herbs listed below that are marked with an asterisk prefer shade, while the rest will grow in full sun to partial shade:

Chamomile* (*Chamaemelum nobile*). A low-growing perennial with apple-scented, daisylike flowers; used as a tea herb and medicinally.

Chervil* (*Anthriscus cerefolium*). A white-flowered annual; used as a culinary herb.

Coriander/cilantro (*Coriandrum sativum*). An annual grown for its pungent seeds (coriander) and foliage (cilantro); both used as culinary herbs.

Common witch hazel* (*Hamamelis virginiana*). A shrub with autumn flowers whose petals look like small yellow ribbons; used medicinally.

Dill (*Anethum graveolens*). An annual grown for its seeds and foliage; both used in cooking.

Lemon balm (*Melissa officinalis*). A white-flowered member of the mint family; used for fragrance and teas.

Mints (*Mentha* spp.). Rampant-growing herbs with pungent foliage; used medicinally and for fragrance and teas.

Sweet cicely* (*Myrrhis odorata*). A plant with ferny, fragrant foliage that smells of licorice; used as a culinary herb.

Sweet violet* (*Viola odorata*). A spreading plant available in many colors; used for fragrance.

Sweet woodruff* (*Galium odoratum*). A low-growing plant with white flowers; excellent groundcover; dried foliage and flowers used for fragrance.

Wintergreen* (*Gaultheria procumbens*). A creeping evergreen with tasty leaves and berries; used medicinally and for teas.

they will accept as little as six hours of sunlight a day. Incorporate compost or other organic matter into the soil regularly. Cultivate carefully to keep out weeds. Mulch everything except the Mediterranean plants (marjoram, oregano, rosemary, sage, winter savory, and thyme) with a fine, thick material that neither acidifies the soil nor keeps out the rain. Avoid pine bark (chipped or shredded) and peat. Mediterranean plants prefer being weeded to being mulched, since they are used to growing on rocky hills with no accumulation of vegetable matter around their woody stems. In the colder areas of the country, protect your plantings of catmint, horehound, lavender, rue, thyme, winter savory, and sage with evergreen boughs in the winter.

Gardeners who grow their plants out in the sun and wind will have little trouble with disease or insect damage. Basil is sometimes subject to attack by chewing insects, but if you follow good cultural practices and grow enough plants, the damage can be ignored. You'll rarely have the need to take measures to control insect pests on herbs. It's best never to apply botanical insecticides to culinary herbs.

## OVERWINTERING TENDER HERBS

To overwinter frost-tender herbs such as rosemary (*Rosmarinus officinalis*), sweet bay (*Laurus nobilis*), myrtle (*Myrtus communis*), pineapple sage (*Salvia elegans*), scented geraniums (*Geranium* spp.), and lemon verbena (*Aloysia triphylla*), you can either grow them permanently in pots or take cuttings of plants at the end of the season, root them, then pot them and hold them over the winter indoors until the following spring. This method works well for nonwoody herbs like basils and pineapple sage. Most herbs prefer a bright, airy spot with a temperature between 50° and 70°F. Keep the soil evenly moist, and provide a good level of humidity

by grouping pots together and setting them on shallow trays filled with wet gravel.

These plants don't really object to being grown in pots, but they don't tolerate being indoors very well. You may have to help them fight off bugs and disease during the winter months. Potted herbs in the house may become afflicted with scale, aphids, or other pests. (Scented geraniums are the exception; these plants tend to shrug off pests.) Keep a close watch for signs of infestation. Here are some herbs that usually adapt well to indoor culture:

Basils (*Ocimum* spp.)
Bay (*Laurus nobilis*)
Catnip (*Nepeta cataria*)
Chervil (*Anthriscus cerefolium*)
Chives (*Allium schoenoprasum*)
Coriander or cilantro (*Coriandrum sativum*)
Elfin herb (*Cuphea hyssopifolia*)
Myrtle (*Myrtus communis*)
Oregano (*Origanum heracleoticum*)
Patchouli (*Pogostemon cablin*)
Rosemary (*Rosmarinus officinalis*)
Sages (*Salvia* spp.)
Scented geraniums (*Pelargonium* spp.)
Summer savory (*Satureja hortensis*)
Sweet marjoram (*Origanum majorana*)

In spring, move the plants outside. Within a few days, their relief will be visible, and they'll start growing happily again.

Before bringing herbs in for the winter, turn them out of their pots and put them into larger ones, adding new soil mixed with compost. When, after some years, the pots have reached the limit of what you want to lift, turn out the plants and root-prune them. If the roots form a solid, pot-shaped lump (as they certainly will in the case of rosemary), take a cleaver or large kitchen knife and slice off an inch or two all the way around. Fill in the extra space with fresh soil and compost. Cut back one-fourth to one-third of the top growth to balance what you have removed from the bottom.

Stimulate new growth and keep your plants in good shape by pruning your herbs regularly. Herbs such as pineapple sage (*Salvia elegans*), basil, scented geraniums, and thymes quickly become spindly without pruning or harvesting. So if your herb plants are strictly ornamental, plan to prune and shape them at least once each month when they're actively growing during warm summer months. If you have culinary herbs, harvest from them as needed or trim them on the same schedule as your ornamentals.

# HARVEST AND STORAGE

Cut and use your herbs all summer while they are at their very best. The flavor of herb leaves is at its peak just as the plants begin to form flower buds. Cut herbs in midmorning, after the sun has dried the leaves but before it gets too hot. You can cut back as much as three-fourths of a plant without hurting it. (When harvesting parsley, remove the outside leaves so that the central shoot remains). Remove any damaged or yellow foliage. If the plants are dirty, rinse them quickly in cold water and drain them well.

You will want to save some herbs for the

**Hanging herbs to dry.** Tie herbs in small bunches and hang them. To keep them clean and out of direct sunlight, you can cover the plants with brown paper bags. Cut holes in the bags to ensure proper ventilation. Herbs harvested for seeds also must be covered with a paper bag to catch the seeds as they dry.

---

 **Fridge-Dried Herbs**

To preserve your leafy green herbs while retaining much of their flavor and color, try drying them in the refrigerator. Harvest as usual, rinse, and pat dry. Remove the leaves from the stems if desired. Put the leaves or leafy stems in a brown paper bag in the refrigerator. They'll dry in three or four weeks. This technique is particularly effective with tarragon, basil, chervil, savory, parsley, and celery leaves.

winter months. Drying is an easy way to preserve herbs, although you can also freeze them in plastic bags or preserve them in olive oil.

## DRYING TECHNIQUES

Start your herb drying by picking herbs from the garden after they have dried off from the morning dew. (Avoid harvesting after a rain.) Since your goal is to dry the herbs, you don't want to delay the process by starting with wet plants. Next, determine which drying method you'll use: air-drying, which is the least labor-intensive on your part; or oven or microwave drying, both of which will help to shorten the

 **Harvesting Tips for Success**

Whether cutting herbs to use fresh or gathering bunches of them for drying, it's important to harvest herbs with care. Here's how:

■ On each trip to the garden, no matter the purpose, carry your shears or clippers and make sure to stop by the herb patch. You may not have planned on harvesting today, but there's almost sure to be something (a snip of this, a blossom of that) you can trim and bring indoors to add to the next meal.

■ It's best to cut the herbs in the morning of a cool, cloudy day. Wait until the dew has dried, but harvest before the sun has become very bright. Usually the best time is around 9:00 A.M. Only cut the amount of material you will be able to handle that day so you won't waste any.

■ Keep small rubber bands looped around the neck of your herb scissors. They'll be easy to find when you're harvesting bunches in the garden.

■ As you're cutting, keep the herbs fresh and unwilted by placing them in a bucket of cool water.

■ If the plants are clean and free of pesticides, you can bundle them immediately after picking. If not, wash them in water and pat dry with a towel.

■ To keep fresh herbs fresh, place them in bunches in jars filled with an inch or two of water, covered loosely with plastic wrap, and refrigerate. They'll last this way for about two weeks. Wrap smaller sprigs of herbs in paper towels, sealed in plastic bags, and place them in the crisper drawer of the refrigerator, where they'll last for about two weeks. Be sure the leaves are completely dry, or brown spots may develop.

■ Use sharp pruning shears and cut the plant so that it will still look beautiful even after it has been pruned. On some plants such as parsley or chives the leaves are cut right back to the base; cut the outside leaves all the way around the plant to encourage further growth. The entire clump of chives can be cut to 1 inch high; it will grow again.

■ If you plan to dry the herbs by hanging them upside down suspended from a line or cord, you'll need to separate them into small bunches and fasten them together with string or a rubber band at the base. Don't make the bunches too large, for there is a risk that they won't dry properly and will mildew if not enough air is able to reach the leaves.

■ You can also dry herbs by laying them flat on screens or baskets to dry. In fact, if you are drying flower petals, such as roses, it's best to dry them in this manner because they need good air circulation to dry evenly. With flowers, it's a good idea to occasionally move them around gently to avoid moisture buildup.

drying process considerably.

**Air Drying**   Dry herbs as quickly as possible in a dark, airy place. Attics and barns are ideal, but any breezy room that can be kept dark will do. Hang the branches by the stems, or strip off the leaves and dry them on racks through which air can circulate. Drying on racks is the best way to handle large-leaved herbs such as sweet basil or comfrey. It's also good for drying rose petals or other fragrant flowers for pot-pourris.

To keep air-dried herbs dust-free and out of the light while drying, you can cover them with brown paper bags. Tie the cut herbs in loose bunches, small enough so that they don't touch the sides of the bag, then tie the bag closed around the ends of the stems. Label the bag.

After a few weeks, test for dryness. When the leaves are completely dry and crisp, rub them off the stems and store them in tightly sealed jars out of the light.

**Oven Drying**   You can also dry herbs on racks made of metal screening in a gas oven that has a pilot light. Turn twice a day for several days. Or dry in an electric oven at very low heat—150°F or lower. When herbs are crisp, remove the leaves from the stems and crumble them into jars.

**Microwave Drying**   Microwave-dried herbs retain excellent color and potency. Start by laying the herb foliage in a single layer on a paper towel, either on the oven rack or on the glass insert. Cover the leaves with another paper towel and microwave on high for 1 minute. Then check the herbs, and if they are still soft, keep testing at 20- to 30-second intervals. Microwave ovens differ in power output, so you'll have to experiment. Keep track of your results with each kind of herb.

Microwave drying is a bit easier on plant tissue than oven drying because the water in the herb leaves absorbs more of the energy than the

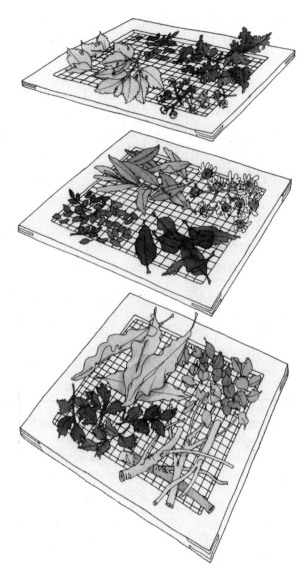

**Screen drying.** Herbs, rose petals, and other ingredients destined for potpourri can be spread on screens and left in a warm, dark, dry place.

plant tissue does. The water in the leaves gets hot and evaporates—that's why the paper towels get damp during the drying process—leaving drying plant tissue behind. The plant tissue heats up a little because of contact with water, but the water absorbs most of the heat. In a conventional oven, all the plant material gets hot, not just the water.

# USING HERBS

If you have only a tub or two in which to grow herbs, you might plant a few culinary herbs or lavender for fragrance. If you have a big garden, you can experiment with medicinal plants as well as with material to dry for winter bouquets, wreaths, and potpourris.

## COOKING WITH HERBS

If you're not accustomed to using herbs in cooking, start out by exercising restraint. If you overdo it, you might find you have overwhelmed the original flavor of the meat or vegetable whose flavor you meant to enhance. Remember that dried herbs are more powerful, ounce for ounce, than fresh ones. Study herb cookbooks, and when you've learned the usual combinations (French tarragon with fish or chicken, or basil with tomatoes and eggplant, for instance), experiment on your own. You could invent some new and wonderful dishes. See "Selecting and Growing Herbs" on page 267 for a list of herbs to get you started.

## USING FRESH HERBS

To serve four people with a sauce, soup, stew, or sauté, use about 2 teaspoons of minced fresh herbs. To reach the fullest aroma, rub the leaves between your hands, then mince them using a sharp knife or by snipping them with kitchen shears. Mince large amounts of herbs in a food processor.

Whole fresh leaves should be rubbed between your hands to release flavor before adding to marinades, soups, stews, and punches. The amount of leaves to add will vary depending on their size, but use the 2-teaspoons-for-4-servings rule and try to visualize how many whole

leaves will make that amount.

For the best flavor in long-cooking foods like soups and stews, add fresh herbs during the last 20 minutes or so of cooking.

## USING DRIED HERBS

Generally use about 1 teaspoon of dried herbs to serve four people, or about half the amount you would use of fresh. Smell the herbs before using them to make sure they're aromatic. Then rub them between your hands or grind them coarsely in a spice grinder, coffee grinder, or with a mortar and pestle. Use immediately.

## USING FROZEN HERBS

Clever chefs are learning that the herbal pantry is not limited to fresh or dried herbs. The freezer provides a hospitable environment for many herbs and spices because its low temperature helps them keep their flavors longer.

Tough-stemmed herbs like basil, tarragon, and sage should have their leaves removed for freezing. Brush off the soil with a stiff paintbrush rather than washing because too much water may dilute flavors. Once the leaves have been brushed and removed, lay them out flat on a cookie sheet and freeze them for several hours. Then place them gently into freezer containers or bags, and they'll be easy to remove individually as needed.

The big question when freezing herbs is whether or not to blanch. Although the color of the herbs will usually stay greener if they have been blanched, flavor and aroma will often be sacrificed.

Basil is an exception: It should be blanched, or it will turn black. Most other herbs will freeze well unblanched for up to six months if they are frozen just after harvesting. After that time, blanched or unblanched, they'll begin to deteriorate.

To blanch, simply place the leaves in a strainer

and pour boiling water over them for one second. Then lay them on paper towels and let them cool in the air before freezing. Don't be tempted into cooling the leaves by plunging them into ice water because it could dilute their flavor.

Delicate herbs like thyme and dill freeze well in sprigs. Simply arrange them in freezer containers or bags and seal. Use whole frozen sprigs or snip them as needed.

Many frozen herbs can be used as you would fresh—about 2 teaspoons to serve four people. Take the herbs from the freezer and toss them (without defrosting) into soups, stews, and sauces. If you're using frozen herbs in salads or other uncooked foods, defrost and drain them first. (Frozen minced herbs will need more draining than sprigs.) Note that flavors can change during freezing, so be sure to taste and,

if necessary, adjust before serving.

Herbs can also be minced by hand or with a food processor and frozen in ice cube trays. When the cubes are frozen, transfer them to plastic bags and use as needed.

Another way to freeze minced herbs is by making herb pastes. Add fresh leaves or sprigs to a food processor and begin to mince. While the motor is running, add oil, a bit at a time, until the mixture has formed a paste. Freeze the paste in ice cube trays or in tablespoon amounts wrapped in plastic.

## MAKING FLAVORED OILS

Flavored oils can be a dieter's dream. The secret is that you can use less because the oil is more flavorful. For example, on a salad to serve four people, you might make a dressing using 2 tablespoons of oil. But if you use a flavored oil, you can cut the amount in half—the dressing will be so flavorful that nondieters will be jealous.

Gently heat olive oil, peanut oil, or other vegetable oil until it's warm and fragrant. This will take three to five minutes, depending on how much oil you're heating. Then pour the oil into a glass jar to which you have added fresh herb sprigs, herb leaves, garlic, or chilies. Use about three 2-inch sprigs, one clove of garlic, or one chili for each cup of oil. Let the oil cool, cover, and store it in a cool, damp place for about six months. Use the oil to sauté and in marinades and salad dressings.

## MAKING HERB BUTTERS

Like flavored oils, herb butters allow calorie counters to use less because there's more flavor. They also jazz up a breakfast table or an appetizer tray with wonderful colors and tastes. Try serving herb butters in tiny ramekins (crocks), shaping them in butter molds, or cutting them with a butter curler.

Combine about 1 tablespoon of minced fresh

 **Tasty Combinations**

If you use basil and thyme together in cooking, why not preserve them together, too? Here are some ideas for other tasty combinations of herbs:

- Basil, thyme, and Italian parsley
- Marjoram, lovage, and thyme
- Coriander leaf and chilies
- Chives and dillweed
- Dill, mint, and parsley
- Oregano, thyme, and Italian parsley
- Tarragon and lovage
- Sage, thyme, and chives
- Lemon verbena and tarragon
- Mint, lemon balm, and dill
- Dill, lovage, and chives
- Oregano, basil, and thyme
- Chives and marjoram
- Oregano, epizote, and parsley
- Mint and zatar

herbs with ½ cup of softened sweet butter. Wrap the mixture in plastic and store it in the refrigerator for about a month or in the freezer for about three months. Use the butter on warm biscuits or toast, steamed vegetables, poached chicken, or fish. Use it to sauté.

## HERB-AND-SPICE COMBINATIONS

Here are some other classic herb combinations that you may have heard of. Try one or more of these mixes to make the most use of your herbal bounty.

**Bouquets Garnis**  These are the little bundles of aromatic herbs and spices used to flavor soups, stews, and sauces. The idea behind a bouquet garni is to keep the herbs contained so that flavor, but not flecks, will permeate the food. The little bundles can be made up of several fresh herb sprigs tied together with string; fresh or dried herbs tied in a cheesecloth bag; fresh or dried herbs placed in a tea ball; or fresh or dried herbs tucked between two pieces of celery and tied with string. When using a bouquet garni that is tied together with string, make the string long enough that you can tie the loose end to the pot handle. Then when you need to remove the bouquet, it will be easy to find.

Classically, bouquets garnis contain parsley, thyme, and bay with occasional additions of whole peppercorns, whole allspice, whole cloves, celery leaf, tarragon, and marjoram. Be encouraged to expand on the bouquet concept by creating your own removable bundles. For instance, combine cinnamon stick, orange peel, lemon peel, and nutmeg to flavor warm apple cider. Or use lemon peel, whole peppercorns, and garlic together to spice up simmering vegetables.

Bouquets garnis can be made ahead in cheesecloth bags and frozen. Add them to simmering food directly from the freezer.

**Fines Herbes**  This is a combination of chervil, parsley, thyme, and tarragon, freshly minced and added to omelets, sautés, cheese sauces, and other recipes at the very last minute of cooking. The allure of fines herbes is in the freshness of the herbs and the satisfying flavor they create when combined.

**Quatre Épices**  This means "four spices" and is used in French haute cuisine to flavor roast meats, poultry, hardy vegetables, or desserts. The four spices are a ground combination of any of the following: cloves, mace, nutmeg, ginger, cinnamon, black pepper, or white pepper. Without the peppers, quatre épices

## Maximizing the Flavor

Here's how to get the most flavor from your dried and fresh herbs:

■ To develop the flavor of dried herbs, soak them for several minutes in a liquid that can be used in the recipe—stock, oil, lemon juice, or vinegar.

■ When using herbs in salad dressings, allow the flavor of the ingredients in the combination to develop by soaking for 15 minutes to an hour.

■ Work the flavors of herbs into meat, poultry, and fish by rubbing them in with your hands before cooking.

■ For steamed or boiled vegetables, add the herbs to melted butter and allow to stand for ten minutes before seasoning the vegetables with it.

■ To intensify the flavors of whole spices, toast them briefly in a dry, heavy skillet before using.

■ Dried and fresh herbs may be used interchangeably in most recipes. Use two to three times more fresh herbs than dried, depending on the strength of the herb.

becomes good old American pumpkin pie spice.

**Curry Powder**  This is an aromatic combination of many ground spices that can include coriander seed, cumin seed, nutmeg, mace, cardamom seed, turmeric, white mustard seed, black mustard seed, fenugreek seed, chilies, ginger, white peppercorns, black peppercorns, garlic, allspice, cinnamon, cayenne, and fennel seed. Curry powder is famous in East Indian cooking and Southeast Asian cuisines, especially Thai. Thai curries generally omit the sweeter spices like cinnamon, ginger, nutmeg, and mace and include lots of fresh basil. Thai curry powders are commonly combined with a liquid and used as pastes.

**Chili Powder**  This is a combination of ground spices and herbs that always contains dried chilies plus a selection of garlic powder, oregano, allspice, cloves, cumin seed, coriander seed, cayenne, black pepper, turmeric, mustard seed, and paprika. As with all dried spice and herb combinations, chili powder is best when ground as needed and heated before eating. If you must make chili powder ahead, store it in a tightly covered glass jar and keep the jar in a cool, dark place.

**Chinese Five-Spice Powder**  This is a dried, ground combination of Szechuan peppercorns, cinnamon, cloves, fennel, and star anise. It's used as a seasoning for pork and chicken and as a condiment. Five-spice powder is most flavorful ground as needed and heated before serving.

## Simple Herbal Vinegars

Making herbal vinegars is a fast and easy way to preserve your harvest. Just fill a clean glass jar with your favorite fresh culinary herbs, and cover them with warm (not boiling) vinegar. (Choose white vinegar, white wine vinegar, red wine vinegar, apple cider vinegar, or rice vinegar, depending on the herbs you're adding.) Let the vinegar cool, then cover the jar. (If you are using a metal cap, line it with plastic wrap first.)

For best results, store the jar in a cool, dark place and use as needed. If you want your vinegars for display, strain out the herbs, pour the vinegar into decorative bottles, and add a few sprigs of fresh herbs. Deeply colored herbs like purple basil can add a beautiful hue to your finished product. Here are some combinations to try:

■ Rosemary, raisins, orange peel, garlic, and white wine vinegar

■ Sage, parsley, shallots, and red wine vinegar

■ Borage, dill, shallots, and white wine vinegar

■ Chilies, garlic, oregano, and cider vinegar

■ Mint, honey, cardamom seed, and white wine vinegar

■ Coriander leaf, garlic, and rice vinegar

■ Dill, nasturtiums, garlic, and cider vinegar

■ Savory, chive blossoms, and cider vinegar

■ Fennel leaf, garlic, parsley, and white wine vinegar

If you're using five-spice powder as a condiment, toast it first in a dry sauté pan. If you must store five-spice powder, keep it untoasted in a tightly covered glass jar in a cool, dark place.

**Pickling Spice** This often includes dillweed and/or dill seed plus a choice of dried chilies, mustard seed, bay, allspice, white peppercorns, black peppercorns, cinnamon, cloves, coriander seed, turmeric, cardamom, ginger, celery seed, garlic, mace, and nutmeg. Sound confusing? Simply choose your spices according to what you're pickling. For instance, for cucumber pickles, use dillweed, dill seed, mustard seed, celery seed, garlic, and black peppercorns. Now imagine that you're pickling carrots. Think about what flavors enhance them. You could choose cinnamon, nutmeg, bay, and peppercorns.

## USING HERBS FOR TEAS

While you're gathering herbs for the kitchen, include some to use for tea. Herbal teas can be soothing, stimulating, or simply pleasant. Many of them are wonderful aids to digestion or for allaying cold symptoms. Some, such as lemon balm, pineapple sage, and lemon verbena, make refreshing iced tea or additions to iced drinks.

You can make herb tea with dried or fresh leaves, flowers, or other plant parts. To make herb tea, place leaves into an earthenware or china pot or mug. Start with 1 tablespoon of dried herbs or 2 tablespoons of fresh herbs per cup, and adjust the quantity to suit your own taste as you gain experience. Then add boiling water, and steep for 5 to 10 minutes before straining. Serve herb tea with honey, lemon, orange slices, or fresh herb sprigs. To make iced tea, follow the same procedure, except use 3 tablespoons of fresh herbs or 2 tablespoons of dried herbs. The extra amount allows for melting ice.

Herb teas can be frozen in ice cube trays and used to chill refreshing summer beverages. You can also freeze sprigs of herbs, like mint, in ice cubes for flavoring and decorating beverages. One word of caution: Not all herbs are suitable for making tea. If you're interested in experi-

 **Pick Your Favorite Pesto**

There's more to pesto than just basil! Try substituting other culinary herbs in your basic pesto recipe, and create a taste sensation that will win over even the most devoted basil lovers. You can, for example, add tender garlic tops in early spring, before other herbs begin producing. Or substitute the basil with thyme, coriander (cilantro), or a combination of parsley and rosemary. If the flavors are too strong, replace one-half of the strong herb with the relatively mild-flavored parsley. For an added twist, try substituting ricotta or grated mozzarella for the Parmesan cheese. Here's a basic pesto recipe that will work with any culinary herb:

2–3 cups packed herb leaves
2 cloves garlic
½ cup olive oil
2 tablespoons pine nuts, walnuts, or cashews (optional)
1 teaspoon salt (optional)
½ cup finely grated Parmesan cheese (optional)

Blend together the herb leaves, garlic, and oil with the nuts and salt (if using) in a blender or food processor until thoroughly pureed. Transfer to a small bowl and stir in the cheese (if using). Serve over hot pasta, spread lightly on fresh bread, add to leafy salads, or use in any recipe that lists pesto as an ingredient.

Yield: 1 cup sauce

menting with herbal-tea making, remember that some herbs can make you ill if ingested. Research before you drink. See "Ideas for Tea Blends" on this page for a list of herbs you can safely brew and sip.

## USING HERBS AS MEDICINES

Until quite recently in human history, herbs were the only medicines available. Herbal medicine has a rich and fascinating history.

### Ideas for Tea Blends

Try any of the combinations below for a refreshing drink:

- Spearmint, elderberry, and lemon balm
- Tansy, sage, and rosehips
- Marjoram, anise, and lemon verbena
- Angelica, clove, orange peel, and nutmeg
- Anise, chamomile, and costmary
- Lemon verbena and borage
- Blueberry leaf, beebalm, and ginger
- Savory, lemongrass, and scented geranium
- Thyme, sassafras, and strawberry leaf
- Lemongrass, rosemary, and thyme
- Rose petals, rose hips, and raspberry leaf
- Nettle, ginger, and hyssop
- Horehound and chamomile
- Jasmine, orange peel, and sage
- Fennel and goldenrod
- Chicory, ginseng, and cinnamon
- Elderberry, rosehips, and bay
- Chamomile and valerian
- Basil, lemon verbena, lemongrass, and lemon thyme
- Pennyroyal, peppermint, and ginger
- Chamomile and apple mint

For example, the Roman "Doctrine of Signatures" theorized that the shape of a leaf or flower indicated the human organ a plant was designed to heal; thus, hepatica, having liver-shaped leaves, was thought to cure diseases of that organ. Pliny, a first-century Roman scholar, listed 70 diseases for which leeks were used as medicine. While we wouldn't agree today with the old Roman doctors as to the great healing power of leeks, it is astonishing to find how many of the herbs we use in cooking have medicinal as well as culinary value.

Marjoram, mint, oregano, sage, and thyme all help in digestion. Garlic is an antiseptic, as well as being an effective aid in the treatment of colds, influenza, and bronchitis. Onions are said to lower blood pressure, reduce blood cholesterol, and aid circulation. Coriander, parsley, rosemary, savory, and sorrel have been and are still being used as remedies for minor ills. It's comforting to think that as we add herbs to our food to enhance the flavor, we are promoting our health at the same time.

Through centuries of searching and experimenting, we have found certain plants that contain elements to help heal many of our ills. Some of them have long been part of our pharmacopoeia and remain so today: Digitalis, from common foxglove (*Digitalis purpurea*), for example, has been used to treat heart disorders for hundreds of years. In Europe and America, herbs are usually used only by healers outside the mainstream of Western medical practice; in Asia, herbs are still an important element in all healing. Since so many of our medicines come from plants, the search goes on for substances that will help our bodies fight afflictions. This is one of the reasons scientists are so alarmed at the rapid destruction of unique plant communities such as the rain forests.

While amateur herbalists may safely soothe

their digestive systems by drinking mint tea, beware of doctoring yourself or others with extracts or infusions of plants whose properties you do not fully understand. A "remedy" from a wild plant is not necessarily safe, because "natural" substances are not automatically benign. Overdoses or even small doses of a plant such as foxglove can kill rather than save. See "Common Home Remedies" on this page for suggestions for safe herbal treatments.

## USING HERBS FOR REPELLING INSECTS

Planting herbs as companion plants in the vegetable and flower garden is a time-honored but not infallible way of helping to deter some pests. For more on companion planting, see "Cultural Controls" on page 111.

## USING HERBS FOR FRAGRANCE

Flowers release their perfume into the air so freely, you need only walk past to enjoy the scent of roses, lilacs, honeysuckle, clove pinks, or any other highly fragrant flower. Occasionally, we can detect the scent of lavender or thyme when they are baking in the hot sun. But plants with aromatic leaves do not, as a rule, release the odor of their oils unless you rub a leaf, walk on the plant, or brush against the branches while working around them.

The leaves of scented geraniums (*Pelargoni-*

---

###  Common Home Remedies

Home remedies can save money, and some are very effective. Be sure to check and double-check the identity of a plant before using it as a remedy. Here are some common herbal cures:

Aloe (*Aloe barbadensis*): The juice of cut leaves soothes small burns and insect stings.

Broadleaf plantain (*Plantago major*): The crushed leaves soothe the itch of insect bites and poison ivy.

Chamomile (*Chamaemelum nobile*): Tea made from flowers aids digestion and upset stomachs.

Cranberry (*Vaccinium macrocarpon*): Drinking cranberry juice helps prevent/cure bladder infection; taking two to four cranberry capsules with lots of water is also effective.

Dandelion (*Taraxacum officinale*): The leaves are a rich source of vitamins. Dried root is a mild laxative.

Flax (*Linum usitatissimum*): Crushed seed wrapped in a cloth may be used as a poultice for sores or insect bites.

Garlic (*Allium sativum*): Raw garlic or the juice from crushed cloves mixed with hot water or honey is a cold and sore throat remedy.

Hens-and-chickens (*Sempervivum* spp.): The juice from cut leaves soothes burns and insect stings.

Horehound (*Marrubium vulgare*): Tea made from dried leaves helps soothe coughs and acts as an expectorant.

Peppermint (*Mentha × piperita*): Tea made from leaves can soothe an upset stomach.

Rosemary (*Rosmarinus officinalis*): Tea made from leaves and flowers is good for colds and indigestion.

Roses (*Rosa* spp.): Tea made from rose hips is high in vitamin C and good for colds. It also acts as a laxative.

Sage (*Saliva officinalis*): Tea made from the foliage is good for indigestion and colds.

Sweet fern (*Comptonia peregrina* var. *asplenifolia*): The juice from crushed stems stops itching of poison ivy.

um spp.)—just one example of the many fragrant-foliaged herbs—are wonderful to rub. They come in a wide variety of scents, including lemon-rose, lemon, mint, nutmeg, rose, and ginger. Their many different fragrances and leaf and flower variations, make them fascinating to collectors and gardeners alike.

Lavender, lemon balm, lemon verbena, scented geraniums, and sweet woodruff are among the best-known herbs grown for fragrance. All can be preserved by air drying (see "Harvest and Storage" on page 256 for directions). For more suggestions of herbs to grow for fragrant flowers, foliage, or fruit, see "Fragrant Herbs" on this page.

Sachets and potpourri are two good ways to preserve the scent of herbs for winter. Sachets are made with combinations of dried herb leaves and, frequently, crumbled or ground rose petals. You can dry rose petals by spreading them on sheets or screens in a dark, airy place. Petals of apothecary's rose (*Rosa gallica* var. *officinalis*) are the most fragrant.

Potpourri is a mix of petals and leaves used whole; it can be made with fresh or dried leaves and petals. Some potpourris include dried orange or lemon peel and spices such as cloves and allspice. Experiment with different combinations and see which ones you prefer. The fragrance is usually set with a fixative, such as orris root.

---

 ## Fragrant Herbs

Rub a leaf and use your nose to find what smells best to you! Here are some of the herbs that can be used, fresh or dried, for herbal crafts such as wreaths, potpourris, sachets, or arrangements:

Bee balm (*Monarda didyma*): blossoms and foliage used in wreaths, potpourris, and teas

Jerusalem oak (*Chenopodium botrys*): fluffy gold branches good for herb wreaths

Lavender (*Lavandula angustifolia*): flowers and foliage used in many herbal crafts

Lavender cotton (*Santolina chamaecyparissus*): used in herb wreaths; odor of gray foliage may be too medicinal for sachets or potpourri

Lemon balm (*Melissa officinalis*): used in teas, food, potpourri, and commercially in soap and toilet water

Lemon verbena (*Aloysia triphylla*): highly prized for potpourri and tea

Mints (*Mentha* spp.): fragrant foliage used in teas, potpourris, wreaths, and other herbal crafts; orange mint probably best for fragrance

Pineapple sage (*Salvia elegans*): wonderfully fragrant leaves and scarlet flowers used in wreaths and other herbal crafts

Rosemary (*Rosmarinus officinalis*): fragrant, needlelike leaves used for tea, cooking, and winter sachets

Scented geraniums (*Pelargonium* spp.): fragrant leaves used in sachets and potpourris

Southernwood (*Artemisia abrotanum*): dried branches traditionally hung in closets to repel moths

Sweet woodruff (*Galium odoratum*): leaves especially fragrant when dried; used in potpourri, wreaths, and as a tea

Sweet wormwood (*Artemisia annua*): sweetly aromatic flowers and foliage make good filler material for herbal wreaths

Thymes (*Thymus* spp.): leaves and tops used in sachets and wreaths

## Selecting and Growing Herbs

The plants we call herbs are among the most useful in the garden. They are essential ingredients for flavorful dishes, and also in such diverse activities as crafts and medicine. The following are the most common culinary herbs. Give them a try in your garden!

| Herb | Description | Culture | Comments and Uses |
|---|---|---|---|
| **Basil, sweet** (*Ocimum basilicum*) | Bushy annual with fragrant, oval, 2"–3"-long leaves. Yellow-green leaves; maroon cultivars available. 1'–2'. | Full sun. Rich, moist, well-drained soil. Propagate by seeds. | Excellent fresh or dried in tomato-based dishes; pesto. Plant in herb or flower gardens. Thought to benefit tomato plants when grown near them. |
| **Chamomile, German** (*Matricaria recutita*) | Annual with fuzzy, featherlike leaves and daisylike flowers. 2'–3'. | Full sun. Sandy, well-drained soil. Sow outdoors in spring or fall. Will reseed. | Makes a soothing tea. Adds applelike fragrance of leaves to sachets or arrangements. Fragrant when crushed. |
| **Chervil** (*Anthriscus cerefolium*) | Annual with delicate, fernlike foliage and small white flowers. 1'–2'. | Partial shade. Humusy, moist soil. Propagate by seeds sown where the plants are to grow. Seed requires light to germinate. | Add to soups, stews, just before serving for best flavor. Flowers are used in bouquets. Sow seeds at 2-week intervals for consistent supply. |
| **Chives** (*Allium schoenoprasum*) | Clump-forming, grasslike perennial. Flowers borne in round, $\frac{1}{2}$" clusters. 1'–1$\frac{1}{2}$'. | Full sun. Average, sandy, dry, well-drained soil. Propagate by division, seeds. Zones 4–10. | Use leaves fresh or dried for mild onion flavor. Dried flowers attractive in arrangements. Ornamental for borders, edging. |
| **Coriander** (*Coriandrum sativum*) | Annual with fragrant carrot-like foliage, called cilantro. 2'–3'. | Full sun to partial shade. Moderately rich, light, well-drained soil. Will reseed. | Leaves are added to foods for a bold flavor. Seeds have citrus taste. Attractive plant for borders. |
| **Dill** (*Anethum graveolens*) | Annual with feathery, blue-green foliage. Flat, pale yellow flower clusters yield seeds also used for flavoring. 2$\frac{1}{2}$'–3'. | Full sun. Moderately rich, moist, well-drained soil. Propagate by seeds sown where the plants are to grow. Will reseed. | Seeds and leaves are used in all types of cooking for their strong, tangy flavor. Flowers and leaves dry well. Can be stored frozen. |

*(continued)*

## Selecting and Growing Herbs – Continued

| Herb | Description | Culture | Comments and Uses |
|------|-------------|---------|-------------------|
| **Fennel** (*Foeniculum vulgare*) | Nonhardy perennial with feathery, blue-green foliage with a mild, aniselike flavor. Usually grown as annual. 3'–4'. | Full sun. Average, well-drained soil. Propagate by seeds sown where the plants are to grow. Will reseed. Zones 9–10. | Use fresh leaves in salads; seeds in desserts, breads, beverages. Stems can be eaten like celery. |
| **Garlic** (*Allium sativum, A. ophioscorodon*) | Pungent perennial bulb with blue-green foliage that is also edible. 2'–3'. | Full sun. Deep, rich soil. Plant cloves in fall 4"–6" apart; 1"–2" deep. Harvest when leaves turn brown in summer. | Use fresh leaves for seasoning or pesto. Cure bulbs in a hot, dry, airy place for 2 weeks after harvest. Use chopped in sauces, stews. |
| **Lemon balm** (*Melissa officinalis*) | Loosely branched perennial with square stems and scented, toothed, roundish leaves that are 1"–3" long. $1\frac{1}{2}$'–2'. | Full sun to partial shade. Average, well-drained soil. Propagate by division, cuttings, layering, seeds. Zones 4–5. | Fresh leaves used in cooking for their minty lemon taste. Add dried leaves to potpourris. |
| **Lemon verbena** (*Aloysia triphylla*) | Fragrant, nonhardy shrub with lance-shaped leaves and pale purple flowers. 5'–10'. | Full sun. Rich, moist soil. Propagate by cuttings. Zones 9–10. | Dried leaves make a lemon-lime tea and are good in potpourris. Grow as a houseplant in containers in colder climates. |
| **Marjoram, sweet** (*Origanum majorana*) | Bushy perennial often grown as an annual. Fuzzy, gray green leaves. Tiny white or pink flowers. 1'–$1\frac{1}{2}$'. | Full sun. Light, dry, well-drained soil. Propagate by division, cuttings, seeds. Zones 9–10. | Use fresh or dried leaves and flowers for a mild oregano flavor. Add to potpourris or wreaths. |
| **Mints** (*Mentha* spp.) | Square-stemmed perennials with fragrant leaves and spikes of tiny flowers. 1'–3'. | Full sun to partial shade. Rich, moist, well-drained soil. Propagate by division or cuttings. Zones 5–10. | Many types available—spearmint, pineapple mint, peppermint, apple mint. Use in tea, jelly, candy. Attractive, but can be invasive. |

| Herb | Description | Culture | Comments and Uses |
|------|-------------|---------|-------------------|
| **Oreganos** (*Origanum* spp.) | Perennial with oval, aromatic leaves and spikes of tiny white flowers. 1'–2'. | Full sun. Average, well-drained soil. Propagate by division, cuttings. Zones 5–10. | Used in cooking—tomato sauce, egg dishes. Fragrance and flavor vary; plant named cultivars or strains selected for flavor. |
| **Parsley** (*Petroselinum crispum*) | Biennial with finely cut foliage that comes in curly or flat-leaved forms. 1'–1½'. | Full sun to partial shade. Rich, moist, well-drained soil. Propagate by seeds. | Rich in iron, vitamins A and C. Blends well with other flavorings. Adds color to foods. Used as a garnish. |
| **Rosemary** (*Rosmarinus officinalis*) | Evergreen shrub with aromatic, gray-green, needlelike leaves and purplish blue flowers borne in spikes. 5'–6'. | Full sun to partial shade. Light, well-drained soil. Propagate by division, cuttings, layering. Zones 8–10. | Excellent flavoring in lamb, veal, beef, vegetables. Good in sachets. Can be grown in containers. |
| **Sage, garden** (*Salvia officinalis*) | Wiry-stemmed, low-growing shrub with fuzzy, aromatic gray-green leaves. 1'–2½'. | Full sun. Moderately rich, well-drained soil. Propagate by division, cuttings, layering, seeds. Zones 4–8. | Used as flavoring alone or with other herbs. Leaves dry well. Attractive in gardens. Variegated forms available. |
| **Savory, summer** (*Satureja hortensis*) | Bushy annual with soft, gray, linear leaves. 1'–1½'. | Full sun. Average soil. Propagate by seeds. | Used in cooking for its peppery-thyme flavor. Blends well with other flavorings in vinegars, herb butters, and vegetables. |
| **Tarragon** (*Artemisia dracunculus*) | Perennial with linear, fragrant leaves on wiry stalks. 1½'–2'. | Full to partial shade. Rich, loamy or sandy, well-drained soil. Propagate by division, cuttings. Zones 4–10. | Adds strong flavoring to fish, beef, lamb, vegetables, sauces. Plant near vegetables for healthy growth. |
| **Thyme, common** (*Thymus vulgaris*) | Small prostrate shrub with tiny, roundish, aromatic leaves that are hairy underneath. 9"–12". | Full sun to partial shade. Light, dry, well-drained soil. Propagate by division, cuttings, layering. Zones 5–9. | Adds delicate flavoring to lamb, veal, beef, butter, vegetables. Dried flowers repel insects. Leaves and flowers good in sachets. |

# Chapter 12

# FLOWER GARDENS

What can brighten a yard like flowers? They add color to any yard, whether you use them along the front of your foundation planting, to line a walk leading to a patio, to brighten a shady spot, or throughout your entire landscape. A cutting garden can bring the beauty of flowers into your home—watch a winter-bare bed erupt with purple crocuses and golden daffodils, or the late autumn sun set behind a planting of purple asters and yellow goldenrod, and you won't be able to resist growing more.

In this chapter, you'll learn how to plan and grow a garden full of flowers—annuals, perennials, biennials, bulbs, and roses. You'll also learn how to maintain your garden and keep away pests and diseases, create a meadow, and grow the best flowers for cutting and drying.

Before you get started, you'll find it's helpful to learn about the different types of flowers. See "Words to Know" on the opposite page for more information.

## LANDSCAPING

Although you can use all types of flowers throughout your yard, there are ways to use perennials, annuals, and bulbs to best advantage. Here are some suggestions that will help you plan ways to use them in your landscape.

### LANDSCAPING WITH PERENNIALS

Perennials are all-purpose plants—you can grow them wherever you garden and in any part of

your garden. There's a perennial to fit almost any spot in the landscape, and with a little planning, it's possible to have them in bloom throughout the frost-free months. In addition to an endless variety of sizes, shapes, colors, and plant habits, there are perennials for nearly any cultural condition your garden has to offer.

Most perennials prefer loamy soil with even moisture and full sun. Gardeners who have these conditions to offer have the widest selection of plants from which to choose. However, there are dozens of perennials for shady sites, too. See "Light Up the Shade" on page 273 for more information on growing perennials in shady sites.

Perennials add beauty, permanence, and seasonal rhythm to any landscape. Their yearly growth and flowering cycles are fun to follow—it's always exciting to see the first peonies pushing out of the ground in April or the asters braving another November day. Here are some ways to use perennials effectively in your yard.

**Borders:** If you have a fairly long area that could use some color, such as a fence, a rock wall, or the side of a building, consider a perennial border. Group plants with similar requirements for soil, moisture, and sunlight. Also plan for pleasing color combinations and arrange them by height, form, and texture to create garden pictures. (For more on how to do this, see "Designing a Garden" on page 276.)

**Beds:** Another way to use perennials is in beds. A bed differs from a border in that it is freestanding, without an immediate background

**Words to Know**

**Annual:** An annual is a plant that completes its life cycle in one year; it germinates, grows, flowers, sets seed, and dies in one growing season. Many plants we grow as annuals, such as zonal geraniums, are actually tender perennials.

**Hardy annual:** An annual that tolerates frost and self-sows. Seeds overwinter outside and germinate the following year. Examples: annual candytuft, cleome.

**Half-hardy annual:** An annual that can withstand light frost. Seeds can be planted early. Plants can be set out in fall and will bloom the following year. Often called winter annual. Examples: pansies, snapdragons, sweet peas.

**Tender annual:** An annual that is easily killed by light frost. Most annuals are in this category. Examples: marigolds, petunias.

**Biennial:** A plant that completes its life cycle in two years, producing a rosette of foliage the first and flowers the second. Biennials can reseed and come back year after year like perennials. Examples: foxglove, sweet William.

**Bulb:** A diverse group of perennial plants, including true bulbs, corms, rhizomes, and tuberous roots—all structures that store nutrients to support growth and bloom.

**True bulb:** True bulbs have layers of food-storing scales around a flower stalk and leaves in the center. They're often covered with a papery skin, called the *tunic*. Examples: onions, daffodils, tulips, lilies, hyacinths.

**Corm:** A corm is a rounded, swollen stem covered with a papery tunic. Corms are solid, with a bud on top that produces leaves and flowers. Examples: crocuses, gladioli.

**Tuber:** Tubers are fleshy underground stems that have eyes or buds from which leaves and flowers grow. Some tubers, such as caladiums

and tuberous begonias, are cormlike. Unlike corms, tubers sprout roots from the sides and top. Examples: potatoes, anemones.

**Tuberous root:** Tuberous roots are swollen, fleshy roots. They have a pointed bud on top; roots sprout from the bottom. Example: dahlias.

**Rhizome:** Rhizomes masquerade as roots, but are actually thick, horizontal stems with roots on the bottom and leaves and flowers on the top. Examples: callas, cannas, bearded irises.

**Little bulbs:** A general term used to refer collectively to the many species of small, hardy bulbs, especially spring-blooming ones. Examples: crocuses, snowdrops, squills, grape hyacinths.

**Perennial:** A plant that flowers and sets seed for two or more seasons. Short-lived perennials like coreopsis and columbines may live 3 to 5 years. Long-lived perennials like peonies may live 100 years or more.

**Tender perennial:** A perennial plant from tropical or subtropical regions that can't be overwintered outside, except in subtropical regions such as Florida and Southern California. Often grown as annuals. Examples: zonal geraniums, wax begonias, coleus.

**Hardy perennial:** A perennial plant that tolerates frost. Cold tolerance of hardy perennials is ranked by zone.

**Herbaceous perennial:** A perennial plant that dies back to the ground each season. Most garden perennials fall into this category.

**Semiwoody perennial:** A perennial plant that forms woody stems but is much less substantial than a shrub. Examples: lavender, some varieties of thyme.

**Woody perennial:** A perennial plant such as a shrub or tree that does not die down to the ground each year.

**Flowers in the landscape.** Most gardens have more than one ideal spot for displaying annuals, perennials, bulbs, and roses. Use a border of flowers to soften a fence, or set them off against a backdrop such as an outbuilding or a hedge of evergreens or shrubs. Use island beds the way you would an ornamental pool or specimen shrub—floating gracefully in the lawn. Specimen plants work as an exclamation in the landscape, drawing the eye. Choose large, dramatic-looking plants like Siberian iris (*Iris sibirica*).

such as a fence or wall. Plant beds to add color and drama to the sides of a path, use them to define the edge of a patio or deck, or create an island bed in your lawn to relieve all that green with a bright splash of color. Plant the tallest plants in the center of the bed, using progressively shorter plants toward the edges.

**Specimen plants:** Larger perennials make striking specimen plants. You can use them in the landscape wherever you want an accent but don't want to feature something as large or heavy-looking as a shrub or tree. Try a large clump of peonies at the corner of the house or use a specimen plant to point visitors to a specific view of the yard or mark the beginning of a path. For example, use a bold accent like a very large-leaved hosta at a bend in a shady garden path to attract attention and pull visitors into the garden.

## LANDSCAPING WITH ANNUALS

When most people think of annuals they think of color, and lots of it. Annuals are garden favorites because of their continuous season-long bloom. Colors run the spectrum from cool to hot, subtle to shocking. Plants are as varied in form, texture, and size as they are in color.

Annuals have as many uses as there are places to use them. They are excellent for providing garden color from early summer until frost. They fill in gaps between newly planted perennials. They are popular as cut flowers. Annuals

##  Light Up the Shade

You can use flowers to turn problem shady sites where lawn grass won't grow, such as under trees or between buildings, into an asset by creating a shade garden. Many perennials tolerate shade, but remember that shade plants often have brief periods of bloom. For the most successful shade garden, you should count on the plants' foliage to carry the garden through the seasons. The most engaging shade gardens rely on combinations of large-, medium-, and small-leaved plants with different leaf textures. For example, try mixing ferns with variegated hostas, astilbes, Virginia bluebells (*Mertensia virginica*), and shade-tolerant groundcovers like Allegheny foamflower (*Tiarella cordifolia*) and creeping phlox (*Phlox stolonifera*) to create a diverse mix of size, foliage, and texture. See "Classic Groundcovers for Shade" on page 333 for more ideas for shade-loving groundcovers.

There are dozens of choice perennials to brighten a shady site. Most prefer woodland conditions: rich, moist, well-drained soil and cool temperatures. Plants that tolerate deep shade include species of *Brunnera*, *Cimicifuga*, *Epimedium*, *Heuchera*, *Hosta*, *Mertensia*, *Polygonatum*, and *Pulmonaria*. Many plants in this list grow well in partial shade; the plant name is followed by bloom time and color:

Columbines (*Aquilegia* spp.); spring to early summer; all colors, bicolors

Alumroots (*Heuchera* spp.); spring to summer; pink, red, white, green

Astilbes (*Astilbe* spp.); late spring to summer; red, pink, white

Bergenias (*Bergenia* spp.); early spring; rose, pink, purple, white

Bleeding hearts (*Dicentra* spp.); spring; rose, pink, white

Bugbanes (*Cimicifuga* spp.); summer to fall; white

Epimediums (*Epimedium* spp.); spring; pink, red, yellow, white

Hellebores (*Helleborus* spp.); early spring; white, rose, green, purple

Hostas (*Hosta* spp.); early to late summer; violet, lilac, white

Jacob's ladders (*Polemonium* spp.); spring to summer; blue, pink, white, yellow

Lungworts (*Pulmonaria* spp.); spring; purple-blue, blue, red

Siberian bugloss (*Brunnera macrophylla*); spring; light blue

Solomon's seals (*Polygonatum* spp.); spring; white, white-green

Virginia bluebells (*Mertensia virginica*); spring; blue, white

Most spring bulbs, like daffodils, and little bulbs, like crocuses, do beautifully in shade gardens. They also provide color in early spring before most perennials get started.

And don't forget annuals and biennials to perk up your shady sites throughout the entire summer season. The jewel-like tones of impatiens or coleus will brighten even the darkest areas under trees. It's surprising how many annuals do tolerate shade. Impatiens, lobelia (*Lobelia erinus*), and wishbone flower (*Torenia fournieri*) will all tolerate full shade. Pansies, wax begonias, Madagascar periwinkle (*Catharanthus roseus*), summer forget-me-not (*Anchusa capensis*), and sapphire flowers (*Browallia* spp.) are all outstanding annuals for partially shaded sites. Biennials for shade include foxglove, forget-me-nots, Canterbury bells (*Campanula medium*), and money plant (*Lunaria annua*).

can make even the shadiest areas of the late-summer garden brighter. And since you replace annuals every year, you can create new garden designs with different color schemes as often as you would like.

You can use annuals alone or in combination with perennials or other kinds of plants. Bedding out is the traditional way of using annuals. The Victorians created extensive, colorful displays, usually with intricate patterns against emerald lawns, called bedding schemes. That's why annuals are often called bedding plants.

You can take a tip from the Victorians and create formal or informal designs in island beds or in borders. Fences, hedges, and brick or stone walls all make attractive backdrops for annual gardens. Annuals are also a good choice for outlining or edging garden spaces. Petunias, marigolds, begonias, and zinnias are ideal for beds in the sunny garden.

Many perennials are slow-growing by nature, so the average perennial garden takes up to three years to look its best. Annuals are perfect for filling in the gaps between new perennials

---

 **Perennials for Dry Soil**

These tough plants tolerate both heat *and* dry soil, making them useful for spots that the hose can't reach and nice for sunny meadow gardens. Some actually grow invasive and weedy in rich, moist soils, while others survive drought but suffer in humid conditions. All prefer well-drained soil, regardless of the amount of water they receive. The plant name is followed by bloom time and color:

Artemisias (*Artemisia* spp.); summer; gray, white, yellow

Baptisias (*Baptisia* spp.); spring to summer; blue, white, yellow

Blanket flower (*Gaillardia* × *grandiflora*); summer; red, yellow

Blue flax (*Linum perenne*); spring; blue

Common thrift (*Armeria maritima*); summer; pink, white

Coneflowers (*Rudbeckia* spp.); summer; yellow

Coreopsis (*Coreopsis* spp.); spring to summer; yellow

Daylilies (*Hemerocallis* spp.); spring to summer; all colors except blue

Globe thistle (*Echinops ritro*); summer; dark blue

Golden Marguerite (*Anthemis tinctoria*); summer; yellow, orange

Goldenrods (*Solidago* spp.); late summer to fall; yellow

Lamb's-ears (*Stachys* spp.); spring; purple

Pinks (*Dianthus* spp.); spring; pink, red, white, yellow

Sages (*Salvia* spp.); summer to fall; all colors

Sea hollies (*Eryngium* spp.); summer; blue, silver-blue

Sedums (*Sedum* spp.); spring to fall; yellow, pink, white

Spurge (*Euphorbia* spp.); spring to summer; yellow, red

Statice (*Limonium* spp.); summer; blue, red, white, yellow

Tall gayfeather (*Liatris scariosa*); summer; purple, white

Torch lilies (*Kniphofia* spp.); late spring; red, orange

Yarrows (*Achillea* spp.); spring to summer; yellow, white, red

Yuccas (*Yucca* spp.); summer; white

and carrying the garden through the first few seasons. Take care not to crowd or overwhelm the permanent plants—try mid-season pruning or staking of overly enthusiastic annuals.

## LANDSCAPING WITH BULBS

In spring, most gardeners' fancies turn to thoughts of bulbs—especially crocuses, daffodils, and tulips. But bulbs light up the garden throughout the year. Dahlias, lilies, glads, and many other familiar flowers are classified as bulbs. Here are some effective ways to use bulbs in your landscape:

**Bulbs with groundcovers:** Bulbs grow beautifully in groundcovers. There's nothing like a dark green groundcover background to make daffodils sparkle. Try them with pachysandra, English ivy, prostrate junipers or common periwinkle (*Vinca minor*). Lawn grass is one groundcover that does not combine well with tall spring bulbs like daffodils. The reason is simple: Bulb foliage needs 8 to 12 weeks to ripen after bloom so the bulb can store enough food for the following season. By the time the

---

 **Perennials for Moist Soil**

Grow these perennials where you have a poorly drained or boggy spot in your yard. True to their streamside origins, most of these perennials prefer at least partial shade and cool nights. Species of *Caltha, Chelone, Filipendula, Iris, Lobelia, Lysimachia, Rodgersia,* and *Thalictrum* tolerate full sun, while *Hibiscus, Tradescantia,* and *Vernonia* demand it. The plant name is followed by bloom time and color:

Astilbes (*Astilbe* spp.); late spring to summer; red, pink, white

Bee balm (*Monarda didyma*); summer; red, white, pink, purple

Bonesets (*Eupatorium* spp.); late summer to fall; purple, blue, white

Bugbanes (*Cimicifuga* spp.); late summer to fall; white

Common sneezeweed (*Helenium autumnale*); late summer; yellow, bronze

Globeflowers (*Trollius* spp.); spring; orange, yellow

Goat's beards (*Aruncus* spp.); late spring; creamy white

Great blue lobelia (*Lobelia siphilitica*); late summer; blue

Japanese iris (*Iris ensata*); summer; pink, blue, purple, white

Japanese primrose (*Primula japonica*); late spring; pink, red, white, purple

Loosestrifes (*Lysimachia* spp.); early to late summer; yellow, white

Marsh marigold (*Caltha palustris*); spring; yellow

Meadow rues (*Thalictrum* spp.); summer; lilac, pink, yellow, white

Meadowsweets (*Filipendula* spp.); summer; pink, white

Rodgersias (*Rodgersia* spp.); late spring to summer; creamy white, red

Siberian iris (*Iris sibirica*); spring; blue, white, purple, wine red

Spiderworts (*Tradescantia* spp.); summer; blue, pink, white, red

Virginia bluebells (*Mertensia virginica*); spring; blue, white

White turtlehead (*Chelone glabra*); summer; white with red tinge

Yellow flag (*Iris pseudacorus*); early summer; yellow

daffodil or tulip foliage is ripe, the grass would be knee-high! If you enjoy the sight of blooming bulbs in your lawn, plant low-growing species like crocuses because their foliage generally matures before grass needs cutting.

**Bulbs with perennials:** With the exception of tender bulbs like cannas (*Canna* spp.) and dahlias that must be dug every year or treated as annuals, bulbs are perennial and should be used like perennial flowers. In fact, they're ideal companions for perennials. In spring, bulbs add color to the perennial garden when little else is in bloom, and perennials hide unsightly bulb foliage while it ripens. Peonies, hostas, daylilies, irises, and asters are especially good with bulbs.

**Bulbs with trees and shrubs:** Don't forget the beautiful show spring-blooming bulbs make under deciduous trees and shrubs. For best results, avoid planting bulbs under trees such as beeches and some maples that have very aggressive surface roots, which will out-compete the bulbs.

**Bulbs with annuals:** Annuals are perfect plants for covering dying bulb foliage or gaps in the flower border left by dormant bulbs. Marigolds, snapdragons, wax begonias, impatiens, and zinnias are all good "filler" annuals.

**Bulbs with other bulbs:** Don't forget about planting bulbs with bulbs. Clumps of mixed daffodils, or scatterings of other types of spring-blooming bulbs such as tulips or crocuses are well-known signs of spring.

# DESIGNING A GARDEN

Designing a flower garden—especially one that features perennials—may seem overwhelming at first since there are so many to choose from. But chances are your growing conditions are right for only a fraction of what's available. Let

---

 **Flowers for Containers**

To add color and excitement to a deck, patio, balcony, or entryway, try containers filled with annuals and perennials. You can mix several types of annuals or perennials together, combine the two, or plant just a single perennial per container.

Annuals are perfect container plants. Their fast growth, easy culture, and low cost make them irresistible for pots, window boxes, and planters. You can start container gardening in early spring with pansies. Summer and fall bring endless choices for sun or shade. Zonal geraniums, ornamental cabbages, and snapdragons remain attractive until hard frost. Tender perennials that are usually grown as annuals, including zonal geraniums, coleus, and lantana (*Lantana* spp.) can also be pruned and brought indoors for the winter.

Many perennials also grow well in containers. Try a daylily in a half barrel in a sunny spot or hostas with variegated foliage in a shady one. Ornamental grasses make very attractive container specimens, as do most herbs. Since containers dry out quickly, choose plants that tolerate some dryness for best results.

Whatever you plant, select as large a container as you can comfortably manage. Small containers dry out far too quickly and create extra work. Be sure all the containers you use have drainage holes. Choose a light soil mix that drains well but holds moisture. Don't overplant: Crowded plants don't bloom well and require constant watering. Fertilize containers regularly with a balanced organic fertilizer.

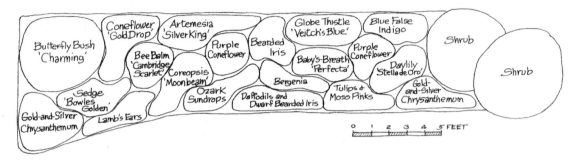

Butterfly Bush 'Charming'

Coneflower 'Gold Drop'

Artemesia 'Silver King'

Bee Balm 'Cambridge Scarlet'

Purple Coneflower

Bearded Iris

Coreopsis 'Moonbeam'

Globe Thistle 'Veitch's Blue'

Blue False Indigo

Baby's-Breath 'Perfecta'

Purple Coneflower

Daylily 'Stella de Oro'

Shrub

Shrub

Ozark Sundrops

Bergenia

Daffodils and Dwarf Bearded Iris

Tulips & Moss Pinks

Gold-and-Silver Chrysanthemum

Sedge 'Bowles Golden'

Gold-and-Silver Chrysanthemum

Lamb's Ears

0  1  2  3  4  5 FEET

**Making a bubble diagram.** When you have an idea for the size and shape of your garden, draw its outline to scale on graph paper (1 inch on paper equals 1 foot of ground is a good scale for most gardens). Use a pencil so you can "move" things around easily, and don't be afraid to make changes. Then draw in circles or "bubbles" to represent your plants, making the scale of each bubble match the mature width of the plant. Write in the plant name, color, and bloom season in each bubble if you have room, so you can see at a glance how the combinations are likely to look.

your moisture, soil, and light conditions limit the plants you choose. If you have a garden bed that gets full sun and tends toward dry soil, don't plant shade- and moisture-loving perennials like hostas and ferns. Instead, put in plants that like full sun and don't like wet feet, like daylilies and ornamental grasses. And don't forget to choose plants that are hardy in your area.

The first step in planning a flower garden is to choose the site you'd like to plant. If you're determined to grow sun-loving plants, the site should receive six to eight hours of direct sun. It's also best to select a site with good air circulation and shelter from strong winds. Take some time to examine your chosen site and learn about its soil and other characteristics so you can select plants that will grow well there. For more information on site and plant selection, see "Sizing Up Your Site" on page 5 and "Plants and Design" on page 10.

When you've picked a site, outline the shape and size of your proposed bed right on the spot with a garden hose or string. Next, draw a rough sketch showing the shape of the bed, then measure and record the dimensions. Indicate north on your sketch with an arrow. Next,

draw the shape of your bed or border to scale on a piece of graph paper. A good scale to begin with is one that assumes 1 inch on paper equals 1 foot of garden area. If your garden is extremely large, use a formula such as 1 inch equals 2 feet or 1 inch equals 3 feet. To make a plant list and draw a design, you'll also need regular and colored pencils or crayons, a tablet of paper (for plant lists), tracing paper, and a soft eraser.

To get an idea of how many plants you'll need, consider the approximate size at maturity of the types of plants you want to include in your garden. Perennial plants generally need 2 to 4 square feet at maturity; that means you can fit between 30 and 60 of them in a 125-square-foot garden. Shrubs and small trees may need 9 to 25 square feet or more.

## SELECTING PLANTS

While it's relatively easy to plan and plant an annual garden, selecting plants for a perennial garden is a challenge. There are literally thousands to choose from and a confusing array of flower colors, sizes, shapes, and textures. Start with a list of favorite plants, then add ones you've admired in other gardens, nurseries,

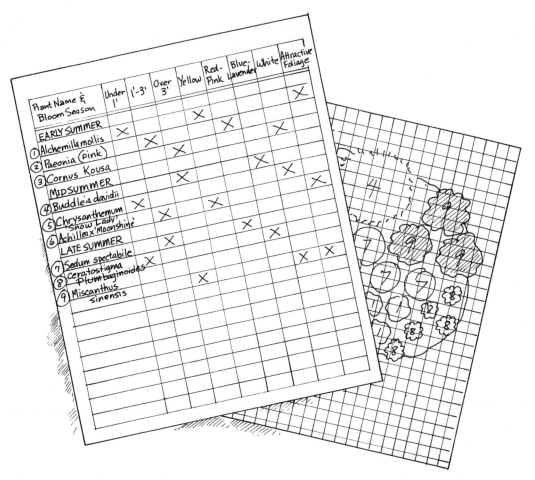

**Drawing your design.** Make a chartlike plant list that's organized according to season of bloom, and indicate plant height and color. Then use the list to locate plants on your design.

photographs, books, magazines, and nursery catalogs. Leave plenty of space between plants for making notes. Jot down plant descriptions, growing tips, bloom time, height, color, hardiness, and culture.

Keep an eye out for perennials with good foliage and a long season of bloom. Trees and shrubs with winter interest—like evergreens or ones with ornamental bark or branching habits—are also invaluable. Don't worry about making your list too long.

Periodically review your list and cross off plants that won't grow well in the site and don't fit your needs. If you have only shade to offer, cross off plants that need full sun. Do you want only easy-care plants? Eliminate those that need staking or deadheading to look their best. Do you want to save on water bills? Cross off any that may need supplemental watering.

## CHARTING YOUR SELECTIONS

Next, make a chart to help identify plants that will add the most to your design. On a clean sheet of paper, make a column on the left labeled "Plant Name and Bloom Season." Draw lines across the page at intervals to indicate sections for each season of bloom (see the illustration on the opposite page). If you have a large garden, you can use a separate sheet for each bloom season. Write down the bloom seasons you want in the first column—early, mid-, and late summer, for example. Leave enough space under each season to list plant names.

Divide the right side of the paper into three or four columns to indicate plant heights and another three or four columns to indicate flower colors. Add an extra column to indicate plants with attractive foliage or winter interest.

Starting with the first plant on your list, enter it under the appropriate bloom season on your chart. Then indicate height and color with an "X" in the appropriate columns. Repeat this process for each plant on your list. When you finish, look the chart over to make sure you have a fairly equal representation of "X's" under each column. Will some flowers of each color be blooming in each season? Are there a variety of heights? Add and subtract plants until you have a balance in all the categories and a manageable number of plants to grow. Last, number the plants on your list. Use these numbers to fill in the spaces as you draw your garden.

## DRAWING YOUR DESIGN

To draw your design, use tracing paper over the scale drawing of your garden that you made on graph paper. That way, you can start over easily if you need to. Begin drawing shapes on the paper to indicate where each plant will grow. Try to draw them to scale, based on the sizes you charted as described above. Instead of drawing neat circles or blocks, use oval or oblong shapes that will flow into one another.

Arrange plants, especially perennials and small shrubs, in clumps of several plants. Because of the basic design principles of balance and repetition, you'll want to repeat clumps of at least some species. As a general rule, you'll probably want half as many species of plants on your list as the number of individual plants you can fit in your border. In the example on page 277, that would mean 15 to 30 species.

Beginning with the first plant on your list, study its "profile" and decide where you want to plant it in the garden. Transfer its name or number to the corresponding shape—or shapes if you want to repeat it in more than one spot—on your diagram. Do this with all the plants that are on your list.

As you work, you'll have to decide how many of each plant you want to grow. You may wish to follow the "rule of three" for perennials that are relatively small at maturity. Three plants will make an attractive clump when mature. For large plants, such as peonies, you may want only one plant; for others, two. See "Basic Design Principles" on page 9 for more information on balance, proportion, and other design strategies. Also consider color combinations as you work, and avoid large masses of single colors. The illustration on page 280 shows some ways you can visualize your design.

As you grapple with these problems and refine your design, be sure to make changes on both the tracing paper and your master diagram. Expect to have to redo your design several times before you feel you have it right. Each sheet of crumpled paper brings you closer to your goal of creating a beautiful garden.

When you're ready to make your garden plan a reality, it's time to head out to the nursery or pick up the plant catalogs and buy your plants. For a detailed discussion of buying and planting, see Chapter 5.

# MAINTAINING THE GARDEN

Your flower garden will need basic routine care to keep it in top-notch form. If you've prepared the soil well before planting, planted carefully, and mulched your garden, you'll be well on your way to a healthy, vigorous garden. Here are some points for keeping your flowers looking their best. You'll find more information on caring for your plants in Chapter 8.

## START WITH THE BASICS

Weeding, watering, staking—these are just a few of the regular chores required to keep your flower garden blooming beautifully. The care

## Make a Design Reality Check

To visualize how your garden will look at each season, put a sheet of tracing paper over your completed design. Check your plant list to find out which plants bloom in early summer, for example. Trace the plants blooming at that time onto your tracing paper. Then use crayons to color them the appropriate color. Do the same for the other seasons of bloom, using a separate sheet of tracing paper for each season's drawing.

Ideally, you'll want a balanced composition in every season, with the colors evenly distributed during each bloom period. Are all the reds or yellows off to one side so that the design looks lopsided? Are the color combinations pleasing to you? Are major color combinations repeated at rhythmic intervals to tie the border together? Would it help to add more plants of a particular color?

Another way to check your design, shown here, is to make a paper garden with color cut from plant catalogs and magazines.

**A design reality check.** To make sure your paper garden really works, put a sheet of tracing paper over your bubble diagram. Using the bubbles as a guide, draw in the shapes of your plants—shrubby, spiky, mounded, and so forth. Make a copy for each bloom season. To see if the colors really work well together, find color photos of all the plants in your design. Cut out strips of each photo and position them on the design according to bloom season, with spring-blooming plants on one copy, summer-blooming plants on another, and so on.

you lavish upon your flower garden throughout the year will pay off with strong growth and flowering year after year. Here's a rundown on the basics of garden care.

**Weeding** Weeds compete for water, nutrients, and light, so weeding is a necessary evil. Catch them while they're small and the task will seem easier. A light mulch of bark or shredded leaves allows water to infiltrate and keeps the weeds down.

**Watering** Most plants need 1 inch per week for best growth. Bog and pond plants require a continual supply of water. Dry-soil plants are more tolerant of a low water supply, but during the hottest summer months, even they may need watering. Water with a soaker hose where possible and mulch to conserve soil moisture and cut down on watering.

**Staking** Staking may be necessary for thin-stemmed plants such as coreopsis, yarrow, and garden phlox. Extremely tall plants such as delphiniums require sturdy stakes to keep flower spikes from snapping off. Heavy, mounding flowers like peonies may need hoop supports (circular wire supports set up on legs) to keep their faces out of the mud. You can also stake up a clump of plants by circling it with twine, then tying the twine to a sturdy stake. The illustration on page 207 shows several different staking options.

**Pinching** Pinching keeps plants bushy. Plants like chrysanthemums and asters have a tendency to grow tall and flop. Pinch them once or twice in the spring to encourage production of side shoots. Early pinching promotes compact growth without sacrificing bloom.

**Thinning** Plants like delphiniums and phlox produce so many stems that the growth becomes crowded and vigor is reduced. Cut out excess stems to increase air circulation and promote larger flowers on the remaining stems.

**Disbudding** Disbudding is another technique used to increase flower size. Peonies and chrysanthemums produce many buds around each main bud. Simply pinch off all but the largest bud to improve your floral display.

**Deadheading** Removing spent flowers will help promote production of new buds in many plants. Just pinch or cut off faded flowers, or shear bushy plants just below the flower heads if the plant blooms all at once. Some perennials like baptisias and 'Autumn Joy' sedum will not rebloom, and their seed heads are decorative. Leave these for winter interest in the garden.

**Winterizing** In autumn, begin preparing the perennial garden for winter. Remove dead foliage and old flowers. After the first frost, cut down dead stems and remove to the ground other growth that will die. (Leave ornamental grasses and other plants that add winter interest.) After the ground freezes, protect plants from root damage as a result of frost heaving with a thick mulch of oak leaves or marsh hay. Evergreen boughs are also good for this purpose. Snow is the best insulator of all, but most of us can't count on continuous snow cover. Mulching helps keep the ground frozen during periods of warm weather.

## ❀ Don't Starve Your Bulbs

Spring bulbs need at least eight weeks of leaf growth after bloom in order to produce food for the next season's blooms. Don't braid foliage or bind it with rubber bands while waiting for it to ripen. This actually harms the bulbs—it cuts off sunlight and air, hampers flower production, and encourages rot. Instead, allow bulb foliage to die naturally. Don't rush to mow or cut it off. Wait until the foliage begins to turn yellow and fall over, then cut it.

**Pinching, disbudding, and deadheading.** Pinch out the growing tips of each stem of perennials like this chrysanthe-mum (*left*) for bushier plants with more flowers. To disbud perennials like this dahlia (*center*) for fewer but larger blooms, pinch out side buds, leaving only the central or highest bud in each cluster. Deadhead flowers like this daylily (*right*) by pinching or cutting off spent flowers.

**Dividing**   Sooner or later, even the slow-growing perennials become crowded and need dividing. Divide plants in spring or fall in the North and in the fall in the South. (Some plants, such as peonies, should only be dug in the fall.) Some fast growers like bee balms, chrysanthemums, and asters should be lifted every 2 to 3 years. Other perennials such as peonies, daylilies, and hostas only need dividing when they've become overgrown. You'll know a clump is overgrown because it looks crowded, doesn't have as large or as many blooms as it used to, and may have died out in the center. See Chapter 6 for instructions on dividing perennials.

**Controlling Pests and Diseases**   The best way to avoid problems is with good cultural practices, good maintenance, and early detec-tion. Healthy plants develop fewer problems. Here are a few simple tips:

■ Water early in the day to enable plants to dry before evening. This helps prevent leaf spots and other fungal and bacterial problems.

■ Don't overwater. Waterlogged soil is an invitation to root rot organisms.

■ Remove old flowers and yellowing foliage to destroy hiding places for pests.

■ Remove plants that develop viral infections and dispose of them.

■ Never put diseased plants in the compost.

■ Early detection of insects means easy con-trol. Many insects can be controlled by treating the plants with a spray of water from a hose. Treat severe infestations with appropriate organic control such as a soap-spray solution. Follow label recommendations.

See the illustrations on pages 284 and 285 for information on some of the most common flower garden pests and diseases. For more on pest and disease control, see Chapter 7.

# GROWING ROSES

The rose is the best-loved flower of all time, a symbol of beauty and love. Roses have it all—color, fragrance, and great shape. Many roses produce flowers from early summer until frost, often beginning the first year of planting.

The members of the genus *Rosa* are prickly stemmed shrubs with a wide range of heights and growth habits. There are as many as 200 species and thousands of cultivars, from miniatures less than 6 inches tall to rampant climbers growing to 20 feet or more. And you can find roses in gardens in just about every climate around the world.

Over the years, roses have gained a reputation for being difficult to grow. But many of the "old roses," plus a great number of the newer cultivars, are disease-resistant, widely adaptable plants able to withstand cold winters and hot summers.

## SELECTING ROSES

With so many roses available, deciding on the ones you want may be the hardest part of growing them. To begin making choices, it helps to understand the differences among roses. This large, diverse genus can be divided into three major types: bush, climbing, and shrub roses.

**Bush Roses**  Bush roses form the largest category, which has been divided into six subgroups: hybrid tea, polyantha, floribunda, grandiflora, miniature, heritage (old), and tree (standard) roses. Here's a rundown:

■ Hybrid tea roses usually have narrow buds, each borne singly on a long stem, with large, many-petaled flowers on plants 3 to 5 feet tall. Hybrid teas bloom repeatedly over the entire growing season.

■ Polyantha roses are short, compact plants with small flowers produced abundantly in large clusters throughout the growing season. Plants are very hardy and easy to grow.

■ Floribunda roses were derived from crosses between hybrid teas and polyanthas. They are hardy, compact plants with medium-sized flowers borne profusely in short-stemmed clusters. They bloom all summer long and are easily grown.

■ Grandiflora roses are tall (5 to 6 feet), narrow plants bearing large flowers in long-stemmed clusters from summer through fall.

■ Miniature roses are diminutive, with both flowers and foliage proportionately smaller. Most are quite hardy and bloom freely and repeatedly.

■ Heritage (old) roses are a widely diverse group available prior to 1867, the date of the introduction of the first hybrid tea rose. Plant and flower forms, hardiness, and ease of growth vary considerably; some bloom only once, while others flower repeatedly. Among the most popular of the old roses are the albas, bourbons, centifolias, damasks, gallicas, mosses, and portlands; also some species roses.

■ Tree (standard) roses are created when any rose is bud-grafted onto a specially grown trunk 1 to 6 feet tall.

**Climbing Roses**  Roses don't truly climb, but the long, flexible canes of certain roses make it possible to attach them to supports such as fences, arbors, and trellises. The two main types are large-flowered climbers, with thick, sturdy canes growing to 10 feet long and blooms produced throughout the summer; and ramblers, with thin canes growing 20 feet or

*(continued on page 286)*

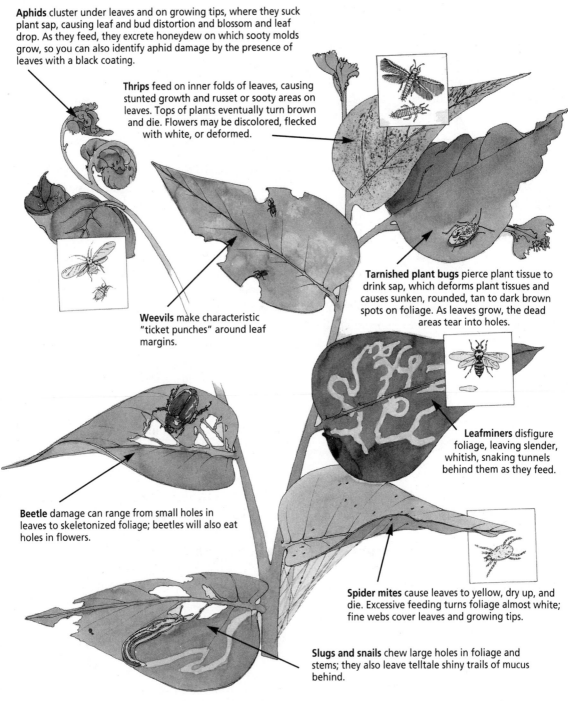

**Aphids** cluster under leaves and on growing tips, where they suck plant sap, causing leaf and bud distortion and blossom and leaf drop. As they feed, they excrete honeydew on which sooty molds grow, so you can also identify aphid damage by the presence of leaves with a black coating.

**Thrips** feed on inner folds of leaves, causing stunted growth and russet or sooty areas on leaves. Tops of plants eventually turn brown and die. Flowers may be discolored, flecked with white, or deformed.

**Weevils** make characteristic "ticket punches" around leaf margins.

**Tarnished plant bugs** pierce plant tissue to drink sap, which deforms plant tissues and causes sunken, rounded, tan to dark brown spots on foliage. As leaves grow, the dead areas tear into holes.

**Leafminers** disfigure foliage, leaving slender, whitish, snaking tunnels behind them as they feed.

**Beetle** damage can range from small holes in leaves to skeletonized foliage; beetles will also eat holes in flowers.

**Spider mites** cause leaves to yellow, dry up, and die. Excessive feeding turns foliage almost white; fine webs cover leaves and growing tips.

**Slugs and snails** chew large holes in foliage and stems; they also leave telltale shiny trails of mucus behind.

**Flower pests—an overview.** You can often identify pests by the type of damage they cause. Here's a look at the most common garden pests and their destructive ways.

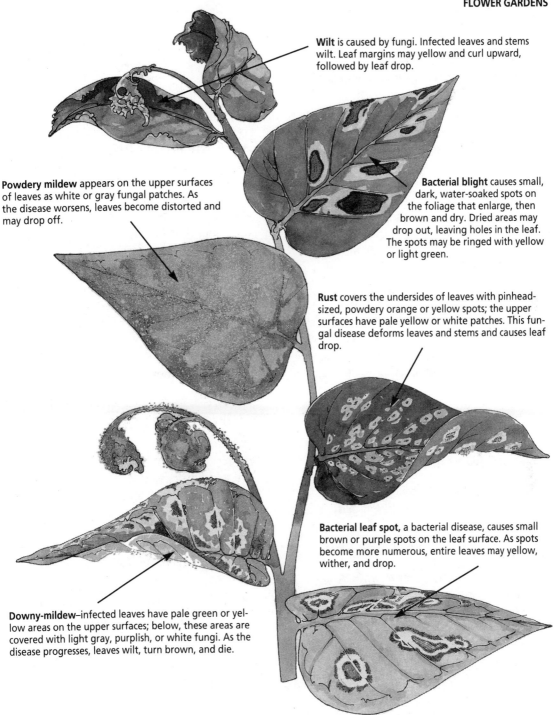

**Wilt** is caused by fungi. Infected leaves and stems wilt. Leaf margins may yellow and curl upward, followed by leaf drop.

**Powdery mildew** appears on the upper surfaces of leaves as white or gray fungal patches. As the disease worsens, leaves become distorted and may drop off.

**Bacterial blight** causes small, dark, water-soaked spots on the foliage that enlarge, then brown and dry. Dried areas may drop out, leaving holes in the leaf. The spots may be ringed with yellow or light green.

**Rust** covers the undersides of leaves with pinhead-sized, powdery orange or yellow spots; the upper surfaces have pale yellow or white patches. This fungal disease deforms leaves and stems and causes leaf drop.

**Bacterial leaf spot,** a bacterial disease, causes small brown or purple spots on the leaf surface. As spots become more numerous, entire leaves may yellow, wither, and drop.

**Downy-mildew**–infected leaves have pale green or yellow areas on the upper surfaces; below, these areas are covered with light gray, purplish, or white fungi. As the disease progresses, leaves wilt, turn brown, and die.

**Flower diseases—an overview.** You can treat diseases most effectively if you learn to recognize their symptoms. Here's a look at flower disease symptoms.

more and flowers borne in early summer.

**Shrub Roses**  Shrub roses grow broadly upright with numerous arching canes reaching 4 to 12 feet tall. Most are very hardy and easily grown. Some only bloom once in early summer, while others bloom repeatedly during the summer. Many produce showy red or scarlet fruits called hips. Some species roses are considered shrub roses.

**Groundcover Roses**  Groundcover roses are sometimes included with shrub roses. These have prostrate, creeping canes producing low mounds; there are once-blooming and repeat-blooming cultivars.

## USING ROSES IN THE LANDSCAPE

To grow well, roses need a site that gets full sun at least 6 hours a day, with humus-rich soil and good drainage. If these conditions are met, you can use roses just about anywhere in the landscape. Try roses in foundation plantings, shrub borders, along walks and driveways, surrounding patios, decks, and terraces, or in flower beds and borders. Combine roses with other plants, especially other shrubs or perennials. You'll get the greatest visual impact by massing roses of a single color or cultivar.

Use climbing roses to cover walls, screen or frame views, or decorate fences, arbors, trellises, and gazebos. Grow groundcover roses on banks or trailing over walls. Plant hedges of shrub, grandiflora, and floribunda roses. For a single-row hedge, space plants 2 feet apart; for a wider hedge, stagger rows with 1½ feet between rows and 2½ feet between plants.

You can also grow roses in containers. For all roses except miniatures, choose a container at least 14 inches deep and 1½ feet wide. You can grow miniatures in pots as small as 6 inches in diameter. Use a soilless potting mix; fertilize and water regularly. In all but frost-free climates, overwinter pots in an unheated garage or basement.

## GROWING GOOD ROSES

The key to growing roses successfully is to remember that they need plenty of water, humus, and nutrients.

**Soil**  Prepare a new site in fall for planting the following spring, or in summer for fall planting. If you plan to grow roses with existing plants, then no special preparation is needed. For a new site, dig or till the soil to a depth of at least 1 foot. Evenly distribute a 4-inch layer of organic material such as peat moss, compost, leaf mold, or dehydrated cow manure over the soil surface. Also spread on fertilizer. A general recommendation is to add 5 pounds of bonemeal and 10 pounds of greensand or granite dust per 100 square feet. Dig or till the fertilizer and soil amendments into the soil.

**Planting**  For much of the West Coast, South, and Southwest, or wherever winter temperatures reach no colder than 10°F, the best

---

## Know Your Roses

Whether they're sold locally or by mail order, roses are sold by grade, which is based on the size and number of canes. Top-grade #1 plants grow fastest and produce the most blooms when young; #1½-grade plants are also healthy and vigorous. Avoid #2-grade plants, which require extra care.

You can buy either dormant, bareroot roses or container-grown plants. Both mail-order companies and local outlets sell dormant plants, offering the widest range of cultivars. Healthy dormant plants have smooth, plump, green or red canes; avoid plants with dried-out, shriveled, wrinkled, or sprouted canes.

time to plant bareroot roses is January and February. In slightly colder areas, fall planting gives roses a chance to establish a sturdy root system before growth starts. In areas with very cold winters, plant bareroot roses in spring, several weeks before the last frost. For all but miniature and shrub roses, space roses 2 to 3 feet apart in colder areas; 3 to 4 feet apart in warmer regions where they'll grow larger. Space miniatures 1 to 2 feet apart; shrub roses 4 to 6 feet apart.

To plant bareroot roses, dig each hole 15 to 18 inches wide and deep, or large enough for roots to spread out. Form a soil cone in the planting hole. Removing any broken or damaged roots or canes, position the rose on the cone, spreading out its roots. Place the bud union (the point where the cultivar is grafted onto its rootstock) even with the soil surface in mild climates and 1 to 2 inches below the soil surface in areas where temperatures fall below the freezing point.

Add soil around the roots, making sure there are no air pockets, until the hole is three-fourths full. Fill the hole with water, allow it to soak in, and refill. Make sure the bud union is at the correct level. Finish filling the hole with soil and lightly tamp. Trim canes back to 8 inches, making cuts ¼ inch above an outward-facing bud and at a 45 degree angle. To prevent the canes from drying out, mound lightly moist soil over the rose bush. Gently remove it when growth starts in one to two weeks.

Plant container-grown roses as you would any container plant. For more on this technique, see Chapter 5.

**Water** Ample water, combined with good drainage, is fundamental to rose growth. The key is to water slowly and deeply, soaking the ground at least 16 inches deep with each watering. Water in the early morning, so if foliage gets wet, it can dry quickly. Use a soaker hose, drip irrigation system, or a hose with a bubbler

attachment on the end. Roses grown in containers must be watered much more frequently. Check containers daily during the summer.

**Mulch** An organic mulch conserves moisture, improves the garden's appearance, inhibits weed growth, keeps the soil cool, and slowly adds nutrients to the soil. Spread 2 to 4 inches of mulch evenly around the plants, leaving several inches unmulched around the stem of each rose.

**Fertilizing** Feed newly planted roses 4 to 6 weeks after planting. From then on, for roses that bloom once a year, fertilize in early spring. Feed established, repeat-blooming roses three times during the growing season: in early spring just as the growth starts, in early summer when flower buds have formed, and about six weeks before the first fall frost. The last feeding should have no nitrogen.

Use a commercial balanced organic plant food containing nitrogen, phosphorus, and potassium, or mix your own, combining 2 parts blood meal, 1 part rock phosphate, and 4 parts wood ashes for a 4-5-4 fertilizer. Use about ½

---

 **Disease-Resistant Roses**

Thinking of adding roses to your yard? According to a survey by the American Rose Society, the following cultivars are among the best for disease resistance:

**Miniatures:** 'Baby Betsy McCall', 'Gourmet Popcorn', 'Little Artist', 'Rainbow's End', 'Rose Gilardi'

**Grandiflora:** 'Queen Elizabeth'

**Floribundas:** 'Impatient', 'Sunsprite'

**Shrub Roses:** 'All That Jazz', 'Carefree Wonder'

**Hybrid Teas:** 'Duet', 'Olympiad', 'Smooth Lady'

**Aphids.** These ⅛″ insects cluster on new growth, causing deformed leaves and buds with sticky residue. Control with insecticidal soap, pyrethrins, or rotenone.

**Borers.** Larvae of various insects bore holes in canes; new growth wilts. Prune off damaged canes and seal ends with paraffin or nail polish.

**Beetles.** Japanese and other beetles chew leaves and flowers. Remove and destroy by hand, treat soil with milky disease, or control with pyrethrins, rotenone, or ryania.

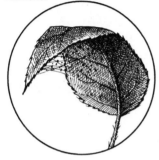

**Spider mites.** These tiny, spiderlike pests cause yellowed, curled leaves with fine webs on undersides. Spray all leaf surfaces in early morning with a strong jet of water for three days, or use insecticidal soap.

**Powdery mildew.** Causes white powder on deformed growth. Provide good air circulation, prune off infected plant parts, apply lime sulfur to dormant plants, and treat with fungicidal soap.

**Rose midges.** Very tiny white maggots cause deformed, blackened buds and leaves. Prune and destroy all damaged parts.

**Blackspot.** Disease causes black spots on yellow leaves and defoliation. Prune off all damaged plant parts, don't wet foliage when watering, and spray with fungicidal soap.

**Rust.** Disease causes red-orange spots under leaves; yellow blotches on top surfaces. Prune off infected plant parts; spray with fungicidal soap.

**Rose pests and diseases.** Your best defense against rose problems is to buy healthy, disease-resistant roses and be diligent about preventive maintenance, such as destroying diseased foliage and flowers immediately and cleaning up around roses in the fall. Control pests as soon as you see them. When dusting or spraying, apply controls early in the morning and cover both sides of the leaves.

cup for each plant, scratching it into the soil around the plant and watering well. As an alternative, apply dehydrated cow manure and bonemeal in the spring and use fish emulsion or manure tea for the other feedings. (See "Tea Time for Your Plants" on page 177.)

**Pruning**   Prune in early spring to keep hybrid tea, grandiflora, and floribunda roses vigorous and blooming. Many of the newer shrub-type roses need very little pruning. Heritage, species, and climbing roses that bloom once a year bear flowers on the previous year's growth. Prune these as soon as blooming is over, cutting the main shoots back by one-third and removing any small, twiggy growth. Remove suckers coming up from the rootstock of any rose whenever you see them.

In the first pruning of the season, just as growth starts, remove any dead or damaged wood back to healthy, white-centered wood. Make each pruning cut at an angle ¼ inch above an outward-facing bud eye, which is a dormant growing point at the base of a leaf stalk. This stimulates outward-facing new growth. Also remove any weak or crossing canes. Later in the season, remove any diseased growth and faded flowers on repeat-blooming roses, cutting the stem just above the first five-leaflet leaf below the flower.

**Winter Protection**   In areas with winter temperatures no lower than 20°F, no winter protection is necessary. Elsewhere, apply winter protection after the first frost and just before the first hard freeze. Many shrub roses as well as some of the polyanthas, floribundas, and miniatures need only minimal winter protection. Hybrid teas, grandifloras, and some floribundas and heritage roses usually require more.

Remove all leaves from the plants and from the ground around them and destroy them. Apply a fungicidal soap spray containing sulfur. Apply ¼ cup of greensand around each plant

and water well. Prune plants to one-half their height and tie canes together with twine.

Where winter temperatures drop to 0°F, make an 8-inch mound of coarse compost, shredded bark, leaves, or soil around the base of each plant. In colder areas, make the mound 1 foot deep. Provide extra protection with another layer of pine needles or branches, straw, or leaves. Where temperatures reach -5°F or colder, remove the canes of large-flowered, repeat-blooming climbers from supports, lay them on the ground, and cover both the base and the canes.

# ATTRACTING BUTTERFLIES

Color on the wing is waiting to fill your garden with a fluttering rainbow. Nearly every locale across the country offers some butterflies that you can attract into your garden by meeting just a few of the insects' basic needs.

If you want to add the living color of butterflies to your garden, start by using some of the recommended plants on page 290. Use low-growing groundcovers such as clovers and grasses

 **More About Roses**

For more information about roses, contact the American Rose Society, P.O. Box 30,000, Shreveport, LA 71130-0030. They also publish the *Handbook for Selecting Roses*, updated yearly, with an alphabetical listing of rose cultivars rated for quality. The *Combined Rose List* lists all roses available, with their sources. For a current price, write to Beverly Dobson, 215 Harriman Road, Irvington, NY 10533. The best book on roses for the backyard gardener is Rayford Reddell's *Growing Good Roses*.

to provide sunning spots for adults to warm themselves. Shallow depressions that remain moist naturally or through regular watering offer drinking sources. Walls, hedgerows, and similar windbreaks add protected spots that nearly all butterfly species will appreciate.

Plants may serve as nectar sources for butterflies, as host plants for caterpillars, or as food for both adults and larvae. To increase the number of butterflies flitting about your garden, plant as many host plants and nectar sources as you can in your yard.

Blend butterfly-attracting weeds such as alfalfa, clovers, Queen-Anne's-lace, nettles (*Urtica* spp.), teasel (*Dipsacus fullonum*), or mustard family members like field mustard (*Brassica rapa*) into a wildflower patch. And plant some extra parsley just for the larvae of the beautiful swallowtail butterflies. Some plants that butterflies appreciate are garden pests. These include dandelions and thistles, which will attract lovely painted lady butterflies. But the airborne seeds of these weedy plants will settle in other areas of your garden. Use common sense when creating your butterfly garden.

A reliable field guide to butterflies is helpful in planning a butterfly garden. Look for a book with information about the plants that caterpil-

---

 **Plantings for a Butterfly Garden**

This listing of flowers, trees, and shrubs will get you well on your way to planning a garden that will attract butterflies. The suggestions here are suitable for all parts of the country.

### Flowers

Ageratum (*Ageratum houstonianum*)
Asters (*Aster* spp.)
Bee balms (*Monarda* spp.)
Bonesets, Joe-Pye weeds (*Eupatorium* spp.)
Butterfly bushes (*Buddleia* spp.)
Common heliotrope (*Heliotropium arborescens*)
Common sneezeweed (*Helenium autumnale*)
Coneflowers (*Rudbeckia* spp.)
Coreopsis (*Coreopsis* spp.)
Daylilies (*Hemerocallis* spp.)
Fleabanes (*Erigeron* spp.)
French marigold (*Tagetes patula*)
Goldenrods (*Solidago* spp.)
Gumweeds (*Grindelia* spp.)
Hollyhock (*Alcea rosea*)
Ironweeds (*Vernonia* spp.)
Lavenders (*Lavandula* spp.)

Milkweeds, butterfly weeds (*Asclepias* spp.)
Mints (*Mentha* spp.)
Oxeye daisy (*Chrysanthemum leucanthemum*)
Phlox (*Phlox* spp.)
Purple coneflower (*Echinacea purpurea*)
Sages (*Salvia* spp.)
Shasta daisy (*Chrysanthemum × superbum*)
Showy stonecrop (*Sedum spectabile*)
Sunflowers (*Helianthus* spp.)
Sweet alyssum (*Lobularia maritima*)
Thymes (*Thymus* spp.)
Verbenas (*Verbena* spp.)
Zinnias (*Zinnia* spp.)

### Trees and Shrubs

Basswood (*Tilia americana*)
Blueberries (*Vaccinium* spp.)
Common lilac (*Syringa vulgaris*)
Gray rabbitbrush (*Chrysothamnus nauseosus*)
Honeysuckles (*Lonicera* spp.)
Privets (*Ligustrum* spp.)
Sumacs (*Rhus* spp.)
Willows (*Salix* spp.)

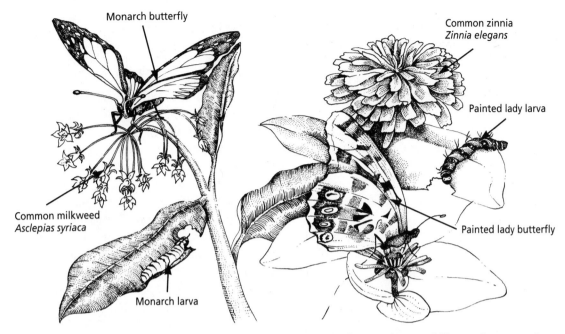

Monarch butterfly

Common zinnia
*Zinnia elegans*

Painted lady larva

Common milkweed
*Asclepias syriaca*

Painted lady butterfly

Monarch larva

**Flowers to attract butterflies.** Monarch butterflies are attracted to the flowers of many wildflowers for nectar. They depend on milkweeds for their larvae. Painted lady adults and larvae relish flowers and foliage of daisy-family members, including zinnias.

lars eat, the plants from which the adults take nectar, drinking and sunning habits of the adults, and special information about other unique habits. Detailed, full-color illustrations of the caterpillar and adult stages, and information about the geographical area in which the insects normally are found, are also valuable. *Butterflies: How to Identify and Attract Them to Your Garden* by Marcus Schneck is a good guidebook that includes color illustrations of many species plus information on habitat, host plants, and nectar sources. A local natural history museum, college entomology department, or butterfly club can give you more pointers.

# COTTAGE GARDENING

Cottage gardening originated during the Middle Ages, when people cultivated gardens outside the doorsteps of their thatched stone and wood cottages. They grew a patchwork of herbs, flowers, vegetables, and fruit trees. These joyful cottage gardens can still be found along the lanes of English villages.

Even if you don't live in a cottage, you might want your own cottage garden—its cheerful disorder looks surprisingly contemporary. For the most authentic look, locate the garden in a sunny plot surrounding a path to the front or kitchen door, and enclose the yard, or part of it, with a rustic fence. A decorative gate or arbor at the garden's entrance would add a charming touch. A cottage-style garden could also work well along the side of the house or beside a garage, barn, or toolshed.

The delightful informality of a cottage garden makes it a perfect place for accessories. A swing, chaise, or bench is at home there, and so is a sundial, beehive, windchime, or other ornament. Add a birdbath to welcome the many birds and butterflies that will visit your profusion of herbs and flowers, or a rustic birdhouse on a pole. Remember not to overload your cottage garden with ornaments, though—the emphasis should always be on the flowers.

Traditionally, the path leading through a cottage garden proceeded in a straight line from the lane to the door—its purpose was functional, not decorative. However, you might prefer to make a meandering path through your garden. Cover the path with bark chips, old paving bricks, or cobblestones. Or create a fragrant path with stepping stones nestled among scented "path plants" such as woolly thyme (*Thymus*

*pseudolanuginosus*), chamomile, or Corsican mint (*Mentha requienii*).

## PLANTING A COTTAGE GARDEN

If you have room, consider a small flowering tree or two along the fence for year-round structure. Old-fashioned fragrant flowering shrubs such as lilacs, sweet mock oranges (*Philadelphus coronarius*), and shrub roses in the corners add structure and enhance the garden's homey feeling. And don't forget a butterfly bush (*Buddleia* spp.) for the butterflies.

Choose flowers that fit the casualness of the cottage garden style, like self-sowing annuals and spreading perennials. Mix flowers right in with your favorite herbs. Dill, parsley, and

---

 **Best Cottage Garden Plants**

These cheerful flowers will give your cottage garden a joyful, exuberant look. The annuals self-sow freely, returning to your garden each year. And many of these spreading perennials have adorned cottage gardens for hundreds of years. Cottage garden plants aren't fussy; they prefer full sun and average soil.

### Annuals

Baby-blue-eyes (*Nemophila menziesii*)
Browallias (*Browallia* spp.)
Cornflower (*Centaurea cyanus*)
Corn poppy, Shirley poppy (*Papaver rhoeas*)
Cosmos (*Cosmos bipinnatus*)
Delphiniums (*Delphinium* spp.)
Four-o'clock (*Mirabilis jalapa*)
Garden forget-me-not (*Myosotis sylvatica*)
Honesty (*Lunaria annua*)
Johnny jump-up (*Viola tricolor*)
Love-in-a-mist (*Nigella damascena*)
Morning-glories (*Ipomoea* spp.)

Pot marigold (*Calendula officinalis*)
Rocket larkspur (*Consolida ambigua*)
Spider flower (*Cleome hasslerana*)
Sweet alyssum (*Lobularia maritima*)

### Perennials

Bee balm (*Monarda didyma*)
Common yarrow (*Achillea millefolium*)
Daylilies (*Hemerocallis* spp.)
Feverfew (*Chrysanthemum parthenium*)
Italian bugloss (*Anchusa azurea*)
Lady's-mantle (*Alchemilla mollis*)
Moss pink (*Phlox subulata*)
Perennial pea (*Lathyrus latifolius*)
Rose campion (*Lychnis coronaria*)
'Silver King' artemisia (*Artemisia ludoviciana* 'Silver King')
Sneezeweed (*Achillea ptarmica*)
Sundrops (*Oenothera pilosella*)
Threadleaf coreopsis (*Coreopsis verticillata*)
Woolly blue violet (*Viola sororia*)

coriander will self-sow and look pretty with the flowers. If you want to add mints to your garden, keep in mind that they are very invasive; add them to your garden in pots.

To complete the cottage-garden effect, drape climbing roses, goldflame honeysuckle (*Lonicera × heckrottii*) or Jackman clematis (*Clematis × jackmanii*) over a fence or arbor. Pop in vegetables wherever you find a spot, and use herbs such as lavender and parsley as edging plants along the walk.

## CARING FOR THE COTTAGE GARDEN

Because part of its charm comes from its informal design, a cottage garden requires less work to maintain than more manicured gardens. But weeding can be a challenge in spring, when you have to decide which are self-sown annual and herb seedlings and which are weeds. Thin or transplant flower seedlings as needed.

Add a topdressing of compost and mulch each year after seedlings are well established. Pick off any spent flowers of annuals early in the season to encourage more blooms, but allow flowers to ripen into seed heads in late summer so that they can disperse seeds to start next year's garden.

# ORNAMENTAL GRASSES

Ornamental grasses are great plants for adding four-season interest to your flower garden—they produce clumps of vertical or fountainlike foliage in spring, bloom in summer, set attractive seed heads and turn color in fall, and hold their form throughout the winter. Many have handsome white, cream, or yellow stripes, which contrast beautifully with the rounded or oval variegated foliage of perennials like hostas and Bethlehem sage (*Pulmonaria saccharata*). Others have steel blue or red foliage.

Because ornamental grasses range in height from creeping (as low as 2 inches tall) to towering (some are over 10 feet tall), they can fill every garden niche from groundcover to large "shrub." Use them in the front, middle, and back of a flower border to add sparkle and contrast. Or site a tall grass like Japanese silver grass (*Miscanthus sinensis*) or switchgrass (*Panicum virgatum*) in the center of an island bed or at the ends of a border to anchor the planting.

Besides providing forms and textures that work well with flowers, oranamental grasses have two very desirable traits that make them valuable in gardens: They catch the light, which seems to shine through the foliage and flower heads, making them glow; and they shimmer in the breeze, moving with every air current. Use these features to add excitement to your garden.

Remember to choose clumping grasses like the fountain grasses (*Pennisetum* spp.) or feather reed grass (*Calamagrostis arundinacea*) rather than running grasses when you include ornamental grasses in a flower garden. As their name implies, clumping grasses form increasingly large clumps but stay in one place, while running grasses send out creeping stems or roots, which spread like weeds all over the garden (think of crabgrass). If you want to include a running grass like 'Feesey's Form' ribbon grass (*Phalaris arundinacea* 'Feesey's Form') because its pink, white, and green variegations are so beautiful, plant it in a deep, sunken bucket with the bottom cut out, or sink a wide metal edging around it to control its spread.

Grasses can adapt to a variety of soil textures, from sand to clay. Most grasses are drought-tolerant. A site with moist but well-drained, loamy soil of average fertility will suit most of these plants. At least a half day of full sun is usually ideal, although some grasses, such as hakonechloa grass (*Hakonechloa macra*), grow well with more shade. In general, those grasses with thin, wide leaves appreciate more shade and are less drought tolerant.

Grasses require very little maintenance. Fertilize only if you have very sandy soil. Pests and diseases are rarely a problem. You may want to cut the plants back close to the ground once a year (generally in early spring). If you leave seedheads for winter interest, the grass may self-seed. Cultivate lightly around clumps in spring to uproot unwanted seedlings.

Grasses are easy to propagate by seed or division. Sow seed of annuals indoors about four weeks before the last frost. Transplant (or sow seeds directly) into the garden after danger of frost is past; thin to 6 to 12 inches apart.

To propagate cultivars or renew old clumps, divide existing plants. Lift plants from the ground, separate them into smaller clumps, and replant. To learn more about this technique, see "Division" on page 94. Divide or plant warm-season grasses in spring, just as they are starting to grow; move cool-season grasses in either spring or fall.

# A MEADOW GARDEN

Meadow gardening fiction: All you need do to create a beautiful wildflower meadow is to scatter wildflower seeds over an established lawn and stop mowing. Meadow gardening fact: Seeds of any kind—even of hardy wildflowers—need some help to grow into established plants. And typical turf grasses will overwhelm meadow flowers because their mat-forming roots crowd out any other plants.

Fortunately, it's also a fact that it's easier to

---

 **Eight Great Grasses**

The plants listed below are eight of the best perennial clump-forming grasses:

Blue oat grass (*Helictotrichon sempervirens*). A cool-season grass that grows 1½ to 2 feet high and wide. Flowers bloom in spring over tufts of blue foliage. Zones 5–9.

Compact pampas grass (*Cortaderia selloana* var. *pumila*). A cool-season grass growing 4 to 6 feet high and wide. Flowers bloom in fall over mounds of gray-green foliage. Zones 7–9.

Feather reed grass (*Calamagrostis acutiflora* var. *stricta*). A warm-season grass growing 3 to 4 feet high and wide. Flowers bloom in summer over arching clumps of medium green foliage that turns orange-brown in fall. Zones 4–9.

Fountain grass (*Pennisetum alopecuroides*). A warm-season grass growing 3 to 4 feet high and wide. Flowers bloom in summer over mounds of green foliage with yellow-brown fall color. Zones 5–9.

Giant feather grass (*Stipa gigantea*). A cool-season grass growing 2 to 3 feet high and wide. In spring, showy flowers appear over mounds of gray-green foliage. Zones 7–9.

'Morning Light' miscanthus (*Miscanthus sinensis* 'Morning Light'). A warm-season grower reaching 4 to 6 feet high and 3 to 4 feet wide. Flowers appear in late summer over upright arching clumps of gray-green foliage; orange-brown fall color. Zones 5–9.

Northern sea oats (*Uniola latifolia*). Sometimes called *Chasmanthium latifolium*, this warm-season grass grows 2 to 3 feet high and wide. Flowers appear in summer over upright arching clumps of light green foliage that bronzes in winter. Zones 4–9.

Quaking grass (*Briza media*). A cool-season grass that grows 1 to 1½ feet high and wide. Showy flowers appear in spring over tufts of green foliage. Zones 4–9.

create a beautiful, self-perpetuating meadow than a flower bed. To make your own meadow, just follow the same soil preparation, timing, sowing, and watering methods you'd use to establish a new lawn.

A meadow garden mimics the beauty of a natural meadow, and part of that beauty comes from meadow grasses. The meadow grasses—mostly clumping, warm-season species that grow slowly in spring and fall, thrive in the heat of summer, and go dormant in winter—stabilize the soil and provide support for the flowers. The grasses add color and texture to the meadow, especially when they change color in fall.

## EVALUATING SEED MIXES

A meadow garden should be composed of native warm-season grasses and flowering annuals, biennials, and perennials that will spread and self-sow to create a self-maintaining field of flowers and foliage. Unfortunately, most of those lavish packaged meadows sold in shaker cans contain no grass seed at all. If grass seed isn't in your mix, purchase it separately; you can find sheep's fescue (*Festuca ovina*) at many farm supply centers, and it works well in meadow gardens in most areas of the country if sown at 1 pound per 1,000 square feet.

Choosing a seed mix can be tricky. Don't let the pretty pictures seduce you—read the label. Don't purchase any meadow mix that doesn't list the species in it—all of them. And be sure the mix is a regional one that has been specially formulated for your area of the country.

Many commercial seed mixes include both annuals and perennials. The annuals will bloom the first year and make a pretty meadow that first growing season, but they rarely reseed as expected. For splashy annual color every year, overseed with annuals each spring to ensure a consistent show. Meanwhile, during that first season the perennials are sprouting, putting

down sturdy roots, and just getting themselves established. The perennials should flower the second season and get even better as the years pass, particularly if mixed with protective grasses. They may even self-sow. If you're impatient for perennial flowers—and have the funds—plant container-grown or bareroot perennials in a newly seeded or established meadow, or grow your own transplants.

## SEEDS AND WEEDS

Natural meadows occur in full sun—make sure you site your wildflower meadow in full sun, too. The meadow soil can be average, and you don't have to fertilize or improve it at all—

 **Meadow-Growing Basics**

Follow these guidelines and your wildflower meadow will be off to a good start:

■ Clear the soil of all vegetation and then till to prepare a seedbed.

■ Use a mixture of perennial and annual flowers along with native clump-forming grasses. Sow at a heavy application rate, as much as twice the rate on the package directions, and cover thinly with soil.

■ Mix seed with equal portions of clean river sand to facilitate even spreading.

■ Keep the seedlings moist. You may need to irrigate the meadow during its first year.

■ Weed diligently the first year.

■ Cut the meadow to 6 inches high in late winter to prevent invasion by woody plants and to help disperse flower and grass seed.

■ Sow seeds of annual flowers every year for a good show. This means some yearly soil preparation when sowing.

unless it is extremely sandy or clayey. Ordinary soil will give you the best meadow because meadow plants feed lightly.

Your greatest adversary in establishing a successful meadow garden will be weeds. The battle begins at planting time and continues for at least one to two seasons. An established meadow garden, especially one with grasses, should have thick enough foliage to shade out most weeds *if* you get rid of aggressive species like Johnsongrass, thistles, and bindweeds early on.

The fight is most fierce at the start because the newly cleared soil offers an open invitation to airborne seed and because weed seed lying dormant in the soil springs to life when the ground is cleared. Soilborne weeds are particularly troublesome if you till the soil when sowing the meadow mixture, because dormant seed lying too deep to germinate comes to the surface and sprouts. One way to handle this is to till the soil (either by hand or with a power tiller), wait several weeks until weed seeds have sprouted, and then till, hoe, or disk the soil *shallowly* to disrupt the weed seedlings. (Shallow disking is essential because deeper tilling brings up more weed seed.) You may have to repeat the process.

Once the soil is tilled and weeded several times, sow the meadow garden. Do this in either spring or fall, depending on your climate. In the South and Mid-Atlantic, fall sowing works best; in the North, spring sowing is better. It is essential to sow the seed thickly—often at twice the recommended rate on the

---

##  Best Plants for Meadow Gardens

These wildflowers and grasses are the most dependable native annuals and perennials for meadows across the country. Look in a wildflower gardening book, check with a wildflower society, or refer to seed catalogs to find the plants that do best in your area. Plants marked with an asterisk (*) are non-native species that can be successfully naturalized.

### Wildflowers for Meadow Gardens

Bee balm (*Monarda didyma*)
Black-eyed Susan (*Rudbeckia hirta*)
Blanket flower (*Gaillardia pulchella*)
Blue false indigo (*Baptisia australis*)
Butterfly weed (*Asclepias tuberosa*)
Canada lily (*Lilium canadense*)
Common sneezeweed (*Helenium autumnale*)
Common yarrow* (*Achillea millefolium*)
Coreopsis (*Coreopsis* spp.)
Cornflower* (*Centaurea cyanus*)

Crimson clover* (*Trifolium incarnatum*)
Foxglove penstemon (*Penstemon digitalis*)
Goldenrods (*Solidago* spp.)
New England aster (*Aster novae-angliae*)
Oxeye daisy* (*Chrysanthemum leucanthemum*)
Purple coneflower (*Echinacea purpurea*)
Shooting-star (*Dodecatheon meadia*)
Showy evening primrose (*Oenothera speciosa*)
Spike gayfeather (*Liatris spicata*)
Wild lupine (*Lupinus perennis*)
Yellow cosmos* (*Cosmos sulphureus*)

### Grasses for Meadow Gardens

Broomsedge (*Andropogon virginicus*)
Fescues (*Festuca* spp.)
June grass (*Koeleria cristata*)
Little bluestem (*Schizachyrium scoparium*)
Miscanthus (*Miscanthus* spp.)
Sideoats grama grass (*Bouteloua curtipendula*)
Switchgrass (*Panicum virgatum*)

package—to keep out weeds. Rake over the area two to three times to settle the seeds into the soil. Once the meadow is up and growing, hand-weed as needed. Keep your meadow watered throughout the first growing season to help the plants get established.

To keep woody plants from taking over your wildflower meadow and shading out the flowers, mow it back to about 6 inches from the ground each year in late winter. A regular lawn mower won't do the job because it cuts too low—use a scythe or a small tractor.

# A Cutting Garden

With the cost of cut flowers these days, it makes more sense than ever to grow your own. With your own cutting garden, you can grow the flowers you love in the colors you want, and make sure you have a selection of flowers for cutting year-round.

There are two ways you can grow flowers for cutting: with all the plants of each species grown together in rows or raised beds, as in a vegetable garden, or mixed in ornamental borders and beds. Each plan has its advantages. If you already grow vegetables, you'll find that adding cut flowers to the vegetable garden makes it glow with vivid colors. Cut flowers are as easy to tend as vegetables when grown in blocks, too.

If you want to grow cut flowers in an ornamental garden, interplant annuals and perennials, including ornamental grasses, with bulbs, roses, and herbs to create spectacular mixed beds and borders. To make sure the flowers you cut won't leave holes in your border, grow at least three plants of each perennial and six or seven of each annual.

Use the rest of your landscape to supplement your cutting garden. Grow roses with other shrubs in a foundation planting, as a border or screen at the edge of the property, or around a deck or patio. Train vines on arbors, trellises, or fences to supply graceful stems for arrangements. Trees and shrubs provide foliage, flowers, berries, and branches for cutting. You can turn a shady spot into a lovely garden of ferns and hostas that will supply foliage for arrangements.

## CHOOSING PLANTS

When you're deciding which plants to include in your garden, remember to grow a variety of plant shapes, so you'll always have the right shapes for any arrangement. Satisfying arrangements generally have three primary elements: tall, spiky flowers and foliage for line; large, flat, round flowers and foliage for focal points or mass; and small, airy flowers and foliage for fillers.

Choose plants that bloom for a long period and hold up well as cut flowers. Many annuals bloom almost nonstop during the summer; most perennials flower for a week to a month or more. Make sure you grow flowers that bloom at different seasons to have bouquets indoors throughout the year. Other important considerations are color, height, and fragrance.

Think first about color when selecting the flowers you'll grow. The most effective arrangements coordinate with the colors in your home. If one color predominates in your house, grow flowers that complement that color.

Height also matters when choosing plants for cutting. For flower arrangements, it is easier to use longer stems. New cultivars of annuals and perennials frequently are shorter, more compact-growing plants. As you choose plants, note the mature or blooming height.

Growing fragrant flowers makes both gardening and flower arranging more pleasurable. Scented flowers that are good for cutting include hyacinths, lilies, lilies-of-the-valley, peonies, and phlox. Nicotiana ( *Nicotiana* spp.), pinks (*Dianthus* spp.), stocks (*Matthiola* spp.), sweet peas (*Lathyrus odoratus*), and tuberoses (*Polianthes tuberosa*) are also good choices. Don't overlook flowering trees and shrubs like lilacs, magnolias, and roses.

Most herb foliage, flowers, and seed heads provide fragrance as well as form to arrangements.

Among the best hardy bulbs for cutting are daffodils, hyacinths, irises, lilies, tulips, alliums (*Allium* spp.), and grape hyacinths (*Muscari* spp.). Tender bulbs that make great cut flowers include caladiums, dahlias, gladioli, tuberous begonias, agapanthus (*Agapanthus* spp.), and montbretias (*Crocosmia* spp.).

To grow cut flowers successfully, choose the planting site carefully and prepare the soil well. Most of your plants will thrive if you site your cutting garden where they'll get well-drained, humus-rich soil and full sun. Check the cultural requirements of the plants you want to grow; group plants with similar needs together.

Give your plants the care they need: adequate watering and fertilizing, diligent weeding and deadheading (removal of faded flowers), and winter protection and pest control when necessary. An organic mulch, such as compost or shredded leaves, conserves moisture, inhibits weeds, and keeps flowers and leaves clean and mud-free. Commonsense care and careful plant selection will give you a constant supply of beautiful cut flowers all season.

**Feature foliage in arrangements.** Don't overlook foliage when you're out cutting flowers for arrangements. Adding beautifully colored, textured, shaped, or variegated foliage can integrate the different shapes and colors of your flowers and give an arrangement added charm and sophistication.

## MAKING CUT FLOWERS LAST

There's nothing more disheartening than to spend the time carefully cutting and arranging flowers only to find them limp and brown a few days later. Your flowers will last a lot longer if you use some common sense when cutting

them. Start by cutting your flowers early in the day, and choose only those that aren't fully open. Cut the stems cleanly with sharp scissors or pruners.

If you're cutting more than just two or three stems, bring along a bucket of lukewarm water and plunge the stems into the water as soon as they're cut. The water should come at least halfway up the stems, but not reach the blooms. Set the bucket in a cool, shady place.

When you bring your flowers inside, before adding them to an arrangement recut the stems on a slant and strip off all leaves and buds that would be underwater. Be sure to use lukewarm water in your arrangement—don't shock your flowers with icy water. Treat foliage like artemisias, ivy, and lamb's-ears the same way you treat flowers.

Some flowers need special treatments. Flowers that drip milky sap from their cut ends, including poppies, spurges (*Euphorbia* spp.) and buttercups (*Ranunculus* spp.), last longer if you sear the cut end of the stem in a flame for a second or dip it in boiling water for a minute. Flowers with hollow stems like daffodils, delphiniums, lupines (*Lupinus* spp.), and alliums (*Allium* spp.) last longer if you fill each stem with water, then plug the end with cotton.

---

##  Best Flowers for Cutting

A garden of annuals and perennials can provide months of colorful cut flowers. Most cutting-garden flowers prefer full sun with average soil and moisture. Include different colors and shapes in your garden so you'll have a variety of flowers to work with. Flower shapes can be grouped by their use in arrangements: linear, for line and height; round, for mass or a focal point; and filler, to add an airy look and unify the other elements. Plant names are followed by flower shape and color.

### Annuals

Calliopsis (*Coreopsis tinctoria*); round; yellow, red

China aster (*Callistephus chinensis*); round; white, yellow, pink, red, blue

Cosmos (*Cosmos* spp.); round; white, pink, red, yellow

Pot marigold (*Calendula officinalis*); round; yellow, orange

Snapdragon (*Antirrhinum majus*); linear; white, pink, red, orange, yellow

Statice (*Limonium sinuatum*); filler; white, pink, purple-blue, yellow

Stock (*Matthiola incana*); linear; white, pink, rose, lavender

Zinnia (*Zinnia elegans*); round; white, pink, red, yellow, orange

### Perennials

Artemisias (*Artemisia* spp.); filler, linear; silver-gray

Asters (*Aster* spp.); round; white, pink, red, lavender, blue

Baby's-breath (*Gypsophila paniculata*); filler; white

Bellflowers (*Campanula* spp.); round, linear; white, pink, blue

Blanket flowers (*Gaillardia* spp.); round; yellow, red, orange

Chrysanthemums (*Chrysanthemum* spp.); round; white, pink, red, orange, yellow

Coneflowers (*Rudbeckia* spp.); round; yellow

Delphiniums (*Delphinium* spp.); linear; white, blue, purple

Gayfeathers (*Liatris* spp.); linear; white, purplish pink

Globe thistles (*Echinops* spp.); round; blue

Phlox (*Phlox* spp.); round; white, pink, red, orange, lavender

Pinks (*Dianthus* spp.); round; white, pink, red

Purple coneflower (*Echinacea purpurea*); round; mauve, white

Sages (*Salvia* spp.); linear; purple-blue

Sweet rocket (*Hesperis matronalis*); round; white, purple

Yarrows (*Achillea* spp.); round; yellow, pink, white

# Chapter 13

# TREES AND SHRUBS

Trees, shrubs, and vines form the foundation, framework, and walls of a landscape. They can focus our attention on lovely views or shut out ugly ones. Trees also help to modify the microclimate in our yards by casting shade or serving as a windbreak. They can act as barriers to block the noise and commotion of street traffic.

While trees and shrubs can be expensive, they are true investments that can raise the value of your property. Before you spend money buying trees and shrubs, though, spend time learning about the best plant choices for your site and about how to care for the plants you select. Consult books, local gardening organizations, and county extension agents. Find a reliable nursery, and ask the owner or manager for advice. And for a dose of inspiration, visit public gardens and arboretums.

In this chapter, you'll find advice on selecting and caring for trees and shrubs, as well as how to use trees, shrubs, and vines for best effect in the home landscape. See Chapter 5 for tree and shrub planting information.

## TYPES OF TREES AND SHRUBS

Trees are woody perennials, usually with a single trunk, ranging in height at maturity from 15 feet to giants exceeding 100 feet. A plant thought of as a tree in some parts of the country may be considered a shrub in others. Crape myrtle (*Lagerstroemia indica*) exceeds 15 feet in the South, where it is grown as a small flowering tree, but in the mid-Atlantic area, it may die back to the ground after cold winters and only reach shrub height.

Some of the most familiar and beautiful plants around our homes are shrubs. The graceful sweep of forsythia and the stately form of a privet hedge show the diversity of these woody perennials. Shrubs have multiple stems and range in height from a few inches to approximately 15 feet at maturity, although individual shrubs may grow as high as 30 feet. A shrub trained to a single stem, called a standard, resembles a miniature tree. Here's a look at the types of trees and shrubs most commonly found in home landscapes:

**Deciduous trees:** These drop all of their leaves at the end of the growing season and grow new leaves the following spring. They are good choices for fall color. Once they drop their leaves, with the exception of some limited root growth, they generally are dormant for the entire winter.

**Evergreen trees and shrubs:** These hold most of their leaves year-round. Although many people think "Christmas tree" at the mention of evergreens, all plants that retain their green color throughout the year can properly be called evergreens, and there is a broad range of shapes and sizes. Evergreen can mean a 60-foot fir tree—or the diminutive rug junipers used as groundcovers.

Evergreens are divided into two groups according to the general shape of their leaves. Narrow-leaved or *needle* evergreens include plants such as junipers, pines, and yews. Most needle evergreens are very hardy and can be successfully grown over much of the United States. Some of these, like pines and spruces, are also known as conifers because they bear cones. But not all coniferous trees are evergreen: Larches (*Larix* spp.) and bald cypress (*Taxodium distichum*) are deciduous conifers.

Broad-leaved evergreens usually have showy flowers or fruit, and are generally not as cold-hardy as other evergreens. But some types, such as azaleas and rhododendrons (*Rhododendron* spp.), hollies (*Ilex* spp.), and Japanese barberry (*Berberis thunbergii*) are widely adaptable. Tender evergreens, such as gardenias (*Gardenia* spp.), are grown only in the warmest regions of the country. Broad-leaved evergreen trees include southern magnolia (*Magnolia grandiflora*) and live oak (*Quercus virginiana*).

If you live in a warm area, you may be able to select a third type of "evergreen" tree. Palms are categorized as evergreens, although they are monocots, not dicots like other trees. A dicot forms annual growth rings that increase the trunk's diameter, and their crown is formed of branches. Palms don't form annual growth rings, and they generally don't branch, either—their crowns are made up entirely of their large leaves.

**Semi-evergreen trees and shrubs:** These keep at least part of their leaves well into the winter. Shrubs such as glossy abelia (*Abelia* ×

---

 **Words to Know**

**Clump:** A tree grown with several closely growing trunks. Birches are often sold as clumps.

**Vase-shaped:** A tree with upswept branches, narrower in silhouette near the base than at the top, such as American elm.

**Globe-shaped:** A tree with a rounded, usually low-growing silhouette, such as crab apple.

**Oval:** A tree with branches that form an oval silhouette, such as 'Bradford' flowering pear.

**Columnar:** A tall, somewhat narrow form, such as 'Columnare' Norway maple.

**Pyramidal:** A cone-shaped tree, such as spruces or American arborvitae.

**Conical:** Cone-shaped, but with a narrower profile than a pyramidal tree, such as 'Wichita Blue' juniper.

**Weeping:** A tree with branches that droop toward the ground, such as a weeping willow.

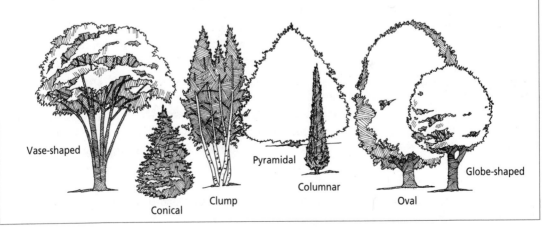

Vase-shaped

Conical

Clump

Pyramidal

Columnar

Oval

Globe-shaped

grandiflora) are evergreen in the South and semi-evergreen farther north. And certain cultivars of Chinese or lacebark elm (*Ulmus parvifolia*) keep many of their leaves well into the winter. They may be fully evergreen in the South.

## SELECTING TREES AND SHRUBS

Your trees and shrubs will be a part of your life for a long time. Choose them with care. Think about what you want from a tree or shrub. In a design sense, trees and shrubs have a variety of uses. They can be used to screen and filter views, soften hard edges, enclose spaces, and visually connect buildings to the ground. In a good design, they also create an atmosphere that is comforting and restful.

Landscape plants provide visual interest, a catchall term that not only refers to flowers, fruit, fall foliage, and bark, but also to the interesting patterns, textures, and contrasts they create. And a cherished plant that might have been part of childhood, or reminiscent of a favorite place or time, is a soul-satisfying presence.

Trees, shrubs, and other vegetation soak up noise and glare, filter atmospheric impurities, and offer shelter from winds. They also invite wildlife and bring coolness by casting shade, by transpiration, and by wind channeling. These benefits should offer inspiration to gardeners to plan and plant their home landscapes with loving attention and to give them the best possible year-round care.

Before you head to the nursery or garden center to buy shrubs, make a list of desired features. What should your trees and shrubs do— form a windscreen, complete your foundation planting, shade your house, serve as an accent for a flower garden, provide food for wildlife, or serve as a specimen? Would you rather have a display of flowers in spring, brightly colored leaves in fall, showy bark, or persistent fruit in the winter? How big can the shrub or tree get,

how often will you have time to prune it, and what showy features do you want? Here are some suggestions for ways to use trees and shrubs in your landscape:

■ Use groups of trees and shrubs to block unwanted views or accent desirable ones, both on and off your property, and to give privacy. Evergreens provide year-round concealment. Privet (*Ligustrum* spp.) is a classic hedge plant, but many others also make good hedges. A low-growing hedge, such as common boxwood (*Buxus sempervirens*), can direct traffic around walkways and define borders of flower and herb beds. Plant larger shrubs, such as spireas (*Spiraea* spp.) and viburnums, singly or in groups. They can frame outdoor spaces, provide privacy, hide unsightly views, and buffer against wind and noise. See "Growing Hedges" on page 307 for more on hedges.

■ A unified group of trees and shrubs in a single bed looks better than a widely separated planting, and the arrangement helps protect the trees from lawn mower nicks and gouges.

■ Specimen or accent plants are used alone to call attention to an attractive feature such as the finely cut leaves of full-moon maple (*Acer japonicum*), or the showy flowers of saucer magnolia (*Magnolia* × *soulangiana*). Unusually textured bark, bright fall color, or an interesting shape are other good reasons to showcase a tree or shrub as a specimen plant.

■ Use ground-covering shrubs, such as rockspray cotoneaster (*Cotoneaster horizontalis*) or shore juniper (*Juniperus conferta*), to control erosion and ease maintenance on steep banks.

■ Low-growing Japanese hollies (*Ilex crenata*) or abelias (*Abelia* spp.) make good foreground plants for foundation plantings. Medium and tall shrubs, such as yews (*Taxus* spp.) and Chinese junipers (*Juniperus chinensis*), serve as background plants for foundation plantings, as well as for perennial beds.

■ Be sure to learn the mature height and spread of the foundation plants you are considering. The rule is patience: Allow time for your new small plants to mature and fill the space you have planned. If you make the mistake of planting cute little arborvitaes (*Thuja* spp.) under the window, or a white pine close to the house, you'll be continually pruning or cutting them down when they outgrow their space.

■ Many medium- and tall-growing shrubs have naturally occurring or cultivated forms that are smaller and slower-growing. These dwarf and miniature forms, such as dwarf nandina (*Nandina domestica* 'Nana') and dwarf mugo pine (*Pinus mugo* var. *mugo*), generally do not grow more than 3 feet tall. Use them when your planting site is small, or when you want less pruning maintenance.

■ Trees supply food, shelter, and nesting sites for birds and other wildlife. Those with berries or other fruits are especially welcome. See "Attracting Wildlife" on page 17 and "Attracting Birds" on page 19 for more ideas for attracting these garden residents.

■ You may want to add trees and shrubs to your landscape that will provide food for you, not just for wildlife and birds. Many common fruit trees, such as apples, pears, peaches, and plums, are available in dwarf sizes that fit neatly into a small corner or even a large container.

## ❀ Shrubs and Small Trees for Mixed Borders

Woody plants add drama and sophistication to a perennial garden. They also anchor the garden, giving it a sense of permanence. Choose trees and shrubs that will mature at a size that fits your garden. Trees with a loose, open branching habit are less likely to shade out your garden as they mature—reserve large trees with dense canopies for the yard. Here are some good choices:

Bayberries (*Myrica* spp.). Scented leaves and fruit; 10 feet tall and wide

Blueberries (*Vaccinium* spp.). Shrubs with red fall color; exfoliating bark

Bottlebrush buckeye (*Aesculus parviflora*). 8- to 12-foot-tall shrub; white flowers

Bumald spirea (*Spiraea* × *bumalda* cultivars). 2- to 3-foot shrub; white or pink flowers in summer

Butterfly bushes (*Buddleia* spp.). Shrubs with arching branches; purple, pink, yellow, or white flowers attract butterflies

Catawba rhododendron (*Rhododendron catawbiense*). Broad-leaved evergreen shrub; 6 to 10 feet tall; lavender flowers

Eastern redbud (*Cercis canadensis*). Small tree, 30 to 40 feet tall; reddish flowers in spring; heart-shaped leaves

Golden-rain tree (*Koelreuteria paniculata*). 30- to 40-foot tree; dangling yellow flowers

Kousa dogwood (*Cornus kousa*). 20- to 30-foot tree; white flowers; raspberry-like fruits

Oakleaf hydrangea (*Hydrangea quercifolia*). 4- to 6-foot shrub; red in fall; white flowers

St.-John's-worts (*Hypericum* spp.). Bushy shrubs; 1½ to 5 feet tall; striking yellow flowers

Viburnums (*Viburnum* spp.). 4- to 15-foot shrubs, flowers usually white, some fragrant; red or bluish black fruit

White fringe tree (*Chionanthus virginicus*). Shrub or small tree; white, fragrant flowers

Winterberry (*Ilex verticillata*). 6- to 10-foot shrub; red fruit in fall and winter

Witch hazel (*Hamamelis* × *intermedia*). 15- to 20-foot shrub; yellow, orange, or red

See Chapter 10 for more on growing fruit.

■ For fleshy fruit to be eaten fresh or cooked, try pawpaw (*Asimina triloba*), common persimmon (*Diospyros virginiana*), and Japanese persimmon (*D. kaki*).

■ For small, fleshy fruits for jams and jellies, try blueberries, cornelian cherry (*Cornus mas*), crab apples (*Malus* spp.), and wild cherries and plums (*Prunus* spp.).

■ For nuts, try hickories (*Carya* spp.), walnuts and butternuts (*Juglans* spp.), pecans (*Carya illinoinensis*), filberts (*Corylus* spp.),

---

 **How Hardy Are You?**

There is no guarantee that the plant you buy will flourish in its new site. Mother Nature may work against you. Referring to the USDA Plant Hardiness Zone Map, shown on page 336, can help you choose appropriate plants. To find out which zone your home is in, find your state and the approximate location of your town on the map. Use the key in the bottom righthand corner of the map to determine your zone.

When buying expensive plants or trees and shrubs, it's wise to choose those that are hardy *one zone farther north* than your location. For example, if you're in Zone 6, choose plants that are hardy to Zone 5. For less-prominent or inexpensive plants, you can choose those hardy to your zone as well.

Keep in mind that the current zone map is a revision of a map dating from the 1960s. While each zone still represents the same range of average annual minimum temperature, where the zones fall has shifted on the new map. So if you thought you lived in Zone 7, for example, you may now find that you live in Zone 6.

---

and chestnuts (*Castanea* spp.). See "Growing Nut Trees" on page 235 for advice on selecting and growing nut trees.

■ For beekeepers interested in a new taste to their honey, try sourwood (*Oxydendrum arboreum*), lindens (*Tilia* spp.), and water tupelo (*Nyssa aquatica*).

Be realistic about the amount of maintenance you're willing to do. Do you want to plant trees and forget them, or do you enjoy pruning and raking up baskets of leaves on a brisk fall day? For some gardeners, the beauty of the tree or the bounty of the crop outweighs the extra work. See "Nuisance Trees" on page 311 for information on trees that require extra work to maintain.

## MATCHING PLANT TO SITE

Consider the characteristics of your site before you head for the nursery. For healthy, vigorous trees and shrubs, match the cultural requirements of the plants you buy to the conditions of your site. Refer to the map on page 336 to determine your hardiness zone, and make sure the tree you want is compatible. While most nurseries stock plants that are hardy in their area, borderline-hardy plants are sometimes offered with no warnings. It's always a good idea to ask. Remember to check catalogs for hardiness information.

Know your soil—its pH, fertility, and consistency. Take a close look at drainage; choose another site if you see standing water at any season. Check the amount of light the plant will receive.

If you're planting trees, be sure to scout out overhead wires, nearby walkways, or other limiting factors. Think about the size of your tree or shrub in 5, 10, or 20 years.

Also remember that as a tree grows, so does the area of ground that it shades. Some trees, such as thornless honey locust (*Gleditsia tria-*

##  Showy Trees and Shrubs

Trees and shrubs can add color and diversity throughout the year. Flowering trees bring the beauty of flowers to your landscape, while many shrubs add four-season interest with their attractive foliage, colorful berries, or unusually colored or textured bark.

### Small Flowering Trees

The list that follows is arranged by time of bloom, beginning with trees that flower in early spring and progressing through summer-blooming trees. The plant name is followed by flower color:

Serviceberries (*Amelanchier* spp.): white
Cornelian cherry (*Cornus mas*): yellow
Eastern redbud (*Cercis canadensis*): pink
Chinese redbud (*Cercis chinensis*): magenta
Star magnolia (*Magnolia stellata*): white to pale pink
Saucer magnolia (*Magnolia* × *soulangiana*): white to wine
Flowering dogwood (*Cornus florida*): white, pink
Callery pear (*Pyrus calleryana*): white
Crab apples (*Malus* spp.): white, pink, red
Carolina silverbell (*Halesia carolina*): white
Kousa dogwood (*Cornus kousa*): white
White fringe tree (*Chionanthus virginicus*): white
Japanese snowbell (*Styrax japonicus*): white
Golden-chain tree (*Laburnum* × *watereri*): yellow
Japanese tree lilac (*Syringa reticulata*): white
Golden-rain tree (*Koelreuteria paniculata*): yellow
Japanese pagoda tree (*Sophora japonica*): creamy white
Crape myrtle (*Lagerstroemia indica*): white, pink, lavender
Sourwood (*Oxydendrum arboreum*): white
Japanese stewartia (*Stewartia pseudocamellia*): white
Franklinia (*Franklinia alatamaha*): white

### Showy Shrubs

To add year-round interest to your home landscape, try planting a few of the plants from this list. The plant name is followed by features and seasons of interest:

Barberries (*Berberis* spp.): summer and fall foliage, flowers, fruit; all seasons
Blueberries (*Vaccinium* spp.): flowers, fruits, autumn color; summer, fall
Burning bush (*Euonymus alata*): fall foliage, winged bark; fall, winter
Crape myrtle (*Lagerstroemia indica*): flowers, fruits, bark; all seasons
Harry Lauder's walking stick (*Corylus avellana* 'Contorta'): leaves, flowers, twisted stems; all seasons
Mahonias, Oregon grapes (*Mahonia* spp.): evergreen leaves, flowers, fruits; all seasons
Oakleaf hydrangea (*Hydrangea quercifolia*): leaves, flowers; all seasons
Pieris (*Pieris* spp.): flowers, evergreen foliage; all seasons
Red-osier dogwood (*Cornus sericea*): flowers, bark; spring, winter
Rockspray cotoneaster (*Cotoneaster horizontalis*): flowers, fruit, growth habit; all seasons
Rugosa rose (*Rosa rugosa*): flowers, fruits; spring, summer, fall
Smoke tree (*Cotinus coggygria*): leaves, flowers; all seasons
Viburnums (*Viburnum* spp.): flowers, fruits; spring, fall

*canthos* var. *inermis*), produce only light or filtered shade; grass and other plants generally
have enough light to grow under or in the
shade of these trees. Other trees, like the sugar
and Norway maples (*Acer saccharum* and *A.
platanoides*), produce very dense shade in which
even shade-tolerant grasses have trouble growing. You'll need to use shade lovers such as ivy,
hostas, or ferns—or a mulch—to cover the

ground beneath such trees.

Even shade-tolerant plants may have difficulty growing under or near a tree, particularly a
large one. If the crown of the tree is dense, as
with maples, most rain is shed off the canopy
of the tree. The ground immediately below
may be dry even after a rain and tree roots
absorb much of the available water. See "Classic
Groundcovers for Shade" on page 333 for a list

---

 ## Forcing Flowering Trees and Shrubs

During the long dark days of late winter, nothing lifts the spirits as much as the sight of a few
branches of golden forsythia or coral-colored
quince.

Branches of spring-flowering trees are easy
to force for indoor display. You can force
almost any spring-blooming tree or shrub from
mid-January or early February on. Earlier than
this, most forcing fails because buds have not
had sufficient chilling to break their natural
winter dormancy.

Experiment with a variety of plants from
your garden, cutting heavily budded branches
on a mild day. Select stems of medium thickness
or better, since these contain large quantities of
stored sugars needed to nourish flower buds.
Use a sharp knife or pruning shears to cut the
branches; slice diagonally just above a bud. Cut
branches at least 2 to 3 feet long; shorter
branches are less effective in arrangements.
Keep plant health and form in mind as you harvest branches for forcing: Cut as carefully as you
would when pruning. To ensure a steady supply
of flowers, cut fresh branches every week or so.

After you bring the branches indoors, strip
flower buds and small twigs from the bottom
few inches of the stems. Slit up the stem ends a
few inches or crush slightly with a hammer to

encourage water absorption. Some may bloom
faster if you submerge them completely in a
tepid water bath for a few hours before making your arrangement. Recut stems and change
the water in the containers every few days.

Besides forsythias, pussy willows, and fruit
trees such as apples, cherries, plums, and
almonds, some proven favorites for forcing are
flowering quinces (*Chaenomeles* spp.), lilacs
(*Syringa* spp.), witch hazels (*Hamamelis* spp.),
hawthorns (*Crataegus* spp.), mock oranges
(*Philadelphus* spp.), spireas (*Spiraea* spp.), wisterias (*Wisteria* spp.), spicebush (*Lindera benzoin*),
alders (*Alnus* spp.), and horse chestnuts (*Aesculus hippocastanum*). Most of these will burst
into bloom within two to six weeks of cutting if
forced at temperatures between 60° and 70°F.
The closer it is to the plant's natural blooming
period when you cut the branches, the less time
it will take for them to open. You can control
blooming time to some extent by moving
branches to a cooler room to hold them back,
or placing them in a warm, sunny window to
push them ahead.

When arranging branches in containers,
keep in mind the beauty of stems as well as
flowers. Don't crowd them together so tightly
that the interesting tracery is obscured.

of plants that will tolerate these conditions.

Make a second list of the conditions of your site—soil, water, and exposure. For healthy, vigorous shrubs, match the plant to the site. Combine your two lists to discover the shrubs that best fill your needs.

With your list in hand, you're ready to buy. Remember that shrubs are a long-term investment. It's well worth your time and money to seek out and buy good-quality shrubs. Don't base your selection on price alone.

# GROWING HEDGES

Plant a hedge for a privacy screen to block out unwelcome views or traffic noise or to add a green background to set off other plantings. Hedges also provide excellent wind protection for house or garden. Thick, tall, or thorny hedges make inexpensive and forbidding barriers to keep out animals—or to keep them in.

A formal hedge is an elegant, carefully trimmed row of trees or shrubs. It requires exacting and frequent pruning to keep plants straight and level. The best plants for formal hedges are fine leaved and slow growing—and tough enough to take frequent shearing. An informal hedge requires only selective pruning and has a more natural look. A wide variety of plants can be used, many of which have attractive flowers or berries.

## PLANTING AND PRUNING HEDGES

It's best to plant young plants when starting a hedge. Full-grown specimens are more apt to die from transplanting stress, and finding an exact replacement can be difficult. It's easier to fill a gap in an informal hedge.

For an open, airy hedge of flowering shrubs, allow plenty of room for growth when planting. For a dense, wall-like hedge, space the plants more closely. You may find it easier to dig a

trench rather than separate holes. To ensure your hedge will be straight, tie a string between stakes at each end to mark the trench before digging. See "Trees and Shrubs" on page 84 for details on preparing planting holes and setting plants.

Broad-leaved plants used as a formal hedge need early training to force dense growth. For a thick, uniform hedge, reduce new shoots on the top and sides by one-third or more each year until the hedge is the desired size. Cutting a formal hedge properly is a challenge. Stand back, walk around, and recut until you get it straight—just like a haircut. Shear often during the growing season to keep it neat.

Needled evergreens require a different technique. Avoid cutting off the tops of evergreens until they reach the desired height. Shear the sides once a year, but never cut into the bare wood. See "Pruning Evergreens" on page 317 for more pruning tips.

 **Tough Trees for Windbreaks**

If you need a tree that will stand up to extreme cold, heat, and wind, try these three. They were tested over several decades in the Great Plains and will make excellent windbreaks:

Box elder (*Acer negundo*); a fast-growing, rounded tree that grows 30 to 50 feet tall. Zones 2 to 9.

Green ash (*Fraxinus pennsylvanica*); a large tree that grows up to 60 feet tall. Its green leaves may turn a nice yellow in fall but not reliably. Zones 3 to 9.

Silver buffalo berry (*Shepherdia argentea*); a thorny shrub or tree with silvery leaves and red or yellow edible fruit. It grows to 18 feet tall. Zones 2 to 6.

Prune informal hedges according to when they bloom. Do any needed pruning soon after flowering. Use thinning cuts to prune selected branches back to the next limb. Heading cuts that nip the branch back to a bud encourage dense, twiggy growth on the outside. To keep informal hedges vigorous, cut two or three of the oldest branches to the ground each year.

For fast, dense growth, prune in spring. This is also a good time for any severe shearing or pruning. For more about when and how to prune, see "Pruning and Training" on page 310.

# GROWING VINES

Versatility is the hallmark of vines. All scramble or climb, but that's where their similarity ends.

You can grow vines for shade, for food, or for beauty of foliage, bloom, or fruit. Vines range from tough, woody grapes and wisterias to annuals like morning-glories and garden peas. Other favorite vines include climbing roses, clematis, Boston and English ivies, Virginia creeper, climbing hydrangea, bittersweet, and passionflowers.

You can find a vine for almost any kind of site—sun, shade, loam, or sand; boggy or dry; fertile or poor soil. You're better off matching the vine to the situation than trying to alter the environment to suit the specific plant. In general, most vines are tolerant of a wide range of cultural conditions. It is the exception, such as clematis (which requires cool soil around its roots), that has specialized requirements. Be

---

## ❀ Hedge Plants

Many plants make excellent hedges. Even tall or bushy annuals can make a temporary hedge; plant herbs such as lavender for an attractive low hedge. Most hedges are shrub or tree species; this list is a mix of common and uncommon hedge plants. An asterisk (*) indicates a plant for a formal hedge:

### Evergreen Trees

Canada hemlock* (*Tsuga canadensis*)
English laurel* (*Prunus laurocerasus*)
Junipers (*Juniperus* spp.)
Lawson cypress (*Chamaecyparis lawsoniana*)
Pyramidal arborvitae (*Thuja occidentalis* 'Pyramidalis')

### Deciduous Trees

Beeches (*Fagus* spp.)
Hawthorns* (*Crataegus* spp.)
Hornbeam* (*Carpinus betulus*)

### Evergreen Shrubs

Boxwoods* (*Buxus* spp.)
Cotoneasters* (*Cotoneaster* spp.)
Euonymus (*Euonymus* spp.)
Firethorns* (*Pyracantha* spp.)
Japanese holly* (*Ilex crenata*)
Privets* (*Ligustrum* spp.)
Shrub honeysuckles* (*Lonicera* spp.)
Yews* (*Taxus* spp.)

### Deciduous Shrubs

Barberries (*Berberis* spp.)
Buckthorns* (*Rhamnus* spp.)
Forsythia (*Forsythia* × *intermedia*)
Japanese quince (*Chaenomeles speciosa*)
Mock oranges (*Philadelphus* spp.)
Privets* (*Ligustrum* spp.)
Russian olive (*Elaeagnus angustifolia*)
Shrub roses (*Rosa* spp.)
Viburnums (*Viburnum* spp.)

sure to check the specific needs of any plant before adding it into your garden. For basics on planting, propagating, and pest control, see Chapters 5, 6, and 7.

## LANDSCAPING WITH VINES

Vines' growing habits let you merge boundaries and soften harsh edges. Planting annual vines on fences, gates, and other structures quickly brings an established look to a young garden where the plants have yet to fill in. Use vines to define a garden room: Create green walls by covering fences, mark an entrance with a covered arbor, or provide overhead shade with a pergola.

Vines soften and connect the hard edge between the structures and the plants in a garden. Plant Boston ivy or wisteria to climb up a wall of your home, and you'll link the house and garden. Vines also make the house wall more attractive, provide seasonal interest (in our example, Boston ivy has fall color and berries, and wisteria has early-summer bloom), and if planted on the south side of the house, the vines will help cool it.

Plant vines to screen unsightly walls or views. A planting of wintercreeper will make an ugly concrete wall into a feature rather than an eyesore. A chain-link fence can become an asset if you cover it with trumpet vine (*Campsis radicans*) with its showers of brilliant red-orange blooms in midsummer.

Versatile vines have many other uses as well. Clematis or other vines planted next to lampposts and pillars add interest to any garden. Make the most of a small garden or terrace by "growing up." Grow vines over railings and along windows and door frames to create a magical hideaway. Annual vines can be grown in window boxes and are useful on terraces. Morning-glories (*Ipomoea* spp.), scarlet runner beans (*Phaseolus coccineus*), and black-eyed

Susan vines (*Thunbergia alata*) are good window-box choices. And don't forget attractive vines with edible parts such as cucumbers, pole beans, and peas.

## PRUNING AND TRAINING VINES

Pruning is your opportunity to train and control a vine. Look hard at the plant before cutting. The first step in any pruning operation is removal of dead, damaged, and diseased wood. Always use a sharp tool—a hand pruner, lopper, or saw—and make the cut just above a live bud or nearly flush with the stem. Only after "cleaning up" the plant should you start working on the live wood.

Prune live wood after the vine has finished blooming for the season. This means you'll prune spring bloomers in early summer, summer bloomers in early fall, and fall bloomers in winter or early spring. Remove dead wood anytime. Shape and control annuals by pinching early in the season. Pruning depends on the growth habit of the plant. Clinging vines like English ivy (*Hedera helix*), wintercreeper (*Euonymus fortunei*), and Virginia creeper (*Parthenocissus quinquefolia*) merely need trimming to keep them in bounds. Other vines like wisteria, clematis, and grapes will need annual pruning. For more on pruning techniques, see the Grapes entry on page 243.

# CARE AND MAINTENANCE

The most important thing you can do for your trees and shrubs is plant them in the right spot and with great care. For detailed instructions on choosing healthy plants and starting them out right, see "Trees and Shrubs" on page 84. Carefully selected and planted trees and shrubs need only occasional attention, especially once they become well established.

During the first year after planting, water

each week when less than 1 inch of rain falls, especially in summer and fall. Water to thaw the ground, and provide water for the leaves of evergreen trees during warm winter weather.

The mulch you applied at planting time will gradually decompose. Replenish it as needed, but only use a few inches. To avoid rodent problems and to encourage good air circulation, keep the mulch away from the trunk. To find out more about using mulch to conserve moisture and reduce maintenance, see "Mulching Your Garden" on page 167.

Small, yellow leaves, premature fall coloration, stunted twig growth, or too few flowers or fruits often indicate a nutrient deficiency. Your trees will generally receive enough fertilizer if they are located in a lawn that you regularly fertilize. If your trees are located in isolated beds, in areas surrounded by paving, or in containers, you may need to apply compost or a balanced organic fertilizer. Simply broadcast the needed fertilizer on the soil surface. See "Feeding Your Plants" on page 170 for more information about blended organic fertilizers.

Most trees are too large for you to provide them with special winter protection such as a burlap enclosure. If snow or ice loads bend the trees' branches, avoid vigorously shaking the branches to remove the ice or snow. Frozen, brittle branches can easily break. Either allow the ice or snow to melt away naturally or very gently sweep it off.

 **From Seed to Vine**

You can have beautiful vines for the cost of a seed packet. Try the following five beauties for color from spring until fall. For information on how to grow plants from seeds, see Chapter 4.

Black-eyed Susan vine (*Thunbergia alata*); produces 1- to 2-inch-wide orange, yellow, or white blooms with black eyes. Try planting them in hanging baskets, window boxes, and trellises.

Moonflower (*Ipomoea alba*); grows 8 to 10 feet long and has fragrant white night-blooming flowers. Soak seeds overnight or notch them with a knife or file to break through the seed coat and encourage germination.

Morning glories (*Ipomoea* spp.); will grow up to 25 feet long. They produce red, purple, pink, white, or blue flowers. Soak seeds overnight to promote germination.

Ornamental gourds (*Lagenaria siceraria*, *Cucurbita pepo* var. *ovifera*, and *Luffa aegyptiaca*); grown on a trellis will produce straight gourds in a variety of colors and sizes. Soak seeds overnight to promote germination.

Sweet pea (*Lathyrus odoratus*); bears fragrant pea-shaped flowers in every color but yellow in spring and early summer.

# PRUNING AND TRAINING

Pruning is both a science and an art—and probably the least-understood gardening practice. A properly pruned landscape shows off each plant at its best. Well-pruned trees and shrubs produce more or better fruit and flowers. Pruning can improve the health of an ailing shrub, make trees stronger and safer, channel growth away from buildings or traffic, and restore a sense of order to an overplanted or overgrown yard.

Prune young trees at planting time and as they grow, to correct structural problems and improve their form. Training a young tree with several years of judicious pruning leads to a structurally sound, well-shaped mature tree.

After a few years, begin the limbing-up process if the tree is planted where passersby will walk below it. Remove the lowest branch or two by sawing through the limb just before the branch collar. Repeat every year until the lowest branches are high enough to permit easy passage. About five or six years after planting, thin to open up the canopy, reducing wind resistance and allowing light to reach the interior. If your tree is intended to block an undesirable view, use heading cuts to encourage denser branching.

As your shrubs grow, you'll need to prune them to control their size, rejuvenate old plants, repair damage, remove pests, and control flowering and fruiting.

Maintain the natural form of your shrubs by pruning back to outward-facing buds or removing whole branches. Shearing is faster than naturalistic pruning, but it destroys the natural beauty of the plant—and you'll need to do it often. Learn to read the natural shape and type of a plant and prune accordingly. Many plants combine characteristics and may need more than one pruning technique.

## PRUNING CUTS

Many gardeners think pruning is a complicated task; however, most pruning comes down to making one of two kinds of pruning cuts: thinning cuts and heading cuts. The illustration on page 312 shows the differences between these two kinds of cuts.

**Thinning Cuts** Thinning cuts remove branches totally. They open up a plant but don't make it shorter. Thinning directs growth into alternate patterns. Use thinning cuts to establish good structure of young trees and shrubs, to allow sunlight to reach the plant interior, to remove wayward branches or those that block a view, and to make a plant less likely to break under a heavy snow load.

**Heading Cuts** Heading cuts shorten plants and stimulate latent buds behind the cut to grow, making the plant more dense. Nonselec-

 **Nuisance Trees**

Some trees create problems that outweigh their contributions. Many of the following trees are considered nuisance trees and are even banned or illegal to plant in many cities. The plant name is followed by the nuisance features of the tree:

American elm (*Ulmus americana*); insect and disease problems

Black locust (*Robinia pseudoacacia*); seeds prolifically, insect problems

Black walnut (*Juglans nigra*); produces toxin that poisons many other plants

Box elder (*Acer negundo*); weak wood, pest problems

Common horse chestnut (*Aesculus hippocastanum*); poisonous fruit, disease problems

Eastern cottonwood (*Populus deltoides*); messy fruit, weak wood

Ginkgo (*Ginkgo biloba*); female trees have foul-smelling fruit; plant only males

Lombardy poplar (*Populus nigra* 'Italica'); incurable canker disease kills top

Mimosa (*Albizia julibrissin*); insect and disease problems

Mulberries (*Morus* spp.); messy fruit

Silver maple (*Acer saccharinum*); shallow roots, weak wood, seeds prolifically

Thorned honey locust (*Gleditsia triacanthos*); dangerous thorns; plant only thornless cultivars (*G. triacanthos* var. *inermis*)

Tree-of-heaven (*Ailanthus altissima*); invasive grower, seeds prolifically, leaves and male flowers are foul-smelling

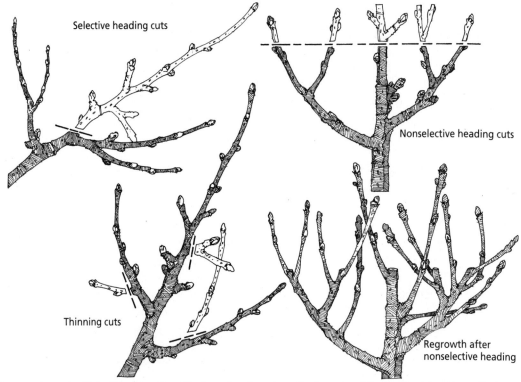

**Making pruning cuts.** Make thinning cuts at the branch collar where the branch originates. Avoid making a flush cut; leave the branch collar intact, but don't leave a stub. Make selective heading cuts back to a point directly above a bud or side branch of significant size that faces the direction you want new growth to take. Make nonselective heading cuts anywhere on the stem to shear branches to a uniform surface.

tive heading is the technique used to shape formal hedges and topiary. Branches are cut back partway along the stem, resulting in rapid, bushy regrowth just below the cut. Nonselective heading is often misapplied—resulting in forlorn, lollipop-shaped shrubs or trees that would look more attractive, and would likely be healthier, if pruned to follow their natural form.

Selective heading, on the other hand, reduces overall size or height of a plant without changing its natural shape. The plant suffers less stress and doesn't regrow as vigorously. Selective heading combines the best of thinning and heading, but it can't be applied to all plants. The older, larger, and woodier the plant, the fewer selective heading cuts should be used.

## PRUNING DOS AND DON'TS

Before you grab your pruning shears and head out the door, be sure you understand basic pruning dos and don'ts—the techniques that work and the mistakes to avoid.

**Proper Technique** Prune from the bottom up and, in the case of large plants, from the inside out. Prune out all dead wood first—an important step for health and good looks. Dead wood is easiest to spot in the summer because the branches have no green leaves.

Next look for a few of the worst rubbing, crossing branches. Leave the best-placed one of any pair. Try to keep any branches that head up and out from the center, as well as ones that fill

## City-Smart Trees

City trees must contend with constricted root space, compacted soil, wind tunnels between buildings, limited moisture and nutrients, high temperatures, and pollutants.

Trees used along streets, in raised planters, in median strips, or in parking lots must survive in the harshest and most stressful of all landscape environments. These often-neglected trees face all the hazards of city trees and must put up with drought, paving heat, and human vandalism. Despite relentless pruning to make them fit under overhead utility lines or within narrow corridors, and even when main branches are whacked off to permit people and cars to pass by, street trees manage to survive. But all these stresses take their toll: On average, street trees live only 10 to 15 years.

In addition to resisting insects and disease, good street trees also share other characteristics. They should be "clean" trees with no litter problems, such as dropping large leaves or fruit, although sometimes, as with sycamores (*Platanus* spp.) and oaks, the litter is overlooked because of other good qualities. Avoid trees with dangerous thorns or spines, such as hawthorns (*Crataegus* spp.); shallow-rooted trees that buckle paving, such as silver maples (*Acer saccharinum*); and thirsty trees, like weeping willows (*Salix babylonica*), whose roots seek water and sewer lines. Trees with branches that angle downward, such as pin oaks, also don't make the best street trees, unless they are limbed up high enough for pedestrians and traffic to pass easily. Here's a list of city-smart trees to consider. These trees are tough enough to tolerate the difficult growing conditions of city streets. All will tolerate poor soil, pollution, and droughty conditions:

### Small Trees

Amur maple (*Acer ginnala*)
Flowering pears (*Pyrus calleryana* 'Aristocrat' and 'Red Spire')
Golden-rain tree (*Koelreuteria paniculata*)
Hedge maple (*Acer campestre*)
Japanese tree lilacs (*Syringa reticulata* 'Ivory Silk' and 'Summer Snow')
Sargent cherry (*Prunus sargentii*)
Tatarian maple (*Acer tataricum*)
Thornless cockspur hawthorn (*Crataegus crusgalli* var. *inermis*)
Trident maple (*Acer buergeranum*)

### Medium to Large Trees

Bald cypress (*Taxodium distichum*)
Chinese or lacebark elm (*Ulmus parvifolia*)
Hackberry (*Celtis occidentalis* 'Prairie Pride')
Japanese pagoda tree (*Sophora japonica*)
Japanese zelkovas (*Zelkova serrata* 'Green Vase' and 'Village Green')
London plane tree (*Platanus × acerifolia* 'Bloodgood')
Sawtooth oak (*Quercus acutissima*)
Silver linden (*Tilia tomentosa*)
Sycamore maple (*Acer pseudoplatanus*)
Thornless honey locusts (*Gleditsia triacanthos* var. *inermis* 'Skyline' and 'Shademaster')
Upright English oak (*Quercus robur* 'Fastigiata')
Upright European hornbeam (*Carpinus betulus* 'Fastigiata')
Upright ginkgo (*Ginkgo biloba* 'Fastigiata')
Willow oak (*Quercus phellos*)

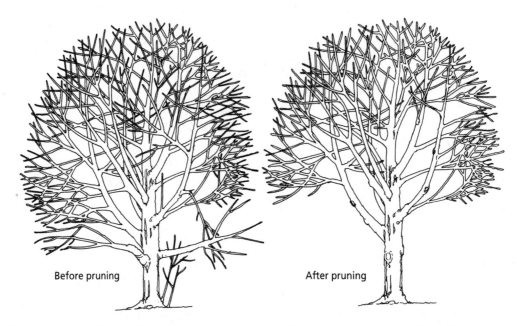

Before pruning

After pruning

**Pruning a mature tree.** If you've inherited a mature tree, some judicious pruning can make it better looking and healthier. If you're not an experienced tree-climber, hire an arborist to rejuvenate your tree. *Before:* Dead and diseased branches, watersprouts, tight crotch angles, and rubbing or crossing branches weaken the tree's structure and make it look neglected. *After:* The tree has been rejuvenated and thinned out, and branches have been headed back to encourage dense new growth.

 **Water in Winter**

Trees and shrubs need extra water during hot summer dry spells, but they also need supplemental water during dry periods in the winter or early spring. Cold, windy weather dries out soil and plants just as it dries and cracks your skin. Unfortunately, plants show less injury from lack of moisture in winter and are more likely to be neglected. Evergreens, which transpire water continuously, are particularly susceptible to winter droughts. It may not be much fun, but if you've had a long stretch without rain or snow, bundle up and haul out the hose or watering can!

an otherwise empty space.

Prune to open up center areas and to clean up the base of shrubs. This improves plant health by admitting light and increasing air circulation. It also has a large impact on the beauty of a plant.

Selectively thin or head back misplaced branches: those that touch the ground, lay upon or crowd other plants, or come too close to the house, windows, and walkways.

Save any heading cuts until the end of a pruning job. Locate the longest, most unruly branch first, follow it down inside the shrub, and cut it off to a side branch or a bud. Next year's new growth will be channeled into the bud or side branch.

**Pruning Mistakes** The most common pruning mistake is to cut back everything in the yard in an ill-fated attempt to make it all smaller again. This stimulates an upsurge of messy regrowth, making the final solution more difficult. Tree topping, indiscriminate shearing, and overthinning are the three major forms of "malpruning."

The cure for badly pruned plants is time. Most will reestablish their natural habits given a few years to recover. Rehabilitative pruning can hasten the process and make plants look better. Meticulously prune all dead wood, removing all stubs. Use thinning cuts to simplify tangled branch ends. Take out entire canes. If treelike shrubs have rampantly produced suckers because of heading cuts, slowly remove the worst of them over a period of years. Let the strongest and best-placed suckers grow back into branches. Some cane-growers, like weigela, can be radically renovated by cutting them entirely to the ground. In about three years they'll regrow to mature size and bloom again. Many lovely but rampant vines, such as autumn clematis, are treated this way.

The majority of needled evergreens will not green up once they are cut back to unneeedled wood. This makes their size difficult to control and radical renovation impossible.

## PRUNING TIMETABLE

Plan your pruning schedule depending on what you want to accomplish. General thinning can be done in any season. Follow these seasonal guidelines:

■ Spring pruning stimulates the most rapid regrowth, so it's a good time for heavy pruning. Prune evergreens in spring, but avoid pruning deciduous trees as they leaf out. Prune spring-flowering shrubs such as azaleas, daphnes, and forsythias when they finish blooming so they'll have time to grow and set new buds during summer. This is essential if you are heading back all the branches to force more blooms.

■ Summer pruning has a less stimulating effect on growth. Hot or dry weather is extremely stressful for plants, so avoid heavy pruning. This is a good time to tidy up plants

 **Words to Know**

**Branch collar:** The part of the trunk that helps hold the branch to the trunk; often recognizable as a bulge at the base of the branch.

**Branch crotch:** The angle where a tree branch meets the trunk or parent stem.

**Break bud:** When a latent bud is stimulated into growing out into a leaf or twig, it is said to break bud.

**Cane:** A long, slender branch that usually originates directly from the roots.

**Leader:** The main, primary, or tallest shoot of a tree trunk. Trees can be single-leadered, such as birch, or multiple-leadered, such as vine maple.

**Pinching:** Nipping out the end bud of a twig or stem with your fingertips to make the plant more compact and bushy.

**Thinning cut:** Cutting a limb off at the base, either at ground level or at a branch collar.

**Heading cut:** Cutting a branch back to a side bud or shoot.

**Skirting or limbing up:** Pruning off the lower limbs of trees. Skirting or limbing up is usually done for easy passage underneath.

**Sucker:** An upright shoot growing from a root or graft union; also, in common usage, straight, rapid-growing shoots or water-sprouts that grow in response to wounding or poor pruning.

**Topiary:** Plants sculpted into tightly sheared geometric shapes or likenesses of animals or people.

and remove suckers and to prune summer-flowering shrubs after they bloom.

■ In mid- to late fall, make only thinning cuts. Heading cuts made late in the season can stimulate soft new growth that is easily damaged in fall freezes. Don't prune plants during the period when their leaves are falling.

■ Late winter is the traditional time to prune dormant plants; leaves have dropped and it's easy to see plant form. Winter pruning stimulates growth, but the results are delayed until spring. This is a good time to prune fruit trees, brambles, grapes, roses, and summer-blooming shrubs, such as butterfly bushes and hydrangeas, that form flowers on the current year's wood.

## GOOD TOOLS FOR GOOD CUTS

Choose pruning tools that cut cleanly and easily. Keep the cutting edges sharp. You'll probably need only three pruning tools: pruning shears for stems and twigs, lopping shears for branches that are finger-size and larger, and a pruning saw for larger branches and crowded areas.

Pruning shears are available in two types. Anvil pruners cut with a sharp blade that closes against a metal plate, or anvil; bypass pruners work like scissors. A leather holster is a wise investment: Your hands are free, but the shears are always handy.

Lopping shears have long handles that extend your reach and give you leverage for more cutting strength. A small rubber shock absorber is a welcome addition on some models. Folding pruning saws fit nicely into a back pocket. New ARS-type saws have multifaceted blades and cut twice as easily as traditional blades. Pole pruners can be used for overhead work, but be careful of overhead wires.

The pruning head can consist of either a saw or a cord-operated hook-type shear, or some combination of the two. You may find that

## I Know You, Bud!

When pruning trees and shrubs grown for flowers or fruits, it's important to be able to distinguish vegetative buds from flower buds. Vegetative buds—those forming leaves—are usually sharper, thinner, and longer than the plump flowering buds.

Terminal or apical buds, found at the tip of a twig, can be vegetative, flowering, or mixed, and they are usually plumper than lateral or axillary buds, which are found farther down the twig.

For correct timing of pruning, it's important to know where flower buds form and when they open. See "Pruning Timetable" on page 315 for information on when to prune flowering shrubs and trees.

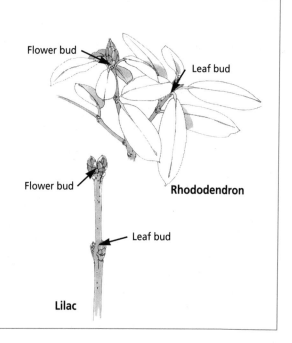

Flower bud

Leaf bud

**Rhododendron**

Flower bud

Leaf bud

**Lilac**

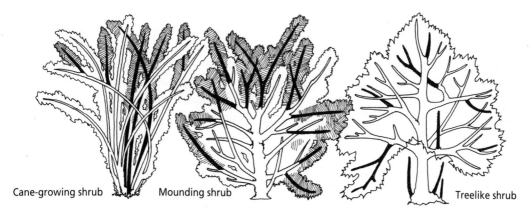

Cane-growing shrub    Mounding shrub    Treelike shrub

**Shrub pruning strategies.** Renew and control cane-growing shrubs such as forsythia, nandina, and roses by removing older canes at ground level. Neaten up and shorten mounding shrubs such as abelias and barberries by using mostly selective heading cuts to remove unruly and overly long branches, hiding cuts in the shrub interior. Prune rhododendrons, witch hazels, viburnums, and other treelike shrubs with thinning cuts to remove dead wood or interfering branches, reduce bulk and clutter, and create definition.

hedge shears are extremely useful for keeping your formal hedges neat.

## PRUNING EVERGREENS

Evergreens that are the proper size for their location need very little pruning. Their natural growth habit is interesting and attractive. To remove unhealthy or errant growth, use a thinning cut, pruning off branches nearly flush against the branch from which they originate. See "Pruning Cuts" on page 311 for more information.

Unlike broad-leaved evergreens, needle-leaved evergreens aren't quick to resprout after pruning. Take care to prune them properly. Follow these steps when pruning evergreens:

■ Thin evergreens by removing branches any time of the year. Cut stray branches far enough to the inside to hide the stub. Branches cut back beyond the green needles will not sprout new growth.

■ Don't cut the central leader at the top of the tree—an evergreen without its central leader will have a drastically different shape.

■ Prune arborvitae, hemlocks, junipers, and yews throughout the growing season.

■ Trim your evergreens gradually. If you cut off more than one-third of the total green on the plant, it may die.

■ One good idea is to hold off pruning your evergreens until a few weeks before Christmas. Then use the trimmings from arborvitaes (*Thuja* spp.), boxwoods (*Buxus* spp.), cedars (*Cedrus* spp.), firs (*Abies* spp.), pines (*Pinus* spp.), rhododendrons (*Rhododendron* spp.), and other evergreens for holiday wreaths and decorations.

## AVOIDING PESTS AND PROBLEMS

Frequent inspection of your trees will help minimize problems. Your best defenses are to buy good-quality, pest-free trees to avoid introducing pests or disease; to plant your trees in proper environments to encourage vigorous growth; to use good maintenance practices; and to minimize environmental stresses.

Biotic or pathological problems are caused by living organisms—insects, mites, fungi, bacteria, viruses, nematodes, and rodents. Abiotic or physiological problems are caused by nonliving things—improper planting and maintenance, poor soil conditions, air pollution, injury, compacted soil, construction damage, and lightning. Far more tree problems are caused by abiotic problems, which weaken trees, allowing boring insects and decay fungi to attack. If your tree shows signs of ill health, check for poor conditions that may have allowed the pest or disease to get a foothold.

The plant family bothered by the greatest number of insect and disease problems is the

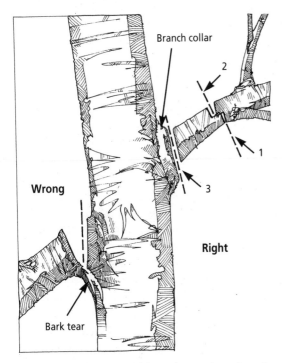

**Pruning large limbs.** Sawed from above, a large branch will tear bark from the trunk as it falls. Use the three-cut method to prevent damage. (1) About 1 foot out from the trunk, cut halfway through the branch from underneath. (2) A few inches in from the first cut, saw off the branch from the top. (3) Remove the stub by cutting along, but never into, the branch collar. On tight crotches, saw from the bottom up.

rose family. This large family includes such trees as crab apples, flowering pears, cherries, peaches and plums, hawthorns, serviceberries, and mountain ash. Crab apples are particularly susceptible to problems; buy only those cultivars that are resistant to the diseases rust, scab, powdery mildew, and fire blight. Other trees, such as flowering dogwood, maples, sycamores, birches, elms, locusts, and oaks, may also have numerous pest or disease problems. Ask your nursery owner for advice before purchasing.

Whenever a disease or insect problem is seen, try to control it by removing the pest or the affected plant part. Don't compost or burn infected plants. Remember to sanitize tools after pruning infested or infected wood by cleaning them with a 10 percent bleach solution (1 part bleach to 9 parts water).

**Insects** Most insect problems of trees are caused by a relatively small number of insects and mites (technically classed as arachnids). These pests have their preferences: Some primarily damage leaves, and others primarily damage branches and trunks.

Insects eat leaves and suck plant sap from them. The larvae of moths and butterflies, such as bagworms, cankerworms, webworms, tent caterpillars, and gypsy moths, are especially voracious leaf-eaters. Highly noticeable webs of Eastern tent caterpillars and fall webworms protect the larvae from predators while they munch your leaves. Although the nests are unsightly, trees usually recover from infestations. Remove and destroy any webs you can reach.

Gypsy moth populations rise to a peak in cycles of several years, causing almost complete defoliation in areas of heavy infestation. Hand-picking and spraying BT (*Bacillus thuringiensis*) are the best defenses against severe attacks of gypsy moths. In winter, check your trees for the light brown egg masses, and scrape them off into a container of ammonia.

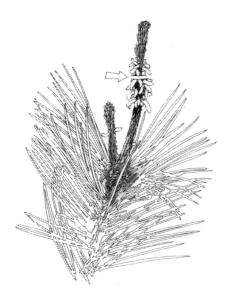

**Pinching pine candles.** Cut back firs, pines, and spruces only in spring when "candles" of new growth appear at the tips of the branches. To encourage denseness or shape the tree, cut off about one-half or two-thirds of the candle.

Other major insect pests that damage leaves are aphids and adelgids, various beetles and bugs, miners, scales, and spider mites.

Insects are always present on trees. Populations must be extreme before the tree suffers any real damage. Don't rush to the sprayer as soon as you spot a caterpillar or two. Remember, the goal is a healthy tree, not complete insect annihilation. Learn to recognize harmful pests and the signs of infestation: curled leaves, stunted growth, deformed flowers.

Try handpicking and pruning off affected branches before you reach for other controls. Even BT is not innocuous. It does kill gypsy moth larvae, tent caterpillars, and other undesirables—but it will also kill any other caterpillar that happens to eat a tainted leaf, including the beautiful luna moth, giant silk moths, and dozens of others.

Stems are damaged when insects such as borers and scales either bore into them or feed on

 **Trees and Construction**

In some cases, you may find it more practical or desirable to leave large trees in place and build around them, rather than transplanting them elsewhere. Be sure that you—and your construction crew—do everything you can to minimize direct and indirect damage to the trees.

Direct tree damage occurs when you cut roots; damage or tear away trunk bark; break, tear away, or incorrectly prune off branches; or tie or nail items to the trees. Indirect tree damage occurs when you strip away topsoil and leaf litter, compact the soil, dump additional fill soil atop the roots, and burn or bury waste materials near the trees. You also indirectly damage the trees by paving over open areas that absorbed rainfall, removing neighboring plants

that provided wind and sun protection, and creating new drainage patterns for rainwater and runoff.

Your top priority is to preserve the natural root environment. If you keep people and equipment away from the tree, you will minimize the chances of damage being done to the tree trunk and branches. If possible, erect fences around the drip line of trees before construction begins to keep vehicles and piles of building materials away from the sensitive root zone and trunk. Once construction is completed, apply mulch to replace leaf litter that was removed, prune structurally weak branches, and provide water and fertilizer to help stimulate new roots.

them. Cicadas cause stem damage when they lay their eggs into slits in twigs. Microscopic worm-like nematodes also cause problems on the roots of many trees. See Chapter 7 for more about controlling insect problems.

**Diseases**  Tree diseases occur on leaves, stems, and roots. Many pathological diseases are difficult to distinguish from physiological problems. For instance, while fungi and bacteria can cause leaf spot diseases, spots on tree leaves can also be caused by nutrient deficiencies, improperly applied pesticides, road salts, and even drought. Be careful to properly identify a tree problem before you look for a control or corrective measure.

Most tree diseases are caused by fungi, although a few major diseases, such as fire blight on pears and other members of the rose family, are caused by bacteria. Flowering peaches and plums are also bothered by viral diseases.

Diseases of tree leaves are generally spots, anthracnoses, scorches, blights, rusts, and mildews. You will see them on your trees most

frequently during moist weather and when plants are under environmental stress. Diseases of tree stems are generally cankers, blights, and decays. You will see these diseases when trees

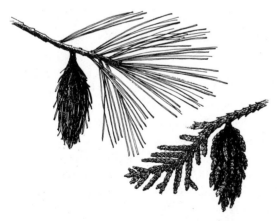

**Bagworms.** These moth larvae chew leaves of many kinds of evergreens. They spin silken bags studded with bits of needles; the bags may resemble pinecones. Hand-pick and destroy the bags in winter. Spray BTK (*Bacillus thuringiensis* var. *kurstaki*) for larvae in spring; catch adult moths in pheromone traps in summer.

 **Girdles Can Kill Trees**

Trees can't die of a broken heart, but they can die of a girdling root. A girdling root is a root that grows in a circling pattern. The root can eventually put so much pressure on a tree trunk that it stops the flow of water and nutrients between the roots and the top, killing the tree.

Symptoms of a root-girdled trunk are weak topgrowth, poor bark development, or a pronounced swelling at the base of the trunk. The leaves on the girdled side may be a lighter green in early fall than the rest of the foliage. Another suspicious condition is a trunk that grows straight up from ground level instead of being flared or buttressed at the soil line. A trunk that is slightly concave on one side can also indicate a girdling root.

What causes girdling roots? Roots can be turned back toward the trunk if they come up against hard, impervious subsoil. Pavement can be the culprit that deflects the roots of street trees. If roots are overcrowded when a tree is first planted, they may interfere with each other's growth and result in a girdling root.

If you suspect a girdling root, do a little detective work, and solve the problem if you uncover one. Gently remove the soil from the roots in the suspect area. Sever any girdling root with a chisel and mallet. Be sure to chop out a gap several inches wide so that the severed root won't rejoin itself. Then cover the area with the soil again.

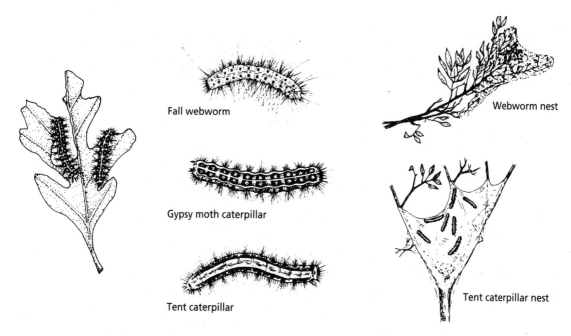

Fall webworm

Webworm nest

Gypsy moth caterpillar

Tent caterpillar nest

Tent caterpillar

**Common tree pests.** Three of the most troublesome pests of deciduous trees are chewing caterpillars. Look for tent caterpillar nests in spring in the crotches of cherries and other trees; fall webworms appear in late summer, their webs festooning branch tips of walnuts and other trees. Hairy gypsy moth caterpillars are hard to overlook in peak years of infestations.

have been damaged by improper pruning, mechanical injury, and other maintenance and environmental factors. The major diseases of tree roots are root rots. Root rots occur when soils are poorly drained and may be intensified if roots have been injured by such things as construction damage and trenching. See Chapter 7 for more information on disease prevention and control.

**Physical Damage** You can damage a tree by nailing items to it or gouging it with a lawn mower. Animals also damage trees. Birds may occasionally break branches or drill branches, looking for sap or insects. Moles damage your trees by cutting the roots as they tunnel, and voles actually feed on the roots. Mice and rabbits damage trees by feeding on the bark. Deer damage trees by browsing on young branch tips and by rubbing their antlers on the trunks and branches.

Handle your trees gently. Avoid lawn mower damage by using mulch or beds of groundcovers to surround the trunk. A cat that patrols outdoors now and then is one way to control rodents. Fence to keep out deer. For more on controlling animals, see Chapter 7.

# Chapter 14

# LAWNS AND GROUNDCOVERS

The goal of most homeowners is to have a lush, green lawn that's free of weeds and, at the same time, easy to maintain. In addition, most of us also want to keep the environment cleaner by cutting down on the use of gasoline-powered lawn mowers, and keep our lawns and our families healthy by avoiding the use of lawn chemicals. An ideal way to cut down on lawn maintenance is to turn some of that green grass into a richly textured bed of easy-care groundcovers.

Whether you're looking for ways to make your lawn healthier, seeking solutions to lawn problems, or looking for alternatives to lawns, this chapter will provide you with a wealth of lawn care and groundcover tips and techniques.

## LAWN CARE BASICS

Healthy green turf makes everything near it look better. A carpet of green grass also makes a great place to play or relax, while preventing soil erosion and enhancing the value of your home. A good lawn is the result of conscientious gardening practices, whether you're starting a new lawn with a carefully selected cultivar or rejuvenating an existing one.

Build a strong lawn by using grass species adapted to your climate. Encourage healthy growth naturally by letting light grass clippings remain where they fall and by applying compost or other organic material. Relying on high-nitrogen chemical fertilizers can lead to problem-prone, shallow-rooted turf that needs mowing more often. These are some of the most widely grown lawn grasses:

- Bermuda grass (*Cynodon dactylon*), a fine-textured, drought-resistant grass popular in warmer climates. Becomes buff brown in the winter. Numerous runners create a wear-resistant turf. Open-pollinated strains are extremely aggressive; modern hybrids are much easier to keep from invading flower beds.

- Buffalo grass (*Buchloe dactyloides*), a creeping, warm-season grass. Tolerates drought and will grow in alkaline soil. Good wear tolerance. Brown in midsummer and fall.

- Centipede grass (*Eremochloa ophiuroides*), a coarser-leaved, warm-season, creeping grass with good drought tolerance. Plant in areas that receive little wear.

- Fine fescues (*Festuca* spp.), dark green, fine-textured, creeping, cool-season grasses with good shade tolerance, often mixed with Kentucky bluegrass.

- Kentucky bluegrass (*Poa pratensis*), a lush, dark green turfgrass with narrow blades that requires substantial sunshine. Favored cool-season lawn grass. May become dormant during summer droughts or during winter freezes. Creeping stolons knit a tough turf.

- Turf-type tall fescue (*Festuca arundinacea*), a coarse, medium green grass good for sun or shade, increasingly popular in the central United States. Updated cultivars remain green most of the year. Drought-resistant. Grows in low clumps and doesn't creep, so is often mixed with other grasses.

■ Zoysia grass (*Zoysia* spp.), a medium green, creeping, fine-textured grass for full sun. Green in warm weather, tan in winter.

## FERTILIZING YOUR LAWN

You don't need to know every grass plant in your yard by name to grow a healthy lawn. The most important thing to note is the time of year when the grass begins to grow rapidly. This is the ideal time to apply a good organic fertilizer. In the North where cool-season grasses have a growth spurt in spring and another in fall, plan to fertilize twice. For warm-season grasses, fertilize in late spring, just as your lawn greens up, and again a few weeks later.

Choose a finely pulverized, weed-free organic fertilizer, such as processed manure or sifted compost, and spread evenly over the lawn just before rain is expected. Mow the grass about a week after you fertilize. Let the nitrogen-rich clippings remain on the lawn.

## MAINTAINING YOUR LAWN

Lawn maintenance involves more than just proper watering techniques. (See "The Way to Water" on page 324.) You also must mow, dethatch, and aerate your lawn regularly to keep it at its best.

**Mowing** Sharpen your mower blade at the beginning of each season to make sure the grass blades are cut, rather than torn, when you mow. Remove only one-third of the grass's top-growth. The exact height for mowing depends on the species of grass. Cut low-growing grasses, such as Bermuda grass and zoysia grass, no shorter than 1 inch. Cut taller grasses, such as bluegrass and tall fescue, no shorter than 2 inches. Mow high during summer droughts. To cut very tall grass, set your mower blade at its highest setting. In the course of the next two mowings, lower the blade until you are cutting at the usual height.

If you mow regularly, let your grass clippings lie where they fall. They will eventually rot and add organic matter to the soil beneath. But don't let large clumps of clippings sit on your lawn—they block sunlight and promote disease. Gather them up and use as mulch in other parts of your yard.

**Dethatching** All lawns have thatch, a layer of clippings and stems that gradually decomposes and feeds the roots. There's no need to remove it if the layer is no thicker than about ¼ inch. Thatch problems often start with overuse of synthetic chemical fertilizers, which make grass grow fast and lush. As clippings build up into a thick layer of thatch, grass plants are unable to get enough air for healthy growth. Use a thatch rake to break up thatch in a small lawn; rent a vertical mower to dethatch a larger area.

**Aerating** Since lawns often bear heavy foot traffic, the soil below them becomes compacted over time. Grass roots have trouble growing down and out and instead concentrate their growth at the surface. Prevent or fix compacted lawns by aerating every two or three years. Aerating a lawn consists of poking tiny holes through the turf into the soil below. Use a step-on core cultivator for small areas; rent a power aerator machine for larger lawns. Mow the lawn and spread a thin layer of organic fertilizer. Aerate in one direction; repeat crosswise. Water the lawn deeply.

## REPAIRING LAWNS

Ruts left by heavy vehicles or scars created when shrubs or trees are removed call for prompt spot repairs. If damage occurs in winter, prepare the soil and cover it with a mulch until spring.

Loosen the soil in the damaged site, setting aside any grass plants that seem healthy. Keep them damp and shaded as you work. Add a ½-inch layer of compost or peat moss to condition the soil, along with enough good topsoil to raise the level of the damaged area 1 inch above the soil level of the surrounding turf. Lightly walk over the spot, and fill in any holes or low places. Reseed or replant, matching the primary species in your yard. Water regularly for a month.

## PLANTING A NEW LAWN

All lawn grasses require at least 4 inches of good topsoil in which to stretch their roots. If your new yard has been scraped down to the subsoil, you will have to spread new topsoil. Site preparation is the same whether you plan to begin with seed or sod: Cultivate new or existing top-soil thoroughly, adding a 1-inch layer of peat moss, compost, or other organic matter. Rake out all weeds and roots, cultivate again, and rake smooth. Use a roller to evenly compact the site and make it level.

Be picky when shopping for grass seed. Improved cultivars of the best lawn grasses cost more than their open-pollinated cousins, but they offer superior performance. Choose named cultivars that have been specially bred for drought tolerance, insect and disease resistance, adaptability to shade, or other traits. Use a mechanical seeder for even distribution. Roll after seeding. Keep constantly moist for two weeks. Start mowing three weeks after seeding.

## The Way to Water

Proper watering techniques will ensure a healthy, lush lawn and will enable you to sustain your lawn's growth even during times of drought. Just follow these steps:

■ Water your lawn with occasional deep waterings to encourage grass roots to penetrate deeply into the soil to draw the soil's water and dissolved nutrients.

■ Avoid frequent shallow waterings. This only leads to shallow grass rooting.

■ During a drought, allow the grass to go dormant by not watering. This allows your grass to "prepare" its natural defenses against a drought.

■ Mow high or don't mow at all during a drought. Dried grass foliage helps insulate the crowns so they'll retain more moisture.

■ Water sparingly after the grass goes dormant. Provide $\frac{1}{2}$ inch of water every two weeks. This will keep some roots and buds alive but won't bring the grass out of its dormant state.

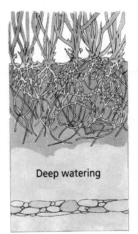

Deep watering     Shallow watering

**How to water your lawn.** Frequent shallow watering leads to shallow rooting. The shallow roots have less of the soil's reserve of nutrients to draw from. Frequent heavy watering can waterlog the soil, also suppressing root growth. Your lawn will be healthiest if you give it occasional deep waterings. The grass roots will penetrate to the depth the soil is wet and can draw water and dissolved nutrients from a larger volume of the soil.

Sod is the fastest way to an attractive lawn, though the cost is higher than seed. It's ideal for spot repairs, especially in high-traffic areas or on slopes. Plant cool-season species in early spring or from late summer to early fall; plant warm-season grasses in late spring to early summer. Use only fresh, green strips. Keep them shaded and damp until planted. Work crosswise along slopes. Roll or walk on the strips after planting to push the roots into the soil. After planting, water newly laid sod every two or three days for three weeks.

## PLANTING OPTIONS

Whether you're starting a new lawn or repairing one you've already got, you have several grass-planting options:

**Spreading seed:** If you're seeding a lawn area, use a spreader to distribute seed evenly. A broadcast-type spreader throws the seeds in a wide swath, so it does the job faster than a drop-type spreader will. When working near flower beds or other nonlawn plantings, the drop type is preferable because it won't cast the seed into your flower beds. Make two passes when seeding an area. On your second pass, walk at a 90-degree angle to the first pass.

**Planting grass plugs:** Plugs can restore a damaged lawn area. Begin by raking the area to level it and remove debris. Water thoroughly the night before you plan to plant. Use a plugger, auger, or spade to make 3-inch-diameter planting holes in a checkerboard pattern. For good establishment, place 1 teaspoon of blended organic fertilizer in each hole before planting. Plant a plug in each hole. The spacing you use will determine how long it takes for the grass to fill in and form continuous cover. Water again after planting and regularly for the first few weeks. Fertilize your new lawn six to eight weeks after planting.

**Laying sod:** When laying sod, fit the strips as close together as possible. Be sure to stagger the seams between strips so that they do not line up from row to row. Use a sharp knife to cut sod to fit around walks, edgings, or other obstacles. Rolling sod after laying it improves contact between the roots and the underlying soil and gets the sod off to a good start. On a slope, always lay the rows of sod across the slope, not up and down.

Do any sod patching on the inside. Pieces along the periphery should be whole. If you're patching here and there as part of a renovation (perhaps to cover where a tree has come down or to resod a patch lost to weeds), you should

 **Low Maintenance Lawns**

For the best lawn in the least time, follow these tips:

■ Limit the amount of lawn in your landscape.

■ Keep lawn in large, continuous swaths. Join trees and shrubs with a bed of mulch or groundcovers instead of mowing around and between. Don't plant lawn in hard-to-mow corners.

■ Replace aggressive old strains of grass with an improved cultivar or mixture.

■ Use lawn edgings and mulch to separate grass from flower beds and trees.

■ Accept clovers in your lawn as beneficial nitrogen-fixers, not weeds.

■ Where conditions are too steep, too shady, or otherwise unsuitable for a good lawn, choose alternatives such as ornamental grasses or groundcovers.

■ During droughts, water modestly once a week. Provide sufficient water to keep your grass alive, but not enough to coax it out of heat-induced dormancy.

## Lawn Grass Pest Patrol

When your lawn starts to show yellow or brown patches, you can be sure that lawn pests are living in your green carpet. Here's a look at the four most common lawn pests and what you can do to combat them:

**Sod webworms:** Webworms sever grass blades and cause irregular dead patches in the lawn. Hot, dry conditions and thatch buildup encourage the pests.

Control webworms by saturating infested areas with a soap drench (2 tablespoons liquid dish soap to 1 gallon water) to drive the larvae to the surface. Rake the pests into a pile and dump them into a bucket of soapy water. Apply BTK (*Bacillus thuringiensis* var. *kurstaki*) or drench the soil with parasitic nematodes when pests are in their larval stage (usually about 2 weeks after moths appear). Spray severely infested areas with pyrethrin if all other attempts at control fail.

**White grubs:** These curved, fat, whitish larvae of Japanese beetles and other beetle species

chew on grass roots, leaving sections of lawn that appear burned. Lift out damaged turf.

**A check for white grubs.** Use a blunt-ended spade to cut through three sides of a square-foot flap of lawn. Gently pry up the roots, and roll the flap back to look underneath. Count the grubs in the ground, and then tamp the turf back down. Ten or more grubs per square foot is a serious infestation. Give the flap a little extra water for a week or two to be sure it reroots.

Walk the turf in spiked sandals (available through mail-order catalogs) that will pierce and kill the grubs. For a large lawn, apply milky disease spores according to package directions; this treatment will eliminate Japanese beetle grubs over a few seasons. Or apply predatory nematodes. Water the soil well before and after application to improve results.

**Billbugs:** Billbug larvae are white grubs with yellow-brown heads that feed on grass stems, causing shoots to turn brown and die. In warm weather the grubs tunnel into the soil and feed on roots and rhizomes. Billbugs are brown or nearly black $\frac{1}{4}$- to $\frac{1}{2}$-inch weevils. Control grubs by aerating the lawn, watering deeply, removing thatch, and adding organic matter. Reseed or overseed with resistant cultivars.

**Chinch bugs:** Chinch bugs and their larvae are common lawn pests virtually everywhere except the Northwest and Plains states. The bugs and the larvae are about $1\frac{1}{2}$ inches long. The bugs have a distinctive inverted-V pattern on their wings.

If your lawn shows ragged yellow or brown patches, you may have a chinch bug problem. Treating problem areas with insecticidal soap is generally effective.

**A check for chinch bugs.** Cut both ends from an empty coffee can and push the can halfway into the lawn. Pour soapy water into the can and wait 10 to 15 minutes. Then count the number of chinch bugs and/or larvae that float to the top. If you see more than 12, you need to take steps to control the pest.

use whole blocks of sod, even if the spot in need is smaller than that. The smaller the piece, the harder it is to keep alive, so cut out a spot big enough to lay in an entire block of sod.

**Making spot repairs:** Where weeds or lawn pests have caused damaged patches, a partial lawn renovation will usually solve the problem. Clean out weeds and dead grasses with a shovel and rake, till the soil, and amend it with an organic fertilizer. The cultivated patch of soil will compact and settle over time, so rake it into a flat-topped mound slightly higher than the surrounding turf. Plan on planting seed or sod that matches the rest of your lawn, unless you've decided on a shade- or drought-tolerant lawn grass for a particularly troublesome area. After sowing or sodding, be sure to firm the soil to ensure good soil contact. Water repaired spots as necessary until the new grass shows strong new growth.

### COPING WITH PROBLEMS

A healthy lawn is naturally more resistant to weed, insect, or disease problems. A tight cover of vigorous grass will outcompete weeds. Loose, well-drained soil helps prevent disease problems. Proper fertilization goes a long way toward preventing lawn problems since it encourages growth of strong, healthy turf. Most updated turfgrass cultivars offer genetically improved resistance to diseases and some insects. If you have lawn areas that are chronically problematic, consider replanting them with an improved cultivar or trying an alternative to lawn grass. See "Groundcovers" on this page for suggestions of plants that work well as substitutes for lawns.

There are a few simple steps to take if your lawn develops weed or pest problems. Use a small, sharp knife to slice off any established weeds about 1 inch below the soil surface. If more than half of the plants in your lawn are

weeds, it is best to completely renovate the lawn by replanting.

Subterranean insect larvae, such as white grubs, occasionally cause serious damage when they feed on grass roots. Apply milky disease spores for long-term control of these pests. Biological insecticides that utilize parasitic nematodes control numerous insects likely to feed beneath your lawn. For more ideas on reducing pests and disease, see Chapter 7.

# GROUNDCOVERS

Groundcovers are the original landscape problem solvers. Where lawn grass won't grow easily or well, groundcovers come into their own. You can use plants like pachysandra to cover bare spots in the dense shade and dry soil under

---

 **Groundcovers with Bulbs**

Spring bulbs also make a nice contrast planted among common groundcovers like English ivy and Japanese pachysandra (*Pachysandra terminalis*). Daffodils work best because they naturalize easily, bloom in light shade, and grow tall enough to reach through the mat of groundcover. However, you may have to thin around the bulbs every two or three years to keep them from being choked out. Common periwinkle (*Vinca minor*) has a light root system, and daffodils do well planted among it without a lot of thinning.

You can also consider interplanting bulbs with perennial groundcovers that emerge later in spring, such as hostas, Siberian bugloss (*Brunnera macrophylla*), and daylilies. As the perennials come up, their expanding foliage hides the yellowing leaves of the bulbs.

trees. Choose tough, deep-rooted groundcovers like daylilies to stabilize slopes. Plant Chinese astilbes (*Astilbe chinensis*) or Japanese primroses (*Primula japonica*) in wet, boggy sites instead of mowing a quagmire.

For weed control and reduced yard maintenance, groundcovers can't be beat. But they're also excellent for covering up plants that are past their peak. For example, hostas will mask dying daffodil foliage so it can ripen in peace without becoming an eyesore. You can also use groundcovers like periwinkle (*Vinca* spp.) under spring bulbs, ferns, and perennials—its uniform green will set off taller and more colorful plants.

You can use any low-growing plant as a groundcover as long as it meets certain requirements: It should look attractive all season, spread quickly to carpet the ground, require a minimum of maintenance, and keep down weeds. Don't limit your choices to the obvious ivy, pachysandra, and periwinkle, though all three make excellent evergreen groundcovers. Wildflowers, perennials, ornamental grasses, annuals, and low shrubs can all be used as groundcovers. For most situations, choose plants that hug the ground or grow up to 3 feet tall; the most useful groundcovers are generally 6 to 18 inches tall.

 **Let the Lawn Breathe**

Don't let fallen leaves stay on the lawn all winter. They mat down and smother the grass below. Shred the leaves, and then add them to the compost pile. If you don't have a shredder, you can chop dried leaves with your lawn mower instead. Just rake the leaves into a pile, and run your mower over them in a criss-cross pattern until they're cut into small pieces.

## USING GROUNDCOVERS

Why use groundcovers when you can just grow grass? For adaptability, resilience, and uniformity, you can't top lawn grasses. They withstand heavy foot traffic, rough play, and all the abuse a family can muster. However, it can require a lot of effort to keep lawn grasses healthy and attractive. They won't grow well under trees and shrubs or in wet sites. You'll save yourself time and work—and create a more dynamic landscape—if you reduce your lawn to the smallest size you need for outdoor activities and turn the rest of your yard over to groundcovers, decks, patios, and ornamental plantings.

Another good way to use groundcovers is to grow them in islands under trees. With a planting of groundcovers around your trees, you won't injure the trunks by scraping them with the lawn mower or waste precious gardening time hand-trimming around each trunk. A mixed planting of hostas, with their beautiful leaf patterns and colors, looks wonderful under trees. So do ferns and astilbes (*Astilbe* spp.), or try blue-green lilyturf (*Liriope* spp.) for a cool contrast to the lighter lawn grass.

Underplanting trees with groundcovers makes your landscape more interesting, too. You can tie individual plants together by surrounding them with an island of groundcover plants, or tie separate groups of plants together by underplanting them with the same groundcover. Try uniform or mixed plantings of groundcovers under shrubs and next to lawn areas, too. You'll find that your yard looks more appealing when everything looks connected—suddenly it will look like a landscaped garden, and all because of a few groundcovers!

You can also grow groundcovers instead of lawn grass where you want to limit water use. As anyone who's spent evenings or weekends holding a hose knows, lawns are very thirsty.

Xeriscaping, a landscape philosophy based on water conservation and minimizing damage to the landscape, uses extensive plantings of tough, drought-resistant groundcovers. These adaptable plants reduce environmental impact, save water, and cut maintenance time. For more on water-wise gardening techniques, see "Watering Your Garden" on page 180.

Groundcovers also can perk up the landscape in the off season. Think about fall and winter in your garden. Many groundcovers take on beautiful hues as cool weather returns. Some, like lilyturf and bearberry (*Arctostaphylos uva-ursi*), display colorful fruits. Seed heads of ornamental grasses are loveliest late in the season. Evergreen foliage shines against light snowfalls.

Don't forget to go beyond problem solving when you're using groundcovers—after all, you have to look at them, too. A yardful of pachysandra may get the ground covered, but it's not nearly as appealing as a combination of groundcover plants. Think about mixing shape, texture, and color in exciting combinations. Feathery ferns with white-variegated hostas and low, glossy-leaved European wild ginger (*Asarum europaeum*) will make a shady site much more interesting than any one of the three alone. A mix of ajugas (*Ajuga reptans*)—perhaps 'Pink Beauty' (a pink-flowered, green-leaved cultivar) with the bronze-leaved 'Bronze Beauty' and large-leaved, blue-flowered 'Catlin's Giant'—will add more sparkle to a sunny spot than a single cultivar.

Don't be afraid to try something new if a combination falls flat. If a plant doesn't work where you've put it, just move it: Your best design tool is your shovel.

## CHOOSING GROUNDCOVERS

The cardinal rule in gardening is to match the plant to the site. To get the best performance from a groundcover, you must give it the grow-ing conditions it needs. Plant shade-loving, shallow-rooted Bethlehem sage (*Pulmonaria saccharata*) to cover a bare area in the shade of a maple tree, and sun-loving, deep-rooted yarrows (*Achillea* spp.) to stop erosion on a dry, sunny bank.

Don't forget maintenance. Plant rampant growers like ivies or sedums where you need dense cover to control weeds, not in a small space where they would quickly get out of control. For a small space that's not weed-prone, choose airy plants like Allegheny foamflower (*Tiarella cordifolia*) or chamomile (*Chamaemelum nobile*) that won't be in a hurry to overgrow the site. In both cases, a well-chosen groundcover will reduce your yard work, while a badly chosen groundcover will pitch you into a losing battle.

When you're looking for a good groundcov-

 ## Start with Small Plants

Starting groundcovers in a large area can be expensive because you must buy many plants. You can reduce the cost by starting with young plants. Groundcovers such as English ivy (*Hedera helix*), Japanese pachysandra (*Pachysandra terminalis*), and common periwinkle (*Vinca minor*) are often sold in flats of rooted cuttings (also called plugs). They will take a little more pampering than those grown in 4-inch pots but may cut your costs by half or more. You can also start mondo grass (*Ophiopogon japonicus*), blue lilyturf (*Liriope muscari*), and many perennial groundcovers from plugs. Another shortcut you can take is to pull apart large clumps of blue lilyturf or mondo grass either from an established planting or from plants purchased in larger pots.

er, let your needs limit your choices. Focus on the plants that suit your garden and your design. First, define your needs by asking yourself a few key questions:

■ Is your site shaded, partially shaded, or in full sun?

■ Is your site moist or dry?

■ Do you need a ground-hugging plant for the site, or would a taller plant look better?

■ Do you want bold or fine texture?

■ How important are flowers? Flower color?

■ Can you use variegated foliage to brighten things up?

■ Should the plant you choose be evergreen or deciduous?

You'll find lists of groundcovers for special situations at the end of this chapter.

## PLANTING AND MAINTENANCE

When you're trying to grow a good groundcover, thorough soil preparation is essential, especially in difficult sites. Plants will take off and grow faster if you give them a head start, so you'll have less trouble with weed competition. If you haven't had a soil test, consider it; you'll learn a lot about your gardening conditions. (To find out more about soils and soil

testing, see Chapter 2.)

First remove existing sod or undesirable growth from your site. Double dig the soil to a minimum depth of 18 to 20 inches. (For more on this technique, see page 40.) Spread a generous layer of compost, shredded leaves, or other organic matter over the soil. Add an organic fertilizer and other amendments as needed. (You can find out more about fertilizers in Chapter 8.) Turn the soil again, incorporating all the amendments thoroughly. Level the soil surface with a garden rake. Break up any remaining clods. Water to settle the soil, and you're ready for planting.

Space plants according to their growth rate and size at maturity. Plant fast-growing perennials, ornamental grasses, and other herbaceous plants 1 to 3 feet apart, depending on the mature size of the plant. Plant junipers and other large woody plants 3 feet apart. Plant slow-growing woody plants like wintergreen (*Gaultheria procumbens*) 1 foot apart.

Arrange the plants within the bed according to your design. For each plant, dig a hole large enough to accommodate the loosened root ball. If you're using container plants, make sure the plants are positioned at the same level at which they grew in the containers. Soak the roots of bareroot plants for several hours before planting. Remove the plants from the water one at a time and spread the roots evenly over a dome of soil in the bottom of the planting hole. Check the level of the crown to make sure it's at the right planting depth. (For more how-to-plant techniques, see Chapter 5.)

Mulch the site after planting to control weeds and reduce moisture loss. Water newly set plants thoroughly. Groundcovers need regular watering until they are well established—an entire growing season for woody plants. Pull weeds early to avoid competition.

 **Save Time, Mulch First**

Trying to lay mulch between plants in a newly planted expanse of groundcover can be a long, tedious task. You can save yourself some time by laying the mulch first. This is especially helpful when planting groundcover plugs or plants in small pots. After laying the mulch, you can easily plant through it with a trowel without pulling up too much soil on top of the clean mulch.

**Planting groundcovers on a gentle slope.** Where the ground slopes gently, you can plant groundcovers directly in the bank, then mulch around them until they're established.

**Planting groundcovers on a steep slope.** On a steep slope, plant from the top down. Put up a wooden barrier where you want a plant, pile soil behind the barrier, and plant. Once the plants are established, remove the barriers.

Groundcovers as a group are tough, trouble-free plants. But some pest and disease problems are inevitable in any garden situation. Prevention is the best control. Keep plants healthy, well watered, and mulched. Remove weeds that can harbor pests. If pest or disease problems arise, consult Chapter 7.

## GROWING GROUNDCOVERS

Groundcovers are a diverse group of plants. Propagation techniques vary according to whether you're dealing with a shrubby, vining, or perennial groundcover. Most groundcovers can be grown from seed started indoors or direct-seeded outdoors. But you'll get quicker results from fast-growing groundcovers if you take cuttings or divide them.

Take cuttings from perennial groundcovers like English ivy (*Hedera helix*), spotted lamium (*Lamium maculatum*), leadwort (*Ceratostigma plumbaginoides*), pachysandra, periwinkle, and sedum in early to midsummer. You can divide groundcovers in spring or fall. If the plant is a vine or creeper like ajuga, creeping phlox (*Phlox stolonifera*), English ivy, Allegheny foamflower, periwinkle, or wintercreeper (*Euonymus fortunei*), sever rooted plantlets from the parent stem. Lift clumps of perennials like astilbe, bergenia (*Bergenia* spp.), blue fescue (*Festuca caesia*), crested iris (*Iris cristata*), daylily, and hosta, and separate the crowns.

A slow but easy method of propagating woody groundcovers like cotoneasters (*Cotoneaster* spp.) and junipers is layering—encouraging branches to root where they touch the ground. For more on propagation, see Chapter 6.

**Classic Groundcovers for Sun**

There are so many great groundcovers for sun that it can be hard to choose the best. The list below covers some of the most popular sun-loving groundcovers, with their botanical names, common names, brief descriptions, and hardiness zones. Unless otherwise noted, these plants will grow in average, well-drained soil. Try a few of these on a sunny slope or along a bright path:

Bearberry (*Arctostaphylos uva-ursi*). White bell-shaped flowers in spring, followed by red berries, over small evergreen leaves. Prefers evenly moist, acidic soil. Zones 2–6.

Chamomile (*Chamaemelum nobile*). Tiny white daisies in summer over mats of ferny bright green foliage. Zones 5–9.

Cranesbills (*Geranium* spp.). Showy white, blue, purple, or pink flowers in spring to early summer; spreading, mounded, or slightly upright clumps of scalloped to deeply cut leaves. Zones 3–8.

Creeping juniper (*Juniperus horizontalis*). Needle-like green, blue-green, or gray-green foliage. Zones 2–10.

Crispleaf spirea (*Spiraea bullata*). Rosy red flower clusters in summer over crinkled blue-green leaves. Zones 4–8.

Crown vetch (*Coronilla varia*). Pink flowers in summer over ferny green leaves. Zones 3–9.

Daylilies (*Hemerocallis* spp.). Trumpet-shaped summer flowers in a range of colors over fans of strap-shaped leaves. Zones 3–9.

Hens-and-chickens (*Sempervivum* spp.). Fleshy rosettes of green or red-tinged leaves. Zones 3–10.

Lamb's-ears (*Stachys byzantina*). Fuzzy gray flower spikes topped with tiny purple-pink blooms in spring to summer; soft, fuzzy, oblong gray-green leaves. Zones 4–8.

Moss pink (*Phlox subulata*). White, pink, or lavender flowers in spring over mats of needle-like evergreen leaves. Zones 3–8.

Perennial candytuft (*Iberis sempervirens*). Clusters of white spring flowers over spreading mounds of narrow, dark green evergreen leaves. Zones 4–8.

Pinks (*Dianthus* spp.). Single or double flowers in pink, red, white, or yellow in spring or summer; mats or rosettes of grassy gray or green leaves. Zones 3–8.

Rockspray cotoneaster (*Cotoneaster horizontalis*). Tiny white flowers in spring, followed by bright red berries over small deciduous or evergreen leaves. Zones 5–8.

St.-John's-wort (*Hypericum calycinum*). Bright yellow flowers in summer on shrubby stems with evergreen leaves. Zones 6–9.

Sedums (*Sedum* spp.). Clusters of starry yellow, pink, or white flowers in spring, summer, or fall; mats or rosettes of succulent green, blue-green, or purplish leaves. Zones 3–10.

Shrubby cinquefoil (*Potentilla fruticosa*). Yellow flowers in spring and summer on a rounded, twiggy shrub. Zones 2–7.

Snow-in-summer (*Cerastium tomentosum*). Small white flowers in late spring to early summer over mats of silvery leaves. Zones 2–7.

Strawberry (*Fragaria* × *ananassa*). White spring flowers and edible red fruit; rosettes of three-parted green leaves. Zones 3–9.

Thymes (*Thymus* spp.). Tiny white to pink flowers over mats or clumps of small, often fragrant, leaves. Zones 5–9.

Wall rock cress (*Arabis caucasica*). Fragrant white spring flowers; spreading clumps of fuzzy light green evergreen leaves. Zones 4–7.

## Classic Groundcovers for Shade

Groundcovers for shady spots can be green and restful or colorful and exciting. The list below includes groundcovers that will thrive in at least partial shade, along with a brief description and their hardiness zones. Most shade-lovers will grow in average, well-drained soil, but most appreciate some extra moisture and humus. For year-round interest, look for evergreen species. For extra color, underplant groundcovers with spring bulbs like crocus and daffodils. Try some of these for your shady sites:

Ajuga (*Ajuga reptans*). Spikes of blue, pink, or white flowers over rosettes of green, purple, or variegated leaves. Zones 4–8.

Allegheny foamflower (*Tiarella cordifolia*). Spikes of white spring flowers over evergreen clumps of heart-shaped leaves. Zones 3–8.

Bergenias (*Bergenia* spp.). Spikes of pink flowers in spring; glossy evergreen leaves often turn burgundy in fall. Zones 4–8.

Chinese astilbe (*Astilbe chinensis* 'Pumila'). Plumes of rose-pink summer flowers over clumps of fernlike foliage. Zones 4–8.

Common periwinkle (*Vinca minor*). Blue or white flowers in spring over glossy evergreen leaves. Zones 5–8.

Creeping phlox (*Phlox stolonifera*). Clusters of blue, pink, or white blooms in spring over rosettes of green leaves. Zones 2–8.

English ivy (*Hedera helix*). Dark green or variegated evergreen leaves. Zones 5–9.

Epimediums (*Epimedium* spp.). Sprays of tiny yellow, red, pink or white flowers in spring; clumps of heart-shaped green leaves all season. Zones 3–8.

Fringed Bleeding Heart (*Dicentra eximia*). Nodding pink flowers in spring over mounds of fernlike bluish green leaves. Zones 3–8.

Himalayan sarcococca (*Sarcococca hookerana*). Tiny fragrant white flowers in spring; glossy dark green evergreen leaves. Zones 6–8.

Hostas (*Hosta* spp.). Spikes of trumpet-shaped violet, lilac, or white flowers over heart-shaped leaves in summer or fall. Zones 3–8.

Japanese pachysandra (*Pachysandra terminalis*). Spikes of white flowers in spring over evergreen leaves. Zones 4–9.

Lamiums (*Lamium* spp.). Small pink or white flowers over heart-shaped green-, yellow-, or white-variegated leaves. Zones 3–9.

Lily-of-the-Valley (*Convallaria majalis*). Sprays of fragrant white flowers in early spring; broad green leaves all season. Zones 2–8.

Liriopes (*Liriope* spp.). Spikes of violet-blue or white flowers in late summer; clumps of grassy evergreen foliage. Zones 6–10.

Lungworts (*Pulmonaria* spp.). Blue-pink spring flowers over clumps of dark green leaves, often with gray or silver spots. Zones 3–8.

Paxistima (*Paxistima canbyi*). Small dark green evergreen leaves may bronze in winter. Zones 3–7.

Strawberry geranium (*Saxifraga stolonifera*). Sprays of tiny white summer flowers over rosettes of rounded, silver-veined green leaves with reddish undersides. Zones 6–8.

Wild gingers (*Asarum* spp.). Rounded glossy dark green leaves; some species are evergreen. Zones 3–8.

Wintercreeper (*Euonymus fortunei*). Glossy evergreen leaves may bronze in winter. Zones 4–8.

Yellow archangel (*Lamiastrum galeobdolon*). Yellow flowers in spring over heart-shaped green- and white-variegated leaves. Zones 4–9.

# RECOMMENDED READING

## GENERAL GARDENING

Bradley, Fern Marshall, and Barbara W. Ellis, eds. *Rodale's All-New Encyclopedia of Organic Gardening.* Emmaus, Pa.: Rodale Press, 1992.

Damrosch, Barbara. *The Garden Primer.* New York: Workman Publishing, 1988.

Ellis, Barbara W., and Fern Marshall Bradley, eds. *The Organic Gardener's Handbook of Natural Insect and Disease Control.* Emmaus, Pa.: Rodale Press, 1992.

Martin, Deborah L., and Grace Gershuny, eds. *The Rodale Book of Composting.* Emmaus, Pa.: Rodale Press, 1992.

Roth, Susan A. *The Weekend Garden Guide.* Emmaus, Pa.: Rodale Press, 1991.

## FRUITS, VEGETABLES, AND HERBS

Bartholomew, Mel. *Square Foot Gardening.* Emmaus, Pa.: Rodale Press, 1981.

Hill, Lewis. *Fruits and Berries for the Home Garden.* Rev. ed. Pownal, Vt.: Garden Way Publishing, 1992.

Michalak, Patricia S. *Rodale's Successful Organic Gardening: Vegetables.* Emmaus, Pa.: Rodale Press, 1993.

*Rodale's Illustrated Encyclopedia of Herbs.* Edited by Claire Kowalchik and William H. Hylton. Emmaus, Pa.: Rodale Press, 1987.

Whealy, Kent, ed. *Fruit, Berry and Nut Inventory.* 2nd ed. Decorah, Iowa: Seed Saver Publications, 1993.

## FLOWERS AND OTHER ORNAMENTALS

Appleton, Bonnie Lee, and Alfred F. Scheider. *Rodale's Successful Organic Gardening: Trees, Shrubs and Vines.* Emmaus, Pa.: Rodale Press, 1993.

Greenlee, John. *The Encyclopedia of Ornamental Grasses.* Emmaus, Pa.: Rodale Press, 1992.

Loewer, Peter. *The Annual Garden.* Emmaus, Pa.: Rodale Press, 1988.

Phillips, Ellen, and C. Colston Burrell. *Rodale's Illustrated Encyclopedia of Perennials.* Emmaus, Pa.: Rodale Press, 1993.

Schultz, Warren. *The Chemical-Free Lawn: The Newest Varieties and Techniques to Grow Lush, Hardy Grass.* Emmaus, Pa.: Rodale Press, 1989.

## SPECIALTY GARDENS

Creasy, Rosalind. *The Complete Book of Edible Landscaping.* San Francisco: Sierra Club Books, 1982.

Gessert, Kate Rogers. *The Beautiful Food Garden: Creative Landscaping with Vegetables, Herbs, Fruits, & Flowers.* Pownal, Vt.: Storey Communications, 1987.

Kourik, Robert. *Designing and Maintaining Your Edible Landscape Naturally.* Santa Rosa, Calif.: Metamorphic Press, 1986.

Loewer, Peter. *The Evening Garden.* New York: Macmillan Publishing Co., 1993.

Schneck, Marcus. *Butterflies: How to Identify and Attract Them to Your Garden.* Emmaus, Pa.: Rodale Press, 1990.

————. *Your Backyard Wildlife Garden.* Emmaus, Pa.: Rodale Press, 1992.

Uber, William C. *Water Gardening Basics.* Upland, Calif.: Dragonflyer Press, 1988.

# SOURCES

Here's a list of mail-order companies for seeds, plants, and gardening supplies. Some catalogs are free, but write and inquire since many do charge a fee and prices may change.

## GARDEN SUPPLIES

Gardener's Supply Co.
128 Intervale Road
Burlington, VT 05401

Gardens Alive!
5100 Schenley Place
Lawrenceburg, IN 47025

Peaceful Valley Farm Supply
P.O. Box 2209
Grass Valley, CA 95945

## GENERAL GARDENING

W. Atlee Burpee and Co.
300 Park Avenue
Warminster, PA 18974

Henry Field's Seed and
Nursery Co.
415 North Burnett Street
Shenandoah, IA 51602

Gurney Seed & Nursery Co.
110 Capital Street
Yankton, SD 57078

Hastings Seeds
P.O. Box 115535
Atlanta, GA 30310-8535

Park Seed Co.
P.O. Box 31
Greenwood, SC 29647

Pinetree Garden Seed
Route 100
New Gloucester, ME 04260

## VEGETABLES

The Cook's Garden
P.O. Box 535
Londonderry, VT 05148

Johnny's Selected Seeds
310 Foss Hill Road
Albion, ME 04910

Shepherd's Garden Seeds
30 Irene Street
Torrington, CT 06790

## HERBS

Companion Plants
7247 North Coolville Ridge Road
Athens, OH 45701

Nichols Garden Nursery
1190 North Pacific Highway
Albany, OR 97321

Richters
357 Highway 47
Goodwood, Ontario
Canada L0C 1A0

## FRUITS

Country Heritage Nursery
P.O. Box 536
Hartford, MI 49057

Edible Landscaping
P.O. Box 77
Afton, VA 22920

Raintree Nursery
391 Butts Road
Morton, WA 98356

St. Lawrence Nurseries
R.R. 5, Box 324
Potsdam, NY 13676

Stark Bro's Nurseries
P.O. Box 10
Louisiana, MO 63353

## ORNAMENTALS

Kurt Bluemel, Inc.
2740 Greene Lane
Baldwin, MD 21013

Holbrook Farm & Nursery
P.O. Box 368
Fletcher, NC 28732

Milaeger's Gardens
4838 Douglas Avenue
Racine, WI 53402-2498

Andre Viette Farm and Nursery
Route 1, Box 16
Fishersville, VA 22939

Wayside Gardens
1 Garden Lane
Hodges, SC 29695

White Flower Farm
Litchfield, CT 06759

## BULBS

McClure & Zimmerman
P.O. Box 368
Friesland, WI 53935

Dutch Gardens
P.O. Box 200
Adelphia, NJ 07710

## WATER GARDENS

Lilypons Water Gardens
P.O. Box 10
Buckeystown, MD 21717

William Tricker, Inc.
7125 Tanglewood Drive
Independence, OH 44131

# USDA Plant Hardiness Zone Map

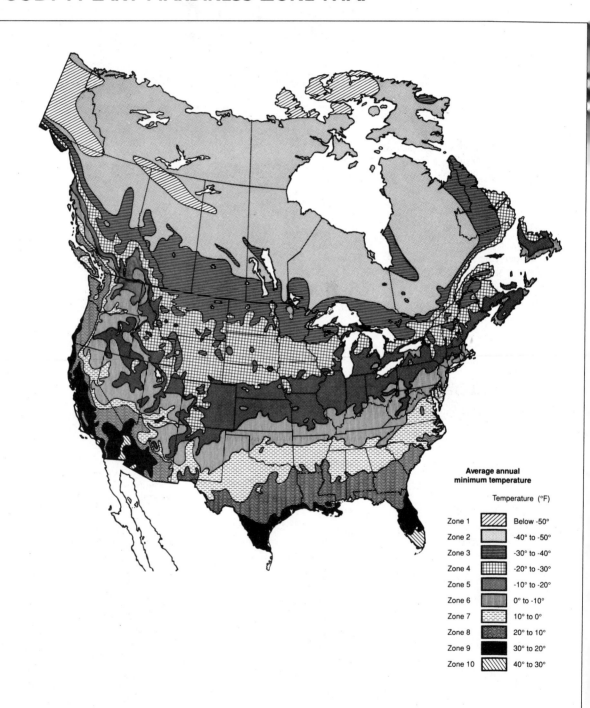

**Average annual
minimum temperature**

Temperature (°F)

| | | |
|---|---|---|
| Zone 1 | | Below -50° |
| Zone 2 | | -40° to -50° |
| Zone 3 | | -30° to -40° |
| Zone 4 | | -20° to -30° |
| Zone 5 | | -10° to -20° |
| Zone 6 | | 0° to -10° |
| Zone 7 | | 10° to 0° |
| Zone 8 | | 20° to 10° |
| Zone 9 | | 30° to 20° |
| Zone 10 | | 40° to 30° |

# INDEX

Note: Page references in *italic* indicate tables. **Boldface** references indicate illustrations.